D1266113

A Harmony of the Gospels
MATTHEW, MARK AND LUKE
VOLUME I

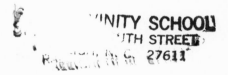
CALVIN'S COMMENTARIES

CALVIN'S COMMENTARIES

A Harmony of the Gospels
MATTHEW, MARK
AND LUKE

VOLUME I

Translator
A. W. MORRISON

Editors
DAVID W. TORRANCE
THOMAS F. TORRANCE

WM. B. EERDMANS PUBLISHING COMPANY
GRAND RAPIDS   MICHIGAN

Translation © The Saint Andrew Press 1972

Published in 1972
by The Saint Andrew Press
121 George Street, Edinburgh

ISBN 0 8028 2038 7

Printed in Great Britain
by R. & R. Clark Ltd.

INTRODUCTION

Chief Editions of John Calvin's Commentaries on a Harmony of the Gospels, Matthew, Mark, and Luke, and on the Epistles of James and Jude.

On a Harmony of the Gospels

The first edition appears in 1555, attached to his earlier Commentary on John (1553):

> Harmonia ex / tribus Euangelistis composita, / Matthaeo, Marco & Luca: adiuncto seorsum Iohanne, quod pauca cum / aliis communia habeat, / Cvm Ioh. Calvini Commentariis. / [Device] / Oliua Roberti Stephani / M.D.LV.

The same works were published in French in 1555 by Conrad Badius—'Concordance qu'on appelle Harmonie etc.' —and in English in 1584 by Thomas Dawson; the translation of the Harmony into English was made by 'the Lord's most unworthie minister, lame Eusebius Paget'.

The Calvin Translation Society version is by the Rev. Wm. Pringle, Edinburgh, 1845-46 (3 vols.).

On James and Jude

Calvin produced a Commentary on Jude in French in 1542—'Exposition sur l'Epistre de sanct Iudas Apostre de nostre Seigneur Iesus Christ.' This is not translated here, but that found in the Commentaries published together in 1551:

> Ioannis Calvini / Commentarii in Epistolas / Canonicas, vnam Petri, / vnam Ioannis, / vnam Iacobi. / Petri alteram. / Ivdae vnam. / Ad Edvardum VI. Angliae Regem. / Additus est sententiarum et locorum index. / [Device] / Genevae, / Ex officina Ioannis Crispini. / M.D.LI.

The same works were published in French 'chez Jean Gerrard' in 1551, who had published James separately the previous year. The first translation of Jude appears (undated) with I John, by 'W.H.'—'imprinted at London by Jhon Kyngstone, for Jhon Harrison the yonger.' The earliest version of James seems to be one (unnamed) which was published in Aberdeen, 1797, and printed by J. Chalmers and Co.

The Calvin Translation Society version is by the Rev. John Owen, Edinburgh, 1855.

Selections from the Commentaries with introduction appear in the Library of Christian Classics (vol. 23), S.C.M. Press, London 1958; translator and editor J. Haroutunian.

This translation is made on the basis of the Berlin edition (Tholuck) of the Commentaries, 1834, with reference to *Corpus Reformatorum*. The scripture text (except where Calvin's own comments demand a variant reading) is that of the Revised Version.

A.W.M. translates from The Dedicatory Epistle to Matt. 10.41, T.H.L.P. from Mark 6.12 to Luke 19.43, and A.W.M. translates from Matt. 21.10 to the end in Volume II. A.W.M. is responsible for the remainder of the Harmony and for James and Jude in Volume III.

A. W. M.

Dedicatory Epistle

John Calvin to Their Excellencies the Presidents and Council
of the noble city of Frankfurt

If there was ever advantage in setting out examples of virtue for men to copy, to stimulate the idle and sluggish and dawdlers in the race, we may affirm that both the carelessness and the downright apathy of this very corrupt generation make it essential that the greater part of mankind be prompted by shame, if nothing else, to discharge their responsibilities, for far from making progress, they appear rather to lose ground. It is the universal spectacle, both in private and public life, that men are devoted to a crude form of rivalry, that no monarch should appear to drag behind his neighbours in any degree of craft, industry, resource or audacity in extending his boundaries by any means: that no state or republic yield its reputation for cunning and general trickery to any other: that no individual in his dedication to self-seeking fall down in any branch of the evil arts. In a word, each incites the other in a mutual, and unproclaimed, contest of vice, and the worst behaviour of one readily sets the whole crowd headlong by his example, while in the general reign of vice a mere handful of right acting men are to be found. From this I judge there is added advantage, when outstanding virtue is seen in persons of distinction, for them to be praised to the skies in appropriate terms for the widest notice to be taken, that many may be stirred to follow their lead. This, my most gracious lords, I confess to have been my first thought in desiring to publish this work of mine under the inscription of your name. Though I would reckon it a splendid achievement if my work should lend some extra haste to those who make good headway on their own, yet I had more thought for those others who might make equal progress with yours, or at least pursue the same path. I do not intend, however, to draw up a full list of all the virtues in which you excel, but let it for the present suffice for me to praise one, which has bound me, and many servants of Christ, to you with a bond of especial sanctity. We were impressed greatly, five years ago, when all suffered the rage of terror, and the defeat we met seemed to threaten appalling distress for the churches of Germany, the virtual ruin of the Gospel, but you, exposed as you were to the very first onslaught stood so firmly by your free confession—then so obnoxious—and held the true pattern of belief which you had received with such constancy, that it was plain for the world to see that in all the crisis and alarm there was no greater ideal for you than to soldier beneath the standards of Christ. However, of even nobler record is the fact that not only do you foster pure religion amongst yourselves, and perform faithful work, to keep your citizens within the paths of Christ, but you also gather in the tattered fragments, the refugees of the persecuted church driven from other places. I can assure you it gave me no small comfort at a time of great pain to hear that devout worshippers of God, coming to you as exiles from England and other parts, had been given your kind hospitality; more than a haven for their unhappy exile, a fine honour to the Son of God, that His Gospel should be heard in your city in foreign tongues. I compare the recent humanity of the Council of Zürich towards the poor folk of Locarno, not only opening their city to them, when they were not allowed to worship Christ in their own according to their desire, but also assigning them a church building in which to hold their religious services; nor were they deterred by the diversity of speech, but wished to have Christ's Name spoken in their midst in the Italian tongue. To return to yourselves, from the moment I heard of your kindness in granting permission to men of our tongue to establish a church there, I felt a sense of obligation to you on my own account and determined that my gratitude should be attested in the gift I now offer. While the condition of our people is indeed lamentable—the sacrilegious tyranny of Papal rule making their home-land a virtual banishment from the Kingdom of God, one must at the same time rejoice that there is some place to settle in a foreign land where they may practise proper worship of God. Doubtless this sanctified hospitality, offered not so much to men as to Christ Himself, will bring you the distinction of rewards from God (I hope) beyond your present prosperity, and will continue their uninterrupted course amongst you: certainly, as I have just affirmed, it has brought me to dedicate this work of mine to you.

It is a commentary I have worked out on a Harmony composed from the three Evangelists, with extreme fidelity and equal diligence: what the exertion has cost me in sweat, there is no point in discussing at length, and what the achievement has been, must be left to the judgment of others. I mean fair, skilled, and genuine readers, such as are not put off from the outset by a brutish contempt for learning, but devoted to the common good. There are twisted and malicious rogues (not just the hooded monks, who wage open warfare against us to defend the Pope's tyranny, but the low-down villains who slip in amongst us, trying by all means to conceal their own ignorance, who would quench every light of doctrine) . . . I say no more. However coarsely they yap at me, I can step aside at will, as I am not liable by divine or human law to stand under the judgment of men who for their foul stupidity deserve a caning, and for their impenetrable obstinacy, ill will and ill nature, deserve to be flogged. As far as being profitably employed for the Church of God, I may say without any sort of boasting that I have offered a faithful contribution. Two years ago my interpretation of John was produced, and I believe satisfied a need. So I have attempted, as far as my prowess allowed, to magnify the progress of Christ on His four-horse chariot, like one of His attendant heralds, and honest readers who have been helped by my efforts will not mind confessing that some success has met my endeavour. I compare the Gospel story quite deliberately to the *quadriga*, being set out as God willed by four witnesses. In this fitting and harmonious manner God appears to have chosen to prepare a triumphal passage for His Son, by which He may ride conspicuous before the whole assembly of the faithful, and swiftly circle the world around. One appreciates Augustine's wise comparison of the four Evangelists to four trumpets, whose blast fills all the quarters of the globe, that from East and West, South and North, the Church may be hailed to holy unity in the faith, and make congress. Which makes quite insufferable the vulgar ingenuity of men who not content with these heaven-sent messengers push rotten trash under the title of Gospel, that altogether stains the purity of faith and exposes the Name of Christ to the mockery and ridicule of the ungodly.

Your excellencies, as you have shown that you abhor any leaven that would corrupt the true sincerity of the Gospel, and make plain that nothing is more to your heart than to protect and defend the simple teaching that was revealed in Christ, I am quite convinced that this study which interprets the riches of the Gospel will meet with your highest approval and being dedicated to your name will be a welcome sign of my respect for you. Farewell, my noble Lords. May Christ ever guide you with His Spirit, stablish you by His power, defend you with His protection, and fill your city and republic with full store of blessings.

GENEVA, 1st August 1555.

THE THEME
OF THE GOSPEL OF JESUS CHRIST

According to Matthew, Mark and Luke

In order to make profitable study of the Gospel narrative, it is very important to grasp the actual meaning of the word *Gospel*. Thus we may determine the purpose behind the writing of these divine witnesses, and say where the matters related by them are leading. The title was not imposed on their work by an outside hand, but so inscribed by the authors themselves, as we see from Mark, who expressly declares that he is giving 'the beginning of the Gospel of Jesus Christ'. A firm and unmistakable definition of Gospel is best found in a passage of Paul (Rom. 1.2), where he says that it was 'promised by God in the Scriptures through the Prophets concerning His Son, who was born of the seed of David, revealed to be the Son of God with power, according to the Spirit of holiness, by the resurrection of the dead'. First, he describes it as a testimony to the revealed salvation which had been promised of old to the Fathers through continued succession of generations. Thus a distinction is set between the promises which held the hopes of the faithful in suspense, and this glad news, wherein God testifies that He has brought to pass that event which before He had made the object of hope. Likewise, he tells a little later how the righteousness of God was here openly manifested after having its testimony given in Law and Prophets. Elsewhere again in the same Apostle (II Cor. 5.20), it is called an Embassy, by which the reconciliation of the world with God, once for all accomplished in the death of Christ, is daily conveyed to men. Secondly, he means that not only is Christ the pledge of all benefits that ever God has promised, but that we find in Him their full and substantial revelation; as he says in another place, 'All the promises of God find their Yea and Amen in Him.' Certainly, that free adoption by which we are made sons of God, as it derives from the eternal good-pleasure of the Father, so it was displayed to us in Him, in that Christ (in His nature the only-begotten) put on our flesh and took us to Himself as brothers. The atonement whereby sins are cleared, that the curse and judgment of death should no longer weigh upon us, is to be sought precisely in His sacrificial death. Righteousness, salvation and entire felicity are based upon His rising again. Thus the Gospel is the solemn proclamation of the presence of the Son of God revealed in the flesh to renew a fallen world, to restore men from death into life.

Rightly then are these good and glad tidings, since they contain complete happiness, for the end is that the Kingdom of God once begun in us, clearing away the corruption of the flesh, should bring us renewed in spirit to the glory of heaven. For this reason it is often called the Kingdom of Heaven, and the renewed life of blessedness offered in Christ sometimes called the Kingdom of God, as when Mark (15.43) says Joseph 'looked for the kingdom of God', referring doubtless to the coming of the Messiah. This makes it plain that the title Gospel properly applies to the New Testament, and that there is a lack of discernment in those writers who make it common to all ages, and reckon that the Prophets no less than the Apostles were its ministers. Christ speaks quite differently, teaching how the Law and the Prophets flourished up till John (Luke 16.16), then declaring that from that time was preached the beginning of the Kingdom of God, while Mark, as we have just noted, made the Gospel begin at the preaching of John.

Now the title was quite deliberately given to the four narratives which describe Christ's working out of the office of Mediator. For as the birth, death and resurrection of Christ contain in themselves the whole sum of our salvation, indeed are so much its substance, it is right and proper to use the word Evangelists of those who set before our eyes Christ, sent by the Father, that our faith may recognize in Him the Author of the life of blessedness. The actual force and effect of His coming are more stressed in other books of the New Testament. In fact John differs in this respect quite considerably from the other three in that he devotes himself very much to describing the character and influence of Christ as it comes from Him to us, while they concentrate more on the one point, that our Christ was that Son of God, the Redeemer promised to mankind. They do include teaching on the role He played, to let us understand the nature of His grace, and the reason for its coming upon us, but they deal particularly with what I have said, how in the Person of Christ Jesus were fulfilled the things that God had promised from the beginning. They had no intention or plan by their writings to do away with the Law or the Prophets, in the manner that some crazed folk imagine, making the Old Testament now superfluous, since the truth of heavenly wisdom has been revealed to us through Christ and the Apostles: rather they point the finger to show how Christ is to be sought therein, from His tokens in Law and Prophets. We come to a useful and fruitful study of the Gospel when in fact we learn to combine it with the former words of promise.

As regards the three writers of Gospel story whom I am taking as my subject, Matthew is well enough known, while Mark is believed by some to have been the close disciple of Peter, and to have written down the Gospel as Peter dictated it to him, thus serving merely as amanuensis or secretary. We need not make a great fuss over this, as it has little significance for us, once we realize he was a witness of standing and of divine appointment, publishing nothing except by the previous dictation of the Holy Spirit. But Jerome's comment makes no sense at all, that it was a shortened form of the Gospel written by Matthew. He does not consistently follow Matthew's order, and from the very start has a different approach in his handling; he relates certain matters omitted by the other, and at times gives a fuller account of the same event. I think it is much more likely, and a conjecture closer to fact, that he never set eye on Matthew's book when he wrote himself: so far was he from wishing to put down a set condensation of that work. I would make the same judgment regarding Luke. We should not say that the diversity which appears between the three was consciously simulated, but that as each in good faith determined to put to writing what he accepted as certain and factual, so each arranged it as he thought would be best. There was nothing fortuitous about it, of course, for it happened rather under the control of divine providence; the Holy Spirit has given such wonderful unity in their diverse patterns of writing that this alone would almost be enough to win them authority if a greater authority from another source did not supply it. Luke is clear witness that he was that particular companion of Paul's. It is a childish comment given in Eusebius that Paul was the author of the Gospel which bears Luke's name, just because he speaks in another context (II Tim. 2.8) of 'my Gospel'. As if it were not perfectly evident from what follows that he is speaking not of a particular book but of the whole proclamation. He says, 'Wherein I suffer hardship unto bonds'. Quite certainly he was not convicted of having written a particular book, but because he was an outspoken minister and herald of the message of Christ. It shows us that Eusebius was a man of great industry, but rather lacking in judgment, to string together an indiscriminate lot of dull trifles. I would like readers to take warning from this, in case they should be put off by other ineptitudes of this sort which abound in his work.

I have chosen a manner of exposition which may not at first sight win general approval, and I must give an explanation which will satisfy devout and reasonable readers. There is no disagreement, first, that one can make no intelligent or apt comment on one of the three Evangelists without comparing the other two. For this reason faithful and skilled commentators have expended most of their efforts on reconciling the three accounts. But as limited minds find the comparison hard to grasp, continually having to turn up this place and that, I thought it would be a welcome and useful short-cut to treat the three narratives together in a continuous line, on one form so to speak, where readers could see at a glance the points of likeness and difference. So I shall omit nothing which is found written in one of the three, and shall put the material of two or three into one context. Whether or not this will have the value I anticipate will be judged by the use readers make of it. There is no question of my seeking the credit for the innovation—I freely confess (in the character of an honest man) that the method derives from imitation of others. I have particularly copied Bucer, that man of holy memory, outstanding doctor in the Church of God, whom I judge to have pursued a line of work in this field which is beyond reproach. As he was aided by the efforts of an older generation who had gone before him in this enterprise, so his industry and research have given me considerable assistance. And should I at times dissent from him (as I have freely allowed myself to do as occasion demanded) he would be the last, if he were still alive on earth, to take it unkindly.

A COMMENTARY ON THE HARMONY
OF THE GOSPELS

Forasmuch as many have taken in hand to draw up a narrative concerning these matters which have been fulfilled among us, even as they delivered them unto us, which from the beginning were eyewitnesses and ministers of the word, it seemed good to me also, having traced the course of all things accurately from the very first, to write unto thee in order, most excellent Theophilus; that thou mightest know the certainty concerning the things wherein thou wast instructed. (Luke 1.1-4)

Luke alone gives his Gospel a preface, to show briefly the reason that led him to its composition. It seems strange to address it to one man, when his real object should be to trumpet abroad that summons which called all men alike to faith. Therefore it appears out of place to send instruction privately to his own Theophilus, when it should be shared by all, not kept to one or two. The result is, that some believe the name to be generic—all faithful men being called 'friends of God—*theophili*', from the love of God that is in them. This argument, however, is refuted by the epithet which, at once, he adds. Nor, in fact, is there anything to feel strange about, that should lead them to seek such a solution. Paul's instruction applies no less to all, though he dictated certain Epistles to particular towns and particular men. Indeed, if we pause to consider the state of those times, we shall admit that the decision Luke made was good and wise. There were tyrants on all sides, threatening to obstruct the course of the true teaching by terror and oppression. It was a time for Satan and his crew to spread clouds of error all over, to spoil the true light. And as the commonalty had little concern for preserving the purity of the Gospel, and few took careful note of what Satan plotted, the danger that lurked in such deceptions, so it was that any man who stood out for his exceptional faith and distinctive gifts of the Spirit had to take the responsibility of greater study and care upon himself, to play a man's part in keeping religious truth free and unspotted from any corrupting influence. Such men were chosen of God, not unlike holy guardians of the law, faithfully to hand down to future generations the heavenly teaching entrusted to them. With this in view, Luke dedicates his Gospel to Theophilus, enlisting him as its faithful custodian: the same role that Paul lays on his Timothy, with the same trust, in his second Epistle. ch. 1.14 and 3.14.

I

Luke 1. *Forasmuch as many.* The reason he puts forward for his writing, is one that ought apparently to restrain his pen: it was unnecessary labour to repeat a tale told by many, if in fact they had properly dealt with their task. Now, he does not charge them with one word of deception or negligence or any kind of fault: so he must appear to be saying that he will do a thing done before. The answer is, that although he spares the others who had written before him, he does not altogether approve their work. He does not expressly say that they wrote with insufficient information, but his own claim of certainty over facts is a gentle derogation of their trustworthiness and indubiety. One may object, that he should rather have taken them roundly to task for their errors; but I say, that perhaps their transgression was slight, due more to hasty enthusiasm than to mischief, and so no cause for his attacking them more fiercely. We may certainly believe that there were certain notions in embryo, not then greatly damaging, which might have caused serious damage later on if they had not been checked in good time. It is well worth remarking the admirable purposes of God, in calling Luke to deal with these superfluous documents, in order that, when the rest had been by general consent repudiated, those alone should win respect which retained the glowing light of His holiness and His majesty. What an intolerable crime it is for men to peddle out upon the world rotten fables, so-called works 'of Nicodemus', or some such!

Matters which have been fulfilled among us. The participle Luke uses— πεπληροφορημένα—means things that are properly established, without any doubt. Previous interpretation went astray at this point more than once, and ignorantly spoiled several passages for us. Consider Romans 14.5, where Paul bids every one be certain in his own mind, or his conscience will be tossed by various opinions this way and that, and make him unsteady and unsafe. Hence we have the word πληροφορία, which is ill-translated 'fulness', seeing that it is that firm assurance of faith upon which devout minds may rest secure. As I have said, there is a tacit antithesis: when he claims for himself the authority of a faithful witness, he lessens that of those who give a different account. *Among us* has the same force as *unto us.* It may appear that confidence in human narratives is not well-founded, when it should rely on the Word of God alone; and certainly the πληροφορία of faith is ascribed to the seal of the Spirit. I would say, that unless God's authority holds pride of place, faith will never be satisfied with the testimonies of men, but when the inward assurance of the Spirit has led the way, it may subsequently allow them some standing, in an historical knowledge of events (*in historica rerum notitia*). I mean by an historical knowledge, one which we conceive from events which either we have seen ourselves or have heard from others. With the manifest works of God, we are as much to listen to eye-witnesses as to trust our experience. Besides, Luke is not dealing with private sources, but men who were ministers of the Word (*sermonis ministri*). He gives them a distinction that places them above the rank of human authority: he means, that they who gave him testimony on the Gospel had been divinely entrusted with the role of publishing it. Hence that security (to which he refers a little later) which, unless it rests on God, will ever be disturbed. It is of great weight that he draws his Gospel from those whom he calls ministers of the Word, for the faithful may infer from this that they are, as lawyers say, witnesses beyond all exception, whom it would not be right to reject. Erasmus—who borrowed from Virgil for his translation, reckoning it had some bearing—does not take sufficient account of the worth and importance of the calling of God. It is not in everyday terms that Luke speaks. He bids us look to the command of Christ, through the person of his Theophilus, that we may reverently hear the Son of God speaking through His Apostles. Impressive as it is to call them spectators, by naming them ministers he raises them above the common rank of humanity, to fix our faith on the ground of heaven, not of earth. All in all, it is Luke's desire that what once we had learned orally, we should have carefully consigned to script, and so rest more securely on the instruction we had received. It is clear that God promised by all means, that our faith should not toss about at the mercy of men's shifting ideas. The world's ingratitude is the more unpardonable, for almost deliberately it seeks out those vague and recklessly published stories, for constant change: this is plain insult to the goodness of God. Let us, at least, hold to the shining criterion which the Lord has set in our midst, and not suffer vain credulity to trade under the sign of faith. Then we may leave the world, as it deserves, to swallow the bait of foolish curiosity under Satan's deception, yes, let it be hooked completely with impostures.

Luke 1.2. *Having traced the course of all things accurately.* Previous interpretation takes it as, 'All things in their course'. And the Greek verb—παρακολουθεῖν—is taken metaphorically of those who follow tracks, lest anything escape them. It is the painstaking regard for enquiry that Luke wishes to express, exactly as Demosthenes uses the word in examination of an embassy, which he prosecutes, and boasts that he was as diligent in looking into their affairs as if he had been an eye-witness himself.

There was in the days of Herod, king of Judaea, a certain priest named Zacharias, of the course of Abijah: and he had a wife of the daughters of

3

Aaron, and her name was Elisabeth. And they were both righteous before God, walking in all the commandments and ordinances of the Lord blameless. And they had no child, because that Elisabeth was barren, and they both were now well stricken in years.

Now it came to pass, while he executed the priest's office before God in the order of his course, according to the custom of the priest's office, his lot was to enter into the temple of the Lord and burn incense. And the whole multitude of the people were praying without at the hour of incense. And there appeared unto him an angel of the Lord standing on the right side of the altar of incense. And Zacharias was troubled when he saw him, and fear fell upon him. But the angel said unto him, Fear not, Zacharias: because thy supplication is heard, and thy wife Elisabeth shall bear thee a son, and thou shalt call his name John. (Luke 1.5-13)

Appropriately, Luke begins his Gospel with John the Baptist, just as one who is to speak on daylight might begin with the dawn. For he preceded the Sun of righteousness, then at the point of rising, exactly as the day-break. The others do in fact make some mention of him, but introduce him when his ministry has begun. Luke allows him some dignity even before his birth, declaring the signs of divine power around his nativity, and showing that he was a Prophet of heaven's appointment, before men could ever know what he would turn out to be: and the intention is to gain him a greater hearing and respect, when his public career leads him out to proclaim the glory of Christ.

Luke 1.5. *In the days of Herod.* This was the son of Antipater, who had been brought to the throne by his father, and had laboured so strenuously for its increase, and with such energy, that he was afterwards given the title 'the Great'. Some believe that he is named by Luke, because he was the first foreign King: therefore the time of redemption was ripe, for the sceptre had passed to an alien race. Those who speak this way are not taking sufficient note of the prophecy of Jacob, where the coming of Messiah is not promised simply upon the Jews being robbed of their kingdom, but upon the loss of it by the tribe of Judah. Though it was not the wish of the holy Patriarch, the tribe of Judah had to lose its leadership before Christ should come; but the government of the people would find stability in that tribe right up to Christ, and ultimately in His person it would continue firm for ever. Even at the time when the Maccabaeans flourished, the tribe of Judah was almost reduced to non-ruling status, and shortly afterwards John, their last leader in that line, was killed. Yet their influence was not totally extinguished, for the Sanhedrin was still left, that is, the select council drawn from the family and descendants of David, whose authority was supreme. This lasted up till Herod, who took vengeance

4

upon it for a penalty once inflicted on himself, by wickedly slaying the judges. (He had been convicted of murder, and been forced to go abroad into voluntary exile, to escape execution.) So the fact that Herod's reign was alien did not break the sceptre of the tribe of Judah; rather it was when by daylight robbery he snatched from it what dignity the tribe still had left. The dignity of the throne had collapsed many years before, and its prestige had slowly crumbled, but this break is not inconsistent with the prophecy of Jacob. God had made two particular promises: that the throne of David would be eternal, and after it was destroyed, He would rebuild its ruins: the power of the kingdom would be eternal, yet a young branch would come out of the stem of Jesse; and both of these must be fulfilled. So God allowed the rule of the tribe of Judah, which He had fostered, to collapse in due time, that the people might wait for the reign of Christ with increased expectancy. Then at the moment when the failure of the council almost shattered the hopes of the faithful, God instantly burst upon them. This reference belongs to the historical sequence, in noting the time of the events, but it was reasonable, in making mention of the King's name, to record the miserable state of the times, so that the Jews might realize that now they must turn their eyes towards the Messiah, if indeed they waited on God's covenant in good faith.

Zacharias, of the course of Abijah. We know from the sacred history that the families of priests were allotted by David to certain orders. In doing this David made no contravention of the Law. God had conferred the priesthood on Aaron and his sons: the remaining Levites He had appointed to lesser duties. Nothing of this was changed by David, but he made a plan partly to prevent crowding that could lead to a violent disorder, and partly to anticipate ambition, at the same time arranging that a few should not take all the work to themselves, and leave the majority to sit at home idle. In this distribution, Abijah son of Eleazar had the eighth course of duty. So Zacharias was of priestly family, and indeed was descended from Eleazar, who succeeded his father to the high priesthood. How Elisabeth, being of the daughters of Aaron, could be kinswoman to Mary, I shall explain in due place. Luke records Elisabeth's family as a mark of distinction. According to the Law, Zacharias was allowed to marry any ordinary Levite's daughter. From the equality of this match, it is plain that the man was of some standing in his order.

Luke 1.6. *They were both righteous before God.* He gives them the glowing testimony, that they were not only holy and upright in their dealings with men, but also they were righteous in the sight of God. This righteousness Luke briefly defines as, walking in the commandments of the Lord. Both merit our careful attention: though the object of commending Zacharias and Elisabeth is to tell us that the lantern, which shone in front of the Son of God, was taken from no mean house, but from a particularly holy place, at the same time, we are shown by their example what is the rule of devout and righteous living. This is the first thing in ordering our lives aright, to approve ourselves before God with every effort. We know that He seeks above all the sincere heart and the pure conscience. So it is a reversal of priorities if we delay the matter of our heart's integrity, and arrange our outward scheme of existence in terms of obedience to the Law. We must remember that God, whom we are bidden to keep before our eyes, looks chiefly at the heart, not at the outward features of works. The next thing is obedience. We must not construct for ourselves our own favourite new pattern of righteousness apart from the Word of God, but must allow ourselves to be ruled by God's command. Nor are we to neglect this definition, that the righteous are those who form their lives according to the precepts of the Law. This implies, that all pretended cults are nothing in the sight of God, and that the course of human life is uncharted and unsound as soon as it departs from His Law.

The difference between *commandments* and *ordinances* is this, that the latter properly refers to the practices of devotion and divine worship, while the former is more general, applying as much to the worship of God as to the duties of charity. The word חקים which Hebrew uses to signify decrees and statutes, is translated into Greek as ordinances (δικαιώματα): חקים in Holy Scripture means rites, which the people employed in their worship of God and in their confession of faith. Now there are hypocrites who are over anxious and punctilious in this direction, but they are nothing like Zacharias and Elisabeth. True worshippers of God, as these two were, do not snatch at empty, vain ceremonial, but practice it inwardly, in their spirits, aiming at sincerity. False and two-faced men may weary themselves endlessly on external rites, but as they do not practise them as they were bidden by the Lord, they make a mockery of their efforts. In sum, Luke has embraced the whole Law in these two words.

Well then, if Zacharias and Elisabeth were without reproach in their observance of the Law, had they no need of the grace of Christ, for the full observance of the Law brings life, and where there is no transgression, the offence ceases? The answer is, that the splendid commendation which God's servants enjoy must be taken with a proviso. We should consider how it is that God deals with them—that is, according to the covenant that He has made with them, whose first article is free reconciliation, and daily forgiveness, by which He covers their sins. Men are reckoned righteous and blameless, because their whole life testifies that they are devoted to righteousness, that the fear of God

6

directs them, with some evidence of holy living meanwhile. Yet their pious efforts are far removed from perfection, and they can never please God without forgiveness. The righteousness that is praised in them depends upon the free kindness of God, whereby He does not lay to their charge such unrighteousness as lies in them still. This is the way we must expound whatever the Scriptures say of human righteousness, so as not to undermine the remission of sins, upon which the whole structure entirely relies for its foundation. The simple exposition that Zacharias and Elisabeth were justified by faith, because they gratuitously pleased God, for the Mediator's sake, distorts Luke's words. And as for the sense itself, it expresses something, but not the whole. I agree that the righteousness ascribed to them must be taken as theirs not on account of their merit, but on account of the grace of Christ, but it was because the Lord did not impute their sins to them, that He granted their holy—though imperfect—lives the distinction of righteousness. One can refute the folly of the Papists without trouble when they contrast the righteousnesss of faith with what is ascribed to Zacharias. The latter certainly flows from it, but it should be dependent and secondary to it—subordinated, as they commonly say—so as not to conflict with the other. The smoke-screen they create over one word is ridiculous. Ordinances, ('justifications') they say, mean the precepts of the Law: therefore they justify us. As if we deny that true righteousness is brought to us in the Law, or blame its doctrine for not justifying us, as though the fault were not really in the weakness of our flesh. Let us say it a hundred times: our life is set within the precepts of the Law, but nothing comes to men from that source, for by nature, they are utterly averse to the Law, and even under the regeneration of the Spirit of God, men are far from observing it completely.

Luke 1.7. *And they had no child.* God provided, by an exceptional decision, that John should be conceived beyond the ordinary and usual rule of nature. This was done also for Isaac, in whom God determined to give a rare and memorable example of His grace. In the flower of her years, Elisabeth had been barren: now came old age, that closes the womb even of fruitful women. So a twofold sign of divine power is displayed over two obstacles, and to this end, that the Lord should testify to the sending of his Prophet, as by a hand stretched out from the skies. A mortal man is born of earthly parents, yet beyond nature, if I may say so; the means commending him no less, than if he had flown down from heaven.

Luke 1.9. *According to the custom of the priest's office.* The Law ordained that incense be burned twice daily, that is, at morning and evening. The way the priests cast lots among themselves was according to the institution of David, as we have just described: what is done here

7

with incense is strictly upon the instruction of God's Law. The rest began with David, that individual families should take their turns, although David instituted nothing outside the order of the Law: he had merely demonstrated a pattern by which each could fulfil the task laid on him by God. The word 'temple' is here used of the Holy Place: we must note this, for at other times it includes the court also. Zacharias is said to have entered the temple, where only the priests were allowed to tread. So Luke says that the people stood far off, and between them and the altar of incense was a long distance, as the altar on which victims were offered stood in the middle. Note that Luke says, *before God*, for as often as the priest went into the Holy Place, it was like entering into the sight of God, to be a mediator between Him and the people. The Lord wished His people to have this testimony—that no mortal man may make his approach to heaven without a priest going before him. As long as men live on this earth, they may not gain the heavenly throne to find grace from it, unless in the person of a Mediator. Now seeing there were many priests, it was not permitted that two at a time should carry out the due office of intercession for the people: this was the reason for their being allocated to orders, that one only should enter the Sanctuary, thus only one at any one time should be priest. It was moreover intended by the burning of incense, to show the faithful that the breath of their prayers only ascended to heaven through the sacrifice of a Mediator. How these symbols apply to us is to be sought in the epistle to the Hebrews.

Luke 1.12. *Zacharias was troubled.* God does not appear to His servants deliberately to terrify them, but there is benefit, indeed necessity, for them to be struck with fear, that they may learn to show Him due honour after their confusion. Luke does not simply say that Zacharias was afraid, he adds that fear fell upon him, meaning that he was frightened to the point of collapse. The fear that comes in God's presence teaches men to reverence Him but also humbles the pride of their flesh, which is always so arrogant that they never submit to Him without being overcome by force. We see that only in the absence of God (that is, when they withdraw themselves from His sight) can men act in pride and self-conceit. If they kept God before their eyes, they would have to yield at once. If this was the experience of Zacharias, praised for his righteous living, at the sight of an angel, a spark of the divine radiance, what will become of us poor creatures if God's majesty makes us advance into His brilliant light? Let us take a lesson from the example of the holy fathers, that the only experience of the real sense of the presence of God is felt by men who fear and tremble in His sight; those who hear Him speak without a qualm, are dull and stupid.

Luke 1.13. *Fear not, Zacharias.* See how the glory of God makes

His saints tremble, not to the extent that they are dissolved in panic, but that they throw off their empty assurance, and receive Him humbly. As soon as God has quenched the pride of the flesh in His faithful, He reaches out an arm to raise them up: not so with the wicked. When they are haled to the judgment seat of God, total despair seizes them; this is the just reward God pays them for their empty consolations, their intoxicant cups of sin. To see the Angel's approach to Zacharias should be a welcome comfort for us. We must not be afraid, when God shows us His favour. What a great deception—to seek to enjoy peace by hiding from the presence of God—when our peace is to be found in Him. *Thy supplication is heard.* Zacharias might seem to have acted amiss, and contrary to the rule of his office, if he had entered the Sanctuary in the name of all the people and prayed like a private individual for the gift of a child. When a priest assumes his public office (*suscepta publica persona*), he should forget himself and make prayer for the well-being of the Church in general. If we were to say that there would be nothing out of place in Zacharias completing the main part of his intercession, and thereafter thinking of his personal needs, it would be a reasonably good solution. But it is hardly likely that Zacharias was at that time making prayer to get a son, for which he had lost hope, on account of his wife's advanced years; nor in fact must any particular moment be inferred from the words of the angel. So I simply interpret, that at last a prayer was heard, which long since he had poured out in the presence of God. The desire to raise up offspring—as long as it be without excess—may be inferred from Scripture as perfectly proper and holy; this is not reckoned least among the blessings of God. *Thou shalt call his name John.* I believe that the name set on the Baptist was to commend the exercise of his mission. יהוחנן, which Greek renders by 'John', means to the Hebrew *grace of God*. Many think that Zacharias' son was so called as meaning 'beloved of God.' I believe the grace commended was not that which God gave him as an individual, but that which his mission was to take to all men. The timing adds to the force and effect of the name, for even before he is born, God sets the mark of His grace upon him.

And thou shalt have joy and gladness; and many shall rejoice at his birth. For he shall be great in the sight of the Lord, and he shall drink no wine nor strong drink; and he shall be filled with the Holy Ghost, even from his mother's womb. And many of the children of Israel shall he turn unto the Lord their God. And he shall go before his face in the spirit and

9

power of Elijah, to turn the hearts of the fathers to the children, and the disobedient to walk in the wisdom of the just; to make ready for the Lord, a people prepared for him. (Luke 1.14-17)

Luke 1.14. *And thou shalt have joy.* The angel means a joy greater than any Zacharias might take in the new child, for he wishes to say that the son will be to him what he would never have dared to expect. And he goes on to say more—that the joy will be more than domestic, as parents know it themselves, or as is contained within their own four walls. It will be shared with outsiders, who will have access to the product of this birth. It is exactly as if the angel said, that it would not be just a son born to Zacharias alone, but a Teacher and a Prophet to the whole people. This passage has been abused by Papists, who introduce a pagan practice at their celebration of the birth of John. I need not tell how their lust for dissipation, with dances and reels and all sorts of frenzy, makes a quite ridiculous occasion of the day, which they make out to be a holy one, besides the games they allow, with magic arts and devil's tricks, just as at the mystic rites of Ceres. For the present, it is sufficient for me to remark briefly, that they have boorishly misapplied the angel's message to an annual birthday celebration, whereas the angel simply is proclaiming the joy that will come to all pious souls from the fruit of his teaching. They rejoiced that a Prophet was born to them, by whose ministry they were led to the hope of salvation.

Luke 1.15. *For he shall be great.* He confirms what he said on joy, for John was destined to win a great and unusual achievement. Here it is not so much the virtues in which he excelled that are praised, as the greatness and excellence of his office that are extolled: as Christ (Matt. 11.11) in affirming that he is the most outstanding of the sons of women, refers not so much to the holiness of his life as to his ministry. What follows directly, *he shall drink no wine nor strong drink*, is not to be taken in the sense that it was an exceptional virtue of John to be abstemious, as that God wished by this plain sign to set a mark on His servant, by which the world would recognize the life-long Nazaraean. Priests also abstained from wine and strong drink when they took their turns in the temple. The same abstinence was prescribed for Nazaraeans, until they had fulfilled their vow. God showed that John was dedicated to Him as a Nazaraean for his whole life—a distinctive token, just as we read was the case with Samson. Now this is not to be used as a pretext for concocting a cult of God by abstinence from wine, in the way that imitators snatch up something to emulate from their forebears. Let all observe moderation: let those who suffer ill effects from drinking wine choose to abstain, and let those who have none bear the lack of it with equanimity. As for the word *sicera* (strong drink), I readily adhere to the opinion which holds that the Hebrews used the word שֵׁכָר for any kind of wine.

He shall be filled with the Holy Ghost. I think these words simply mean that a character will be revealed in John which shall show promise of the greatness to come. I say character, not in the sense vulgarly employed in business, but as fits his exalted calling. The sense is, then, that the power and grace of the Spirit will come out in him not only at the time when he steps out on his life's work, but straight from the womb he will excel in the gifts of the Spirit, which shall be as tokens to show what he will turn out to be. *From his mother's womb* just means from his early infancy. I admit that the virtue of the Spirit worked upon John while he was still shut in his mother's womb, but there, in my opinion, the angel means something different, namely that, while John was still an infant, he would be, so to speak, led into the arena with the unusual approbation of the grace of God. As to the question of fulness, there is nothing to discuss too minutely, or rather to trifle over with sophists. The Scripture only uses the word to express the nobility and pre-eminence of the abundance of the gifts of the Spirit. We know that to Christ alone was the Spirit given without measure, that from his fulness we may all drink (John 1.16), while to others there is distribution within a certain limit (I Cor. 12.11; Eph. 4.7). But those who are gifted with richer grace, beyond the common capacity of the crowd, are said to have been 'filled' with the Spirit. Now as the richer power of the Spirit was an extraordinary gift of God in John's case, you must note that the Spirit is not conferred on all from boyhood, but when it is God's will. John, from the womb, gave token of future renown: Saul the cattle-man long showed no sign at all of royalty, till suddenly elected king he changed into a new man (I Sam. 10.6). The instance teaches us how from early infancy to extreme old age, the working of the Spirit upon men is free.

Luke 1.16. *And many of the children of Israel shall he turn.* These words reveal the wretched wastage that then existed in the Church. They must have been quite fallen away, for there to have been occasion of turning back to God. In truth, there was such corruptions, such depraved morality, such disordered government, that one should look on it as a miracle that even a few adhered to religion. If the decay of the old Church was so terrible, it is not competent for the Papists to defend their superstitions on the frivolous pretext that the Church shall never be in error—assuming that they do not apply the term to the true and elect sons of God, but to the rabble of wrong-doers. Does this passage attribute more to John than a man can carry? When conversion to God restores men to their spiritual life, this is not only God's own activity, it is actually a greater work than the very creation of man. On

11

this basis, ministers might seem to be equated with God, and even put above Him, inasmuch as He is Creator, since it is a greater thing to be born again to the life of heaven than to come into mortal life upon earth. The solution is easy: when the Lord accords such praise to outward teaching, He is not speaking of it apart from the secret virtue of His own Spirit. As God chooses men to be His ministers, using their efforts in the building-up of His Church, at the same time He works through them by the hidden power of His Spirit, to make their labours effective and fruitful. As often as Scripture commends the effectiveness of men's ministry, let us learn to acknowledge the welcome grace of the Spirit, without which the voice of man would have spent itself on thin air. So Paul (II Cor. 3.6), while he boasts that he is a minister of the Spirit, claims nothing for himself alone, as though he by his voice could reach into a man's heart; it is the power and grace of the Spirit that he puts forward in his ministry. These expressions are worthy of note, for Satan strains with amazing cunning to weaken the effect of teaching by reducing the grace of the Spirit that goes with it. I agree that, of itself and by itself, outward preaching can do nothing; but as it is an instrument of divine power for our salvation, and an instrument made efficacious through the Spirit, then what God has joined together, let us not put asunder. Further, that the glory of conversion and faith may remain firmly with God alone, the Scripture often warns us that ministers are nothing in themselves, but goes on to compare them with God, in case anyone should falsely steal the honour from God and transfer it to them. In short, those whom God turns to Himself by the work of His minister, the minister is said to convert as being nothing else than the hand of God; and both points are wisely put over in the present passage. Enough has now been said on the efficacy of teaching. As for its not being in the minister's choice and hand to convert men to God, we may see that John did not convert all wholesale (and no doubt he would have done, if they had yielded to him in all points as he willed); he only converts those whom it pleased the Lord effectively to call. In short, the angel gives the same lesson here as Paul passes on to the Romans (10.17), Belief comes of hearing, but the illumination of faith only comes to those who have inward revelation of the aim of the Lord.

Luke 1.17. *And he shall go before his face.* These words define what the task of John will be, and by this sign distinguishes him from the other Prophets, each of whom received a definite and particular call, in that John was sent only to walk before Christ, as one that prepares the way of the king. Thus the Lord speaks in Malachi (3.1), 'Behold, I send my messenger, and he shall make level the way before me'. Altogether, John's mission had the single aim of making a hearing for Christ, and preparing disciples for him. There is no actual mention of Christ here, but the Angel makes John the fore-runner or standard-bearer of the eternal God—so we infer the eternal Godhead of Christ.

In the spirit and power of Elijah. 'Spirit and power' I take to mean that Power or Excellence of the Spirit, with which Elijah was endowed. We need have no resort here to the stupid idea of Pythagoras, and pretend that the soul of the Prophet migrated into the body of John; but understand that the very Spirit of God, which had worked mightily in Elijah, later exerted a similar force and efficacy in the Baptist. The name is added to explain and expound the particular grace in which Elijah supremely excelled, namely, under the direction of heavenly resource, to restore the broken worship of God in a wonderful way: reformation of this order took more than human virtue. What John began was no less marvellous: so it is natural that he in turn should be awarded the same gift.

To turn the hearts of the fathers. Here the angel notes the greatest resemblance John had to Elijah. He declares the object of his mission to be the gathering together of a scattered people into unity of faith: to 'turn fathers to sons' means drawing them back to grace, out of dissension—so we may take it that there had been a division that split the people, tore them apart in fact. We know how terribly the people fell away in Elijah's day, how shamefully they lapsed from their fathers' standards, that they could scarcely ever be called by rights 'children of Abraham', being so very different from them: this was the people that Elijah brought back to reverence and order. Just such a gathering-in of the fathers with the children began again with John, and Christ in the end made it perfect. So Malachi, speaking of this 'turning', means that the condition of the Church would be all upset when the second Elijah would come. Of its state in these days we are more than adequately informed in the histories, as we shall see clearly in the appropriate places. The message of Scripture was stained with innumerable falsifications, the worship of God was corrupted with the most foolish superstitions, religious life was divided by various sectarian interests, the priests were blatant sinners and *Bon Viveurs*, the common people itself had fallen into all kinds of dissolute living—in a word there was no health in them. The expression here, *hearts of the fathers to the children*, is inexact, for there was more need for the children to be converted, as they had broken covenant and defected from the wholesome faith of their fathers. But though the way of the conversion is not accurately expressed by the Evangelist, his sense is perfectly plain: God would achieve things through John that would re-unite in holy concord elements formerly divided against themselves. In the Prophet, it reads both ways, but his one intention was to emphasize the mutual agreement.

Considering how men often make common purpose, that leads

different parties further away from God, the angel goes on to define the promised conversion as 'recalling the disobedient to the wisdom of the just'. His point is, that we should not use a false air of harmony to lead us into frivolous involvement with the godless. As the word 'peace' has a winning and attractive sound to it, the Papists seize on it, wherever it is found in Scripture, to pour ill repute on us, as though we, in our efforts to bring the world from its traitorous lapse back to Christ, were the authors of its discords. Their lack of understanding is nicely refuted by this passage, since the angel defines the manner of true and proper conversion as having, for support and binding, the 'wisdom of the just'. A curse on peace and unity, that unites men—and leaves out God! Further, there is no doubt that by the wisdom of the just we must understand faith, as by contrast the disobedient are called unbelieving. It is a shining tribute to faith, teaching us that we are really wise unto righteousness when we obey the Word of the Lord. The world has its own wisdom, but perverse, yes, fatal, under the condemnation of vanity: it is implied by the angel that the shadowy wisdom in which the children of this generation indulge is debased and accursed in God's sight. We are sure that conciliation among men starts with a return to peace with God. What follows, about preparing a people perfect for the Lord, agrees with that phrase where John is to be the herald of Christ, to walk before His face: the object of his preaching was to make the people alert to hear the teaching of Christ. The participle κατεσκευασμένον does not so much mean 'perfection' in Greek as 'composition and harmony', in which things fall into place. This meaning fits the present passage well enough: John is to be sent to adapt and shape the people to Christ, who otherwise were rough and coarse, never ready to be taught.

And Zacharias said unto the angel, Whereby shall I know this? for I am an old man, and my wife well stricken in years. And the angel answering said unto him, I am Gabriel, that stand in the presence of God; and I was sent to speak unto thee, and to bring thee these good tidings. And behold, thou shalt be silent and not able to speak, until the day that these things shall come to pass, because thou believedst not my words, which shall be fulfilled in their season. (Luke 1.18-20)

Luke 1.18. *And Zacharias said unto the angel.* Now comes Zacharias' hesitation, and the penalty God exacted for his lack of faith. He had prayed for a son, yet here at its promise, he seems to have forgotten his prayers and his faith, and is diffident. At first sight it might seem hard that God is so gravely offended at his answer. He protests his advanced years. Abraham did the same, and his faith is so greatly praised that Paul says (Rom. 4.19), he did not regard his own body as good as dead, nor the deadness of Sarah's womb, but simply made his confidence in the truth and power of God. Zacharias asks by what means, by what proof, he can be sure. Gideon (Judges 6.17) is not blamed for asking for a double sign. In fact, we soon find mention of Mary taking similar exception, 'How shall this be, seeing I know not a man?' Yet the Angel covers it, as though there were no fault in her words. So how does it transpire that Zacharias is sharply punished by God, convicted apparently of a most serious sin? I would say, that if we are to look only at the words, his fault was either equal to them all, or that there was no sin in Zacharias. However, while we may reasonably reckon men's deeds and words according to natural feelings, we must ultimately stand by the judgment of God, who can penetrate the hidden places of the heart. No doubt the Lord saw something worse in Zacharias than his words reveal, and this was the reason for His anger, when he turned back in diffidence from the grace promised to him. It is not our place to prescribe rules for God; He must be free to punish a failing in one man which in others He forgives. Yet it is easily seen that Zacharias' case is different from that of Abraham, Gideon and Mary. This does not appear from their words. The understanding must be God's, for His eyes pierce to the very depths of the heart. Thus God distinguishes Sarah's laugh from Abraham's, though there is no difference in the kind of laugh (Gen. 17.17, 18.10). The reason for Zacharias' failure to believe, was that bounded by the limits of his natural existence, he attributed less to God's power than he ought. Men think too narrowly and meanly of the works of God when they believe He will do no more than they can believe in natural terms, as though His hand were restricted to our senses, or were limited by earth's measures. The feature of faith is to extend belief far beyond the dictates of the possibilities of carnal order. Zacharias had no hesitation whether this were the voice of God or not, but, as he was too earthbound, his mind allowed the doubt to creep in—would the words come true? His action caused God great hurt; it was just as if he were disputing with himself whether God was to be relied upon for truth, after agreeing that it was He who had spoken. Yet we must realize that Zacharias was not so unbelieving as to abandon his faith. There is faith in general, accepting the promise of eternal salvation and the testimony of free adoption. But, just as once God has taken us into His favour, He makes many particular promises—that He will feed us, rescue us from dangers, defend the cause of our innocence, protect our life—so there is a particular faith, that responds to each promise of this kind. It will sometimes happen that a man who has faith in God over remission of sins, and his salvation,

15

may be weak in another part: perhaps he will tremble too much at the fear of death, perhaps he will be over anxious for his daily sustenance, perhaps he will be too much confused in his own plans. This was Zacharias' incredulity; he held on to the roots and foundation of his faith, but hesitated on the one matter—whether God would give him a son. We must remember that men whose uncertainty over one particular affair disturbs and shakes them do not fall away, or lose their faith, nor are those branches tossing in the changing winds the sign of a failure at the roots. Zacharias had not the least intention to call in question the faith of the divine promise. In general he was sure that God was true, but he was drawn by the craft and wiles of Satan to make an unworthy point of difference. We must be all the more watchful and alert. Which of us shall be unscathed by Satan's traps, when we see a man of such rare sanctity caught up in them, after a life-time of vigilance, taking heed to himself?

Luke 1.19. *I am Gabriel.* By those words the Angel shows that it is distrust, not of himself, but of God who sent him, whose command he carries; Zacharias is reproved for contempt of God. *Stand in the presence of God,* has the effect of being ready for service. In other words, he is no mortal man, but a heavenly spirit; he has not made a self-willed descent to earth, but has faithfully fulfilled his task as becomes a servant of God. It follows that God, the Author of the promise, has been shamefully injured and despised in the person of His messenger. Christ is making the same point in the words (Luke. 10.16), 'He that rejecteth you, rejecteth me,' etc. Though the preaching of the Gospel is not carried to us from the skies by angels, yet as God has so often testified that it comes from Him by marvellous signs, and Christ, Chief and Head of the angels, proclaimed it once for all from His own lips to be for ever fixed, it should have no less honour than if all the Angels appeared in heaven to shout aloud its evidence. Compare how the Apostle, in the Epistle to the Hebrews, is not content to equate the voice of the Gospel, which sounds in the voice of men, to the Law brought by angels, but goes on to lead his argument from lesser to greater: for if the word, he says, spoken through angels was not rejected with impunity, far less shall they escape their reward who today despise the voice of Christ, which will shake heaven and earth (Heb. 2.2, 12.25). Our lesson is to bring God the obedience of faith, which is of more avail than many sacrificial victims.

Gabriel means the strength or fortitude or chieftaincy of God, and this name was given the angel for our sake, that we might learn to ascribe nothing to angels in themselves, for all their virtue is divine. The participle παρεστηκὼς is past tense, but it is well known with words of this kind that the past is used for the present, especially when a con-

16

tinuing activity is described. The angel, as we have just said, claims in these words to be God's constant servant. Speaking of bringing good tidings increases Zacharias' blame, for he shows God ingratitude, while He kindly holds forth a matter full of gladness and expectation.

Luke 1.20. *And behold, thou shalt be silent.* This was a suitable kind of penalty to inflict on Zacharias, to await the outcome of the promise without speech, seeing that when he ought to have listened in silence, he broke in with his objection out of turn, Faith keeps its silence, to give attention to the Word of God. Its chance to speak comes after, in replying, Amen; compare Hos. 2.23, 'I will say to them, Thou art my people: and they shall say to me, Thou art our God.' As Zacharias has rashly contradicted the Word of God, this favour is refused him; he may not break out into thanksgiving, but rather, for a time loses the power of his tongue, which had been in too great haste. Yet God gently mitigates the penalty. First, He limits it to ten months: second, He does not allow Zacharias to lose the favour, which he did not deserve. The same kindness He shows to us daily. Our faith is narrow, we throw many obstacles in the way, and the truth of God has to find some means to force its way through, to win its way towards us. This is the aim of the angel, when he rebukes Zacharias' lack of faith, and yet proclaims that the thing he has failed to believe will still come to pass. It was a great relief to Zacharias to hear this, to know that the faithfulness of God is not made of no account by his short-coming, but indeed falls out all the greater at last. It happens some times, that the Lord offers and fulfils what He has promised to the unbelieving in spite of their resistance. A memorable example is given us in King Ahaz, who, for all he rejected the promise of salvation, was still delivered from his enemies (Isa. 7.11). In his case, the outcome brought forward the salvation of the chosen people, at no benefit to himself. It is different with Zacharias, to whom God pardons the failure of faith and provides a way of correction.

And the people were waiting for Zacharias, and they marvelled while he tarried in the temple. And when he came out, he could not speak unto them: and they perceived that he had seen a vision in the temple: and he continued making signs unto them, and remained dumb. And it came to pass, when the days of his ministration were fulfilled, he departed unto his house.

And after these days Elisabeth his wife conceived; and she hid herself five months, saying, Thus hath the Lord done unto me in the days where-

in he looked upon me, to take away my reproach among men. (Luke
1. 21-25)

Luke 1.21. *And the people were waiting.* Luke tells that the people
witnessed this vision. Zacharias lingered in the temple longer than was
usual. Hence suspicion arises that something out of the ordinary has
affected him. When he comes out, he shows by gestures and by signs
that he has been made dumb. We may well believe that fear showed in
his face. They infer that God has revealed Himself to him. Visions in
that age were rare, or non-existent, but the people remembered that
they were once frequent in the days of their fathers. Right enough
then, by the plain signs, do they make their judgment: it was no
human accident, to become speechless all at once, without being ill, and
to emerge from the temple after an extraordinary delay in a state of
shock. The word *temple* (as we have already said) is used of the Shrine,
where the incense altar stood. The priests used to come out from
there, when the rite was over, into their courtyard, to give the people a
blessing.

Luke 1.23. *When the days . . . were fulfilled.* Λειτουργίαν is Luke's
term for Ministration, which came to each in due turn, as we have
explained. The fact that Zacharias is said to have returned home after
the completion of his period of duty tells us that the priests stayed away
from their homes while they were on the roster, obviously to be completely devoted and set upon the worship of God. For this reason
floored apartments were set in the sides of the temple, to serve as
cubicles (I Kings 6.5). The Law did not prohibit a priest from his
home, but, as it did not permit a man who feeds on holy bread to have
contact with his wife (I Sam. 21.4), it is likely that when holy things
were often handled with too little reverence here was a means devised
to keep them away from all distractions, and preserve them clean of any
stain. Not only was it forbidden them to lie with their wives, but also
to take wine or strong drink. Since then they had to alter their way of
living, it was useful not to leave the temple at all, but to let the sight of
the place itself remind them that they were to keep pure, in the way
God prescribed. It was useful too, for all occasion of self-indulgence to
be cut off, to give them more attention to their duties. On this pretext
the Papists today defend their tyrannical rule of celibacy. This is their
argument: as priests of old were bidden to keep away from their wives
at the season of their sacred service, it is right now for perpetual continence to be asked of priests, who sacrifice daily, and not at set times—
especially as the rites are now of far greater worth than under the Law.
But I should like to know why they do not abstain from wine and
strong drink? They have no right to separate precepts that God put to-

gether, and keep one half while the other is neglected. Lying with wives is forbidden no less explicitly than drinking wine (Ezek. 44.21). If the Pope commands his ministrants to be celibate, under pretext of the Law, why does he allow them wine? On the same lines he should have all his ministrants huddled in some back corners of the temples, to lead a prison existence all their lives apart from the intercourse of women and the world. No, it is obvious, they have no good purpose in putting forward the Law of God, when they depart from it. The full answer comes from a right distinction of Law and Gospel. The priest stood in God's sight for the expiation of the people's sins, to be a kind of mediator of God and men: the role given him made him require to have some mark to exempt him from the common run of men, so that the character of the true Mediator might show through. This also was the purpose of holy vestments and anointing. There is nothing like this involved for the ordinary ministers and pastors of the Church: I speak of the ministers that Christ has appointed to feed His flock, not those whom the Pope initiates, more as butchers for the slaying of Christ than as ministrants. Let us accept the verdict of the Spirit, which states, 'Let marriage be had in honour among all' (Heb. 13.4).

Luke 1.24. *And she hid herself.* This might seem out of place, as though she were ashamed of the blessing from God. It is the opinion of some that she did not dare go out in public while there was no certainty, in case she should be exposed to mockery if the hope she had conceived were disappointed. I am sure she was so convinced of the promise received, that she had no doubt about the outcome. When she considered the heavy penalty her husband got for his careless slip of the tongue, is it likely that she would continue to harbour a similar hesitation in her mind for five months? And her words show clearly that her hope was not tentative or uncertain. When she says, 'Thus hath the Lord done', she explicitly and fearlessly declares that she acknowledges His favour. There could be two reasons for concealment: the first, not to expose God's miracle, before it was unmistakable, to the idle play of human gossip—the world is always ready to talk idly and with scant respect of the works of God. The second, to make men, who should see her suddenly with child, the more eager to give praise to God. When the works of God reveal themselves by degrees, often the process itself cheapens them in our eyes. It was not for her own sake that Elisabeth kept hidden, but more in respect of other people.

Luke 1.25. *Thus hath the Lord done unto me.* She goes over God's goodness in private, till the time for making it known ripens. We may believe that she was informed of the promised child in writing from her husband, so that she might more surely and more earnestly declare

God to be the Author of this favour, as her next words show, *wherein he looked upon me, to take away my reproach.* She knows the reason for her barrenness was that God's favour had been turned away from her. Scripture places this among the chief earthly blessings of God—that God grants us offspring: rightly so. If increase given to dumb animals comes of His goodness, how much greater is the propagation of the human race, and how much more is human fertility to be understood as a work of grace. It is no slight or common honour for God, who alone is, and alone deserves to be reckoned, Father, to admit the sons of earth into a share of the title. It is a lesson to be carefully observed, that children are an inheritance which come from God to us, and the fruit of the womb is His reward (Ps. 127.3). Elisabeth sees more in it, however, for in barrenness and old age, against the usual way of nature, she had conceived in a singular miracle. *To take away my reproach.* Sterility was always held as a reproach, and not without reason, as the womb's blessing was held to be among the highest testimonies of God's love. Some believe this was particularly regarded among the ancient people, because Christ was to be a descendant of the seed of Abraham. But this only had respect to the tribe of Judah. Others say, more correctly, that it was for the prosperous and happy increase of the holy people, as was said to Abraham, 'Thy seed shall be as the sand of the sea-shore, and as the stars of the heaven.' We have to hold together the universal benediction extended to the whole human race, and the promise given to Abraham, which applies to God's Church in particular (Gen. 13.15). Parents must learn to thank God for the children they raise up, while those who have no offspring must accept that they are humbled in this regard. Elisabeth relates the reproach only to men, as the chastening is temporary, and brings us no loss in the Kingdom of Heaven.

Now in the sixth month the angel Gabriel was sent from God unto a city of Galilee, named Nazareth, to a virgin betrothed to a man whose name was Joseph, of the house of David; and the virgin's name was Mary. And he came in unto her, and said, Hail, thou that art highly favoured, the Lord is with thee. But she was greatly troubled at the saying, and cast in her mind what manner of salutation this might be. And the angel said unto her, Fear not, Mary: for thou hast found favour with God. And behold, thou shalt conceive in thy womb, and bring forth a son, and shalt call his name JESUS. He shall be great, and shall be called the Son of the Most High: and the Lord God shall give unto Him the throne of his father David: and he shall reign over the house of Jacob for ever; and of his kingdom there shall be no end. (Luke 1.26-33)

Luke 1.26. *Now in the sixth month.* We must marvel at the pattern of the divine plan—so utterly diverse from the common judgment of men—in God willing a more distinguished start to be given to the birth of the fore-runner, than to His own Son. The prophecy concerning John was made known in the temple and published on all sides. The promise of Christ came to a virgin in an obscure Judaean town, and the prophecy stayed buried in the heart of one girl only. Clearly from Christ's very nativity there was to be a fulfilment of the words, 'That God through foolishness willed to save them that believe' (I Cor. 1.21). In such a way did He entrust the treasure of this mystery to a virgin, that in good time it might reach all godly men. Such guardianship, I agree, might be despised, but it was the best suited to test the humility of faith, and to resist the pride of the wicked. We must learn for ourselves to submit quietly to God, even though the reason is not at once obvious, and not be ashamed to have as our teacher her who bore in her womb Christ, the eternal Wisdom of God. At all events, we must not let scornful contempt make us fail to understand the incomparable secret, which God deliberately wanted hidden for the little ones and the meek. I believe it is for the same cause that He chose a girl engaged to a man. Origen's conjecture has nothing to it, when he says that it was done to conceal from Satan the salvation He was preparing for men. A screen of marriage was presented to the eyes of the world, that He whom the commonalty reckoned to be Joseph's son might be recognized by the faithful as Son of God. Christ's coming forth was not so entirely without glory that the heavenly Father did not from the beginning shine upon Him the splendour of Godhead. The angel heralded the birth of a Saviour, but their song was only heard by the shepherds and did not travel far. One sign might have become famous, as the Magi who came from the East published it—the star that appeared to them as witness of the birth of a mighty king. Yet we may see how God kept His Son almost in obscurity, until the time of full revelation came: then, as it were, He put Him out onto a stage where He would be seen by all. The participle ἐμνηστευμένην used by the Evangelist means a girl engaged to a man, but not already given in marriage to her husband. It was the rule with the Jews for parents to keep their daughters at home with them for a time after they had betrothed them to men, otherwise the law relating to the corruption of a virgin would have been superfluous (Deut. 22.13). Luke says Joseph was of the house of David, as families are usually reckoned under the names of the men. On this matter there will be more to say elsewhere.

21

Luke 1.28. *Hail, thou art highly favoured.* The angel's mission was so amazing, so incredible indeed, that he opens it with a commendation of the grace of God. And certainly the small degree of our intelligence makes our minds too small to grasp the unmeasured greatness of the works of God, so that this is the best means to stretch them for us, to take in the infinity of His grace. The door to faith is our sense of the divine goodness. Thus the angel does well to follow this approach, and by instilling into the heart of the virgin the thought of the grace of God he widens it to receive a mystery beyond all understanding. The participle κεχαριτωμένη that Luke uses expresses the free favour of God. This is better shown in Eph. 1.6 where Paul, dealing with our reconciliation with God, says that ἐχαρίτωσεν us in His beloved Son, that is, He has taken into His grace, and embraced with His favour, us who before were hostile to Him. Then the angel adds, *the Lord is with thee.* Those to whom God has once granted His love find His loving-kindness shown them, and receive the enrichment and continuance of His benefits. So he adds a third phrase, 'she is *blessed* among women'. He makes the blessing a kind of effect and proof of the divine favour. In my view, this is not spoken to her praise, but rather as a mark of her happiness. It was Paul's way to ask grace first, and then peace, that is all prosperity, for God's faithful people, meaning that we come at last to blessedness and riches, only when we are loved by God, the source of all good things. Now if Mary's happiness, righteousness and life all spring from the freely given love of God, then her virtues and all her excellence are nothing other than the generosity of God. It is quite absurd to teach that we are to seek from her anything which she receives otherwise than we do ourselves. The Papists, with the most crass stupidity, have turned this salutation into a miniature prayer, with some kind of magic charm, and have reached such a pitch of folly that their spokesmen will never get up on a platform and pray for the grace of the Holy Spirit unless they use their 'Hail Mary'. Quite apart from this being no more than a word of congratulation, it is reckless for them to take an office that is not theirs, for God only gave the word to His angel. Their attempted repetition is doubly silly, when they salute one who is not there at all.

Luke 1.29. *But she was greatly troubled.* Luke does not say she was troubled at the sight of the angel, but at his words. Why mention the sight, then? My interpretation is that Mary recognized something of the heavenly glory in the angel and felt a sudden fear from reverence for God. She was troubled because she saw that her greeting came not from mortal man, but from the angel of God. Luke does not say that she was troubled to the extent of being struck dumb: no, he indicates that her mind was alert and well composed, when shortly he goes on to say that she considered what kind of salutation this might be: that is, what was its object, what was its meaning. She realizes at once that the angel is not sent for nothing. Her example teaches us, first, that the works of God are not to make us wonder open-mouthed, second, that our thoughts upon them should start with awe and fear.

Luke 1.30. *Fear not, Mary.* This bidding to put away her fear should always remind us of the frailty of our flesh, so that we cannot but tremble whenever the least spark of the glory of God shines forth. When we seriously take to heart the presence of God, it is impossible to rest idly upon our thoughts. As all are under the scrutiny of His judgment, fear sets us afright, until He reveals Himself as our Father. The holy virgin saw such a foul tide of wickedness in her race, that rightly she trembled for a greater vengeance. To remove her fear, the angel declares that he has come as the herald of exceptional good. Luke uses the Hebrew expression *found favour*, for 'having God propitious'. It is not meant that she found favour in the sense of having looked for it, but as having been offered it outright. Instances of this are quite well enough known, and reference would be superfluous.

Luke 1.31. *And behold, thou shalt conceive in thy womb.* The angel shapes his words first on the prophecy of Isaiah, then on other passages in the Prophets, all the better to reach the understanding of the virgin, for such prophecies as these were known and frequently spoken of among the god-fearing. Note of course that his message is not confined to the hearing of the virgin, but was a Word of Gospel shortly thereafter to be published all over the globe. It was not affected without God's design that there should have been such an explicit agreement between the old prophecies and the present announcement of the appearing of *Christ*.

The word *conceive* is sufficient refutation of the delusions of Marcion and Manichaeus alike. We may immediately infer that Mary brought forth no airy body or ghost, but the very progeny that she had first conceived in the womb. *Shalt call his name Jesus.* The explanation of the name is given by Matthew (1.21), 'For it is he that shall save his people from their sins.' So salvation is promised in His name, and it is shown to what end *Christ* was sent by the Father into the world; just as He declares that He had not come to destroy, but to bring salvation to the world (John 12.47). Let us remember that it was not by man's choosing but by the command of God that this name was appointed by the angel, so that our faith might be founded upon heaven, not upon earth. It derives from ישע, which is 'salvation' in Hebrew, whence the verb הושיע, meaning 'to save'. It is wasted ingenuity to attempt to distinguish the Hebrew name יהושע (*Joshua*). It is accepted that the Rabbis' insistence on writing *Iesu* is done maliciously, in case they do

Christ an honour, or rather to make out that He was some kind of degenerate Judaean. Their writings deserve as much credence as the howling of dogs. As for objections that it is far beneath the dignity of the Son of God to share a name with others, the same might also be objected to 'Christ'. However there is a perfectly easy answer to both, that what was fore-shadowed under the Law came to full and concrete existence in the Son of God, what had been figurative took substance in Him. A further objection is equally trifling. It is said that the name of Jesus cannot be an object of veneration and fear, at which every knee should bow, unless it belong uniquely to the Son of God. But Paul himself does not make a magical name of it (Phil. 2.9), as though majesty were contained in its actual syllables, but rather the effect of his words is that Christ has been given supreme authority by the Father, under whom the whole world should be humble. Say 'good riddance' to notions like these and learn that the name of Jesus was set on Christ, that the faithful might understand to seek from Him what, under the Law, had been a shadow.

Luke 1.32. *He shall be great.* The angel had said the same over John the Baptist, yet he does not wish to equate him with Christ. In his degree the Baptist is great, but the greatness of Christ is described directly in terms that exalt Him above all creatures. He alone has the unique right to be called Son of God, as the Apostle argues in Hebrews (1.5). I agree that sometimes in Scripture angels and kings are honoured with this title, but these are called 'sons of God' generally, for their excellence. Now there is not the least doubt or difficulty in seeing that God raises His Son above all the others, when He particularly addresses Him in the words, 'Thou art my Son' (Ps. 2.7). Here Christ is not confused with angels or with men, as though He were one of a company of sons of God. What is given to Him may not lawfully be taken by any other. Kings are sons of God, not by any natural right, but as God has accorded them this honour. Nor even do angels merit this distinction, except that under a supreme head they are exalted in creation. We too are sons, but by adoption which comes by faith, we do not have it by nature. Christ is unique, and only-begotten. The future tense of the verb is so distorted by that foul dog Servetus as to prove that Christ is not the eternal Son of God, but began to be reckoned so from the time that He assumed our flesh: this is sheer slander. His reasoning is that Christ was not Son of God before He took flesh and came into the world, because the words of the angel were 'He shall be called.' I take it quite differently; the angel's words precisely mean that the Son of God will be such in the flesh as He had been in eternity, for *be called* refers to the open revelation. Now there is a great difference between the two positions, whether He began to be Son of God when He had not been such before, or whether He was revealed to men in order that they should recognize Him promised long since. As God was in all ages invoked by His people as Father, it is deduced that there was in heaven a Son, from whom and through whom that fatherhood might reach down to man. It is too much for men to claim, if they dare boast that they are sons of God, except insofar as they are members of the Son only-begotten. Quite certainly, the holy fathers were emboldened to invoke this honour upon themselves through their reliance upon the mediation of the Son Himself. The fuller application of this matter may be found in Paul: how we may now, without fear, not only call God Father, but cry it out (Rom. 8.15, Gal. 4.5).

Shall give unto him the throne of . . . David. We said that the angel borrowed lofty expressions from the Prophets to commend Christ, to help the holy virgin recognize that He would be the Redeemer promised of old to the fathers. Whenever the Prophets speak of the renewal of the Church, they recall the whole hope of the people to the reign of David, till it became a common-place axiom among the Jews that the salvation of the Church would be established upon the happy ground of that reign, that nothing would more befit and become the office of Messiah than to raise up anew the kingdom of David. Hence the name of David is from time to time applied to the Messiah, as in Jer. 30.9, 'They shall serve the Lord their God, and David their king.' Similarly in Ezek. 34.24 and 37.24, 'And my servant David shall be king over them,' Hos. 3.5, 'And seek the Lord their God, and David their king'. The passages, besides, where He is called son of David are sufficiently known and discussed. All in all, the angel signifies that in the Person of Christ will be fulfilled the prophecy of Amos, on raising up the tabernacle of David, which was ruined and cast down (Amos 9.11).

Luke 1.33. *He shall reign over the house of Jacob.* As salvation was promised to the Jews in particular (according to the covenant struck with their father Abraham) and as Christ was, on Paul's testimony (Rom. 15.8) 'minister of the circumcision', the angel was right to appoint His reign over that race, being His true seat and home. There is no contradiction with other prophecies, that spread Christ's Kingdom abroad and extend it to the farthest limits of the earth. In a new and marvellous act of adoption God brought the nations into the family of Jacob—those who were foreign before: yet so that the Jews, considered as the first-born, should hold a prior place, as we read in Psalm 110.2, 'The Lord shall send forth the rod of thy strength out of Zion.' Thus the throne of Christ was placed in the people of Israel, from which He should subdue all the world to Himself. As many as He gathered through faith into the stock of Abraham are reckoned true Israel.

Though the Jews by their defection have withdrawn from the Church of God, the Lord will preserve some remnant yet to the end, since His calling is without repentance. Certainly the body of the people is cut back to a degree, but we must remember the mystery, of which Paul speaks at length in Rom. 11.25. It will come to pass in future time that God will draw in some Jews from their dispersed state. Meanwhile the Church spread over all the world is the spiritual home of Jacob, since it took its origin from Zion.

For ever. The angel explains in what sense we may take the often repeated promise of the Prophets that the Kingdom of David was everlasting. In his day and in Solomon's it prospered in power and resources, but the third in line, Rehoboam, scarcely kept control over one tribe and a half. After him it fell into a succession of disasters until its ultimate collapse. The angel now declares that when it shall be established in the person of Christ, it will not be liable to fall, and to add force to this he engages the support of Daniel (7.14), 'of this kingdom there shall be no end'. But while the sense of the words is that God will be the protection and guard for ever of Christ's Kingdom and Church, that it may not pass from the earth as long as sun and moon shall shine in the sky, the true perpetuity pertains to the glory to come. In unbroken ranks the faithful thus succeed each other in this life, that finally they may all at one time be brought into heaven, where they shall reign without end.

And Mary said unto the angel, How shall this be, seeing I know not a man? And the angel answered and said unto her, The Holy Ghost shall come upon thee, and the power of the Most High shall overshadow thee: wherefore also that which is to be born shall be called holy, the Son of God. And behold, Elisabeth thy kinswoman, she also hath conceived a son in her old age: and this is the sixth month with her that was called barren. For no word from God shall be void of power. And Mary said, Behold, the handmaid of the Lord; be it unto me according to thy word. And the angel departed from her. (Luke 1.34-38)

Luke 1.34. *How shall this be?* The holy virgin seems to put a false limit upon God's power as much as Zacharias did before. What is beyond the ordinary course of nature, she infers to be an impossibility. Her reasoning is, I do not know a man: how then am I to believe that what you announce will come true? No great effort is required from us to clear her from all fault. By faith she must at once ascend to the unbounded virtue of God, which is not tied down to natural means, but soars over all the earth: here it lights upon the common way of child-bearing. We must realize that there was no thought, in her doubt or inquiry, of lowering God's power or equating it to her own intelligence. She is struck with a feeling of sudden wonder, and so raises the question. We may tell that she embraced the promise with obedience, from the fact that while she might have found many objections, she only hesitates over one point. She might have asked—where then was this throne of David, since all its power and might were long since abolished, the whole splendour of the royal line extinct. Certainly if she had judged the matter by fleshly standards, she might have taken the message of the angel as mere fable. No doubt then that she was quite persuaded of the restoration of the Church and took in with ease a deed that was, to the flesh, incredible. It is likely that at that time the prophecy of Isaiah was well known (11.1), where God says that He will raise up a shoot out of the rejected stock of Jesse. Faith then in the grace of God so worked upon the virgin's mind that she accepted without debate the message brought her concerning the raising up of the throne of David. Someone may say that it was also a prophecy that a virgin should bear a son; I answer, that the understanding of that mystery was in those days uncertain. The Fathers hoped that a King would be born to them, under whom the people of God would be blessed and prosperous, but the means was as hidden as if a veil obscured it from them. So no wonder that the holy virgin puts a question on the matter she does not understand. The way in which some have taken from her words that she had taken a vow of perpetual virginity is too feeble, indeed quite absurd. She would have undergone a treacherous deception to become engaged to her husband, and would have mocked God in her contempt of the holy bond of marriage. Although a cruel tyranny in this quarter has had its range under the Papacy, they have never dared go so far as to allow a wife to take a vow of continence at her whim. It is really a childish comment, inventing a Jewish Monasticism. No, but we must resolve the objection, that the virgin looks to the future, and so signifies that she will have no inter-course with a man. The likely and simple conjecture is that the magni-tude, indeed the majesty, of the matter so overwhelmed the virgin's senses that she was completely tied and caught up in admiration. When she hears that the Son of God will be born, she appreciates that it is no common thing, and that this is a reason to exclude man's intercourse. Hence her astonished cry, 'How shall this be?' And God kindly pardons her, and through the angel makes gracious and courteous reply, for her question was reverent and lowly, and not lacking in wonderment at the divine work, how it should be, seeing that she was persuaded that it must be more sublime than the common and usual way of nature. Her asking, then, was not opposed to faith, for it arose more from admiration than from diffidence.

Luke 1.35. *The Holy Ghost shall come upon thee.* The angel does not define the means, so as to satisfy curiosity, for there was no need. He simply recalls the virgin to consider the power of the Holy Spirit, so that she may wholly yield herself to Him in quietness and peace. The word *come upon* shows that the action will be extraordinary, as the means of nature will not do. The next phrase is added to explain. That the power of the Most High shall overshadow her. The Spirit is, as it were, the essential virtue of God, whose effect comes out and exerts itself both in the general government of the world as in miracles. In the word *overshadow* there is a fitting metaphor: Scripture frequently compares the *power of God* by which He guards and watches over His own, to a shadow. But the particular application in this passage seems to be different, namely that the operation of the Spirit will be secret, as though a cloud should intervene and cover over the sight of men's eyes. As God, in publishing His miracles, keeps back from us the means of His working, so on our part we must adore with restraint, what He wishes to keep hidden from us.

Wherefore also that which is to be born shall be called holy. This is a confirmation of the last sentence. The angel teaches her that Christ must be born without the intercourse of husband and wife, that He may be holy, and Son of God: that is, to excel all creatures in holiness and glory, and not be on the common level of mankind. The heretics who pretend that He was made Son of God only at the time of His human birth, catch on to the causal particle—'He was to be called Son of God', because His conception would be due to the miraculous virtue of the Holy Spirit: but the reasoning is false. Though He was manifested Son of God in the flesh, it does not follow that He was not the Word begotten of the Father before all ages. No rather, He is the same, who was Son of God in the eternal Godhead, that appeared also Son of God in human flesh. Now the passage does not only point out the unity in Christ's Person; it also shows Christ as Son of God in the very role of assuming human nature. As from the beginning the name Son of God belonged to the divine essence of Christ, so now it applies jointly, to both natures at the same time, because the secret and celestial way of His procreation exempts Him from common course of men. Elsewhere He frequently calls Himself Son of man, in order to affirm Himself to be truly man, but it is no obstacle to the truth of His human nature for His divine origin to endow Him with peculiar dignity above all others, namely, that He should be conceived by the Holy Spirit outside the ordinary means of nature. This quite rightly increases our confidence, to dare to invoke God as Father with more freedom, because His only Son put Himself on equal terms with us, wishing to be our brother. Note that Christ is called the *holy seed*, being conceived by spiritual power. Just as He had to be true man to expiate our sins and death, and overcome Satan in our flesh, all in all to be the true Mediator, so it was necessary for Him, in order to cleanse others, to be clear of all uncleanness or spot. Thus though Christ was born of the seed of Abraham, he drew no contagion from that blemished nature, for from the very first, God's Spirit kept Him pure, not merely that He should abound in holiness unto Himself alone, but rather that He should make others holy. The very mode of His conception testifies that He was set apart from sinners to be our Mediator.

Luke 1.36. *And behold, Elisabeth . . . hath conceived.* By the example of her own household the Angel is able to direct Mary's faith to accept the promised sign. If neither the barrenness nor the age of Elisabeth are any obstacle to God in making her a mother, no more should Mary be restricted to the usual limits of nature, when she sees such a token of the divine power in her cousin. He is careful to say that it is the sixth month, for as it is in the fifth that a woman begins to feel the quickening in her womb, the sixth month is beyond doubt. Mary should have been so acquiescent in the mere Word of God that she should not have needed her faith to be supported from any other source, but in case she should have any further hesitation the Lord allows His promise this further reinforcement. By the same thoughtfulness He daily aids and sustains us, indeed more so, for our faith is so much weaker. Lest His truth fail to convince us, He furnishes it on all sides with evidence of assurance to us.

We are asked what kind of relationship connected Elisabeth, who was of the daughters of Aaron, and Mary, descendant of David's line. In fact, this seems inconsistent with the Law forbidding women to marry out into the tribes (Num. 36.6). As regards the Law, if we consider its object, the ban was only upon such marriages as might confuse inheritances. There was no such danger if a woman of the tribe of Judah were to marry a priest, since the inheritance did not pass to a priest. The same reasoning applied if a woman from the tribe of Levi were to contract out of her own tribe. It is possible that the mother of the holy virgin traced her descent from the tribe of Aaron, and so there was a consanguinity between her daughter and Elisabeth.

Luke 1.37. *For no word from God, etc.* If *word* is to be taken in its proper and natural sense, the meaning will be that God will fulfil His promise, since no obstacle can block His might: the argument will be, God has promised this, therefore He will perform it, as no impossibility can be laid against His Word. But as *word* by reference to the Hebraic expression is often taken as *action*, the simpler exposition will be, that nothing is impossible for God. There is however one axiom always to bear in mind, that it is wilful aberration to speculate on anything that might occur within the power of God, beyond His Word. We must so consider His infinity that we give ourselves ground for hope and confidence. It is not only rash, it is quite useless to discuss what may be possible for God without reckoning on His will. The angel does here what God often does in Scripture: he confirms a particular promise with general teaching. This is the true and proper use of general teaching, to apply its diverse promises to the matter in hand, in any time of distress or perplexity. They give cold comfort when they are kept away from their objectives. There is nothing remarkable in the angel declaring to Mary, the power of God, as it is her diffidence that is mostly undermining her acceptance of the promises. Verbally, all confess that God is omnipotent, but let Him promise something beyond our range of thinking, and we pause. How does this come to be, unless we are only allowing Him as much power as our intelligence can conceive? Paul praises Abraham's faith (Rom. 4.20), saying that he gave glory to God, that what He had promised He was also able to perform. Elsewhere, speaking of the hope of eternal life, he sets before himself the power of God. 'I know Him whom I have believed', he says, 'that He is able to guard that which I have committed unto Him' (II Tim. 1.12). It may seem a small part of faith, that no-one however impious may openly take from God the title of omnipotence. Yet those who hold this sovereignty of God well and firmly to their heart will readily overcome other hindrances to faith. Yet note that God's sovereignty must have the effectual apprehension, as I would say, of true faith. God is able, and God wills so to be recognised, that He may display His truth by results.

Luke 1.38. *Behold, the handmaid of the Lord.* The holy maiden does not allow herself further questioning. Yet no doubt many things might have crept into her mind to check her faith, if not altogether to divert her from the angel's words. But objections are given no chance to succeed, when she constrains herself to obedience. This is the real testing of faith, for us to get a grip on our thoughts and hold them captive, so to speak, to stop them from daring to put anything in God's way—give disputation free rein and it will forever foster infidelity. These words, 'Behold the handmaid of the Lord', are of great moment: she offers and dedicates herself wholly to God, for Him to use her freely at His choosing. The unbelieving draw back from His hand and, as far as they can, impede His work. Faith establishes us before God, that we may stand in readiness to serve. Now if the holy virgin showed herself the handmaid of the Lord precisely in submitting herself freely to His command, then it is the greatest insult to deny Him, by fleeing from

Him, such obedience as He deserves and asks. As faith alone makes us obedient servants to God, and puts us under His sway, faithlessness makes us rebels and deserters. *Be it unto me.* This phrase can be expounded in two ways, either that the holy virgin immediately turns herself to devotions and prayers, or that in one complete action she proceeds to yield and give herself over to God. My simple interpretation is that her assurance of God's power and free acceptance of His call lead her straight from receiving the promise to—not simply awaiting the outcome, but—earnestly desiring it.

And Mary arose in these days and went into the hill country with haste, into a city of Judah; and entered into the house of Zacharias and saluted Elisabeth. And it came to pass, when Elisabeth heard the salutation of Mary, the babe leaped in her womb; and Elisabeth was filled with the Holy Ghost; and she lifted up her voice with a loud cry, and said, Blessed art thou among women, and blessed is the fruit of thy womb. And whence is this to me, that the mother of my Lord should come unto me? For behold, when the voice of thy salutation came into mine ears, the babe leaped in my womb for joy. And blessed is she that believed; for there shall be a fulfilment of the things which have been spoken to her from the Lord. (Luke 1.39-45)

Luke 1.39. *And Mary arose.* Taking this journey, as Luke records it, shows that Mary's faith was no feeble flame that let God's promise disappear with the angel leaving her sight, but something dwelling in her mind. Her haste testifies to her intense and burning emotion. We may infer that in estimation of the grace God had shown her, all other things were put aside, to give place to it. Yet we may ask, what was the purpose she had in taking the journey. Certainly it was no mere curiosity, for she cherished the Son of God as much in her heart through faith as in her womb by conception. Nor do I agree with those who say she came to seek congratulation: it seems more likely to me that her reason was partly to increase and confirm her faith, partly to show forth on all sides the grace she had received of God. There is nothing we should reckon odd in her seeking to confirm her faith by going to see that miracle which the angel had effectively brought to her notice. The faithful may be satisfied with the unadorned Word of God, and yet neglect none of His works which they realise provide support for their faith. Mary above all was right to seize upon the help afforded her, if she did not wish to reject what the Lord had deliberately put before her. And after all, to see each other could stir both herself and

31

to Elisabeth greater thankfulness, as is obvious from the whole account. God's power was more notably revealed by seeing a double grace at one sight, for the very comparison added no little splendour. Now Luke does not state in which city Zacharias lived, but simply records that it belonged to the tribe of Judah, and stood in the hill country. It is inferred that it was farther away from the town of Nazareth than Jerusalem.

Luke 1.41. *When Elisabeth heard the salutation.* It is quite natural for the child in the womb of a pregnant women to move at a joyful surprise, but Luke means to indicate something beyond the usual. There is no point in becoming involved in subtle questions, whether the infant sensed the presence of Christ, or whether this were a feeling of devotion: let this suffice, that the infant leapt with a hidden impulse of the Spirit. Luke does not entirely ascribe the impulse as affecting the child itself, but rather means that it was part of God's working in the mother, that the infant rejoiced in her womb. As for saying, 'filled with the Holy Ghost', the meaning is that she was suddenly gifted with a spirit of prophecy, beyond the normal. The Spirit had not been without gifts before, but here was a revelation of far richer and exceptional force.

Luke 1.42. *Blessed art thou.* This appears to place Mary and Christ on equal rank, which would be most unfitting. But I am happy to accept the opinion of those who make the second phrase the controller. It is quite common to use the connecting particle as a causal. So Elisabeth declares the blessedness of her cousin as due to the blessedness of her son. In fact Mary's happiness in bearing Christ in her womb is not the first thing—that honour actually is second in degree to the rebirth into newness of life by the Spirit of Christ. Yet she deserves to be called blessed, for God has accorded her a singular distinction, to prepare His Son for the world, in whom she was spiritually reborn (*in quo spiritualiter erat regenita*). To this day we cannot enjoy the blessing brought to us in Christ without thinking at the same time of that which God gave as adornment and honour to Mary, in willing her to be the mother of His only-begotten Son.

Luke 1.43. *And whence is this to me.* We should notice the restraint of Elisabeth as she considers the excellent goodness of God upon Mary, and the due honour she must give her: yet her praises do not soar too loftily, to God's loss. There are few who succeed in overcoming the world's inborn weakness, and who do not labour under one or other of these errors. Some are so excessively pleased with themselves that in order to shine alone they despise God's gifts in their brothers, while others exalt men with such a degree of superstition that they make idols of them for themselves; which has resulted in Christ being shoved down the bench, so to say, while Mary is given the place of honour. Quite the opposite with Elisabeth, who in singing her praises is so far from obscuring the glory of God that rather she brings all things back to God. Yet at the same time, recognizing one set higher than herself and other women, she bears her no envy for this higher degree, and humbly declares that she is being (herself) given more than she deserves. In calling Mary the mother of her Lord, the unity of person in the two natures of Christ is intended, as if she had said, he who is born a mortal man in the womb of Mary is at the same time the eternal God. We must remember that this woman does not speak from her own intelligence, but only enunciates what was prompted by the Holy Spirit. The title of Lord really belongs to the Son of God revealed in the flesh, to whom all power is given by the Father, and who is appointed highest Governor of heaven and of earth, by whose hand God directs all things. Yet especially He is Lord of the faithful, who submit themselves to His command freely and quietly, for it is of His body that He is head. So Paul says (I Cor. 8.5), 'For though there be that are called gods, yet to the household of faith there is but one Lord.' Now when she extols this favour of God, of which we speak, from the sudden impulse of the child she bore in her womb, then certainly her desire is to testify to an experience transcendent and divine.

Luke 1.45. *And blessed is she that believed.* As it is evident from the earlier witness of Luke that Elisabeth spoke under the hidden prompting of the Spirit, so it is the Spirit that pronounces Mary blessed in that she believed, and in praising Mary's faith gives a universal admonition on where man's true felicity is to be found. Happy Mary, to have embraced in her heart the promise of God, to have conceived and brought into the world for herself and for all—salvation. This was hers, specifically: but as there is not one drop of righteousness, of life, of any benefit that reaches us except as the Lord brings it to us in His Word, it is one faith that draws us up from the depths of want and wretchedness into the community of true happiness.

There is great significance in this phrase, *for there shall be a fulfilment of the things which have been spoken.* It means, that provision is made by faith for the divine promises to find their outcome in us. Of course, God's truth does not depend on man's device, indeed it is more the case (Rom. 3.4) that God may be found for ever true, though all the world (being incredulous and deceitful) try to dissolve His faithfulness: as the unbelieving are not worthy to harvest the fruits of the promises, Scripture deliberately teaches that only by faith shall they be effectual for our salvation. God offers His benefits to all without distinction, but faith opens our arms to draw them to our bosom: lack of faith lets them fall, before they reach us. If Mary had failed in faith, that would not

33

have stopped God fulfilling His purpose by such other means as He determined. But she is called blessed, for by faith she received the blessing offered her, and opened the way to God to fulfil His work. And by contrast unbelief shuts that door upon Him, and holds Him back from His work, that those who deprive her great name of its credit, may not know her as the bearer of salvation. Note the relation between *word* and *faith*, telling us what it is to believe: it is when we subscribe to the voice of God and firmly determine that He will do what He promises us. The words *from the Lord* mean the same as the everyday commercial expression, Representative for God (*ex parte Dei*). The promise had come through the agency of an Angel, but it had come from none other than God. This tells us that whether God uses the ministration of angels or of men, He wills His Word to receive as much honour as if He came down Himself visibly from the skies.

And Mary said,
  My soul doth magnify the Lord,
  And my spirit hath rejoiced in God my Saviour.
  For he hath looked upon the low estate of his handmaiden:
  For behold, from henceforth all generations shall call me blessed.
  For he that is mighty hath done to me great things;
  And holy is the name.
  And his mercy is unto generations and generations
  On them that fear him. (Luke 1.46-50)

Now we are dealing with that noble and memorable canticle of the holy virgin, which clearly shows how much the grace of the Spirit excelled in her. There are three sections to this canticle. In the first, Mary breaks into a moving act of thanksgiving for her mercies she had known from God. Then she acknowledges in wider strains the power and judgments of God. Finally she brings herself to the present matter, and describes the redemption once promised to the Church and now set before it.

Luke 1.46. *My soul doth magnify.* Here, as we have just said, Mary testifies to her gratitude. As many hypocrites swell their cheeks to sing the praises of God, but have no feeling in their hearts, Mary says that she praises God from the inner emotion of her soul. It is certainly nothing but a profanation of the holy Name of God for men to declare His glory with the tongue alone, not with the heart. The terms *soul* and *spirit* are taken variously in Scripture, but taken together apply in particular to two aspects of the soul (*anima*). The spirit (*spiritus*) is used

34

for the intelligence, the soul (*animus*) for the seat of the affections, desires. To understand the holy maid correctly, we should know that what is second in position is here first in priority. For man's inclination to be aroused to praise God, first must come exultation of the spirit: as James teaches us, 'Is any cheerful? Let him sing praise' (5.13). Sorrow and worry prevent both soul and speech from celebrating the goodness of God. Thus when Mary's mind exults for joy, her heart breaks out into the worship of God. She does well to choose for God the title of Saviour, when she speaks from the gladness of her heart, for until God is recognized as Saviour, the minds of men will never enjoy true and unrestrained delight, but will be bogged down in confusion and care. Only the fatherly kindness of God, and the salvation that flow from it, can flood our hearts with gladness. To sum up, the first thing is, that the faithful may boast that their salvation is in God: second, as it should follow, that those who know the Father's benefits should yield Him thanks. The word σωτήρ means more in Greek than *Servator* in Latin, as applying not to a once only rescue, but to the Author of our continuing salvation.

Luke 1.48. *For he hath looked upon.* She explains why her heart's joy is founded upon God, for He had looked upon her of His own pleasure. She calls herself 'lowly' to disown any worth in herself, and to ascribe to God's open goodness the whole substance of her triumph. This *low estate* does not (as ignorant and boorish men have thought) mean submissiveness, modesty, any state of mind, but precisely means a poor and abject condition. So it means: that I was of no account, despised, but this did not prevent God from condescending to cast His eyes upon me. If we contrast Mary's poor estate with high estate (as the matter in fact requires us to, and as the Greek text reveals) we may see that Mary, in emptying herself, elevates God alone. This is no paean of false humility, but the plain and sincere statement of a conviction that she had graven upon her heart. In the eyes of the world she was of no account, and she rated herself no higher.

Henceforth ... blessed. The sense is, that this blessing of God will be commemorated in all generations. And if it will be so remarkable that it should be told everywhere on the lips of all, then truly Mary herself, at the centre of it, could not rightly keep silence on the matter. We see how Mary puts no weight on her own happiness, but only recognizes what she has received of God, and tells of the acceptance of His favour. I shall be reckoned blessed, she says, through all ages. Is it because she sought this renown through her own virtue, her own efforts? Indeed no, it is God's work alone that she celebrates. This shows us how far away the Papists are from her, when they deck her out with thoughtless and vain notions, and virtually disregard the benefits she received at

God's hand. They fill her to the brim with high-sounding, quite over-bearing titles, like queen of heaven, door of life, sweetness, hope, salvation. Yes indeed, Satan has whipped them to such a shameless frenzy that they pass Christ's Kingship over to her: this is the effect of their chant, 'Ask the Father, Bid the Son.' As we know full well that none of these comes of the Lord, let the holy virgin reject them all with one word, fixing all her glory on the benefits of God. If our triumph is on this ground alone, that God did great things with her, then there is no place left for pretended titles that come from other quarters. Any-how, there is nothing more scandalous than to rob the Son of God of His own to dress her up in the sinful spoils. Go on Papists, say that we do hurt the mother of Christ, for we assign to her only the benefits God gave her, and cast off the falsehoods of men. Yet we allow her the greatest honour of all, and they, perverse devotees, take it from her. We gladly receive her instruction, and conform to her teaching and precepts. Her meaning here is clear beyond doubt: but the Papists dis-own it, run it down, as best they may robbing her words of all credence. We are to keep in mind, that there is one rule prescribed for the praises of men and of angels—let the grace of God be glorified: and nothing is of any praise if it does not come from that source. When she says, *For he that is mighty hath done to me great things*, she means that God was not assisted by outside forces, so that His prowess should stand out alone. Here we must repeat what was said already, that she was re-garded, for all that she was poor and wretched. It follows that praises of Mary, where the might and sheer goodness of God are not entirely set forth, are perverse and counterfeit.

Luke 1.49. *And holy is his name*. This is the second part of the can-ticle, in which the holy virgin illustrates the power and judgments and mercies of God in general terms. This part should not be read as being bound up with the previous part, but rather on its own. Mary had extolled the grace of God which she had experienced in herself. This gives her the opportunity to cry out that His name is holy and His mercy flourishes in all ages. Now God's name is called Holy as deserving the highest reverence: as often as one speaks of God, at once His venerable majesty should be felt to stand in our midst. The next sentence, praising the continuance of His mercy for ever, derives from the solemn affirmation of the covenant, 'I shall be a God unto thee and to thy seed after thee.' Again, 'I am God which keepeth mercy to a thousand generations' (Gen. 17.7; Deut. 7.9). These are words that testify not only that He will continue to be consistent with Himself, but express His continuing favour which He shows to His own, to be loving to their sons after they are dead themselves, and to their grand-sons, and to their whole family. This is the unbroken course of love that He has shown the descendants of Abraham, as having once taken their father Abraham into His favour He concluded an eternal covenant with him.   But seeing that not all descendants of Abraham according to the flesh are his true sons, Mary restricts the enjoyment of the promise to the true worshippers of God, as is written in Psalm 103.17, 'But the mercy of the Lord is from everlasting to everlasting upon them that fear him: and his righteousness unto children's children; to such as keep his covenant', etc.   Thus God promises that He will be merciful through- out all generations towards the sons of the saints, while giving no ground to hypocrites for vain assurances, for their boasting in the fatherhood of God is rash and empty, they are a degenerate stock of saints, they have fallen away from their piety and faith.   This provision refutes the vanity and arrogance of those who puff themselves out with a false parade of the grace of God, and are without faith.   God struck a universal covenant of salvation with the family of Abraham, but as stones washed by the rain become no softer, so hardness of heart pre- vents the unbelievers winning the promised righteousness and salva- tion.   All the while God has preserved some seed, that His promise might be firm and valid.   By the *fear* of the Lord there is intended all devotion and worship, which cannot exist without faith.   Here perhaps the objection might be raised, What is the point of God being called merciful, if no-one finds Him so, unless he be deserving of His grace? If the mercy of God is upon them that fear Him, then devotion and a good conscience win His favour for men, and so by this means men by their merits anticipate His grace.   My answer is, that it is included in mercy, that God should inspire His fear and reverence in the sons of the godly.   This is to make no comment on the origin of grace, that might suggest that God were idly to speculate from His heaven who might be worthy of it, but it is a straight blow to the evil self-assurance of the hypocrites, in case they think God is bound to them, because they are by the flesh sons of the saints: the purpose of the divine covenant is quite different from that, its terms are not the same; for He aims always to have some people in the world who may give Him pure service.

He hath shewed strength with his arm;
He hath scattered the proud in the imagination of their heart.
He hath put down princes from their thrones,
And hath exalted them of low degree.
The hungry he hath filled with good things;
And the rich he hath sent empty away.
He hath holpen Israel his servant,

That he might remember mercy,
(As he spake unto our fathers)
Toward Abraham and his seed for ever.   (Luke 1.51-55)

Luke 1.51. *He hath shewed strength (fecit potentiam).* In effect, she said,
He has worked mightily. *Arm* is contrasted with all the other resources
of God, as at Isaiah 59.16, 'And God saw . . . that there was no inter-
cessor: therefore his own arm brought salvation unto him; and his
righteousness, it upheld him.' Mary knows that God relying on His
own power, and taking no assistance for His task, has called on no-one
to bring Him aid. What follows immediately, regarding the proud,
seems to have been added for two reasons: one, that the proud achieve
nothing in their titanic efforts to resist God; again, that God exerts the
power of His arm only to save the humble, and He casts down the
proud who claim so much for themselves. Compare the exhortation of
Peter, 'Humble yourselves therefore under the mighty hand of God,
etc. (I Pet. 5.6). It is worth noticing the expression, *scattered the proud in
the imagination of their hearts.* As their pride and self-seeking is vast, as
their greed is insatiable, their schemes heap up into monstrous piles—to
put it in a word, they build a tower of Babel. Their folly is never
content with this or that exaggerated enterprise, but they are at once
raising further constructions of mad audacity on top of the first. When
God after a time of silence mocks their marvellous edifice from above,
He instantly ruins the entire construction: just like destroying a
building, which before was firm and solid, with the joints all secure,
and scattering it far and wide over the earth.

Luke 1.52. *He hath put down princes (detraxit primates).* In the Old
Latin this translation (instead of *detraxit potentes*) was chosen to avoid
ambiguity. The word δυνάσται in Greek derives from the word for
power but these are actual princes and chief magistrates. *'Potentes'*
(translating δυνάστας) many take to be a participle. Mary declares that
they are taken from their thrones, that in their place may come up the
obscure and unprivileged. Thus she ascribes to the providence and
judgments of God, what profane men call the turns of Fortune. We
must realise that God is not credited with absolute domination, in the
sense of tyrannical power that kicks men to and fro like balls, to knock
up and down, but with fair government, based on a sound plan, however it may often escape us. God takes no such delight in changes as that
he should decide, in sport, to lift a man to the heights simply to toss him
to the ground; but rather, human misdeeds disturb the order of things,
when men fail to see that each man's lot depends on His will and might.
Those who lord it over others not only cause their neighbours heartless
and rude insult, but also do savage hurt to Him who is the source of

their high position. That we may learn from events how all that is high and lifted up in this world is subject to God, and the whole world controlled at His command, some we see are lifted to the highest degree of honour, while others fall from their thrones, and actually come to disaster: this is the reason and purpose David gives (Ps. 107.40), and Daniel (2.21). Truly, we may observe how the princes of the world grow haughty beyond all measure, how they dissipate themselves in luxurious living, how they become bloated with pride, how the sweetness of good fortune makes them drunk. If the Lord should refuse to tolerate such ingratitude, it is no wonder: and this is the reason that often those whom God elevates do not remain long in security. Of course the splendour of kings and princes dazzles the common mob, and a few reckon any superior as a godlike being. Now if princes were to hold the sceptre from the womb, and maintain an unbroken stability in their reigns, at once all knowledge of God and of His providence would disappear. So the Lord, in raising the lowly on high, turns the world's pride to His own triumph, and at the same time educates His own in simplicity and restraint. Now we grasp the point of Mary's saying, it is God who casts down the mighty from their seats, and raises them of low degree. The lesson is, that the world is not turned and spun by the blind impulse of chance, but the reversals that we see are occasioned by the providence of God, and that God Himself directs with utmost equity all law-giving that might disturb and overthrow the whole order of the worlds. As she underlines in the next verse: *the hungry*, she says, *he hath filled with good things; and the rich he hath sent empty away*. From this we infer that change pleases God not for its own sake, but for good reason, namely because the great and rich and mighty, sated with surplus, claim everything for themselves, and they leave nothing for God. We must take great care not to be carried away by prosperity. Beware of the inflated material affluence, that God may not suddenly bring us to nothing, but the faithful, who know their emptiness and sign for God like famished men, take great comfort from this teaching—God fills the hungry with good things.

Luke 1.54. *He hath holpen Israel*. In this last section Mary suits the general ideas to present circumstances. Briefly, God had now presented that salvation which He had once promised to the holy Fathers of old. But first there is in the word *holpen* (*suscipiendi, ἀντελάβετο*) an apt metaphor: the people's state was so down-fallen that no-one by and large hoped for any possible restoration. Therefore Israel is said (literally, to be taken up, for God has stretched out His hand and raised the prostrate, fallen people to its feet). Religion was sick of many disorders. In public preaching there was little sincerity; the government of the Church was so confused as to resemble nothing so much as wholesale gangsterism; civil order was in ruins; the populace was under assault from the Romans and Herods like wild beasts. Restoration came all the more impressively, when things were so low that no-one could possibly expect it. The word *puer* may be taken equally as 'son' and as 'servant', but the latter sense is more suitable. Israel is called God's servant in this passage, as in many others, because it was brought into the family of God.

That he might remember. Mary gives the reason why the people would be accepted by God though declining into ruin, yes, why God would lift them even out of their collapse: it was to give proof of His mercy in saving them. She expressly notes that God remembered His mercy. It might seem that He had somehow forgotten it, since He let His people be so wretchedly wearied and oppressed. This is usual enough, to attribute emotions to God, in the degree that men judge from the event that He must be angry or pleased with them. Human minds cannot conceive the mercy of God except insofar as He presents it and bears witness to it in His word, and therefore Mary recalls herself and others to His promises, and declares that in keeping them God had been constant and faithful. In this sense God is often called kind and true, for we can never determine His fatherly goodness towards us unless we think upon His Word, the bond by which He ties Himself to us, the middle term, so to speak, that links our salvation with God's goodness in a personal relationship. Mary further shows by these words that the covenant which God made of old with the Fathers was gratuitous, for it draws its promise of mercy pure and simple from the source itself. So we learn that this doctrine was rightly treated of in Scripture. There was at that time a common popular expectation of the Messiah, but there were few who had their faith grounded on such genuine appreciation of Scripture.

Luke 1.55. *Toward Abraham and his seed.* If you read this in apposition there seems to be a glaring change of case. One must say 'toward Abraham and his seed' (*ad Abraham et semen eius*) rather than 'to Abraham (*Abrahae*) etc.', but in my opinion the matter is not simple apposition, for Mary does not only intend those fathers to whom God spoke, but extends the force and effect of the promises to all successive generations, provided they are the true seed of Abraham. So it follows that we are dealing with that solemn covenant made particularly with Abraham and his family. The other promises that were given to Adam and to Noah and to others had a general regard for all nations. Yet many of Abraham's sons by the flesh were cut off by their unbelief, and being degenerate were utterly estranged from Abraham's house, and we who were foreign are reckoned by faith to be ingrafted into the true stock of Abraham. Understand this, God spoke in this way to the Fathers of old, that the grace offered to them might come down to later generations also, for then by faith, an adoption was made of all nations, that they too might be spiritual sons of Abraham, who were not by nature.

And Mary abode with her about three months, and returned unto her house. Now Elisabeth's time was fulfilled that she should be delivered; and she brought forth a son. And her neighbours and her kinsfolk heard that the Lord had magnified his mercy towards her; and they rejoiced with her. And it came to pass on the eighth day, that they came to circumcise the child; and they would have called him Zacharias, after the name of his father. And his mother answered and said, Not so; but he shall be called John. And they said unto her, There is none of thy kindred that is called by this name. And they made signs to his father, what he would have him called. And he asked for a writing tablet, and wrote, saying, His name is John. And they marvelled all. And his mouth was opened immediately, and his tongue loosed, and he spake, blessing God. And fear came on all that dwelt round about them: and all these sayings were noised abroad throughout all the hill country of Judaea. And all that heard them laid them up in their heart, saying, What then shall this child be? For the hand of the Lord was with him. (Luke 1.56–66)

The substance of this narrative is that John's nativity was distinguished by several signs from God, to foretell some great and exceptional future for the child himself. God chose to adorn him with rare tokens even from the womb, in case he should later grow into obscurity and become just like someone out of the crowd, when he came to the performance of his prophetic ministry. Luke first tells how Mary spent about three months with her cousin, that is, till the day of her delivery. It is likely that the only reason for such a long stay was to enjoy the sight of the divine favour, which had been presented to her by the angel to confirm her faith.

Luke 1.58. *And her neighbours and her kinsfolk heard.* We cannot be sure whether the folk reckoned it a remarkable grace of God simply from the blessing of a child being born, or whether they had previously heard that the angel had appeared to Zacharias and promised him a son. Certainly it was no commonplace benefit at God's hands for a barren woman of advanced years to bring forth beyond the natural course. It may be that this was enough for them to extol the greatness of God's good-pleasure. At any rate, on the eighth day they gather out of duty, and as is usual out of friendship, and God uses this occasion to make them witnesses and beholders of His power and glory. There is really little doubt that the greater part of the company had assembled in view of the rare birth. It was like a portent, to see a barren, aged woman suddenly appear in pregnancy, but when the child is born, their admiration is renewed and increased. We gather from Luke's account that though they used to circumcise their infants at home, they were not used to doing this without a company and gathering: and rightly so. As it was a common sacrament of the Church (*commune Ecclesiae sacramentum*) it should not be administered in secret or in private.

Luke 1.59. *They would have called him . . . after the name of his father*. We know that names were originally given men, as might arise from events, or from prophetic inspiration, to mark some hidden plan of God. But later, after a long period of time, as the supply of names was more plentiful, though they might have invented them afresh for each occasion, they were satisfied with the old names, those already accepted, and called the younger generation after their elders. Thus before John's father, there was many a Zacharias, and perhaps this one took his origin with the son of Barachiah. We know how it is often true that accepted use and wont are taken as law. So these people argue that the pattern which had lasted should be kept for this infant's name. Now while there is no need to make any superstition over names, no sound person will deny that there is a practice here religiously and usefully held by faithful people, i.e., to give their sons names which shall serve them as instruction and caution, and may borrow more from the holy Fathers (prompting the children to imitate them) than derive from the profane.

Luke 1.60. *And his mother answered*. We cannot tell if Elisabeth were taught by oracle. But it is likely that Zacharias, when he saw himself paying the penalty for being too slow in believing, showed his wife by writing what the angel had told him concerning the name; otherwise he would not have obeyed God's command. Why this name was divinely settled upon the Baptist, I have expounded above. The relatives, though they do not grasp the reason, are impressed by the novelty of the choice, especially as they surmise it has not been made lightly.

Luke 1.64. *And his mouth was opened*. God enhances the birth day of His Prophet by restoring his father's power of speech. No doubt He had deferred the favour deliberately and purposely to that day in order to draw men's attention upon John. It is said Zacharias praised God, not only to testify to his gratitude, but also that his relatives and neighbours might know that the penalty was inflicted on him for being too slow to believe. He was not ashamed, for all his fall from favour, to celebrate the glory of God. So it became known to all around that a child was born not casually nor in the ordinary way, but as promised by the oracle of heaven.

Luke 1.65. *And fear came on all.* This fear, that Luke records, sprang from a sense of the divine power: God's works are to be considered with awe, to strike us seriously. God does not give miracles for amusement, but to stir human senses, when He sees them asleep. Luke says that the story of these happenings was spread all through the hill country of Judaea, but it did many of them no good to have this contact at the time with the power of God, for when John began to fulfil his teaching mission, few remembered the marvels of his nativity, But it was not only for the sake of those who heard that God wished the story of these things to be published, but that in all ages the miracle might be more certain, for being well reported in its day. The old mirror of human ingratitude meets our view here. While empty and trifling matters stick firmly in our minds, the memory of the graces of God that should flourish for ever quickly slips away and is gone. Luke is not speaking of foolish men, nor of downright despisers of God, for he says, they *laid them up in their heart,* that is, they were ready to give these things careful thought. Probably some remembered for a period, but the majority soon after put out of their minds their sense of fright. Yet see how close they were to the mark in referring the miracles they had seen to the future prowess of the child. We have said that this was God's design, to advance John later on with no small commendation. When Luke says, *For the hand of the Lord was with him,* he means that the grace of God was evident in many ways, to show openly that he would be no man of the herd. This is figurative speech, expressing God's virtue revealed as surely as if His hand had been openly shown, so that anyone could leap to the acknowledgement of God's presence.

And his father Zacharias was filled with the Holy Ghost, and prophesied, saying,
    Blessed be the Lord, the God of Israel;
    For he hath visited and wrought redemption for his people,
    And hath raised up a horn of salvation for us
    In the house of his servant David
    (As he spake by the mouth of his holy prophets which have been since
      the world began),
    Salvation from our enemies, and from the hand of all that hate us;
    To shew mercy towards our fathers,
    And to remember his holy covenant;

The oath which he sware unto Abraham our father,
To grant unto us that we being delivered out of the hand of our enemies
Should serve him without fear,
In holiness and righteousness before him all our days. (Luke 1.67-75)

Luke 1.67. *Zacharias was filled with the Holy Ghost.* This is an expression we have recently explained, namely that God's servants receive a richer grace of the Spirit, without being devoid of it at other times. In such a way the Prophets, as we read, received the Spirit, not that they lacked it between times, but as its power exerted itself more forcibly in them when they came forward into the light of day to perform the work that God's hand, as it were, led them to. So note the connection of the two phrases, as Luke has it, that he was filled with the Holy Spirit, and he prophesied. It means on this occasion that he was so unusually inspired by God as to speak no longer as a private individual, but as demonstrating heavenly doctrine alone. Paul also connects prophecy with the Spirit, in I Thess. 5.19, 'Quench not the Spirit; despise not prophesyings.' We may learn that the light of the Spirit may be extinguished by contempt for doctrine. This generosity of God deserves to be considered—Zacharias is not only restored to the use of speech which he had been without for nine months, but his tongue is also made the instrument of the Holy Spirit.

Luke 1.68. *Blessed be the Lord.* Zacharias begins with an act of thanks, but in the prophetic Spirit it is the fulfilment of the old promise of redemption in Christ that he celebrates, from which salvation and bliss derived to the Church. Why he speaks of the God of Israel, on whose command all the world depends, will be evident from the context: it is because the Redeemer was specifically promised to the seed of Abraham. As God had entrusted His covenant to one race, on which Zacharias will go on to speak, he is right to give the name of that race, to which the grace of salvation was properly, or at least primarily, destined. The word *visited* contains a tacit antithesis, since the face of God was for a time turned away from the wretched sons of Abraham. They were so sunk in disaster, so crushed under a heap of woes, that no-one thought to be looked on by God. Now, this visitation of God, which Zacharias relates, is set as the cause and basis of redemption. So work it out like this, that God looked upon His people in order to redeem it. And since those whom God redeems must be prisoners, and this kind of redemption is a spiritual thing, we may infer that not even the holy fathers were made free of sin's yoke or death's tyranny, other than by the grace of Christ. For Christ is said to be sent as Redeemer to the holy and elect people of God. But if redemption were then only brought by Christ when He was revealed in the manner of the flesh, it follows

44

that the faithful who died before His coming were all their lives enslaved to sin and death: and that would be quite wrong. My answer is, that the force and effect of this redemption, which was once displayed in Christ, were in fact shared by all generations.

Luke 1.69. *Hath raised up a horn of salvation.* This is the power that brings salvation. With the destruction of the throne of David and the dispersion of the people, the hope of salvation in particular had fallen. Zacharias alludes to the oracles of the Prophets, in which there is an immediate promise of renewal out of desperate and lost conditions. The form of words comes from Psalm 132.17, where we read, 'There will I make the horn of David to bud: I have ordained a lamp for mine anointed (*Christ*).' Now if God has shown His power to save us only in Christ, it is wicked to turn away from Him in any degree, if we wish to have divine salvation. Note that the horn is salvation to the faithful, while it remains a terror to the godless, a sign to scatter and reduce and crush them. He calls David the servant of God not simply for his devotion to God, as any worshipper, but in another respect, namely that he had been chosen to rule and serve the people, that he and his successors might portray the Person and role of Christ. Though there was by then no trace of kingdom left to the Jews, yet as Zacharias relies on God's promises, he has no hesitation in calling David God's minister, in whom God published an example of the salvation to come. From this it follows that Christ is really established as the Author of salvation for us, when in our midst a throne is set up from which He may govern us.

Luke 1.70. *As he spake.* Fearing that the salvation which he preaches as being brought by Christ may be distrusted for its newness, he calls all the Prophets to witness, who arose in different times but taught with one voice, that salvation was to be hoped for in Christ alone. Zacharias' purpose is not only to praise the faithfulness and constancy of God for giving and fulfilling what He had once promised, but rather he wishes to recall the faithful to the old oracles, in order that they may, with more assurance and energy, embrace the salvation offered them, to which from the beginning all the Prophets had given testimony. Truly our faith in Christ is founded on a firm support when He breaks upon us adorned with the testimonies of all the Prophets. He calls the Prophets holy, to give their words more weight and respect, as if saying, they are not minor or commonplace witnesses, but official, vested with a public trust, as men divinely set apart from the multitude for this end. How each Prophet rendered his testimony to Christ would be too long to set out in detail. Let it suffice for the present, seeing that all observe this, to say that they only gave the people hope that God would be gracious to them by first setting their sights on the covenant, which had its basis in Christ, and speaking plainly enough of a coming redemption, of the kind which was revealed in Christ. This is the effect of many noble passages, which give clear oracles of Christ, and actually point the finger at Him. Yet we must keep that subscription to the covenant in first place, for if any one were to overlook this, he would never make any sense of the prophets, just as the Jews get hopelessly lost in reading Scripture, for with their excessive curiosity over words, they lose the main target.

Luke 1.71. *Salvation from our enemies.* Zacharias unfolds Christ's power and mission more plainly. Indeed it would be little or no benefit to hear that Christ was given to us, if we did not know to what He brought us. For this reason he explains more fully why the horn of salvation is lifted up: it is that the faithful may be delivered from their enemies. There is no doubt that Zacharias realized well enough that the warfare of God's Church is not principally with flesh and blood, but with Satan and all his array, with which he plots our eternal ruin. Although there are also external enemies ranged against the Church, and she is delivered from them by Christ, yet as Christ's Kingdom is spiritual, these words are spoken chiefly of Satan, prince of this world, and of his troops. At the same time we understand how miserable is the condition of men without Christ, how they lie prostrate under the tyranny of the devil, for Christ would not be otherwise freeing His folk from his hand, that is, his government. The passage advises us that as long as the Church is pilgrim in this world, it will chiefly be among foes and be exposed to their assault, except for the present help of Christ as need arises. This is the inestimable grace of Christ, that He is our undoubted, our sure salvation, though enemies surround us on all sides. Though the expression he uses, *salvation from our enemies,* is crude, there is no doubt what it means, that no device or force of hostile power, no stratagem, no onslaught will stand against God and prevent Him continually rescuing and keeping us from them.

Luke 1.72. *To shew mercy.* Zacharias rehearses again the source of our redemption, the mercy and the free covenant of God. He gives as reason for God's pleasure in saving His people, that in memory of His alliance He revealed His mercy. He is said to have been mindful of His Covenant as it might have seemed that forgetfulness accounted for that long delay, under which He had suffered His people to languish, in the grip of heavy torments. We must be careful to note the priority—God was led by sheer mercy to make a league with the Fathers. In making the league, He further bound men's salvation to Himself by His Word: finally, He displayed all His good purposes in Christ, to set the seal on all His promises. Our confidence in these is only endorsed when the accomplishment is revealed in Christ. Remission of sins is promised in the covenant, but it is found in the blood of Christ. Righteousness is promised, but it is offered through the expiation of Christ. Life is promised, but it is only to be sought in the death and resurrection of Christ. And this is the reason why in ancient-times God ordered the very book of the Law also to be spattered with a victim's blood. It is worth noting how Zacharias extends the mercy shown in his day to the fathers that were dead, that they might share its fruit alike. It follows from this that Christ's grace and power are not confined to the narrow limits of this transitory life, but are eternal. They are not stopped by the dying of the flesh, for the souls survive death, and the death of the flesh is followed by resurrection. As neither Abraham nor any of the saints was able to win salvation by his own power or merits, so salvation revealed in Christ is shared with all the faithful, both the dead and the living.

Luke 1.73. *The oath which he sware.* There is no preposition in the Greek, but this common usage of the language is well known, where a noun in the accusative case is put without a governing word, leaving the preposition, by which it is governed, to be understood. He remembers the *oath*, to express better the stability and sanctity of His truth: God condescends to such a degree of kindness that He agrees to put His Name in support of our weakness. If promises alone are not enough for us, let us take thought of this confirmation, which must remove all doubt, unless we are more than ungrateful, or malignant, against His holy Name. *To grant unto us.* Zacharias does not go through each heading of the contents of God's covenant, but expounds the object of God in dealing so kindly with His people according to His mercy that He should redeem them. This was that when redeemed they should devote themselves wholly to Him, and serve Him to the end, in worshipping the Author of their salvation. As the cause and means of man's salvation was the gratuitous favour of God, so the cause and purpose of it was that men might glorify His Name in godly and holy living. We must carefully note, that mindful of our calling we must remember to apply God's grace to its practical end, and, I stress, think upon these precepts: that we are not called to uncleanness but to holiness; that we are redeemed at great price, not to be slaves of the desires of the flesh, or to run riot in wild living, but to have Christ reign over us; that we are by adoption set in the household of God, that in turn we may give the Father the obedience of sons. For in this the grace of God hath appeared, and His φιλανθρωπία (Titus 2.11, cf. 3.4)—kindness—that, denying worldly lusts, we should live soberly and righteously and godly. Paul again, wishing to give the faithful effective encouragement to consecrate themselves to God in newness of life, putting off the old man and shedding their former mind, that they may

47

present a reasonable service, beseeches them by the tenderness of God's mercy (Rom. 12.1). The Scripture is full of this kind of testimony, showing that Christ's grace is made of no effect, unless we aim at this goal.

We must also note what he says, *should serve him without fear.* It means that we can only serve God aright with tranquil minds. Those who toss with anxiety, who struggle with themselves, as to whether they find Him propitious or hostile, whether He welcome their service or reject it, those, in a word, who are floundering between hope and fear, are very concerned and busy over their worship of God, but in no sense submit themselves to Him in sincerity, from the heart. Their fear and distress make Him abhorrent to them: indeed, if it were possible, they would rather wish His presence to depart from them. We know, however, that only the spontaneous sacrifice, the offering of a glad heart, pleases God. Hence for men to worship God truly, it must be that their consciences are first set at rest, as David says, 'But there is forgiveness with thee, that thou mayest be feared' (Ps. 130.4). Peace is declared when God gently invites men to Himself, that they may approach Him gladly, and with a free desire to worship Him. Hence Paul derives the idea that, 'whatsoever is not of faith is sin' (Rom. 14.23). Seeing that God reconciles men to Himself in Christ, that He watches over them with the same protection, in order to relieve them of all fear, seeing that He has laid their salvation in His hand and custody, surely Zacharias is right to proclaim that by His grace we are free from fear. So the prophets particularly ascribe this to His reign, that men may worship Him without fear, and enjoy quietness and gladness.

Luke 1.75. *In holiness and righteousness.* Just as God drew up the rule of good life on two tables, similarly Zacharias here declares that we give God rightful service when at last our life is ordered by holiness and righteousness. There is no doubt that holiness refers to the duties of religion looking to the first table of the Law, as even Plato recognized. Righteousness covers all the duties of charity, for God asks nothing else of us in the second table of the Law, but to render each man his due. *Before him* is added to teach men that it is not enough to order one's life sweetly in the sight of men, to stop hands, feet, all the body from any offence, for men must abide under the will of God, who is not content with external observances, but chiefly regards the heart. Finally, in case any should imagine he had done his stint by serving God over a certain period, Zacharias states that men are redeemed on the basis of pursuing their zeal for God's service all their lives. Certainly, as redemption belongs to eternity, the thought of it should never drift away. As God adopts man to Himself for ever, gratitude should not wither or be short-lived. As Christ died and rose again for men, He

48

deserves to be lord over life and death. Paul, in the passage recently cited (Titus 2.11, f.) bids us live righteously and godly towards the coming of the great God, 'Looking', he says, 'for the blessed hope', etc.

Yea and thou, child, shalt be called the prophet of the Most High:
For thou shalt go before the face of the Lord to make ready his ways;
To give knowledge of salvation unto his people
In the remission of their sins,
Because of the tender mercy of our God,
Whereby the dayspring from on high shall visit us,
To shine upon them that sit in darkness and the shadow of death;
To guide our feet into the way of peace.
And the child grew, and waxed strong in spirit, and was in the deserts till the day of his showing unto Israel. (Luke. 1.76–80)

Luke 1.76. *Yea and thou, child.* Zacharias returns again to commending the grace of Christ, but does it now as under the person of his son, briefly describing the task to which he was appointed of instructing men. Even if he did not perceive prophetic gifts, in a tiny infant of eight days, yet turning his eyes to the counsels of God, he is able to speak as with understanding. *Called* prophet of God is here taken as being so reckoned and openly received. The hidden calling of God had come first; there only remained for him to be displayed to men, to show what he was. As the term prophet is general in sense, he determines from the revelation brought him by the angel that John is to be Christ's fore-runner. *For thou shalt go before the face of the Lord*, he says: that is, you will face this region, to convert men by your tidings to hear the Lord. Why John should have said almost at the end of his course that he was no Prophet of God, is stated at the appropriate place in John's gospel. And what this 'preparing of the way' is, we shall later see.

Luke 1.77. *To give knowledge of salvation.* Zacharias now comes to a leading tenet of the Gospel, in saying that the knowledge of salvation depends on the forgiveness of sins. For as we are all born sons of wrath, it follows that we are by nature condemned and lost, and the reason for our condemnation is that we are guilty of unrighteousness. Wherefore, there is no other means of escaping death than for God to reconcile us to Himself by not imputing our sins to us. That this unique righteousness abides for us in God, is readily inferred from Zacharias' words. Whence comes salvation, if not from righteousness? Now if the sons of God are forbidden to know any other

49

righteousness than that which comes from remission of sins, it follows that righteousness must not be sought elsewhere. So righteousness, which proud men concoct and engineer out of the proceeds of works done, is in fact an imputation of righteousness, whereby God freely clears us of guilt. Besides this, we must note that Zacharias is not speaking of outsiders, but of the people of God. It follows then, that not only does the beginning of righteousness depend on the remission of sins, but the faithful must also be righteous—by imputation, so to speak—in God's sight to the end, or else they could not stand before His judgment seat, if they did not daily bring themselves to the free atonement.

Luke 1.78. *Because of the tender mercy*, or, *heart of mercy*. Considering this great benefit Zacharias, as well he may, proclaims the mercy of God, and is not content merely to name it, but says that the salvation brought by Christ came forth from the very bowels of the mercy of God, so much the more emphatic. Then he adds the metaphor, that there has resulted from the boundless mercy of God a daybreak for them that sit in darkness. *The dayspring* (*Oriens*) here is not a participle: the Greek is ἀνατολή, that is the eastern quarter, as opposed to the west (Occident). Zacharias extols God's mercy for scattering the shadows of death and restoring light to the people of God. In such fashion should our minds be lifted to the vision of God's mercy, whenever we think of our salvation. There appears to be an allusion to Malachi 4.2. where Christ is called the Sun of righteousness with healing in his wings, that is, his rays. As for *light* and *darkness*, there are similar expressions in Isaiah 9.2, 'The people that walked in darkness have seen a great light: they that dwelt in the land of the shadow of death, upon them hath the light shined:' so in many other passages. These words teach us that there is no life-giving light in the world apart from Christ, but all things are under a pall of death's obscurity: as in another place Isaiah declares that this boon belongs to the Church alone, 'Behold', he says, 'darkness shall cover the earth, and gross darkness the peoples: but the Lord shall arise upon thee, and his glory shall be seen upon thee' (60.2). Yet the question is raised, how the Israelites were *sitting in the shadow of death*, when their hearts were always lit by the Lord through faith. I would answer, that the godly who lived under the Law, though they were surrounded on all sides by the shadow of death, saw light far off in the coming of Christ, and were renewed by it, so that they were not overwhelmed by the death around them. Or it may be that Zacharias had regard to the miserable state of affairs in his day. But on the whole, it is true that Christ's coming was a light rising upon all god-fearing men, those who were before and those who came after, that gave them life, for He shed life also upon the dead. *Sit* means just the same as 'lie down'. Thus Isaiah bids the Church arise, for her light is come.

Luke 1.79. *To guide our feet.* In this line Zacharias explains that the perfection of all good, and the summit of happiness, is gained in Christ alone. The word 'Peace' might be taken in its own sense, and it would not be out of place, for the illumination of Christ is able to pacify men's minds, But as *peace* to the Hebrews means a blessed outcome to all things, no doubt Zacharias intends here to make Christ the Author of perfect blessedness, that we need not look elsewhere for any portion of good, but be assured that in every way and in real depth we are blessed in Christ and may rest in Him alone. This is the view of the words of Isaiah, 'The sun shall be no more thy light by day; neither for brightness shall the moon give light unto thee: but the Lord shall be unto thee an everlasting light (Isa. 60.19). Now if Zacharias reached this understanding only from the sight of his infant son, and was able to discourse so splendidly on Christ's grace and virtue before He was born, is it not threefold, yes fourfold, ingratitude to feel less nobly over Christ after His death, His resurrection, His ascension into heaven, that He might sit at the Father's right hand, that is, to weaken the achievement of Him, whose praises were awarded Him even while He was still confined to His mother's womb? For remember what I earlier remarked, that Zacharias does not speak of himself, but under the Spirit of God directing his tongue.

Luke 1.80. *And the child grew.* This is added by Luke to fill out the texture of the narrative. He tells first how John was strengthened by the Spirit, meaning that a rare and unusual aptitude existed in the boy, which was a sign of the heavenly Spirit dwelling in him, yet he says at the same time, that he was concealed in the deserts as of no account to the day of his shewing, that is, to which God had determined to lead him. Thus we see that though John was well aware of his calling, he made no premature attempt, but followed the voice of God.

The book of the generation of Jesus Christ, the son of David, the son of Abraham.

Abraham begat Isaac; and Isaac begat Jacob; and Jacob begat Judah and his brethren; and Judah begat Perez and Zerah of Tamar; and Perez begat Hezron; and Hezron begat Ram; and Ram begat Amminadab; and Amminadab begat Nahshon; and Nahshon begat Salmon; and Salmon begat Boaz of Rahab; and Boaz begat Obed of Ruth; and Obed begat Jesse; and Jesse begat David the king.

And David begat Solomon of her that **had** *been the wife of Uriah;*

Solomon begat Rehoboam; and Rehoboam begat Abijah; and Abijah begat Asa; and Asa begat Jehoshaphat; and Jehoshaphat begat Joram; and Joram begat Uzziah; and Uzziah begat Jotham; and Jotham begat Ahaz; and Ahaz begat Hezekiah; and Hezekiah begat Manasseh; and Manasseh begat Amon; and Amon begat Josiah; and Josiah begat Jechoniah and his brethren, at the time of the carrying away to Babylon.

And after the carrying away to Babylon, Jechoniah begat Shealtiel; and Shealtiel begat Zerubbabel; and Zerubbabel begat Abiud; and Abiud begat Eliakim; and Eliakim begat Azor; and Azor begat Sadoc; and Sadoc begat Achim; and Achim begat Eliud; and Eliud begat Eleazar; and Eleazar begat Matthan; and Matthan begat Jacob; and Jacob begat Joseph the husband of Mary, of whom was born Jesus, who is called Christ.

So all the generations from Abraham unto David are fourteen generations; and from David unto the carrying away to Babylon fourteen generations; and from the carrying away to Babylon unto Christ fourteen generations. (Matt. 1.1-17)

Jesus . . . being the son (as was supposed) of Joseph, the son of Heli, the son of Matthat, the son of Levi, the son of Melchi, the son of Jannai, the son of Joseph, the son of Mattathias, the son of Amos, the son of Nahum, the son of Esli, the son of Naggai, the son of Maath, the son of Mattathias, the son of Semein, the son of Josech, the son of Joda, the son of Joanan, the son of Rhesa, the son of Zerubbabel, the son of Shealtiel, the son of Neri, the son of Melchi, the son of Addi, the son of Cosam, the son of Elmadam, the son of Er, the son of Jesus, the son of Eliezer, the son of Jorim, the son of Matthat, the son of Levi, the son of Symeon, the son of Judas, the son of Joseph, the son of Jonam, the son of Eliakim, the son of Melea, the son of Menna, the son of Mattatha, the son of Nathan, the son of David, the son of Jesse, the son of Obed, the son of Boaz, the son of Salmon, the son of Nahshon, the son of Amminadab, the son of Arni, the son of Hezron, the son of Perez, the son of Judah, the son of Jacob, the son of Isaac, the son of Abraham, the son of Terah, the son of Nahor, the son of Serug, the son of Reu, the son of Peleg, the son of Eber, the son of Shelah, the son of Cainan, the son of Arphaxad, the son of Shem, the son of Noah, the son of Lamech, the son of Methuselah, the son of Enoch, the son of Jared, the son of Mahalaleel, the son of Cainan, the son of Enos, the son of Seth, the son of Adam, the son of God. (Luke 3.23-38)

As there is not complete agreement on these two genealogies, which are recorded by Matthew and Luke, we must see first whether they both draw the genealogy of Christ from Joseph, or whether

Matthew alone does so, while Luke follows Mary. Those who take the latter way may apparently allege a difference over various names, and indeed at first sight nothing seems less likely than that one and the same genealogy is set down, since Luke differs so greatly from Matthew. For from David to Salathiel (Shealtiel), and from Zerubbabel to Joseph, he gives quite different names. Further, they allege that it would be absurd to make so much effort over an unnecessary matter, as to record twice over the family of Joseph, who after all was not the father of Christ. What, they say, is the point of such repetition, which gives no proof relevant to the furtherance of faith? For merely to understand that Joseph was one of the descendants and family of David, will still leave the descent of Christ uncertain. So in their judgment, it would have been superfluous for the two Evangelists to tackle this approach. For Matthew to rehearse the ancestry of Joseph, they make excuse that it was done for the sake of the many who still believed that he was the father of Christ. Yet it would have been ridiculous to encourage their dangerous error with such indulgence, and the context is blatantly opposed to this. For as soon as we come to the end of the genealogy, Matthew says that Christ was conceived in the virgin's womb not by the seed of Joseph, but by the hidden power of the Spirit. If their reasoning were valid, Matthew might be accused of folly or stupidity, for vainly relating the source of Joseph's line. However, this does not remove their objection, that the ancestry of Joseph has nothing to do with Christ.

The usual and popularly known answer is that Mary's line is included in the person of Joseph, since the law ordained that every man married a wife from his own tribe. But they retort, that this rule had been neglected in almost every age; the proofs however on which they rely, are trivial. They take as an instance that occasion when the eleven tribes promised on oath that they would give no woman as wife to the Benjamites. If this had been laid down by the Law, they say, there was no need of the further sanction. I reply, that this exception has been wrongly and ignorantly forced by them into a general rule. It was a case where the body politic was bound to be made defective by the excision of one tribe, if no assistance should come from some other means. This is not to be regarded as a general rule. A further objection is, that Mary the mother of Christ was related to Elisabeth, when Luke has already stated that she (Elisabeth) was of the daughters of Aaron. There is an easy answer here too, that it was permissible for girls from the tribe of Judah or any tribe at all to marry into the priestly tribe, for there was no impediment from the ruling found written in the Law, that a woman shall not transfer her inheritance to anyone other than of her own tribe. Thus the sacred history relates that the wife of Jehoiada the high priest was descended from royal stock (II Chron. 22.11). So there is nothing remarkable or unusual if Elisabeth's mother were married out to a priest. If anyone should say that this cannot convince us so fully that we may affirm that Mary was of the same tribe as Joseph, because she was his wife, I would agree, that it is not simply proven from the mere narrative as here given, were it not for the support of other circumstances.

First, we are to notice that the Evangelists were speaking of things known in their own day. Thus when Joseph's line was drawn back to David, it was easy for anyone to deduce Mary's line from this. There is no doubt that the Evangelists relied on the general understanding of their generation, and so were less particular. If there were any doubtful cases, it would not require hard or prolonged research. Further, they took it for granted that Joseph, being a man of upright and sincere character, would only have married a wife, as the Law prescribed, from his own kin. (Granted that the general rule would not be enough to show that Mary was of royal lineage, Mary might have been descended from the tribe of Judah without deriving from the stock of David.) I conclude that the Evangelists were reckoning on godly people, who would not look for a legal argument, but would recognize Mary's line in the person of Joseph, especially as we have just said there was at the time no doubt. It might however have seemed incredible, that those poor people and their unesteemed partners could be of David's line, that that seed from which the Redeemer would arise was royal. In answer then to the question whether the genealogy as detailed by Matthew and Luke proves clearly and unmistakeably that Mary took her origin from the stock of David, I must admit that it cannot be certainly established, but seeing that at the time the relationship of Mary and Joseph was not obscure, the Evangelists felt more confidence in the matter. Besides, it was the intention of both to remove any stumbling-block that the low standing and small esteem and poverty of both Mary and Joseph might have caused, preventing anything royal at all being seen in them.

Second, the notion that Mary's line is given by Luke, and Joseph's passed over, may easily be refuted. He writes explicitly, Jesus was reckoned the son of Joseph, the son of Heli, the son of Matthat, etc. Certainly, he is not describing Christ's father or grandfather, but he is expressly giving the ancestry of Joseph himself. I know quite well the answer they will produce to try and loose this knot: they say that son stands for son-in-law, and so interpret Joseph being called son of Meli as having taken his daughter to wife. Yet this is quite inconsistent with the course of nature, and there is no such instance ever found in Scripture. No more can Solomon be excluded from Mary's genealogy, without Christ ceasing to be Christ. Whatever is written of his line is founded on that solemn promise, 'A successor shall sit upon thy throne, who shall reign for ever: I shall be to him a father, and he shall be to me a son' (II Sam. 7.13-14; Ps. 132.11). Now it is beyond dispute that Solomon was the instance of this eternal King, who was promised to David. The promise cannot otherwise be applied to Christ, except that His truth was foreshadowed in Solomon. So if Christ's origin is not traced from him, how and by what reasoning can He come to be reckoned son of David? Whoever deletes Solomon from Christ's genealogy is also making a clean sweep of those promises wherein He should be acknowledged as Son of David. (As for the manner in which Luke, drawing the line of descent from Nathan, does not put Solomon out, we shall comment at the right place.)

So looking at these two genealogies all in all, without being too long-winded, I consider that they do agree with each other, but that there are *four points of difference* to be noted. The first is that Luke goes in reverse, as they say, rising from last to first, while Matthew starts actually at the beginning. The second is, that Matthew does not take his account farther than the holy and chosen generation of Abraham; but Luke continues to Adam. The third, that Matthew thinks in terms of legality, and even allows himself to cut some out of the series of descent, because to aid the reader's memory he simply lists three groups of fourteen, while Luke pursues the natural line of descent more exactly. The fourth and last, that occasionally, in speaking of the same men, they are at variance over their names. On the *first* difference, as it contains no difficulty, there is no need to say any more.

The *second* has very good reason to it. As God had chosen the family of Abraham, that the world's Redeemer might be born of it, and the promise of salvation was in some way deposited there, up to the coming of Christ, Matthew is not transgressing the limits set by God. We must bear in mind what Paul says: 'Christ is a minister of the circumcision to bring salvation, which had been promised to the holy Fathers' (Rom. 15.8). This agrees with the saying of Christ, 'Salvation is from the Jews' (John 4.22). So Matthew spot-lights Him as found in that holy family, to which He was truly appointed. So in Matthew's list we must consider God's covenant, in which He selected the seed of Abraham as a people for Himself, to be separated from other nations as by the intervention of a wall. Luke, however, has a deeper perspective: although we know that from the time that

God made a covenant with Abraham, the Redeemer was particularly promised to his seed, we also know that from the very fall of man He was needed by all, as indeed He was from that time destined for all the world. But in the wonderful providence of God, it came that Luke set forth Christ to us as a son of Adam, while Matthew included the same in the one family of Abraham. It would have done us no good for Christ to have been given by the Father as the Author of salvation, if He had not been available to all without distinction. The Apostle's word would not then have been true (Heb. 13.8), 'Christ is the same yesterday and today, yea and for ever,' unless His power and grace extended to all ages from the very creation of the world. We should know that salvation is openly displayed in Christ to all the human race, for in all reality He is called son of Noah and son of Adam. Yet as we must seek Him through God's Word, it is not misleading for the Spirit to recall us through one Evangelist to the holy family of Abraham, where for the time the treasure of eternal life, together with Christ was laid up.

Let us proceed to the *third* difference. There is no doubt that Matthew follows a different order from Luke. The former connects David with Solomon, the latter with Nathan: obviously this sets up a diversity in descent. Good and experienced interpreters reconcile this sort of disagreement on the lines that Matthew departs from the natural lineage, which Luke follows, to give the legal genealogy. By legal genealogy I mean the course that led the right to the throne to Salathiel (Shealtiel). The fact that Eusebius, in the first book of his Church history, prefers on the opinion of Africanus to call the genealogy described by Luke as the legal one, comes to the same sense. He simply means that the kingdom which has been established, in the person of Solomon, came down eventually to Salathiel in legitimate order. But it is more correct and precise to say that the legal order has been set out by Matthew, for in naming Solomon straight after David he does not keep to the succession that led to Christ's birth in terms of the flesh, but shows how He descended from Solomon and other kings to be their legitimate successor, and in His hand the continuity of the kingdom was to be established, according to God's covenant. They are probably right who reckon that the stock of Solomon came to an end with the death of Ahaziah (II Kings 9.27 and 11.1). Several Jewish commentaries refer to an instruction of David, that if ever the family of Solomon should fail, the right to the throne should devolve on the descendants of Nathan—but I leave this open. I only take what is certain, that the succession to the throne was not out of order, but went by distinct stages. When the sacred history relates that after the killing of Ahaziah the kingdom was seized by his mother Athaliah, and the whole royal stock was done away with, it is more than likely that these sinful and outrageous murders were perpetrated by a woman, greedy for power, to prevent herself being reduced to private status, and seeing the throne transferred to another. So if a son had survived Ahaziah, she would have been willing to reign as his grandmother under the pretext of guardianship, quietly without any ill-feeling or danger. The way in which she made herself notorious and hateful for her extreme crimes (II Chron. 22.9 ff.) was a sign of her desperation, in that she could not keep the kingdom in her household. Now Joash is called the son of Ahaziah, and this is because, being next in rank, he is deservedly reckoned to be the true and native heir to the throne. Quite apart from the fact that Athaliah (if we grant her to have been his grandmother) would have readily abused the child's title for herself, can any man of mediocre intelligence think it likely that a natural son of the king could have been concealed by the priest Jehoiada without his grandmother the more urgently finding him out? No, if we take everything into careful consideration, we may readily conclude that the next heir to the throne was born of another lineage. This is the meaning of Jehoiada's words (II Chron. 23.3), 'The king's son shall reign according to the covenant of the Lord with David.' In other words, it was a shameful crime if an outside woman were to snatch the sceptre to herself, when God intended it to remain in the family of David. So there is nothing odd in Luke tracing Christ's lineage from Nathan: for it may well be that the family of Solomon, as far as succession to the throne was concerned, was cut off. So if any were now to object that Jesus cannot be recognised as the Messiah who was promised, unless He come of the descent of Solomon, who was certainly a type of *Christ*, our solution is at hand: though He was not of Solomon's natural descent, He may be reckoned his son in legal order, as He took His origin from the kings.

It is the great *diversity in names* that causes many a good deal of difficulty: for from David to Joseph there is no apparent agreement between the two Evangelists, except over Salathiel and Zerubbabel. The excuse usually brought forward, namely that the difference arose from the Jews frequently using two names, is unwillingly accepted by many. However, since today the method followed by Matthew in tracing and putting together the genealogy is unknown, it is no wonder that we do not grasp how far the two agree or differ over individual names. Yet there can be no doubt, that from the time of the Babylonian exile, they are speaking of the same men in some cases by different names. With Salathiel and Zerubbabel, I believe, the same names were deliberately retained on account of the changed condition of the people, as the majesty of royalty was by then extinct. Since there was such a faint shadow of dominion left, the change seemed very striking, advising the faithful that there was hope of a more distinguished kingdom than that visible kingdom of Solomon which had flourished for a short time. It is also worth noticing this, that it is quite reasonable for Luke to name more in his list than Matthew, since it is usual for there to be a larger number in natural succession than in legal. Besides, Matthew wanted to divide the genealogy of Christ into three sections, putting fourteen members to each section, and felt free to overlook some names which Luke had no right to omit, as he did not tie himself to that rule. I have discussed the genealogy of Christ, all in all, as far as appeared to be useful. If any are diverted by a greater curiosity, I recollect Paul's warning and prefer a level-headed restraint to trifling and worthless sophistry. We know the passage in Titus 3.9, where he tells us to shun foolish questionings and genealogies.

The last point remaining to deal with, is why Matthew set the whole genealogy of Christ *in three periods*, and put fourteen men in each. Those who think he did this to help the reader's memory have expressed a half truth. It is true that a list sticks better in the mind if it is set out in three equal sections, yet at the same time it is agreed that a threefold condition of the people is here being carefully marked, from the time that Christ was promised to Abraham to the time of fulfilment when He was revealed in the flesh. Up to David the tribe of Judah had admittedly surpassed the rest in distinction, but held no princedom. In David, beyond all expectation, the majesty of kingship emerged, and this lasted to Jeconiah. From that time some dignity and influence remained with the tribe of Judah, to keep good peoples' minds sensitive to the coming of the Messiah.

Matt. 1.1. *The book of the generation.* Some interpreters labour over this heading, to no effect, to excuse Matthew for naming his whole narrative after one half of one chapter. But this ἐπιγραφή does not apply to the whole book; the word 'book' is used for 'list,' as though he said, Here follows the list of Christ's generation. He calls Christ son of Abraham and David, in respect of the promises, as God had promised that a seed would arise from Abraham, in which all nations would find blessing (Gen. 12.3). David received a clearer promise, that the kingdom of his house would remain firm to the end of the era, and a King from his seed will sit on the throne, as long as sun and moon shall shine (Ps. 72.5 and 89.29). Hence it was a common manner of speaking among the Jews, to call Christ the son of David.

Matt. 1.2. *Jacob begat Judah and his brethren.* Though Matthew conceals Ishmael, Abraham's firstborn, in silence, and Esau (who in order of nature was senior to his brother Jacob), he is wise to give place in his genealogy to the twelve Patriarchs, since God had accorded them all a like grace of adoption. It means then, that the blessing in Christ is not aimed at the tribe of Judah alone, but is shared by all the sons of Jacob, whom God gathers into His Church, while Ishmael and Esau were made outsiders.

Matt. 1.3. *Judah begat Perez and Zerah of Tamar.* This was the beginning of that self-emptying (*exinanitio*) of which Paul speaks (Phil. 2.7). The Son of God might have kept His lineage free and pure of any crime or mark of shame, but as He came into the world to empty Himself and taking on the form of a servant to become a worm, and no man, a reproach of men and despised of the people (Ps. 22.7), at last to undergo the accursed death of the cross, He did not refuse either this outrage in His own descent—one born from incestuous union, to be counted among His ancestors. Though Tamar was not driven by lust to seek intercourse with her father-in-law, she tried a wrongful course to avenge the wrong she suffered. When Judah wanted a harlot, he chanced upon his daughter-in-law. Yet the incomparable goodness of God strove against the sin of them both, that this adulterated seed might nonetheless win the sceptre.

Matt. 1.6. *Begat David the King.* David alone is honoured with this word of distinction, as God set forth in his person the type of the Messiah who would come to rule. He had started the kingdom earlier with Saul, but as this was achieved in an uprising, by the misguided appeals of the people, it was reckoned a legitimate changeover to David, especially as regards God's covenant, wherein He had promised ever to be the Governor of His own. When the people threw off the yoke of God and unauspiciously, against all the signs, demanded a king for themselves (I Sam. 8.5), Saul was allowed them for a short time. But God directly went on to establish His kingdom to be a pledge of true blessedness under the hand of David. So we should learn, that this marks a second condition of the people, as was appointed by the Lord. At this point the Evangelist includes the human misconduct, which might have spoiled the splendour of that divine blessing: namely that David begot Solomon by Bathsheba, whom he criminally took from her husband; to enjoy her, he treacherously exposed her innocent man to the slaughter of enemy swords. This ugly episode at the start of the kingdom should have stopped the Jews from glorifying in the flesh. But God wished to testify, that in setting up that kingdom, He gave no weight to human merits. In the succession, as Matthew records it, it is clear from the sacred history that three kings have been omitted. We should pay no heed to those who say this was done through forgetfulness, nor is the argument very probable that these were unworthy of inclusion in the genealogy of Christ. The same would apply to many others whom Matthew mixes indiscriminately with the godly and holy. It is more true that as he wished to compile a list of fourteen kings, he was not over-particular in making his selection, for he thought it enough to set the outline of the genealogy before his readers' eyes up to the end of the kingdom. That we only read of thirteen has probably happened through the fault or error of copyists. Epiphanius, in his first book *Against Heresies*, adduces the reason that as the name of Jeconiah was given twice, unlearned hands dared to cross it out in the second section as superfluous. He explains that this should not have been done, as Jehoiakim, father of king Jehoiachin shared the name Jeconiah with his son (Jer. 27.20; II Kings 24.6 and 15). Robertus Stephanus cites a Greek codex where the name Jehoiakim is inserted.

Matt. 1.12. *And after the carrying away to Babylon.* That is, after the Jews were led off into captivity. The Evangelist means that the descendants of David were then made slaves and exiles, after being kings. And as that captivity was a kind of dying, it came to pass by the marvellous providence of God not only that the Jews came together again into one people, but also that some remnants of princedom remained in David's family. Those who came home willingly obeyed the rule of Zerubbabel. So in this manner fragments of the royal sceptre continued to last, until the coming of Christ was upon them, according to the prophecy of Jacob, 'The sceptre shall not depart from Judah, Nor the ruler's staff from between his feet, until Shiloh come' (Gen. 49.10). And no matter how wretched and sad the dispersion of that people, some sparks of the grace of God never ceased to shine. The Greek word μετοικεσία was formerly interpreted 'transmigration,' and rendered as 'exile' by Erasmus; its proper sense is a change of habitation. So it means that the Jews were forced to migrate from their country, to become like residents in another place.

Matt. 1.16. *Jesus, who is called Christ.* By the added name, Matthew signifies His mission, for readers to learn that this was no private individual, but one divinely anointed to fulfil the role of Redeemer. What He should be, and what was the aim of that anointing, I shall not express with many words at this point. But we must understand the word itself: after the kingdom was abolished, it began to refer to that one alone from whom the full restoration of the lost salvation was to be hoped. As long as some majesty flourished in David's family, Kings used to be called Christs. But in case the ugly void that followed should cast the minds of the faithful into despair, God decided to apply the term only to the Redeemer, as is plain from

Daniel. The Gospel narrative shows on many occasions that this was the common way of speaking, at the time when the Son of God was revealed in the flesh.

Now the birth of Jesus Christ was on this wise: When his mother Mary had been betrothed to Joseph, before they came together she was found with child of the Holy Ghost. And Joseph her husband, being a right-eous man, and not willing to make her a public example, was minded to put her away privily. But while he thought on these things, behold, an angel of the Lord appeared unto him in a dream, saying, Joseph, thou son of David, fear not to take unto thee Mary thy wife: for that which is conceived in her is of the Holy Ghost. And she shall bring forth a son; and thou shalt call his name JESUS; for it is he that shall save his people from their sins. Now all this is come to pass, that it might be fulfilled which was spoken by the Lord through the prophet, saying,
Behold, the virgin shall be with child, and shall bring forth a son.
And they shall call his name Immanuel;
which is, being interpreted, God with us. And Joseph arose from his sleep, and did as the angel of the Lord commanded him, and took unto him his wife; and knew her not till she had brought forth a son: and he called his name JESUS. (Matt. 1.18-25)

Matt. 1.18. *Now the birth of Jesus Christ.* Matthew does not here expound the place or manner of Christ's birth, but describes how His heavenly conception was disclosed to Joseph. First he says that Mary was found with child of the Holy Spirit, not to make the hidden working of God publicly known, but to put the power of the Spirit, as yet concealed, alongside men's apprehension. He notes the moment as, 'When she had been betrothed to Joseph, before they came to-gether.' In marital fidelity, once a girl had been promised to a man, the Jews reckoned her as his lawful wife. So the law of adultery condemned those who violated chastity after the contract of betrothal. The word the Evangelist uses is either a modest expression for inter-course, or simply means (*before they came together*) living in one place, making one home and family as husband and wife. Thus it will mean that the virgin was not yet handed over by her parents into the man's hand, but still lived under their control.

Matt. 1.19. *Being a righteous man.* Some interpreters understand it that Joseph's righteousness consisted in wishing to spare his wife, and so they reckon his righteousness as humanity. fair-mindedness disposed to clemency. But others are more accurate, in taking the two parts as contrasted—though Joseph was a righteous man, yet he was concerned for the name of his wife. Accordingly the righteousness here commended consists in a hatred and detestation of wickedness. As he suspected his wife of adultery, indeed was persuaded of it, he did not wish to foster such a crime by leniency. To connive at a wife's misbehaviour makes a man into a procurer. Not only do decent and honest minds abhor such a crime, but the law also treats this supine attitude, as I call it, as scandalous. So Joseph in his zeal for righteousness condemned what he took to be a crime in his wife; at the same time, his mind was disposed to humanity and restrained him from applying the full rigour of the law. The middle course, the more reasonable, was for her secretly to leave him for another. We must understand that he was not of such soft and womanish material as to shelter a crime under his wing on the pretext of compassion: he only held back from the extremity of the law to avoid her facing a shameful sentence. We should be in no doubt that his thoughts were under the restraint of the Spirit's hidden direction. We know the frenzy of jealousy, how violently it tears at men, but even if Joseph had kept too wildly on his headlong action, he would, by miracle, have encountered various threatening hazards in his way, to advise him to change his ground. I have the same thoughts on Mary's silence. Granted that modesty held her back from telling her husband that she was with child by the Spirit, she was restrained more by God's providence than by her own counsel, for if she had spoken, as the matter stood, Joseph would have been more than incredulous, and thought himself mocked. Indeed, it would have been taken up on all sides as a comic tale: nor would the divine oracle have been so impressive if it had come after that. So the Lord allowed Joseph to be brought to a false judgment by ignorance, in order that He might set him back on the road by His own words. Of course we should realize that this was done more for the sake of us all, than for him alone: God wished to avoid by all means any misguided suspicion falling upon His oracle. When the angel approaches Joseph in his total ignorance of the matter, the wicked cannot make a false charge that he did not face God's message with an open mind. He was not wooed by the charms of his wife, the opinion he had formed was not beseiged with voices of protestation, it was not by human appeals that he was swayed to reverse his course, but when his mind was firmly stuck on the false judgment of his wife, God came to him, as coming down out of the skies, to make a more suitable witness and to carry more authority. We see how God, through the angel, wished to teach His servant Joseph, that he might be heaven's messenger to others, a word to speak which he had not taken from his wife, or from any mortal being. As for the mystery not being at once disclosed to a greater number, the reason seems to have been that, as it was an incomparable treasure which lay concealed, it was right to reveal it only to the children of God. And there is nothing strange if the Lord wished, as He usually does, to prove the faith and obedience of His own. Truly, unless a man grudged giving credence to God, or refused to submit to His will, he would be fully content with the testimonies with which God has surrounded this chapter of our faith. It was for the same reason that the Lord allowed him to wed Mary, and to shelter the virgin's heaven-sent conception, hidden under the veil of matrimony, until the time of revelation was ripe; all the while, the unbelieving are kept off the scene, as their ingratitude and ill-nature deserved.

Matt. 1.20. *But when he thought.* Here we see the Lord's way of being near His people in good time, yes on the very dot, as men say. And we realize that though He appears not to see our worries and concerns, yet we are in His view. But He is so concealed, and keeps so quiet, that after holding a trial of our patience, He may assist us at the instant He has chosen. However slow or delayed His help may be thought, it is for our good that it is so deferred. As for the angel appearing in a dream, this was one of the two ordinary means of revelation, as mentioned in Numbers 12.6-8, where God speaks thus, 'By the Prophets who shall be among you, or by a vision, or in a dream shall I make myself known: but I shall not be so with my servant Moses; with him will I speak mouth to mouth.' We must understand that dreams of this kind differ greatly from natural dreams: they are stamped with a character of certainty, and are under divine seal, so as to make their truth unambiguous. The dreams that normally come to men proceed perhaps from their daytime thoughts, perhaps from their natural constitution, perhaps from diseases of the body, or such like, but with divine dreams there is added the accompanying witness of the Spirit, giving firm assurance that it is God who speaks.

Thou son of David, fear not. The angel's exhortation means that Joseph's mind was troubled lest he should stain himself with any uncleanness for accepting his wife's adultery. He dispels any idea of offence, to allow him to live with his wife in a clear conscience. The epithet *Son of David* is suited to the present case, to lift his mind to ponder that supreme mystery, that he belongs to that family, indeed one surviving in a small company, from which salvation for the world is promised. When Joseph hears the name of David, from whom he traced his descent, he should bring to mind that noble covenant of God concerning the restoration of the kingdom, and realize that there was nothing new in the word spoken to him. It is just as though the angel brought the oracles of the Prophets into their midst, to prepare Joseph's mind to embrace the favour before him.

Matt. 1.21. *Thou shalt call his name Jesus.* I have already said a little, as much as was required, on the word itself. I have only one thing to add, that the angel's words refute the mad idea of those who derive the name from Jehovah, the essential name of God, for the Angel gives the reason why God's Son should be thus named, 'For he shall *save* His people.' This etymology contradicts their invention. And it is useless to try and wriggle out of this by pleading that the addition of Christ being the Author of salvation is appropriate and suitable because He was the eternal God. For here it is not only a case of what God bestows on us: we are dealing with the matter of God's Son, receiving the name that the Father laid Him by command, the mission that He bore in coming down to us. It is really very unintelligent when these two words, Jesus and Jehovah, have only two letters in common and are different in other respects, indeed have really no affinity between them, to confuse the two as though they were one. This is the kind of fusion I leave to the alchemists, who are not so very different from these cabbalists, who cook up for us these foul and unedifying sophistries. Thus God's Son, when He came to us in the garment of the flesh, took from His Father a name which should show openly the purpose of His coming, and what was duly to be expected of Him. The root of the name Jesus comes from the Hebrew Hiphil הושיע, meaning *to save*. The pronunciation is different in Hebrew, namely Jehoschua, but the Evangelists writing in Greek followed the accepted manner of speaking. The Greek interpreters both in Moses and in the other books translated Ἰησοῦν. A further proof of the ignorance of those who distort, rather than derive, the name Jesus from Jehovah, for they reckon it exceedingly strange that any mortal man should have shared this holy name with God's Son, and exclaim with pathos that Christ would never have allowed His name to be thus profaned. As though there were not to hand the ἀντίστροφον, the retort, that they shared the name Jesus just as men shared the name Joshua. Now then that we are quite agreed that God's Son is commended to us under the name Jesus as the Author of salvation, let us analyse the angel's words more closely.

He says, *For it is he that shall save his people from their sins.* The first lesson is, that those to whom Christ was sent for salvation were in themselves lost. He is expressly called the Church's Saviour. But if those whom God has joined to Himself, that Christ might restore life to them, are sunk in death and ruin, what is there to say of outsiders upon whom no hope of life ever shone? We must determine

64

that the whole human race was appointed to destruction, since its salvation depends on Christ. We must also note the cause of its destruction: the heavenly Judge does not pronounce us accursed recklessly or without reason. The angels testifies that we were dead and held subject to dread condemnation, because our sins had lost us the privilege of life. So we are shown the corruption and depravity of our nature. If there had been any man perfectly capable of righteous living, he might have done without the deliverance of Christ. Whereas all, to a man, need His grace; therefore are we slaves to sin, and robbed of true righteousness. Again we are taught the way and means of Christ's salvation, namely, that He delivers us from our sins. There are two parts to this liberation. By His act of expiation He offers us free pardon, which exempts us from our fatal guilt and reconciles us with God. Also, sanctifying us by His Spirit He claims us at the hands of Satan's tyrannical rule, that we may live unto righteousness. Christ is not recognized, then, as truly our Saviour, until we learn to embrace by faith the free remission of sins and know that we are counted righteous before God, as men cleared of our guilt. Moreover, we are to seek from Him the Spirit of righteousness and integrity with no confidence at all in our own works or virtue. Doubtless, by Christ's people the angel intends the Jews, over whom He was set as Head and King, but as soon after the nations were to be ingrafted into the race of Abraham, this promise of salvation is extended openly to all who gather by faith into the one body of the Church.

Matt. 1.22. *Now all this is come to pass.* It is a stupid and childish waste of effort for some to urge that it was the giving of the name Jesus to the Son of God that made Him to be called Immanuel. Matthew is not picking up one time alone, but embracing the whole celestial and divine content of the conception of Christ, including also the universal character. Now we must see how appropriate is his reference to the oracle of Isaiah. The passage is sufficiently known and celebrated (7.14), but the Jews with their accustomed ill-will debase it, though they show a hatred of Christ and of truth over this that is as much blind and foolish as it is sinful. Many of their Rabbis have taken their wild comment so far as to expound it of the king Hezekiah, who was then some fifteen years old. For any sake, what kind of urge to falsehood drives them to reverse the natural order and shut back a youth in his mother's womb, to be born at the age of sixteen, all in order to keep the clear light out? Deservedly they are Christ's foes, whom God maddens with the spirit of giddiness, and strikes down in a stupor. Others imagine for themselves some unknown son of king Ahaz, whose birth the Prophet was foretelling.

But I must ask what right had he to be called Immanuel and have the earth subject to his command, if he led all his life as a private citizen, of no distinction: for shortly after the same Prophet appoints that boy, whoever he is, as lord of the earth. It is an equally stupid remark to wish to have this spoken about a son of the Prophet. We have to say that in this matter Christian writers have had an insane delusion, in attaching the oracle that follows in the next chapter to Christ. The Prophet there says that he was bidden in a vision to go in unto his wife, and that a name was appointed by God's order for the son whom he begat, 'Hasten-the-spoil.' All that is referred to there is the storm of war that threatened with terrible devastation. It is easy to work out that the situations are quite different. Let us look for the true sense of the present passage.

When the city of Jerusalem was under siege, king Ahaz was afraid, indeed he was almost dead with fright, and the Prophet was sent to him with the promise that God would be guardian of the city. But the mere promise did not strengthen his perplexed mind (Isa. 7.11), and the Prophet was told to present him with a sign, whatever in heaven or in earth he should ask for. When that godless hypocrite, to conceal his unbelief, rejected a sign, the Prophet berated him quite forcefully, and at last came out with this, 'Yet God will give you a sign: behold, a virgin shall conceive, and bear a son,' etc. We accordingly interpret this as having been said of Christ: All you descendants of David, as best you may, strive to do away with the grace promised you (for the Prophet explicitly lays the shame at the door of the house of David), but your treachery will win you nothing in the end, for God's truth will come out the victor. God promised that His city would be saved from its enemies and unhurt. If His Word is not enough, He is prepared to give a token of assurance of your choice. You refuse both favours and push them away from you, yet God will stand firm by His covenant. The promised Redeemer will come, in whom God will perfectly establish His presence with His people. The Jews object that Isaiah's proposal would have been clumsy and absurd, if he had given a sign to men of that generation which was revealed some eight hundred years after. Their pride over this point is extreme, since through the inexperience, or neglect, of Christians this objection has been overlooked or buried. But I do not think the solution is difficult, as long as we observe that the covenant of adoption was given to the Jews, and all the other benefits of God hang from that. It was then a general promise under which God co-opted the sons of Abraham as a people for Himself, under which all the particular promises were grounded. Again, the Messiah was the foundation of this covenant. We can see now that the reason for the city's deliverance was that it was God's sanctuary, and from it the Redeemer was to come forth. Without this consideration, Jerusalem would have fallen a thousand times. So now let faithful readers consider, when the royal house blatantly rejected a sign offered by God, whether it was not opportune for the Prophet to pass to the Messiah, as if to say, Although this generation be unworthy of the salvation which I promise in the Lord, God will yet be mindful of His covenant and snatch this city out of the hands of the enemy. So though He now gives no particular sign to witness to His grace, this one word will be enough, and more than enough, that the Messiah shall arise from the stock of David. We must note that the Prophet's calling the unbelievers back to the general covenant is a kind of rebuke, in that they would not accept the particular sign. Now I think I have proved satisfactorily, that the Prophet, when the door was shut in the face of all miracles, passed over at the right moment to Christ, to let the unbelievers consider that there was no other cause of deliverance than the covenant begun with the fathers. By this memorable testimony God wished to show to all ages that He had continued the course of all His benefits towards the sons of Abraham, because He had made a free alliance with them in Christ, not on the basis of their merits.

The Jews attempt by another device to evade the sense we give, from what follows shortly in the context of the Prophet, before the child shall know to refuse the evil, and choose the good, the land shall be forsaken by two kings, etc. They infer from this that the birth of a child is promised which cannot be long delayed: otherwise what is said of the near change of kingdoms would not fit—the Prophet declares it will be before the infant is half grown. I answer that as Isaiah promised a sign concerning the future author of salvation, and announced that an infant should be born who would be true Immanuel, or, (to use Paul's words at I Tim. 3,16), God manifested in the flesh, he is using words equally of any children of his age. We can readily support this argument: having first spoken of the general covenant he comes back to the particular promise, for which reason he had been sent. The first passage, looking to the final and full redemption, denotes one certain child, to whom alone the title of God could apply: but the second, referring to a particular favour then at hand, marks the time by the childhood of those who were then recently born or were shortly afterwards to be born.

So far I have had valid and firm reasons, unless I am deceived, to refute the Jews' slanders, by which they endeavour to subvert Christ's glory, and prevent its light shining out from this oracle. It now remains to deal with their allegation over the word עלמה. They take

Matthew to task rudely for proving that Christ was born of a Virgin when the Hebrew word simply means 'girl.' And they laugh at us, deceived by a word mistranslated, for believing that He was born of the Holy Spirit, when the Prophet only says He would be a girl's son. They certainly display their excessive appetite for trouble-making when they insist that the word 'girl' must be understood as a girl who has known a man, for Scripture frequently uses it of virgins. Even its etymology suggests this—it speaks of secretiveness, in the sense of virginal modesty. They refer to a passage in Proverbs (30.19), but it is not really on their side. There Solomon speaks of a girl greatly loved by a youth, but it does not directly follow that she was undone by the young man who loved her. In fact the opposite conjecture would be the more likely. However, granting what they say about the word, the event itself demands and compels our admission that the Prophet is speaking of an unusual and miraculous birth. He declares that the sign comes down from the Lord: and it is no common one, but such as to excel all others. If he were only speaking of a woman about to give birth, would not this splendid introduction be laughable? We may see how the Jews, by their intemperate attitude, have exposed, not themselves only, but the sacred mysteries of God to mockery. Indeed, there is some weight in taking an argument from the context as a whole, A girl shall conceive. Why is there no mention of a man? What the Prophet extols is quite exceptional. The girl is given an instruction for the naming of the boy: in this regard also the Prophet's message is extraordinary. For though Scripture often relates that sons were named by their mothers, it was always done on the father's authority. Thus the Prophet in directing his words to the girl is taking from men, in this boy's case, what the natural order defers to them by right. Let this be taken for certain, that a remarkable miracle of God is the subject of the Prophet's celebration, for all godly folk to ponder with attention and awe, which the Jews unworthily profane, in transferring to an everyday conception the action that is ascribed to the hidden virtue of the Spirit.

Matt. 1.23. *His name Immanuel.* Scripture is used to speaking in these terms, of God being with us, when His help and favour are by us, and He reaches out the power of His hand to protect us. But here is expressed a way of God's communication with men. Apart from Christ, we are estranged from Him. Through Christ, we are not only received into His favour, but are effectively made one with Him. Compare Paul's teaching (Eph. 2.17; cf. Deut. 6.12-17), that the Jews were close to God under the Law, and there was great division between Him and the nations, meaning simply that God gave, at that time, in shadowy and figurative ways tokens of His presence to the people whom He had adopted. For the promise, 'God in your midst,' was a living one and, 'This is my resting-place' (Deut. 7.21; Ps. 132.14). But as this personal union of God with His people depended on the Mediator, who did not in actual terms yet exist, it was outlined with symbols. His seat and resting-place is set between the Cherubim, as the ark was the figure and visible pledge of His glory. But in Christ the presence of God was tangibly displayed to the people, no longer in shadows. For this reason, Paul says (Col. 2.9), 'In Him dwelleth all the fulness of the Godhead bodily.' He would certainly be no true Mediator if there were not in Him an undivided bond of each nature to tie men to God. There is no reason for the Jews to complain, that the Name of God is often attached to those memorial spots where He has shown His presence with the faithful. For we cannot deny that the Name has an implied antithesis in it, contrasting the presence of God in Christ with presence of every sort, such as was revealed before His coming, to the ancient people. If we can anchor the meaning of this Name on the appearing of Christ in the flesh, it follows that in former days God's tie with the fathers was partial, not complete. Which again brings home to us that Christ was God revealed in the flesh. From the beginning of the world He has performed the office of Mediator, but as all this depended on the final revelation, it is right that at the end as in His new Person He puts on the title *Immanuel*, when as Priest He comes onto the scene, to expiate the sins of men by the offering of His body, at the cost of His blood to reconcile them to the Father, altogether to fufil the whole calling of human salvation. So this name must make us think first of the divine majesty of Christ, to bring us to reverence it, as is due to the one and everlasting God. Yet we must not at the same time neglect its fruit, which God determined we should draw and understand of it. As often as we see God and man in the one Person of Christ, we may be certain that we possess God if by faith we are joined to Christ. As for the change of number in the words *they shall call*, this fits quite well with my previous explanation: the Prophet is addressing one woman only, and so uses the second person, Thou shalt call. But from the time that this name was published, this affirmation became the common property of all the faithful, as God gave Himself to us to be enjoyed in Christ.

Matt. 1.24. *And Joseph arose from his sleep*. The readiness to obey, as here described, has the effect both of showing Joseph's certainty of faith, and of praising his obedience, for if every scruple had not been removed and his conscience genuinely settled, he would never have been so quick to change his mind on the instant and take his wife to him, when he had just been thinking that to live with her would be an uncleaness. Some mark of Godhead was impressed upon the dream, that would not allow his mind to waver. Thus the result of his faith came to pass, that recognizing the will of God, he set himself immediately to obey it.

Matt. 1.25. *And knew her not, etc.* Helvidius takes issue with this passage, and caused great disturbance at one time in the Church. He deduced from it that Mary was only a virgin up to her first birth, and thereafter bore other children by her husband. The perpetual virginity of Mary was keenly and copiously defended by Hieronymus. Let one thing suffice for us, that it is foolishly and falsely inferred from the words of the Evangelist, what happened after the birth of Christ. He is called first-born, but for no other reason than that we should know He was born of a virgin. Joseph is said to have had no intercourse with her, until she brought forth, but this too only applies to that same period. What followed after, he does not tell. We know quite well that this is normally Scripture's way. And we may be sure that no-one will ever raise questions on such a matter except from curiosity: and certainly none but a contentious trouble-maker will press it all the way.

Now it came to pass in those days, there went out a decree from Caesar Augustus, that all the world should be enrolled. This was the first enrolment made when Quirinius was governor of Syria. And all went to enrol themselves, every one to his own city. And Joseph also went up from Galilee, out of the city of Nazareth, into Judaea, to the city of David, which is called Bethlehem, because he was of the house and family of David; to enrol himself with Mary, who was betrothed to him, being great with child. And it came to pass, while they were there, the days were fulfilled that she should be delivered. And she brought forth her firstborn son; and she wrapped him in swaddling clothes, and laid him in a manger, because there was no room for them in the inn. (Luke 2.1-7)

Luke relates how it came to pass that Christ was born in the city of Bethlehem even though His mother Mary lived elsewhere nearly to the time of her delivery. First he eliminates human design, by saying that it was to make their returns, by family and tribe, that Joseph and Mary had left home to travel there. If they had moved by their own decision and plan, for Mary to give birth in Bethlehem, then we should only have studied the personal aspect: but as their only purpose was to conform to Augustus' edict, we should properly understand that it was by the hand of God they were led—like blind people—to the place where Christ was to be born. It might indeed appear to be fortuitous, like all else which is not controlled by men's definite planning and is ascribed by profane folk to chance, but here we should not simply consider the course of events. It should occur to us to think of what was predicted many centuries before by the Prophet, where comparison will clearly show, that this was not without the wonderful providence of God, that a census was then ordered by Caesar Augustus, and that Joseph and Mary set foot from home, in order that they might reach Bethlehem at exactly the right moment. Thus we see that there are times when the saintly servants of God, though their purpose be uncertain, and they wander unaware of where their steps lead, yet keep to the right road, as God directs their path. No less does God's amazing providence reveal itself in the fact that a dictator's bidding pulls Mary away from her home, in fulfilment of prophecy. God had appointed a place where (as we shall shortly see) He wished His Son to be born, but if Mary had not been compelled, she would have decided to stay at home. Augustus orders a census to be held in Judaea, everyone to register their name, that they may thereafter pay him the annual tribute, which previously they used to pay to God. Thus a profane man snatches to himself, what God used to exact from His people. It was just as if he claimed the Jews for himself, and forbade them henceforth to be reckoned with the people of God. So when despair had reached its climax, and the Jews seemed forever cut off from the rule of God and alienated, God not only, with haste and against all hope, provides the remedy, but employs that very tyranny in the redemption of His people. For the Governor (or whoever was Caesar's minister), in fulfilling his commands, is God's secret herald, summoning Mary to the place divinely appointed. And in fact Luke's whole narrative takes the view that the faithful may learn how Christ, from His very nativity, was brought forth by the hand of God. It has considerable weight for re-assuring our faith, that Mary, suddenly and apart from her own choice, was taken off to Bethlehem, in order that the Redeemer should proceed from there, just as once was promised.

Luke 2.1. *All the world.* Seeing we find this synecdoche frequently in Roman writers, it should not seem harsh. I have no doubt that this census was shared by all the provinces, to be more tolerable, and less unpopular: though the method of tribute could be different. I believe the enrolment was the first held because, for the Jews at that time, now in virtual subjection, this was the imposition of a new and unaccustomed burden. Others say it was the first from Cyrenius being appointed over Syria, but this is implausible. Tribute was annual, but enrolment was not held annually, so it means that the Jews were then far more severely oppressed. Variation over the name of the Proconsul is nothing odd, where some call him Cyrenius, others Quirinus or Quirinius. We know that the Greeks in rendering Latin names change something in translation. A far greater difficulty arises from another quarter. Josephus in his book of *Antiquities*, 18, ch. 1, records that, Quirinus, on the banishment of Archelaus to Vienna, came as Proconsul, to attach Judaea to the province of Syria. Now the sources agree that Archelaus reigned nine years from the death of his father Herod. So it results that between the nativity of Christ and that census there must have elapsed some thirteen years. (Nearly all follow Epiphanius' account that Christ was born in the thirty-third year of Herod, that is, four years before his death.) There is further confusion in the fact that the same Josephus (3, ch. 18), states that this census occurred in the thirty-seventh year after the victory at Actium. But if this is true, Augustus survived it some seven years at most. This would cut eight or nine years off his life, for it will be evident from Luke 3 that he was then only in the fifteenth year of his reign. But as Christ's age would be too well known to need to be called in question, it is quite likely that Josephus had a lapse of memory on this point, as on many others. The annals certainly record that Quirinius was Consul some nineteen years before Augustus won supreme power by that victory over Anthony: so he would have to have been sent to the province at a very great age. Besides, Josephus counts four Governors of Judaea within eight years, though he admits that the fifth ruled eleven years: this was Valerius Gratus, whom Pontius Pilate succeeded.

But another solution can be adduced, that the census could not be carried through as soon as it was ordered, for Josephus relates that Coponius was sent with an army, to compel the Jews. So we may readily infer that the census was for a time stopped by popular uprising, and Luke's words can bear the interpretation that some time before Christ's nativity an edict went out concerning a census of the people, but the enrolment could not be held without the change in the status of the kingdom, when Judaea was reduced to the condition of a province. So the latter phrase would be added by way of correction: 'This enrolment was first made under the governorship of Cyrenius,' that is, it was then for the first time made effective. This still does not solve the whole question, for what point was there in holding a census of the people, who paid no tribute to the Roman rule when Herod held Judaea? The answer is, that it is quite feasible that Augustus, in order to put pressure on the Jews, who were famous for their obstinate resistance, wished them to have a census under

Herod. Herod's special kingship did not prevent the Jews paying the Roman government some kind of tribute per capita. We know that Herod's reign was quite precarious, and almost puppet-like. I do not know the source of Eusebius' comment, that the census was decreed by Act of Senate.

Luke 2.7. *There was no room for them in the inn.* Here we see not only how poor were Joseph's means, but how severe was the tyranny that allowed no excuse, but forced Joseph to take his wife with him out of season when she was near to her delivery. It is possibly true that those who were of the royal lineage were treated more harshly and insultingly than the rest. Joseph was not so foolish as not to be worried over his wife's confinement, for he would gladly have avoided this enforcement. But as he cannot, he is driven to it, and submits himself in trust to God. We see at the same time what a start God's Son enjoyed, what a cradle received Him. Such was His manner of birth, for He had put on our flesh to the end that He might empty Himself for our sake. So He was pushed into a stable and lodged in a manger, denied a place of hospitality among men, that heaven may lie open to us, not only as a place in which to lodge, but as an eternal home-land and inheritance, and that angels should receive us to dwell with Him.

And there were shepherds in the same country abiding in the field, and keeping watch by night over their flock. And an angel of the Lord stood by them, and the glory of the Lord shone round about them: and they were sore afraid. And the angel said unto them, Be not afraid; for behold, I bring you good tidings of great joy which shall be to all the people: for there is born to you this day in the city of David a Saviour, which is Christ the Lord. And this is the sign unto you; Ye shall find a babe wrapped in swaddling clothes, and lying in a manger. And suddenly there was with the angel a multitude of the heavenly host praising God, and saying,
Glory to God in the highest,
And on earth peace among men in whom he is well pleased. (Luke 2.8-14)

Luke 2.8. *And there were shepherds.* There would have been no benefit in Christ being born at Bethlehem, if this had not been made known to the world. Yet the means that Luke describes appear to men's judgment unfitting. First, Christ is revealed only to a few witnesses, and that at dead of night. Further, while God had at hand many of rank and high ability as witnesses, He puts them aside and simply chooses shepherds, of little account with men, of no reckoning. Here the reasonableness and thoughtfulness of the flesh must look foolish, and we must allow that what is foolishness from God, is higher than what is, or seems to be, wisdom of the world (I Cor. 1.25). This too was part of His self-emptying, not that Christ should lose any glory through it, but only that it should for a time be concealed. And just as Paul warns us, the Gospel is according to the flesh a thing to be despised, that our faith may be established in the power of the Spirit, and not by high words of human wisdom, or in any mundane splendour (I Cor. 2.4), so from the beginning God laid up this incomparable wealth in earthen vessels, the better to test the obedience of our faith. If we desire to come to Christ, we must not be ashamed to follow those whom God chose, from the sheep dung, to bring down the pride of the world.

Luke 2.9. *An angel of the Lord stood by them.* He says that the glory of the Lord shone round the shepherds, by which they recognised the angel. It would have done little good for what Luke relates to have been spoken by the angel, if God had not testified by some visible sign that what they heard derived from Him. So the angel appeared to them, not in any common form, or without nobility, but arrayed in the brightness of heavenly glory, which would impress upon the shepherds' minds that they were to take the message brought to them exactly as from the mouth of God Himself. Hence their alarm, of which Luke goes on to tell, by which God is used to humble men's hearts, to win reverence for His Word, as I have expounded above.

Luke 2.10. *Be not afraid.* The object of the exhortation here is to relieve their fear. Though it may be useful for men's minds to be struck with fright that they may learn to give God His due honour, at the same time they need consolation, in case they are quite overwhelmed. God's Majesty would inevitably swamp the entire world, if its inherent awesomeness were not tempered with a degree of gentleness. The reprobate collapse at the sight of God, for they only see Him as Judge. But the angel, to restore the shepherds' spirits, declares that he was sent for another object, namely to announce the mercy of God. And this word alone not only raises fallen men, but renews the lost also, and recalls them from death to life, when they hear that God is kindly favoured toward them. The angel's first word is that he brings a message of *great joy*: then he gives the cause or substance of the joy, that a Saviour is born. The first lesson of these words is that until men have peace with God and are reconciled through the grace of Christ, any other happiness they conceive is transient and false. The godless often exult in a mad, drunken

74

happiness, but if there is no peace-maker between them and God, they must necessarily suffer the wretched torment of conscience's blind pricks. In the end, however gladly and smugly they sink into their delights, their very lusts are equalled by their pains. So this is the start of real joy, to sense the fatherly love of God toward us, who alone can comfort our minds. And this joy is in the Holy Spirit, in whom Paul sets the Kingdom of God (Rom. 14.17). The epithet, *great*, is added to let us know not only that we are to rejoice principally in the salvation offered us in Christ, but that this boon is so great, so unbounded, that it outweighs by right all the griefs, troubles and worries of this present life. Hence we learn to be so pleased with Christ alone, that the sense of His favour surpasses all the afflictions of the flesh, indeed removes them altogether.

Which shall be to all the people. Though the angel only addresses shepherds, he means that the message of salvation which he brings them extends farther, not for their ears alone, but for others also to hear. Understand that the joy was open to all the people, for it was offered to all without distinction. For He is not the God of this one or of that, but He had promised Christ to the whole family of Abraham. That, in great measure, the Jews have lost the joy that was theirs to hold, resulted from their failure to believe. Today also, God invites all men alike to salvation through the Gospel, but the world's ingratitude makes only a few enjoy the grace, which is set out equally for all. While the joy, then, has been confined to a small number, in respect of God, it is called universal. And though the angel is speaking only of the chosen people, yet now with the partition wall gone the same tidings are presented to the whole human race. Christ announces peace, not only to those who are near, but to those who are far, no less to outsiders, than to those of the house-hold (Eph. 2.17). It is because, up to the resurrection, the alliance was peculiarly with the Jews, that the angel separates them from the remaining nations.

Luke 2.11. *For there is born to you this day.* Here the cause of the joy is stated, as we have just remarked: that there is born the Redeemer, long since promised, who shall restore God's Church to its standing. Of course the angel does not speak of something altogether unheard-of, but takes the heading of his message from the Law and Prophets, a manner of address which would have been wasted on the godless nations: 'a Saviour which is Christ the Lord is born to you.' With the same intention he records that He is born in the city of David, which would be pointless, if it did not renew the memory of the promises at all times known and celebrated among the Jews. And the angel suited his speech to his hearers, who were not quite unaware of the promise of redemption, and brought the Gospel into line with the teaching of the Law and Prophets, as indeed it flows from that source. As the Greek σωτήρ means more, according to Cicero, than the Latin *Servator*, and there is no Latin word that covers it, I thought it was better to use a non-classical term (*Salvator*) than diminish Christ's power in any respect. I have no doubt that translators of the Vulgate and of the early Church came to the same conclusion. Christ then is called *Saviour*, as conferring full salvation. And the pronoun, to *you*, bears great emphasis, for it would be no great joy to hear that an Author of salvation were born if every man did not accept that He was born for him. Compare Isaiah 9.6, 'Unto us a child is born, unto us a son is given.' Similarly, Zechariah 9.9, 'Behold thy King cometh to thee . . . lowly.'

12. *And this is the sign unto you.* The angel anticipates a stumbling-block, that might easily check the shepherds' faith, for what kind of joke is this, for Him to be seen lying in a cradle, who is the King and only Saviour sent from God? So in case this poor and abject condition of Christ should deter the shepherds from faith in Christ, the angel tells them in advance what they will see. This order of dealing, which human judgment might think absurd, if not comic, is daily observed by God in His treatment of us. For by the voice of the Gospel sent down from heaven He bids us accept Christ crucified, and puts signs in earthly and passing elements to lift us to the glory of blessed immortality. He promises spiritual righteousness, and sets a little sprinkling of water before our eyes. He seals the promise of the soul's eternal life with a morsel of bread and a sip of wine. If the shepherds are not put off by the stable from seeking their salvation from Christ, and submitting themselves to His rule, while yet an infant, there is no sign however contemptible that should darken His glory for us, certainly from the time of His ascension into heaven and sitting at the right hand of the Father, that we should not humbly adore Him.

Luke. 2.13. *And suddenly there was with the angel a multitude.* By the angel alone, there was displayed an impression of the heavenly splendour, yet God determined to give His Son a finer spectacle, as much to strengthen us as the shepherds. The testimony of two or three is enough to remove doubt in human course, but here the heavenly host appeared, with one purpose and one voice to testify to the Son of God. What stubborn mind could resist the angels' united hymn and not join in the praise of our Salvation in Christ? We see how hateful must be our incredulity, that breaks the sweet harmony of heaven and earth. Indeed we are convicted of dumbness worse than bestial if this canticle does not fire our faith and zeal for God's praise, as the angels tune their voices with one mind that we should pick up their strain. Besides, by this instance of the melody of heaven, God wills to commend to us the unity of faith, to encourage us to sing His praises on earth with one accord.

Luke 2.14. *Glory to God in the highest.* The angels begin with an act of thanksgiving or praise to God, for Scripture frequently tells us that we are redeemed from death so that with our tongue as with our works we may show our gratitude to God. So remember that this was the cause and purpose that made God reconcile us to Himself through His only-begotten Son, that publishing the riches of His grace and boundless mercy, He should lend lustre to His Name. Today as far as each of us is stirred to celebrate God's glory by the understanding of His grace, so far has he advanced in the faith of Christ. As often as we hear tidings of our salvation, we must know this is like a signal given to prompt our act of thanksgiving and God's praises. *And on earth peace.* This is the more accepted reading, allowing, 'Among men in whom he is well pleased,' to come as a third phrase. Though it does not greatly affect the substance of the matter, however you read it, the separate arrangement seems to suit better, for there is no doubt that these two phrases, 'Glory to God in the highest,' and, 'And on earth peace,' correspond to each other. Unless one opposes men to God, there will not be a complete antithesis. Perhaps the interpreters were deceived by the preposition 'in' (ἐν) as it was difficult to understand the words, that there was 'peace among men'. But as it is superfluous in many passages of Scripture, there is no need for it to get in our way. If any prefer to put it onto the last phrase, the sense will stay the same, as I shall shortly remark.

We must now see what the angels understand by the word *peace*. Certainly they are not speaking of outward peace, as men keep it with themselves, but they mean that the earth has been pacified, when men are reconciled to God inwardly, and are quiet in their own minds. We know that we are born sons of wrath, and by nature are at war with God, and all the time we must be harassed with dread alarm, as long as we feel that God is against us. So the clear and short definition of peace may be obtained by its opposite, that is, by God's wrath and the fear of death. The reference then is twofold, one way to God, the other way to men, for our peace is established with God, when He clears our guilt, and imputes no sin to us, thus beginning to show us favour, while we, acknowledging His fatherly goodness of heart, call on Him with a firm assurance, and glory without fear in the salvation He has promised us. Though in another place (Job 7.1) the life of man upon the earth is called a continual warfare, and events themselves declare it to be the case, that there is nothing more turbulent than our condition, all the days of our earthly life, yet the angels specifically place peace on earth, to assure us that no storms prevent us from entering upon the calm seas of Christ with tranquil minds. Remember, then, in all the tempests of temptation, in all kinds of trials, in violent uprisings, in fighting and in fear, a place of peace is determined, to prevent our faith being shaken by any device, or weakening to the point of collapse. *Among men in whom he is well pleased.* How the genitive case (men of good will) should have crept in, I do not know. Certainly the Vulgate reading, 'to men of good will,' must be repudiated both as an intrusion, and as spoiling the whole sense. Yet some, reading the nominative case, 'Good will to,' etc., go astray in applying it to men, as though it were an exhortation to embrace the favour of God. I quite agree that God's peace, offered to us men, has effect only as we receive it, but as εὐδοκία is frequently taken in Scripture as translating the Hebrew רצון, it was in turn rendered *beneplacitum* (a state of good-pleasure). It is wrong to interpret this passage in terms of receiving grace. Rather it is a declaration of the source of that peace which the angels have announced, that we should know it to be gratuitous, the flowing forth of God's sheer loving-kindness. If we care to read, 'Good will among men,' it will not produce an unsuitable sense, for this will also indicate the cause of our peace, namely that God has granted men His free favour, after His earlier state of disagreement and hostility towards them, If even one read, 'Peace of His good will,' meaning that it is freely offered, I would not object to the exposition. But it is simpler to take εὐδοκίαν as placed in apposition, in order to tell us the source of the peace that comes out to us.

And it came to pass, when the angels went away from them into heaven, the shepherds said one to another, Let us now go even unto Bethlehem, and see the thing that is come to pass, which the Lord hath made known unto us. And they came with haste, and found both Mary and Joseph, and the babe lying in the manger. And when they saw it, they made known concerning the saying which was spoken to them about this child. And all that heard it wondered at the things which were spoken unto them by the shepherds. But Mary kept all these sayings, pondering them in her heart. And the shepherds returned, glorifying and praising God for all the things that they had heard and seen, even as it was spoken unto them.

And when eight days were fulfilled for circumcising him, his name was called JESUS, which was so called by the angel before he was conceived in the womb. (Luke 2.15-21)

Luke 2.15. *When the angels went away.* Here the obedience of the shepherds is set out for us. Seeing that the Lord willed them to be the witnesses of His Son to the whole world, He spoke to them with effect by the angels, that what had been told them should not come to nothing. They were not ordered clearly and explicitly to come to Bethlehem, but as they sufficiently realize that this is God's purpose, they hurry off to see Christ. So today, when we understand that Christ is announced to us, so that our hearts may approach Him in faith, there is no excuse for us if we delay. And Luke intends to point out that the shepherds decided to set forth as soon as the angels left them. We should not, as many do, let God's Word vanish when its sound has gone, but have its roots work lively in our hearts to produce its effect, as soon as its notes have ceased sounding in our ears. We should note besides how the shepherds encourage one another: it is not enough for each to urge himself on, but there are to be mutual words of resolve. Luke stresses his praise of their obedience in saying that they made haste, to lead us also to a promptness of faith. *Which the Lord hath made known unto us.* With knowledge and in truth, they ascribe to God what they had only heard from the angel, whom they acknowledge as God's minister, and also invest with His authority, as though he stood before them in the Lord's Person. For this reason the Lord continually recalls us to Himself, lest the Majesty of His Word should grow shabby in the sight of men. Here we see again how they reckon it unthinkable for themselves to neglect a treasure shown them by the Lord. They argue from the tidings brought them, that they must proceed to Bethlehem to see this. Each of us, likewise, according to the measure of our faith and understanding, should reasonably equip himself to follow whither God wills.

Luke 2.16. *And found ... Mary.* There was no beauty in the scene—of itself it could have turned them against Christ. What more pathetic than believing one to be King of the whole people, who is not ranked worthy of even the lowest place in the crowd? And to hope for a restoration of the kingdom, for salvation, from one who for his poverty and lack of support is turned out into the stable? Yet Luke writes that nothing of that sort prevented the shepherds from praising God in wonder. Surely they had such a clear impression of God deep in their eyes, such reverence for His Word firm set in their minds, as easily to overcome by the depth of their faith whatever in Christ struck them as lacking in glory and honour. Indeed the only real reason why offences, even the slightest, should hinder or actually put us off our course, is that we have been less intent upon God, and are readily swayed this way and that. If this one thought were to control all our emotions, that we have a certain and faithful testimony from heaven, it would be a firm and stable support against all manner of temptations, and defend us well enough against all petty causes of offence.

Luke 2.17. *They have made known concerning the saying*. Luke commends the shepherds for their faith, in that they frankly passed on from their hands to others, what they had received from the Lord, and the use of their testimony for all our sakes was such, that in the confirmation of our faith, the angels have become almost secondary. Luke also instructs us, that their report of what they heard was not unsuccessful. There is no doubt that the Lord gave effect to their speech, for fear they should be laughed at or spurned. The men's own standing would lessen their authority, and the event of itself could sound fictitious. But the Lord, who gave them this role to play, did not let them play it in vain. Though this way of dealing appeals less to human intelligence, that the Lord should have His Word brought to men's ears by feeble folk, yet it is suited for humbling the pride of the flesh and for testing the obedience of faith, and so it is agreeable to God Himself.

All are astonished, but no-one takes a step to reach Christ. Thus we learn how they heard of the power of God, and were impressed, but without serious effect upon their hearts. This account, then, was published abroad less for their salvation, than to make the ignorance of that people inexcusable.

Luke 2.19. *But Mary kept*. Mary's diligence in considering the works of God is told us for two reasons: first, to show us that the guardianship of this treasure was entrusted to her heart, so that what she kept locked up in herself she might in her time make known to others; also, that all the god-fearing might imitate her example. For if we are wise, this ought to be a principal occupation, a supreme interest of our lives, to think over the works of God with all application, as they build up our faith. The word *kept* refers to memory: συμβάλλειν or to *ponder* means to put single parts together, which combine with each other to attest the glory of Christ, as it were, to make one body. Mary could not diligently weigh everything up, to find the value of them all, except by comparing one part with another.

Luke 2.20. *Glorifying and praising God*. It is also relevant to our common experience of faith that the shepherds recognised God's work with certainty. Their ardour in giving glory to God, as they are credited with, is a quiet reproach to our slothfulness, or I should say, ingratitude. If they valued Christ's nativity so highly, that they should rise from that stable and manger to the heights of heaven, should not the death and resurrection of Christ work more powerfully among us, to lift us to God? Not only is Christ raised up from the earth, so as to draw all things after Himself, He also sits at the right hand of the Father, that with all our heart we, who are pilgrims in this world, may think upon the life of heaven. Luke shows the true nature of their devotion when he says that the angel's testimony was like a rule for the shepherds, by which they checked everything. Faith has its proper support from the works of God when it directs everything to one end, namely to make God's truth shine more brightly, in the way it is revealed in His Word.

Luke 2.21. *For circumcising him.* The general import of circumcision may be found by readers at Genesis 17.10. The points that apply to the Person of Christ may be touched upon briefly. God wished His Son to be circumcised that He might come under the Law, for circumcision was a solemn symbol by which Jews were initiated into the observance of the Law. Paul states its objects in Galatians 4.4, where he says that He was made under the Law to redeem those who were under the Law. So Christ by receiving circumcision professed Himself a servant of the Law, to win us our freedom. In this way, not only was the servitude of the Law abolished by Him, but also there was attached to His own solid body the shadow of the rite, that it might in due course reach its conclusion. Though its abrogation depends on the death and resurrection of Christ, this was something of a preliminary, that God's Son underwent circumcision.

His name was called Jesus. This passage proves that it was an accepted custom among the Jews to give their children's names on the day of their circumcision, as is our practice now at Baptism. The Evangelist makes two remarks. The name of Jesus was given God's Son not unthinkingly, nor by men's choosing, but as the angel brought it from heaven; further, that Joseph and Mary obeyed God's command. This is the way our faith connects with God's Word—He leads, and we speak ourselves; our faith answers His promises. Luke particularly commends to us the rule of preaching the Word, when he says that salvation by the grace of Christ had the testimony of men's voices, salvation, as it had been promised by the angel.

Now when Jesus was born in Bethlehem of Judaea in the days of Herod the king, behold, wise men from the east came to Jerusalem, saying, Where is he that is born King of the Jews? for we saw his star in the east, and are come to worship him. And when Herod the king heard it,

he was troubled, and all Jerusalem with him. And gathering together
all the chief priests and scribes of the people, he inquired of them where
the Christ should be born. And they said unto him, In Bethlehem of
Judaea: for thus it is written by the prophet,
> *And thou Bethlehem, land of Judah,*
> *Art in no wise least among the princes of Judah:*
> *For out of thee shall come forth a governor,*
> *Which shall be shepherd of my people Israel. (Matt. 2.1-6)*

Matt. 2.1. *Now when Jesus was born.* Matthew says nothing of how
it came about that Christ was born at Bethlehem. Indeed God's
Spirit, who appointed the Evangelists as recorders, deliberately controlled their pen, so that all should write in complete agreement, but
in different ways. It gave more certainty and light to God's truth
when it was established that His witnesses did not tell a pre-arranged
tale, but each of them, without respect to the other, wrote simply
and freely what the Spirit dictated. Now this story deserves to be
remembered, how God procured magi from Chaldaea, to come to
Judaea, for the purpose of adoring Christ, while He lay in a stable
inglorious and mean. It was certainly a marvellous counsel of God
to determine that His Son should enter the world in obscurity and
humility, yet He gave Him a splendid commendation of praise and
honour, leaving nothing lacking that might help our faith to attest
His divine Majesty. Yet there is a well-ordered harmony to be
observed in this apparent contradiction. A star in the sky foretells
that He is King, whose throne is a cattle stall, for a place among
common men is denied Him. In the East His Majesty shines out,
but in Judaea it is nowhere to be seen, rather soiled with many insults.
How is this? Surely, the heavenly Father wished the star and the
magi to stand out as our guides, to lead straight to His Son. At the
same time He stripped Him of all earthly splendour, that we should
know that His Kingdom was spiritual. Thus this account is useful,
both as showing how God brought the magi to His Son as first-
fruits of the nations, and also how He wished the reign of His Son to
be appreciated by the distinction, which they and the star brought Him,
in case the cheap and spiteful scorn of His own race should make
Him of no account in our eyes.

Magi, as is well known, is the title astrologers and wise men receive
among the Persians and Chaldaeans: we may readily conjecture that
these came from Persia. It is better to say that we do not know how
many they were, as the Evangelist does not state exactly, than rashly
to assert for sure something which is dubious. It is really a childish
error that led the Papists to make the figure three, on the grounds

that Matthew says they offered gold, incense and myrrh. As though he gave each of them a separate task, when he is really saying that the three gifts were offered jointly. That ancient writer, whoever he was, whose incomplete commentary on Matthew is inscribed with the name of Chrysostom—and is reckoned among Chrysostom's works—says there were fourteen. There is not any extra support to this, unless perhaps it came down from patristic tradition, but this itself is unreliable. The Papists are also more than laughable in making them out to be kings, since they read in another passage (Ps. 72.10), the prediction that kings shall come from Tarshish and the Isles and Saba, to bring gifts to God. An ingenious construction here, for to give men a new pattern they are making their first step the readjustment of the world: they have turned South and West into East! No doubt, they are overwhelmed by God's righteous punishment, and their crass ignorance is exposed to the taunts of all mankind, men who have not scrupled to forge and pervert the truth of God. But the question is, whether this star was one of that number which God created in the beginning as ornament for the heavens. Further, did the science of astrology lead the magi to the deduction they formed over the birth of Christ? Though we need no contentious debate over these matters, we do however infer from Matthew's words that it was not a natural star, but extra-ordinary, for it was not of the order of nature (*ex ordine naturae*) to disappear at certain times, and afterwards suddenly to shine again. Further, that it led in a straight path to Bethlehem, and at length stood fixed over the place where Christ was. None of this accords with natural stars. It is more probable that it was like a comet, seen in the atmosphere rather than in the heaven. There is nothing strange in Matthew using the everyday word and speaking, improperly, of a *star*. And this more or less gives us the answer to the second question, for since it is certain that astrology is confined to the limits of nature, the magi could not have been led by it alone to come to Christ. They must have had the hidden aid of the Spirit's revelation. I do not deny that they had some basis or germ in their craft, but I say they must have had assistance from a new and exceptional vision, or it would have come to nothing.

Matt. 2.2. *Where is he that is born King?* I think it is over ingenious for some interpreters to suggest a tacit opposition between *born king* and 'made' or 'created'. I take it more simply, that the magi mean that the king has recently been born and is still an infant—in order to distinguish him from the adult king, who actually held the reins of government, for they go straight on to add that they have not been excited by the fame of his deeds, or by his actual greatness and its spreading report, but by a heavenly omen of a future reign. As the sight of the star had such an effect upon the magi, woe to our sluggish ways, when we seek Christ so half-heartedly, after He has been revealed as King. *And are come to worship him.* The star was displayed to the end that it might lead the magi to Judaea, for them to be witnesses and heralds of the new King. As regards themselves, they had not come to give Christ a show of duty and worship, in the way due to the Son of God, but they intended to salute Him, in Persian fashion, as the highest king. Probably they grasped no more of His character than that He was to be a man endowed with exceptional power and dignity, a man deservedly to win over peoples to admire and reverence Him. It is even possible that they wished to win His favour in anticipation, that He might be favourable and well-disposed towards them, if He should happen to gain the empire of the East.

Matt. 2.3. *Herod ... was troubled.* Herod was not unaware of the prophecies in which a King was promised to Israel, to convert their state of affliction and turmoil into an era of blessedness. He had lived among that people from boyhood, and had an intimate acquaintance of their history. Moreover the rumour was generally current, and could hardly have escaped neighbouring peoples. But he is troubled as if this were a new issue, previously unheard of. Surely because he had put aside any faith in God and His promises, and had thought he could reckon the hope of a Redeemer to be vain, especially as he had imagined, in the way of proud men, with foolish confidence, that his kingdom would be stable in himself and in his line. Since he had earlier carelessly despised prophecies—intoxicated with his own success—now the recollection of them strikes him with sudden terror. No, he would not have been so greatly disturbed by the mere report of the magi, if those oracles had not come into his mind, which formerly had seemed illusory and unimportant. Thus the Lord allows men to sleep in their unbelief, then suddenly shatters their peace. When Matthew says, that *Jerusalem* also was troubled, it may be explained in two ways: either that the people were violently upset by the novelty of the sudden event, even though they were eager to learn that it was a joyful message for them, of a King born; or that being so used to troubles, and hardened by prolonged endurance, they feared the change, in case it brought them to the beginning of further disaster. They were so worn down and near to exhaustion from continual wars, that as long as they had peace, even wretched and cruel slavery would be, not merely tolerable, but desirable. This shows us how ill they had progressed under the scourges of God. They had become deadened in stupefaction, that by now their promised redemption and salvation had somehow gone stale on them.

I have no doubt that it was their ingratitude which Matthew wished to mark for they were broken under the weariness of evil, and had abandoned their longing for the grace promised them.

Matt. 2.4. *And gathering together all the chief priests.* Though there was utter silence on the subject of Christ in Herod's court, as soon as the magi made mention of a King, prophecies came to mind that before lay in oblivion. Herod immediately guesses that this King, for whom the magi seek, is the Messiah of old divine promise. Further evidence then, that Herod was genuinely alarmed when he made anxious inquiry, and no wonder. For since all tyrants are timid, as their savagery strikes more terror upon themselves than on those who suffer it, Herod was bound to have fears beyond them all, recognizing that his reign was opposed to God. His new inquiry reveals how inept his contempt for Christ had been, before the magi came. That the scribes and high priests make honest answer from Scripture (yet later they tried feverishly to subvert all Scripture, to rob Christ of His title) was done because Christ had not yet disturbed them with His Gospel. All godless men readily subscribe to God in general terms, but when God's truth begins to press them more closely, they spew out the venom of their spleen. We have a brilliant instance of this matter in the Papists of our day. They admit, without controversy, that Christ is the only-begotten Son of God, bearing our flesh, and confess one Person of God and man in two natures, but when one comes to Christ's power and task, the argument suddenly blazes up, for they do not allow themselves to be forced into line, and far less to be brought to nothing. All in all, as long as the godless believe they are losing nothing, they allow God and Scripture a measure of respect. But when it comes to close range, and Christ engages in battle with their self-seeking, greed, luxury, false confidence, hypocrisy and deceptions, then they forget all self-control and rush into a frenzy. We must realize then, that the main cause of the blindness of the enemies of the truth lies in their evil desires, which turn light into darkness.

Matt. 2.6. *And thou Bethlehem.* There is no doubt that the scribes faithfully quoted in their own tongue the whole context of these words, as it stands in the Prophet. Matthew was content to note the passage, and as he wrote Greek, he followed the accepted reading. It is from this and similar passages that we may readily gather that the Gospel was not composed by him in Hebrew. We must always observe the rule, that as often as the Apostles quote a testimony from Scripture, although they do not render it word for word, in fact may move quite a way from it, they adapt it suitably and appropriately to the case in hand. So readers should always take care to note the object of the passages of Scripture that the Evangelists use, not to press single words too exactly, but to be content with the one message which they never take from Scripture to distort into a foreign sense, but suit correctly to its real purpose. Further, as it is their plan to nourish infants and novices in faith with drinks of milk, for as yet they could not digest solid food, so there is no impropriety in the children of God going on to seek diligently and accurately what Scripture contains; thus the appetite which the Apostles encourage may lead them to the source.

Now let us return to the oracle at Micah 5.2. Here is the literal message of the Prophet, 'But thou Bethlehem Ephratah, which art little to be amongst the thousands of Judah, out of thee shall one come forth unto me that is to be ruler in Israel.' For Ephratah, Matthew has put Judah, but in the same sense. For Micah only intends by this to distinguish this Bethlehem, of which he speaks, from the other that was in the tribe of Zebulon. There is more difficulty in the rest of the material. The Prophet says that Bethlehem is little, to be reckoned among the districts of Judah. Matthew on the other hand extols its worth, making it one of the chief places. This has moved some interpreters to read the passage in the Prophet as a question. But others are more correct to reckon that Matthew intended, by this alteration, to praise God for His grace, that a slight and obscure little town had been made the birth-place of the supreme King. But though Bethlehem excelled in this sort of honour, yet it did its inhabitants so little good, that it came to a worse end; for there the Redeemer was received with more than a little insult. Matthew combines Ruler with Shepherd. However he expresses both points—Christ is governor of the people, and He is entrusted with the task of tending them.

Then Herod privily called the wise men, and learned of them carefully what time the star appeared. And he sent them to Bethlehem, and said, Go and search out carefully concerning the young child; and when ye have found him, bring me word, that I also may come and worship him. And they, having heard the king, went their way; and lo, the star, which they saw in the east, went before them, till it came and stood over where the young child was. And when they saw the star, they rejoiced with exceeding great joy. And they came into the house and saw the young child with Mary his mother; and they fell down and worshipped him; and opening their treasures they offered unto him gifts, gold and frankin-

cense and myrrh.   And being warned of God in a dream that they should not return to Herod, they departed into their own country another way. (Matt. 2.7-12)

Matt. 2.7.   *Then Herod privily called the wise men.*   The tyrant did not dare admit to alarm or concern, in case he should embolden the people, by whom he well knew he was hated.   In public he makes out that it is no matter, but he makes private inquiry, in order to be ready for the impending event.   Quite apart from his own bad conscience making him afraid, there is no doubt that God had struck his mind with unusual apprehension, that his purposes should fail him, and his mind lose the track, altogether rendering him ineffective for the present.   There would have been nothing simpler than to send one of his friends quite officially to look into the whole affair and report back.   Herod was endowed with no mean intelligence, for he had great breadth of mind.   It is all the more surprising that at this extreme crisis, when the remedy lay in his hands, he lolled about in a daze, like a lifeless body.   Thus we learn that it was indeed by a miracle that the Son of God was allowed to slip from the lion's mouth. No less today does the Lord madden His enemies, to check their thousand devices aimed to hurt the Church and ruin it, so that they may not often seize their chances when they come up.   The trick, that took in the magi, in pretending that he would also come to adore, was diverted by the Lord by another means, as we shall see. Herod's fear of a popular uprising robs him of his senses, but in return a fierce rage drives him not to hesitate to raise revolt against God, nor to dread its consequences.   He knew that if a King were born, he would be appointed by God to restore the fallen throne of David. So he does not turn on men, but insanely dares to wage war on God. We must note both that he was affected by a giddiness of the Spirit, in attacking God, and yet acted as a child, so scattered were his wits, groping like a blind man in the dark.

Matt. 2.9.   *Having heard the king, went their way.*   Was it not shameful apathy in the Jews, that not one went as companion to the foreigners to see the King, promised to their race?   The scribes instruct them upon the way, they indicate the place, where He is born, but they let them go off alone, for no-one moves a foot.   Maybe they feared Herod's displeasure, but this too was criminal ingratitude, not to take a risk for the sake of the salvation offered them, to put the grace of God below giving offence to a tyrant.   I have shortly before described the whole people as utterly degraded, in preferring the oppression of a tyrant's yoke than to experience the upsets of change in their lives. If God had not re-assured the magi's minds by His Spirit, this could

87

have been a fatal deterrent to them. However, their enthusiasm burns as keenly as ever, and they set out without company. They have grounds to confirm their faith, too, in hearing that the King who was shown to them by the star was earlier celebrated in divine oracles. That the star led them right to the spot, once they were on their way, may easily be inferred, for it had only disappeared before, so that they should seek information of the new King at Jerusalem. And this was to remove any excuse from the Jews, who after being taught about the Redeemer sent to them, yet knowingly and willingly despised Him.

Matt. 11. *Saw the young child.* Again they might have been put off by this unbecoming sight, for Christ was so far removed from royal estate as to be poorer and lower than any urchin of the street. But as they are convinced that He is the divinely ordained King, this idea firmly set in their minds is enough to win their reverence for Christ: they look upon His dignity, as yet concealed, in the purposes of God. And as they are quite certain that He will be other than He now appears, they are not ashamed to offer Him royal honour. They testify by their gifts whence they come, for there is no doubt that they have brought these as emblems of their home-land. You must understand that the gifts were not offered by each separately, but all together gave the three that are mentioned. The way practically all interpreters make learned comment on the kingship, priesthood and burial of Christ, making gold the symbol of Kingship, incense of Priesthood, and myrrh of Burial, is not, in my opinion, well-grounded. We know that the Persians made a ritual of bearing a gift in their hand whenever they saluted their kings. Here they bring those three products that grace the East, just as Jacob sent into Egypt precious and select fruits of the soil (Gen. 43.12). While they, in Persian style, adore Him as King, still reckoning Him such in earthly terms, and bring Him the fruits of the land, our duty is to worship Him in spirit. This is our proper and reasonable service, which He demands, that we should consecrate to Him first ourselves, then our all.

And when the days of their purification according to the law of Moses were fulfilled, they brought him up to Jerusalem, to present him to the Lord (as it is written in the law of the Lord, Every male that openeth the womb shall be called holy to the Lord), and to offer a sacrifice according to that which is said in the law of the Lord, A pair of turtle-doves, or two young pigeons. And behold, there was a man in Jerusalem,

whose name was Simeon; and this man was righteous and devout,
looking for the consolation of Israel: and the Holy Spirit was upon him.
And it had been revealed unto him by the Holy Spirit, that he should not
see death, before he had seen the Lord's Christ. And he came in the
Spirit into the temple: and when the parents brought in the child Jesus,
that they might do concerning him after the custom of the law, then he
received him into his arms, and blessed God, and said,

Now lettest thou thy servant depart, O Lord,
According to thy word, in peace;
For mine eyes have seen thy salvation,
Which thou hast prepared before the face of all peoples;
A light for revelation to the Gentiles,
And the glory of thy people Israel. (Luke 2.22-32)

Luke 2.22. *And when the days . . . were fulfilled.* The ceremony of
purification had to be performed on the fortieth day after the birth.
But it is for another reason that Mary and Joseph come to Jerusalem,
namely, to present Him to the Lord, as He was the first-born. In
first place we must speak of purification. Luke makes it common to
Mary and Christ, for the pronoun *their* cannot in any way refer to
Joseph. There is nothing strange in the fact that Christ, who was to
be made a curse upon the cross for us, should take upon Himself our
uncleanness, even to the extent of being accused for our sakes, although
He was free of fault or sin: that is, that the very fountain of purity,
to wash our dirt away, should agree to be reckoned unclean. They
are wrong who think that this was only a civil regulation, as if the
woman would only be unclean to her husband, not to God. No, the
Jews had as much sense of the corruption of nature before their eyes
as they had of the remedy of God's grace. This rule alone is enough
fully to prove original sin, with its clear testimony to the grace of God.
The curse of the human race cannot be displayed more effectively
than when the Lord testifies that an infant comes forth from its
mother impure and stained, to the extent that the mother herself is
polluted by the birth. Certainly, if man were not born a sinner, and
by nature were a son of wrath, and had in him some settled taint of
sin, he would not need purification. So it follows that all are corrupt
in Adam, since by the voice of the Lord all are condemned for uncleanness. It does not contradict this that the Jews are elsewhere
called holy branches from holy stock (Rom. 11.16), for this was an
additional blessing as it were. Even if by the privilege of adoption
they were separated into a chosen people, yet their inheritance of
corruption from Adam is first in order. We should distinguish
between our first nature, and the particular benefit of the covenant,

by which God frees His own from the general curse. This was the object of purification under the Law, to teach the Jews, that by God's grace they were made clean from the dirt which they had got at their coming into the world. And we should learn what a horrible thing is the contagion of sin, which in some measure infects the right course of nature. I agree that childbirth in itself is not unclean, and I also agree that the sin of lust is covered by the sanctity of marriage, but all the same, the springing waters of sin are so profound and full that some faults ever bubble from them, to spatter with dirty marks what was otherwise pure.

Luke 2.23. *As it is written in the Law.* This is a further religious obligation that Joseph and Mary fulfilled. The Lord ordered all males to be dedicated to Him in memory of redemption, for when the angel slew all the first-born of Egypt, he spared the first-born sons of Israel (Num. 3.13): consequently each was allowed to redeem his first-born at a set price. That was an ancient ceremony, but nowadays when the Lord is Redeemer of all, He rightly claims us for Himself from the least to the greatest. There is every point in Luke's repeating frequently that Joseph and Mary did what was prescribed in the Law of the Lord. These words teach us that we are to make no innovations in God's worship from our own choice, but obediently to follow what He prescribes in His Word.

Luke 2.24. *And to offer a sacrifice.* This sacrifice applied to the rite of purification, in case anyone should think that it was offered for the sake of redeeming the first-born. When the Evangelist names a pair of turtle-doves, or two young pigeons, he takes for granted that such was the poverty of Mary and Joseph that their means did not reach to the offering of a lamb. This exception is expressly noted in Leviticus 12.6. If any object, that they had just before had an offering of gold, which could have paid for it, I answer that we are not to imagine a great supply of gold sufficient to turn their poverty to riches on the instant. We do not read of camels loaded with gold, but more credibly, it was a very small offering, brought purely as a token of honour. Nor did the Law formally demand, that those of slim resources should expend them on the sacrifice, but distinguished them from the rich in matters of sacrifice, and lessened their expense. So there will be nothing wrong with saying that Joseph and Mary gave as well as their condition allowed, even if it left them a reserve of money to cover the journey and cost of provisions.

Luke 2.25. *And behold, there was a man in Jerusalem.* This episode is given to show us that, though practically the whole people had turned to irreligion in a wicked contempt for God, there yet remained a few who worshipped Him, and that Christ was known by them from His earliest infancy. This was that remnant which Paul tells us has been preserved, according to God's free election. In this small handful was contained all the Church of God, though the priests and scribes, with as much arrogance as falsehood, claimed the title for themselves. The Evangelist records two who recognized Christ at Jerusalem, when He was brought up to the temple, namely Simeon and Anna. We must speak first of Simeon. We are not told what his position was: it may be that he was just an ordinary man of un- known character. But Luke gives him a good word for his piety and righteousness, to which he adds the gift of prophecy. Piety and righteousness relate to the two tables of the Law: so integrity of life consist in these two parts. The evidence of his piety lay in his expecta- tion of the consolation of Israel, for God is not properly served without the confidence in salvation, which depends both on faith in His promises, and particularly in the restoration promised in Christ. Now that such expectation is commended in Simeon as an unusual virtue shows us that there were few in those days who truly fostered in their hearts the hope of redemption. The Messiah was spoken of on every lip, the happy days enjoyed under the reign of David, but meanwhile hardly anyone bore his present misfortunes with patience, with reliance on the consolation that redemption was at hand for the Church. As Simeon's piety took force from the manner in which he sustained his soul in expectation of the promised salvation, so today, whoever wish to prove themselves sons of God, should sigh with unending supplication for the promised redemption. Endurance is needed till the final coming of Christ.

The Holy Spirit was upon him. He does not speak of the Spirit of adoption, which is common to all the sons of God, granted in dif- fering degrees, but of the particular gift of prophecy, as is more evident from the next verse and the one after, where it is said that he came in response to the Holy Spirit, and by the same Spirit's leading was brought to the temple. Though Simeon was elevated by no public mark of distinction, yet he was arrayed with excellent gifts, piety, innocence of life, faith and prophecy. No doubt that this oracle was taken up by one individual that it might go down from that occasion to assure all godly folk. Jesus is called *the Lord's Christ*, because He was anointed by the Father, and received the honour of Kingship and Priesthood along with the Spirit. Simeon is said to have come into the temple *in the Spirit*, that is, by secret prompting and certain vision, that he might meet Christ.

Luke 2.29. *Now lettest thou.* From this canticle it is plain that Simeon beheld the Son of God with eyes other than the eyes of the flesh. The outward sight of Christ could only induce a feeling of contempt—

at least it would never have satisfied the mind of a saintly man, to lead him happily and in full possession of his prayers' desire to go quickly to the grave. So the Spirit of God illuminated his eyes by faith, that he might perceive the glory of the Son of God, in the miserable and unworthy appearance. When he says, *depart . . . in peace*, he means that he will die with a tranquil mind, as one who has achieved and won all that he longed for. But the question is asked, whether, if Simeon had been forced to leave this life earlier, he would have been taken reluctantly, with alarm and mixed feelings, as the unwilling do. My reply is, to note the circumstance that is added, *According to thy word*. For as God promised him a sight of His Son, rightly enough he was held in suspense, indeed he was bound to live anxiously, until he came to the fulfilment of his hope. We must grasp this point, for many hold out Simeon's case falsely and wrongly, and boast that they will die gladly if it be granted them to enjoy first this or the other thing, while they still wildly allow themselves to conceive desires to suit their own appetites, and make up empty hopes without the Word of God. If Simeon had just said, 'Now may I die with a quiet and composed mind, for I have seen the Son of God,' these words would have betrayed a weakness in his faith, but because he took in the Word, it was open to him according to the rule of faith to escape death till the coming of Christ.

Luke 2.30. *For mine eyes have seen.* Though this manner of speaking occurs often in Scripture, it still seems that in these words the bodily aspect of Christ is expressly denoted as if Simeon said, that now he had the Son of God present in the flesh, while previously he had fixed his mind's eye upon Him. *Thy salvation* I take as being the content of salvation, for in Christ, are found all the parts of salvation and the blessed life. If the sight of Christ while still an infant, had so powerful an effect on Simeon that he could approach death cheerfully and quietly, how much more ground there is for our quietness and peace today, when we may see all parts of our salvation complete in Christ? Christ is not walking on the earth, we may not cradle Him in our arms, but in the Gospel His divine Majesty shines bright and far, and there He shows us His features, as Paul says (II Cor. 3.18), as it were, face to face: no longer in the weakness of the flesh, but in the magnificent power of the Spirit, as He displayed it in the miracles, in the sacrifice of His death, and in the resurrection. In short, He is so absent from us in body, that He may better be seen sitting at the right hand of the Father. If such a sight does not bring us peace, so that we should go to our deaths with eagerness, then we are more than ungrateful to God, and we think meanly of the honour He has bestowed on us.

Luke 2.31. *Which thou hast prepared.* Simeon means by these words that Christ was divinely appointed for all peoples to enjoy His grace, and soon after to be set up on high, that He might draw the eyes of all upon Himself. This word embraces all the oracles that speak of the publishing abroad of the Kingdom of Christ. If Simeon, holding the little boy in his arms, could make his mind reach out to the furthest bounds of the world, to recognize the effect of His influence in every place, then we today should feel all the more grandly about Him, now He has raised His standard upon the nations, and has shown Himself to all the earth.

Luke 2.32. *A light for revelation.* Simeon now shows to what end Christ was to be produced in the sight of all peoples, namely to enlighten the nations, who were before in darkness, and to be the glory of the people, Israel. He had reason to distinguish the former from the latter, for by right of adoption the children of Abraham were near to God, while the nations with whom God had no covenant were outsiders to the Chruch. For this reason, Israel, in another place, is termed not just son of God, but actually first-born (Jer. 31.9). Paul also says (Rom. 15.8), 'That Christ came to be a minister of the circumcision, according to the promises given unto the Fathers.' But Israel is so set before the nations, that they all alike may obtain salvation in Christ. *A light for revelation* has the exact effect of saying, For enlightening the Gentiles. So we infer that men are by nature without light, until Christ the Sun of Righteousness shines upon them. As regards Israel, though it was awarded the highest honour by God, yet Simeon warns that all its glory depends on one fact, that the Redeemer was promised to them.

And his father and his mother were marvelling at the things which were spoken concerning him; And Simeon blessed them, and said unto Mary his mother, Behold, this child is set for the falling and rising up of many in Israel; and for a sign which is spoken against; yea and a sword shall pierce through thine own soul; that thoughts out of many hearts may be revealed. And there was one Anna, a prophetess, the daughter of Phanuel, of the tribe of Asher (she was of a great age, having lived with a husband seven years from her virginity, and she had been a widow even for fourscore and four years), which departed not from the temple, worshipping with fastings and supplications night and day. And coming up at that very hour she gave thanks unto God, and spake of him to all them that were looking for the redemption of Jerusalem. And when they had accomplished all things that were according to the law of the

Lord, they returned into Galilee, to their own city Nazareth. (Luke 2.33-39)

Luke 2.33. *And his father and his mother were marvelling.* Luke does not mean that they were overcome by the novelty, but that they considered reverently, and took in with due admiration, the oracle from Simeon's lips, in order more and more to grow in their understanding of Christ. This example teaches us, when we have had our first taste of the right faith, that we must gather whatever supports tend to confirm it. Really, true progress in God's Word comes to the man who does not cease to marvel, as often as reading or hearing leads him to continue the advance of faith.

Luke 2.34. *Simeon blessed them.* If you apply this to Joseph and Mary, there will be no difficulty, but as Luke seems to have included Christ, it may be asked by what right Simeon usurped His authority, to give benediction: for the lesser is blessed by the greater, as the Apostle teaches. In fact, it seems absurd that any mortal should put up a prayer for God's Son. I would rejoin, that the Apostle is speaking not of all kinds of blessing, but only of the sacerdotal: men exchange mutual greetings on a different basis. It is more likely that Simeon gave them his blessing as a private individual, just one of the people, rather than in an official capacity, for as we have remarked already, he is nowhere said to have been a Priest. There is anyway nothing odd if we should pray for the prosperous outcome of Christ's reign, as the Spirit gives this εὐλογίαν (blessing) to all the faithful in the Psalm.

Behold, this child is set. Simeon's words were directed primarily to Mary, but they affect all god-fearing people. The holy virgin needed this warning, in case (as often happens) she was so happy at the joyful beginning, that she could not so well compose herself to bear the sad events to follow. Nor must she expect that Christ would be received by the general applause of the whole people, but she needed to have an invincible strength of character, to defend her against all hostile assaults. At the same time, the Spirit of God determined to pass on to all the faithful, one common teaching, that when they saw the world resisting Christ with godless contumacy, they should tackle it with equal toughness, and not be broken. We know what a heavy and difficult burden it is for us to bear the world's incredulity, yet we must get on top of it if we are to believe in Christ. Never were human affairs so well composed that the greater part was on Christ's side. Thus a first lesson has to be learnt by those who are to give Christ His name; they must put on these arms, and be firm in His faith. It was by far the most grievous trial, that Christ was not recognized by His own, but was rejected with insult by that very people which boasted itself to be the Church of God, and especially that the priests and scribes, who held the government of the Church, were His most bitter foes. Who would ever take Him as their King, when they saw them spurn Him so unworthily, so shamefully? So Simeon's prophetic words were well justified, that Christ was set for the fall of many, yes, among the people of Israel. This is the meaning: He was divinely ordained to bring down and tumble many.

But we must note that the ruin comes from their turning on Him in unbelief, as is said a little later, where Simeon calls Him 'a Sign which is spoken against'. Thus as unbelievers rebel against Christ, they crash against Him, and their ruin comes from this. The metaphor is taken from the target at which throwers take their aim, as if Simeon had said: men's malice is seen, indeed the depravity of the whole human race, in what seems to be their concerted action to call down and contradict the Son of God. There would not have been such a consensus in the world to speak against the Gospel if there had not been a kind of natural dis-harmony between the Son of God and men themselves. For although the enemies of the Gospel disagree among themselves (self-seeking and wild ideas tear them apart, split them by factions into separate movements, for there is an endless variety of superstitions to divide the parties of idolatry), yet they all agree in this, that they are opposed to God's Son. So it has been truly said, that there is no blatant instance of human depravity which does not from time to time set itself up against Christ. And though it is a fearful and portentous thing that the world should rebel against its architect, yet as the Scripture foretold that it would be so, and as the reason is quite obvious, that men once alienated from God by sin always seek to escape Him, so instances of this kind should never disturb us, but rather our faith should arm itself accordingly and be equipped to fight the contradiction of the world. Moreover, since God has drawn His Israel from all over the world, and there is no longer the distinction of Jew and Greek, the same situation is bound to recur now, as we read happened then. In his own day, Isaiah had said (8.14), 'Behold, the Lord shall be for a stone of stumbling and for a rock of offence to both the houses of Israel.' From that time on, the Jews hardly ever ceased to turn against God, but by far their most violent conflict was against Christ. Now the same fury is copied by those who call themselves Christians, indeed who proudly claim for themselves the primacy in the Church; they often bring all their force to bear on suppressing Christ, but let us remember that all the progress they make is to break themselves and to be crushed.

By the word *falling* the Spirit denotes the penalty that comes on the unbelievers, to teach us to keep as far from them as possible, lest any association should involve us in a like disaster. Christ is no less dear, for all that many tumble at His rise, for the savour of the Gospel does not cease to be pleasant and sweet to God, however deadly it may be to the world. If any ask how Christ should be an occasion of falling to unbelievers who have perished out of His time, the answer is simple, that those who rob themselves of the salvation offered divinely to them perish a second time. Thus falling indicates a twofold penalty, which awaits all unbelievers, once they have knowingly and willingly set themselves against the Son of God.

And rising up. In contrast to the first phrase, here is a word of consolation, to soften the effect of the distasteful matter, for it would be sad news, if it stood alone, that Christ is a stone of offence who by His hard nature will break and crush the majority of mankind. So Scripture turns us to look on the other side of His mission, that men's salvation is fixed in Him, as Isaiah also says (8.13), 'The Lord of Hosts, him shall ye sanctify; and let him be your fear . . . and he shall be for a sanctuary, a defended citadel.' Peter says more plainly, 'Unto whom coming, a living stone, rejected indeed of men, but with God elect, precious, ye also, as living stones, are built up. Because it is contained in scripture, Behold, I lay in Zion a chief corner stone, elect, precious: and he that believeth on him shall not be put to shame. For you therefore which believe is the preciousness: but for such as disbelieve, The stone which the builders rejected,' etc. (I Pet. 2.4-8; cf. Isa. 28.16). Lest the words of praise should make Christ a terror to us, we should immediately draw from the context that He is also called a corner stone, on which all the salvation of the godly is built; and we should consider that the former role is secondary (accidental) while the latter is primary and true to Christ. It is also worth noting, that Christ is not called the support of the faithful, but their resurrection, for men's condition is not one in which it is right for them to rest. One must first rise from death, before beginning to live.

Luke 2.35. *Yea and a sword shall pierce.* This warning should have the power to strengthen the mind of the holy virgin, in case grief overcame her when it came to that bitterest conflict which was to be encountered. Though her faith was tested and shaken by various trials, the harshest contest was at the cross: she was able to look on Christ in death. Though she was never swamped by grief, yet her heart was not made of rock, to prevent her being sore wounded. The constancy of the saints is very different from dumb acceptance. *That thoughts out of many hearts may be revealed.* Some attach this clause to the sentence further back, that Christ was set for the falling, etc. The passage about the sword, which we have just noted, they put in parenthesis, but in my opinion it is quite satisfactory to place it in the whole context. The particle *that* is not truly causal here, but only denotes consequence. For when the light of the Gospel shall arise, and persecutions follow, at the same time the thoughts of hearts previously concealed come into the open: these are the hiding-places where humans pretend that they may easily stay unobserved, out of Christ's range. But Christ scatters all clouds with His light, and strips hypocrisy bare. So it is right to assign Him this role of driving the secrets of the heart into the open. And when to His doctrine there is added His cross, then He probes hearts more to the quick. Those who embraced Christ with outward profession, recoil from bearing a cross, and as they see the Church subjected to troubles of all kinds, they readily desert their post.

Luke 2.36. *And there was one Anna, a prophetess.* Luke only tells of two, by whom Christ was welcomed, and he intended to teach us to prefer what belongs to God, however little it be, above all the world. The scribes and priests of that time had great renown, but as God's Spirit dwelt in Simeon and Anna, and the leaders were quite destitute of it, these two alone deserve reverence, more than their huge company that so highly vaunts its empty façade. And for this reason Anna's age is recorded, and she is given the title of prophetess; and a third mark of honour is given her, by the testimony made to her devoted piety and chaste living. These are qualities which rightly win authority and reward among men. The only ones to be deceived by a glorious façade and empty display are those who by their vanity of mind are addicted to falsehood. She is said to have lived with a man seven years from her virginity, to let us realize that she was widowed in the very flower of her life. She had married as a virgin, and shortly after had lost her husband. That she abstained from a second marriage, while she was still vigorous in her body, is a circumstance which increases the praise of her chaste life. But what follows may be taken two ways, that she had been a widow some eighty-four years, such being the time that had elapsed since she lost her husband, or that her life was of that length. If you reckon eighty-four years from her becoming a widow, it follows that she was over a hundred years old, but this issue I leave undecided. The Spirit of prophecy still shone in a few individuals, and by these 'tokens' was the teaching of the Law and the Jewish religion given assurance, until Christ should come, assuming that in such a state of general wastage God's elect would have to have such assistance, or they would dwindle away.

Luke 2.37. *Departed not from the temple.* It is an exaggerated way of speaking, but its sense is quite plain, that Anna practically stayed in the temple. Luke adds that she served God with continual fastings and supplications. So we gather that she did not frequent the temple as merely wishing to do perfunctory service, but added other offices of piety. And it is worth noting, that the same rule is not prescribed for all, nor should it be forced as an example without regard, that we pursue all the duties that this widow is commended for: we should make a prudent selection of what suits each calling. It is foolish emulation that has filled the world with apes; with more passion than reason, superstitious men have snatched at anything they hear commended in the Saints, as if, alongside the order of ranks, there were not also an order of works to be selected, that each should live up to his own vocation. What is said here of Anna, Paul particularly attaches to widows. Married women would be ridiculous to do this, if they modelled their lives on a pattern that does not apply. There is still an idea that Luke makes fasting part of the worship of God, but we should note, that of the works that pertain to worship, some are quite simply required of us, as necessary, so they say, in themselves. Others, beyond these, are directed to this end—that they contribute to the former. Prayers to God are an essential part of worship. Fasting is an aid on a lower level, and only approved by God, as far as it helps our enthusiasm and earnestness in prayer. So keep this rule, Men's duties are reckoned by their proper and rightful object. We must keep the distinction, that prayers are a direct service to God, but fasting only consequentially. There is no doubt that the holy woman connected her fastings with grief for the present disasters of the Church.

Luke 2.38. *She gave thanks.* The blessed songs that sounded on the tongues of Simeon and Anna are commended by Luke, that the faithful may encourage each other to sing God's praises with one voice, and mutually take up the strain. When he says that Anna spoke to all who looked for redemption, he again indicates how few the godly were. The basis of faith was to be found in this expectation. It seems there were not many who truly fostered it in their hearts.

Luke 2.39. *They returned into Galilee.* I must readily admit that the journey into Egypt came in between, and when Luke says they lived in their own city of Nazareth this is later in time than the flight into Egypt which Matthew relates. If there is nothing strange in one Evangelist omitting what another puts in, then there is nothing to stop Luke counting out the period of which he had decided to make no mention, and making a transit, as we may say, to the following events. But at the same time, I do not at all agree with the comment which asserts that Joseph and Mary, after the sacrifice of purification, returned to pass the time in Bethlehem. It is really silly to believe that this was a home of Joseph, since he had been so little known there that he had been unable to find lodging. Luke is not out of order in calling Nazareth his home, as much as Mary's. We are to infer that he had never lived in Bethlehem, though he was originally of that place. I shall shortly give a fuller account of the order of events.

Now when they were departed, behold, an angel of the Lord appeareth to Joseph in a dream, saying, Arise and take the young child and his mother, and flee into Egypt, and be thou there until I tell thee: for Herod will seek the young child to destroy him. And he arose and took the young child and his mother by night, and departed into Egypt; and was there until the death of Herod: that it might be fulfilled which was spoken by the Lord through the prophet, saying, Out of Egypt did I call my son. Then Herod, when he saw that he was mocked of the wise men, was exceeding wroth, and sent forth, and slew all the male children that were in Bethlehem, and in all the borders thereof, from two years old and under, according to the time which he had carefully learned of the wise men. Then was fulfilled that which was spoken by Jeremiah the prophet, saying,

A voice was heard in Ramah,
Weeping and great mourning,
Rachel weeping for her children;
And she would not be comforted, because they are not. (Matt. 2.13-18)

Matt. 2.13. *Now when they were departed.* How many days intervened between the departure of the magi up till Joseph was bidden to flee into Egypt, we do not know, nor is it very relevant, except that it is likely that the Lord spared Mary until she had gained strength after childbirth, to be able to make the journey. This was God's amazing plan, that He should determine to save His Son by flight. There is no doubt that Joseph's mind was agitated with many risks and trials, when he saw that his only hope lay in flight, for he could not see any kind of divine protection in running away. It did not seem at all fitting, that only by the action of mortal man could He be saved who was to save all men. God preserved a balance in saving His Son, and gave some tokens of His heavenly power, yet did not make it so conspicuous as to avoid the outward appearance of weakness: the time for Christ's open manifestation was not yet ripe. The angel's prediction of a matter concealed and unknown to men is a sure example of divinity. Giving instruction that the boy's life was to be saved by flight into exile belongs to the weakness of the flesh, to which Christ was subject. We are also taught here that God does not save His own always in one way, but at some times gives a powerful display of His strength, and at other times lets little sparks show in dark coverings and shades. We may see how the marvellous way of saving His Son, by means of the cross, shows us how wrong it is to prescribe a fixed method for God. So we may let Him advance our salvation in unequal ways, and not refuse to be humbled, that He may better disclose His glory. Above all, we must not seek to escape the cross, to which He trained His Son from His earliest infancy. This flight is part of the foolishness of the cross, and one that overcame the entire wisdom of this world. For the Saviour of Judaea to come forth at His appointed time, He must escape from it by flight, and Egypt must nourish Him, from which country before nothing but harm had ever come to the Church of God. Who would not be astounded at such unlooked-for working of God?

That Joseph immediately obeys the command of the angel is a further sign of the certainty of the dream: the eagerness that he shows in obedience shows clearly that he had no doubt that he had God as the authority for taking flight. Yet it may appear to be due to diffidence that he made such haste, for to flee by night indicates alarm. But the excuse for this is easy. He saw that the means of salvation set for him were humble and unimpressive: so he trusts that it is right for him (as is the case in extreme dangers) to rush into exile. Thus we should always match our apprehension to God's predictions: if it agrees with them, it will not be opposed to faith.

Be thou there until I tell thee. The angel means by these words that the boy's life for the future will be God's concern, and Joseph needed this assurance, to be quite certain that God would not only lead him on the journey, but would also continue to be his guardian in exile. By this means the Lord wished to relieve the many concerns that could have boiled up in the breast of that holy man, so as to give him peace in Egypt. Otherwise no single moment could have gone by without a pang from some quarter, when he saw how he was cut off from the inheritance promised by God to all the saints, and from the temple, sacrifices, public profession of faith, in the midst of God's worst enemies, living in a sink of profound superstition. Granted he had with him in the Person of the infant all the good that the fathers had ever hoped for, or that the Lord had ever promised them, still he had not yet made such progress in faith and in the knowledge of Christ, but had to be restrained by this order, 'Be there until I tell you,' in case he should find it hard, to languish among the Egyptians, an exile from his native land.

Matt. 2.15. *Out of Egypt did I call.* As Matthew says the oracle was fulfilled, many have thought that the Prophet had no intention beyond that which is expressed, and have imagined that the sense is that the Jews were foolish in opposing God's Son, and in trying to put Him down, because the Father had called Him out of Egypt. In this way they are distorting the Prophet's words (Hos. 11.1), whose intention was to condemn the Jews for ingratitude, in that they knew God, from their first infancy and creation, as a father more than good and loving, yet they continually provoked Him with new sins. We should take it as unquestioned, that the passage may not be restricted to Christ alone. And it is not distorted by Matthew, who cunningly applies it to the present case. The words of the Prophet must thus be understood: when Israel was still a boy, I led him out of his miserable bondage, in which he was plunged. Before, he was as good as dead, and Egypt was like his tomb, but I brought him out of it into the light of life, as though drawn from the womb. And well may the Lord speak in this way, for that liberation was like a birth for His people. The missive of his adoption was openly published, when, by the promulgation of the Law, he was received into God's property, a priestly kingdom, and a holy race. He was set apart from all peoples, and finally God built Himself a tabernacle, that He might dwell in their midst. So the Prophet's words have the effect of saying, that the people were snatched out of Egypt as from the depths of the grave. Now the redemption brought by Christ— what was it, if not a rising up from death, the beginning of new life? For then the light of salvation was near extinct, when God again, in the Person of Christ, brought His Church to birth. Then the Church came out of Egypt under its own Head, as before it was the whole body that had been led out thence. This is the effect of the analogy, that it should not seem odd that Christ passed some part of His childhood in Egypt: it was rather that God's grace and power should be the more glorious, as the light which comes out of the darkness and the depths to break upon us. Perhaps from another angle the rather fleshly objection might be raised here that, of course the Redeemer will be coming out of Egypt: so Matthew is telling us, that this is nothing new or unusual, for God to call His Son thence; rather that this should have the effect of confirming our faith, since as in earlier times, so now afresh, the Church of God is born from Egypt. The only difference is, that formerly the whole people were confined to Egypt as in a jail-house, but at the second redemption, only the Head of the Church, Christ, was concealed there, He who carried within Himself the salvation and life of all.

Matt. 2.16. *Then Herod, when he saw.* Matthew is speaking of the feelings and thoughts of Herod, who reckoned he was deceived

by the magi because they did not wish to assist his wicked cruelty.
Rather he was caught by his own trick, for having treacherously
pretended that he had in mind also to worship the King. Now there
is no mention of this episode in Josephus. Only Macrobius in Book 2
of his *Saturnalia*, speaking of the humour and witty sayings of
Augustus, says, When he heard that on Herod's order children in
Syria up to the age of two years had been slain, and in that number
a son of his had been slain at the same time, he remarked, I would
rather be Herod's pig than his boy. However, the authority of
Matthew alone is fully sufficient for us. But Josephus ought not to
have omitted such a notorious crime, although it is no wonder that
he kept silence over infants, as he only treats with levity and vagueness
the equally detestable instance of savagery that was suffered at about
that same time by the body of Judges, which they called the Sanhedrin, that not a single remnant might be left of the stock of David.
I have no doubt that it was the same fear that drove him to both
killings.

There is some doubt over the time, however. When Matthew says
the two-year-olds and under were killed according to the time he had
asked of the magi, we may gather from this that Christ had then
reached that age, or at least was not far from being two years old.
Some extend this time further, saying that Christ was at or about that
age at the time of the magi's visit. I would say the two are inconsistent. The terror that seized upon Herod when the rumour went
round concerning the birth of a new king, we have seen a little above.
Since his fears at that time prevented him from daring to send some
treacherous spy on the quiet, we need not wonder if for some time
he was restrained from such a hateful and cruel deed, especially as
the recent story of the magi's visit was still going strong. It is a likely
conjecture, that he turned the crime over in his mind, but put it off
till the right opportunity, and it may be that the Judges were disposed
of by him first so that by depriving the people of their leaders, he
with impunity could force them to carry out anything. So we may
well take it, that they rely on a frivolous argument who say that
Christ was two years old when he was adored by the magi, because
Herod slew the children up to two years old, according to the time
that the star appeared. They foolishly take for granted that the star
did not appear until after the Virgin gave birth. But it is far more
probable that they were warned in good time, to set out on their
journey before the actual nativity of Christ, and see the child new
born in the cradle, or the mother's arms. It is a particularly childish
suggestion that they came from some unknown region, as from
another sphere, and so spent nearly two years on the journey. And

Osiander's contribution is still more comic, and can be left without refutation. In the outline of the narrative that I set forward, there is nothing strange. The magi arrived when the time of the child's birth had not yet passed, and they asked for a new-born king, not one in his second year. Joseph, on their return home, fled by night, but still on the way fulfilled the observance due at Jerusalem, as the Lord's Law prescribed (and in such a crowded city where folk came in from all sides he was safe from danger). Then, after he had gone into Egypt, Herod worried and thought over the danger he was in, till at last the boil came to a head and burst, which for more than eighteen months he had fostered in himself. The adverb *then* does not always mean in Scripture continuity of time, but often comes after there has been a long interval between the events.

Matt. 2.18. *A voice was heard in Ramah.* It is certain that the Prophet (Jer. 31.15), is describing the slaughter of the tribe of Benjamin, which happened in his day. For he foretold the cutting off of a tribe of Judah, half of whose complement was the tribe of Benjamin. That he attributes the grief to the dead Rachel is a personification, to increase the sensation of emotion. Not that Jeremiah painted in rhetorical colours merely for the sake of decorating his speech, but because otherwise the hardness and apathy of the living could not be corrected, if somehow the dead were not recalled from their tombs, to mourn over the chastisements of God—a subject they mostly used to make a joke of. As for the oracle of the Prophet being then fulfilled, Matthew does not mean that it contained a prediction of what Herod would come to do, but that at Christ's coming the grief which the Benjamites had suffered many centuries before was renewed: he wished thus to anticipate the shock which might affect many pious minds with alarm, and make them see no hope of salvation in a man at whose birth, for whose sake, infants were slaughtered; indeed, it was an unhappy and doleful presage, that Christ's nativity had kindled a fiercer flame of rage than ever burns at the most bitter times of war. Yet the Prophet promises a restoration for the tribe, which is cut down even to the very infants; and so Matthew shows, that this massacre does not prevent Christ appearing soon after as redeemer of the whole people: for we know that the whole chapter there is crammed with most happy consolations. After that funereal plaint there follows at once, Refrain thy voice from weeping, and thine eyes from tears: for thy work shall be rewarded . . . there is hope for thy latter end, etc. Thus the comparison between the earlier disaster for the tribe of Benjamin, and this other, is made because both were preliminary to salvation soon to be restored.

But when Herod was dead, behold, an angel of the Lord appeareth in a dream to Joseph in Egypt, saying, Arise and take the young child and his mother, and go into the land of Israel: for they are dead that sought the young child's life. And he arose and took the young child and his mother, and came into the land of Israel. But when he heard that Archelaus was reigning over Judaea in the room of his father Herod, he was afraid to go thither; and being warned of God in a dream, he withdrew into the parts of Galilee, and came and dwelt in a city called Nazareth: that it might be fulfilled which was spoken by the prophets, that he should be called a Nazarene. (Matt. 2.19-23)

Matt. 2.19. *When Herod was dead.* These words show the perseverance of Joseph's faith, for he stayed firm in Egypt until at God's command he was called back to his home-land. And we see at the same time that the Lord never disappoints His own, but comes to them, as soon as they need. It is likely that Joseph returned from Egypt directly after the death of Herod, before Augustus Caesar had by decree appointed Archelaus Ethnarch of Judaea. For while by his father's will he was named successor to the throne, he avoided the royal title, declaring that everything depended on the beck and call of Caesar; however, in all matters, he acted as ruler. Then he went to Rome and received confirmation, but the name of king was denied him, until his actions should warrant it. Philip had rule over Galilee, a quiet-minded man, virtually a private citizen. So Joseph came freely under his authority, as the angel said, as there was less danger in the shadow of a ruler who was averse to bloodshed and took good care of his people. We must still remember God's purpose, to keep His Son, from the beginning, under the elements of the cross, as this was to be His means of redeeming the Church. For this reason He underwent our weaknesses, He was brought up to risk, He faced alarms, in order that He might give eternal peace to the Church, and deliver her from these things by His divine power. Thus His risk was our assurance, His alarm our confidence: not that at His present age He could understand fear, but because it was for fear that Joseph and Mary were dragged off here and there, it may well be said that our fears were taken over by Him, that He might obtain untroubled confidence for us.

Matt. 2.23. *Be called a Nazarene.* Matthew does not derive Nazarene from Nazareth, as though this were a true and certain etymology, whereas it is merely an allusion. The word נזיר means holy and consecrated to God, from נזר which is 'to separate.' The Hebrews do use נזר for flower, crown, ornament of a diadem, but there is no doubt that it is the first sense that Matthew intended.

We never read of flower-decorated people being called Nazarenes, but those who were consecrated to the Lord by the Law's ordinance, as contained at Numbers 6.4. So the sense is: though Joseph was compelled by fears to go to a corner of Galilee, yet there was a higher purpose in God's mind, and the city of Nazareth was decreed for Christ's home that He might well be called a Nazarene. It is asked which Prophets gave Christ this title, as there is no extant testimony to this effect. A sufficient reply appears to be that Scripture frequently speaks of the Holy One, but this answer is unimaginative. For Matthew, as we see, presses the word itself, and actually refers to the ancient Nazarenes, whose sanctity was remarkable, as if to say that there had to be a fulfilment in the Person of Christ of what had then been foreshadowed in the Nazarenes, who were like chosen first-fruits to God. Yet we must still see where the Prophets gave the tradition that this would be Christ's name. Chrysostom, being unable to untie the knot, cuts through it, by saying that many books of the Prophets have perished. This is an unappealing reply, for, although we allow that the Lord, to punish His old people's shame, took from it some part of Scripture, or at least cut out the parts least necessary, yet from the coming of Christ there was nothing destroyed. It is not very intelligent to adduce on this question the passage in Josephus where he says that two books were left by Ezekiel. For the oracles of Ezekiel on the new temple and on the kingdom are obviously separate from the earlier ones, and effectively compose a further volume. But if we have today surviving in full order all the books of Scripture that were extant in the time of Matthew, we must look elsewhere to find the testimony which he cites from the Prophets. Bucer, in my opinion, has the best understanding of them all, who believes that the passage from Judges 13.5 is intended. The words there bear on Samson. But as Samson is called redeemer of the people only insofar as he prefigured Christ, and as the salvation won by his hand and service were only a foreshadowing, a prelude, to that full salvation which would at length be shown to the world through God's Son, all that the Scripture tells to Samson's credit must be transferred to Christ by right. To put it more distinctly, Christ is the primary example, Samson is the subsidiary 'anti-type'. So when he put on the role of redeemer, we must know that all the praise that was showered on his noble, indeed divine, achievement was as truly his, as it was properly Christ's. The fathers tasted the grace of re-demption, which is given to us in Christ to drink to the full. We may readily excuse Matthew for speaking of Prophets in the plural: the book of Judges was composed by many Prophets. But I think what is said here of Prophets goes further. Joseph (who in his time was the saviour of the Church, and in many ways prefigured Christ, or indeed was His living image) is called Nazarene (separate) of his brethren (Gen. 49.26; Deut. 33.16). Thus God wished that supreme nobility, which was instanced in Joseph, to shine again in Samson, and gave him the name Nazarene, that the faithful inspired by these first recruits should be the more eager to know the coming Redeemer, who was to be made separate from all, to be the first-born among many brethren.

And the child grew, and waxed strong, filled with wisdom: and the grace of God was upon him.

And his parents went every year to Jerusalem at the feast of the passover. And when he was twelve years old, they went up after the custom of the feast; and when they had fulfilled the days, as they were returning, the boy Jesus tarried behind in Jerusalem; and his parents knew it not; but supposing him to be in the company, they went a day's journey; and they sought for him among their kinsfolk and acquaintance: and when they found him not, they returned to Jerusalem, seeking for him. And it came to pass, after three days they found him in the temple, sitting in the midst of the doctors, both hearing them, and asking them questions: and all that heard him were amazed at his understanding and his answers. (Luke 2.40-47)

Luke 2.40. *And the child grew.* Matthew proceeds straight from Christ's infancy to His manifestation. But Luke gives one incident worthy of note here, that is, Christ giving in mid boyhood an example of His coming character—showing in a single 'practice round' what He would develop into. He first says that He *grew, and waxed strong* in spirit, meaning that with His years, so did His spiritual gifts increase. We infer that these advances or increases are to His human nature. Nothing could be added to His divinity. Yet it is asked whether He did not immediately, from His conception in His mother's womb, excel in all the fulness of spiritual gifts. It seems strange that anything should have been lacking in the perfection of God's Son. We may readily answer that if it takes nothing from His glory that He was utterly 'emptied out' (*exinanitus*), then it was not alien for Him to wish, for our sakes, to grow in body and also in spirit. Certainly when the Apostles tell that He was like us in all points except in sin (Heb. 4.15), there is little doubt that he includes the fact that His mind was subject to ignorance (*anima subiecta fuerit ignorantiae*).

The only difference between us and Him is that He freely, and of His own will, took on the weaknesses that narrow us by necessity. Thus in the degree and process of His age, Christ according to His human nature increased in the free gifts of the Holy Spirit, that from His fulness He might shower them upon us, for we draw grace from His grace. So it is over-timid for people to restrict what is said here to the external form, and to expound that Christ appeared to advance, but in fact made no new addition to His understanding. The words have a different tone, and the error is more patently refuted a little later, when Luke adds, the boy *advanced in wisdom and stature, and in favour with God and men.* We have no business to speculate that there was latent intelligence in Christ that appeared in the course of time. There is no doubt that God's purpose was to make entirely explicit that Christ, in truth and in reality, when He put on our flesh, embraced the full role of brotherly union with men. We must not imagine He was two-faced about this: though He was one Person of *God* and *man*, it does not follow that His human nature was given anything that was properly divine, but as far as concerned our salvation, the Son of God kept His divine power as it were concealed. The words of Irenaeus, that He suffered, while His godhead remained at rest (*quiescente divinitate*), I may interpret not only of His bodily death, but of His incredible grief and torment of mind, as is expressed in His complaining cry, 'My God, why hast Thou forsaken me?' In short, unless we wish to deny that Christ was made true man, we shall not be ashamed to admit that He freely took what cannot be separated from human nature. It is a foolish objection that ignorance, being the penalty of sin, does not fit with Christ for one would have to say the same also of death. Scripture says that He performed the office of Mediator, because whatever penalties we had deserved to pay He took from us and underwent Himself. Anyhow, to make ignorance the penalty for sin is quite stupid and without thought. We must not think that Adam before the fall knew everything or that angels, in their ignorance of some matters, sustain a penalty for sin. Some make the more subtle inference, that there was no trace of ignorance in Christ, because ignorance was a fault. But these too are making, in error, a false and vain pre-supposition: in this case, the angels would need to be equal with God, to avoid being at fault. The fault is the blindness of the human mind, and is deservedly reckoned a part of original sin, whereas the only ignorance here attributed to Christ is such as may occur in a man free of every spot of sin. When Luke says, *waxed strong, filled with wisdom*—by 'spirit' or 'in spirit' he means that all human wisdom, and its daily increase amongst men, flows from that one spring, namely the Spirit of God. The expression that follows is more general, *the grace of God was upon him*, for it includes whatever brilliance shone in His life.

Luke 2.41. *And his parents went every year*. Here the devotion of Mary and Joseph is commended, that they took pains to practise the outward observances of God's worship. It was not by foolhardiness that they undertook this annual pilgrimage, but at God's command. That the Law only instructs males to appear before the sight of God, does not altogether exclude women, but spares them as a favour. This is a mark that distinguishes pure religion from debased superstitions, that the one holds itself within the obedience of God and the ordinance of His Law, while the others wander about, at their choosing, beyond God's Word, with no fixed rule. Though the temple cult was stained with many corrupt deeds, and the priesthood was venal, and the instruction given was tied up with many falsities, yet, as the legal rites were still alive, and the outward practice of the sacrificial service as handed down in the Law was preserved, it was the duty of the faithful to witness to their faith with such exercises. The name of 'father' is improperly attached to Joseph, from the common usage of the people.

Luke 2.44. *Him to be in the company*. It is agreed in many passages of holy Scripture that those who used to come to the temple to worship on festival days travelled in companies. There is no wonder that Mary and Joseph were little concerned about the boy on the first day: after that, they show that they are not idle or careless in their unconcern.

Luke 2.46. *Sitting in the midst of the doctors*. There must have been beams of divine radiance openly shining on the boy for Him to have been allowed to sit by these proud men. Though it is likely that he sat on a bench, and not on the doctor's rank, these haughty men would never have granted Him an audience in public assembly if some divine force had not driven them to it. This was a kind of overture to His calling, for which the time had not yet come to maturity. Yet He wished to give such a taste of it—it at once fell out of men's remembrance, and only Mary kept it hidden up in her heart—that later, with other treasures, He might apply it to the general benefit of the godly. These are the two things to notice, that all admired Him, taking it as a prodigy that a boy should frame His questions so well and aptly; further, that in listening to Christ Himself, they took the part of disciples, rather than teachers. As He was not yet called to this by the Father, to profess Himself in public as a Doctor of the Church, so in humility He put questions to the doctors. But there is no doubt that in this early engagement He attempted to tackle their perverse manner of teaching, for the word Luke puts for *answers* I take, in accordance with Hebrew idiom, to denote some discussion.

And when they saw him, they were astonished: and his mother said unto him, Son, why hast thou thus dealt with us? behold, thy father and I sought thee sorrowing. And he said unto them, How is it that ye sought me? Wist ye not that I must be in my Father's house? And they understood not the saying which he spake unto them. And he went down with them, and came to Nazareth; and he was subject unto them: and his mother kept all these sayings in her heart.

And Jesus advanced in wisdom and stature, and in favour with God and men. (Luke 2.48-52)

Luke 2.48. *His mother said unto him.* In my judgment, those who say that the holy virgin spoke in this way to display her authority are wrong. I think it more probable that on their own, and away from onlookers, she began to expostulate with her son, after He came out of the meeting. Whichever is the case, it was no self-seeking that inspired her, but the weariness of three anxious days was in that complaint. At the same time, her protest on the ground of being unfairly wounded makes plain how we are by nature inclined to defend our own position, and to neglect God's viewpoint. The holy virgin would have died a hundred deaths sooner than deliberately plan to put herself above God, but in indulging a mother's grief, she slips that way through thoughtlessness. Certainly the example warns us how much we should suspect all the emotions of the flesh, how greatly we should beware of holding on to our rights beyond the norm and, from self-interest, of robbing God of His due.

Luke 2.49. *Wist ye not, etc.* Christ is right to reprove His mother, though He does so with restraint and indirectly. In short, the obedience that He owes His Father, God, is far to be preferred to all human duties. Thus His earthly parents are wrong to be sad that they are neglected over against God. There is a general lesson to be gathered here, that duties to men are subsidiary to the first table of the Law, that God may preserve His authority intact. Kings, parents and lords are to be obeyed, but only under God's command, that is, that no loss or diminution be suffered by God, for the gratification of men. There is no loss of dutiful respect on the human side when God's order is given preference. *In my father's house* ('in the things of my father'). These words intend to say that He possessed something more than human scale. He gives the main object of His being

109

sent into the world, which was, to fulfil the task laid on Him by the
heavenly Father. But the wonder is that Joseph and Mary did not
understand this reply, after being instructed by many testimonies
that Jesus was the Son of God. I would answer, that although the
heavenly origin of Christ was not utterly unknown to them, they
had not grasped in every respect that He was intent on pursuing His
Father's bidding, since His vocation had not yet been openly revealed
to them. That Mary preserves in her heart things which her mind's
understanding does not yet comprehend, teaches us to accept with
reverence, and (as a seed is nurtured in the earth from its conception)
to hold in the confines of our souls, such mysteries of God as exceed
the outreach of our intelligence.

Luke 2.51. *He was subject unto them.* This humility in Christ was
assumed for our salvation—the Lord and chief of angels willingly
subjected Himself to mortal creatures. Thus He fulfilled God's
intention, that for a time He should shelter under Joseph's name,
as under a shadow. There was no necessity that compelled Christ
to this subjection. He could have been excused it, but He had assumed
human nature on the terms that He should be subject to His parents.
He had put on the person of man and servant (*hominis ac servi personam*),
and thus for the role of Redeemer this was His rightful state. All the
more freely should we, each of us, undergo the yoke which the Lord
may lay upon our necks.

*And in those days cometh John the Baptist, preaching in the wilderness
of Judaea, saying, Repent ye; for the kingdom of heaven is at hand.
For this is he that was spoken of by Isaiah the prophet, saying,*
  The voice of one crying in the wilderness,
  Make ye ready the way of the Lord,
  Make his paths straight.
*Now John himself had his raiment of camel's hair, and a leathern girdle
about his loins; and his food was locusts and wild honey. Then went
out unto him Jerusalem, and all Judaea, and all the region round about
Jordan; and they were baptized of him in the river Jordan, confessing
their sins.* (Matt. 3.1-6)

  The beginning of the gospel of Jesus Christ, the Son of God.
  Even as it is written in Isaiah the prophet,
  Behold, I send my messenger before thy face,
  Who shall prepare thy way;
  The voice of one crying in the wilderness,

Make ye ready the way of the Lord,
  Make his paths straight;
John came, who baptized in the wilderness and preached the baptism o,
repentance unto remission of sins. And there went out unto him all the
country of Judaea, and all they of Jerusalem; and they were baptized of
him in the river Jordan, confessing their sins. And John was clothed
with camel's hair, and had a leathern girdle about his loins, and did eat
locusts and wild honey. (Mark 1.1-6)

Now in the fifteenth year of the reign of Tiberius Caesar, Pontius Pilate
being governor of Judaea, and Herod being tetrarch of Galilee, and his
brother Philip tetrarch of the region of Ituraea and Trachonitis, and
Lysanias tetrarch of Abilene, in the high-priesthood of Annas and
Caiaphas, the word of God came unto John the son of Zacharias in
the wilderness. And he came into all the region round about Jordan,
preaching the baptism of repentance unto remission of sins; as it is written
in the book of the words of Isaiah the prophet,
  The voice of one crying in the wilderness,
  Make ye ready the way of the Lord,
  Make his paths straight.
  Every valley shall be filled,
  And every mountain and hill shall be brought low;
  And the crooked shall become straight,
  And the rough ways smooth;
  And all flesh shall see the salvation of God. (Luke 3.1-6)

Though the narrative we have followed so far in Matthew and
Luke is part of the Gospel, yet there is something in Mark's decision
to begin his Gospel at the preaching of John Baptist. For, as we find
in the first chapter of John, with him the Law and the Prophets
come to an end. "The Law and the Prophets were until John, from
that time the kingdom of God,' etc. (Luke 16.16). To cite the witness of Malachi (3.1) agrees most aptly with this. That the Lord
might inflame their minds to desire His promised salvation, He decided for a time to deny His people further oracles, and we know that
Malachi was the last of the true and certain Prophets. And to prevent
them from perishing of starvation in the interim, He urges the Jews
to hold firm by the Law of Moses, until the promised redemption is
revealed. He appealed only to the Law, as the Prophets' teaching
held nothing divorced from it, being only a supplement, a fuller
exposition of it, so that the whole system of governing the Church
depended upon it. It is nothing new or unusual in Scripture, that
prophecies are included under the heading of Law, for all are made

in reference to it, as source or end. The Gospel was no inferior addition to the Law, but rather a new form of teaching, abrogating the former. Malachi discerned the double condition of the Church, and set the former under the Law, and the latter to start from the preaching of John. There is no doubt that he means John the Baptist when he says, 'Behold, I send my messenger,' for (as has just been said) there is made here an explicit distinction between the Law and the new order of the Church, the new condition, which was to take its place. In the same sense he had said a little earlier (as is cited by Mark: the passages are almost identical), 'Behold, I send you Elijah the Prophet, before the great day of the Lord come.' Likewise, 'Behold I send you my messenger who shall clear the way before me: the Lord whom ye seek shall suddenly come to his temple.' As in both places a finer condition is held out to the Church than had existed under the Law, so beyond doubt the rise of the Gospel is intended. Yet before the Lord would come forth to restore His Church, a forerunner or herald is said to be coming, who shall announce that He is near. Whence we infer that the abrogation of the Law and the beginning of the Gospel are rightly set at the preaching of John. But as John commends Christ incarnate, both His nativity and the whole narrative of His showing forth are included in the Gospel. Mark here deals with the start of the Gospel's publication. So it is reasonable for him to begin with John, who was its first minister. This was the Father's deliberate plan, that His Son's life should be, as it were, buried in silence, until the full time of revelation came. And it was by God's unfailing providence that the Evangelists pass over the whole period which Christ spent privately at home, and proceed from His infancy rapidly to His thirtieth year, in which He assumed His public role, and was revealed to the world as Redeemer, in which except for the one instance Luke briefly records of His coming vocation, around His twelfth year. What really mattered above all, was that we should know, first, that Christ was true man, second, that He was son of Abraham and of David: the Lord wished us to have this testimony. The other details concerning the shepherds, the magi, and Simeon are intended to prove His divinity. Luke's narrative concerning John and his father Zachariah are a kind of prelude to the Gospel.

In Malachi's words there is nothing odd in the change of person: in the prophet God says, 'I send my angel (i.e. messenger) and he shall prepare the way before me.' But Mark has the Father bring us His Son. We may see, however, that Mark had no other intention than to express the prophet's mind more clearly. Mark gives Christ the title Son of God, when the other Evangelists have witnessed that

He was born of the stock of Abraham and David, that He might also be *Son of Man*. Mark means that redemption was only to be hoped for from God's Son.

Matt. 3.1 *And in those days*. Luke 3.1. *Now in the fifteenth year*. One cannot deduce from Matthew or Mark at what year of his age John began to come out to the public, but Luke clearly enough shows that he was around thirty at that time. That he was born fifteen years before the death of Augustus is practically the universal consensus of the ancient writers of the Church. Tiberius, his successor, had now held power for fifteen years when the same John began to preach. This makes up the thirty years I spoke of. So it follows that he did not long fulfil the office of teacher, but shortly gave place to Christ, for we shall soon see that Christ was baptized in the thirtieth year of His age. And this was His initiation for His undertaking His work. As Christ directly followed upon John, the Sun of righteousness upon the torchbearer, or dawning, it is no wonder that John faded from sight, to make the brightness of Christ alone more conspicuous.

Luke 3.1. *Pontius Pilate*. It is likely that this was Pilate's second year: for from Tiberius' seizure of power, Josephus tells us in his book of *Antiquities*, 18, Valerius Gratus was appointed governor by him of Judaea, replacing Annius Rufus. This replacement could have occurred in his second year. Valerius was governor for eleven years, according to the same Josephus. So Pilate had the province for two years when John began to preach the Gospel. The Herod here whom Luke makes tetrarch of Galilee was the second heir of Herod the great, who succeeded his father through his will. The ethnarchy of Judaea had been given to Archelaus, but when he was exiled to Vienne by Augustus that portion fell prey to Rome. Thus Luke here records two sons of Herod, Herod Antipas made tetrarch of Galilee and controlling Samaria and Peraea, and Philip, who reigned over the tetrarchy of Trachonitis and Ituraea, from the sea of Tiberias or Genesar to the foothills of Lebanon, where the river Jordan rises.

Lysanias has been falsely reckoned the son of Ptolemaeus Mennaeus, who was king of Chalcis, for this man had earlier been killed by Cleopatra, that is, thirty years before the birth of Christ, as Josephus relates (*Ant.* 15). He could hardly even be his grandson, as Josephus calls him the instigator of the Parthian war (*Bell. Jud.* 1). For he would then have been over sixty years old. As it was under Antigonus that he stirred up the Parthians to war, he must at that time have been fully adult. Now Ptolemaeus Mennaeus died not long after the murder of Julius Caesar, at the start of the triumvirate of Lepidus, Antony and Octavius, on the evidence of Josephus (*Bell. Jud.* 14.23).

But as this grandson of Ptolemaeus shared the name of Lysanias with his father, he could have passed it on to his son in turn. So we can refute the error without any debate, if any make out that a Lysanias killed by Cleopatra was alive sixty years after his death!

The name of tetrarch is wrongly applied, as it suggests that the whole region was divided into four parts. Though the initial division of the region was fourfold, other changes occurred subsequently, but the name was kept on for dignity's sake. In the same sense Pliny records seventeen tetrarchies in one area.

Luke 3.2. *In the high-priesthood.* It is quite certain that the priesthood never knew two high priests at any one time. Josephus' evidence is that Caiaphas was appointed high priest by Valerius Gratus, shortly before he left his province. When Pilate was governor of Judaea, we read in Josephus of no change being made by him. Even when he was deposed from office and summoned to Rome to give account of himself, it was only then that Vitellius as governor of Syria brought Caiaphas to heel, and transferred the high priesthood to Jonathan son of Annas (*Ant.* 18). When Luke names two high priests, we are not to take it as meaning that the same title applied to each, but that the honour of the high priesthood rested in half measure on Annas, the high priest's father-in-law. Thus Luke is saying that affairs were so troubled and confused that there was really no one true high priest, but the holy office was torn by self-seeking and tyrannical power.

Luke 3.2. *The word of God came.* Before Luke relates, as the others, that John entered upon his teaching office, he states that he was called to it from on high, to give firm authority for his ministry. I cannot see why interpreters should prefer to alter *unto* John to *over* John, for the sense is quite unambiguous, that the mission was entrusted to him, and he was given the mandate to preach. I have followed the accepted version. Understand from this, that none are true teachers except they have been given their task by God: it is not enough to have the Word of God, unless there come also a particular calling. To reconcile Matthew and Mark, who only speak of the *wilderness*, with Luke's words, we must reckon that John started his teaching work amongst his close neighbours. Then he spread his Gospel more widely, to become further known, which resulted in his fame shortly reaching as far as Jerusalem. Now this region of Jordan may well be called wilderness. It does not mean solitude, but rough and hilly country, which is little inhabited by men.

Matt. 3.2. *Repent ye.* Matthew differs from the other two in this respect, that he sums up John's teaching in John's own words, while they do it in their own. Mark has one word more than Luke's for

he says, *He came, who baptized . . . and preached the baptism of repentance.*
In effect, there is complete agreement, for all attach repentance to
the remission of sins. For the Kingdom of God among men is nothing
else than restoration to the life of blessedness, true and eternal happiness.
So when John says that the Kingdom of God is at hand, he means
that men, estranged from God and exiled from the Kingdom of
Heaven, were again to be gathered in to God, to live under His hand.
This is the effect of His free adoption and pardon for sin, by which
He reconciles the unworthy to Himself. All in all, the *kingdom of
heaven* is simply newness of life, by which God restores us to the hope
of blessed immortality. He snatches us from the slavery of sin and
death, and claims us for Himself, that in our earthly pilgrimage we
should even now possess the life of heaven by faith (cf. Eph. 1.4).
For though we were like dead men, yet we know our life is secure,
being hid with Christ (Col. 3.3). Thus the sermon finds its way to
the source, which is repentance. John does not say, 'Repent ye,'
and by this means the Kingdom of Heaven will come near to you,
but he gives priority to the grace of God, and from that encourages
men, to take thought to themselves. So it is sure, that God's mercy
is the foundation of repentance, by which He sets up those that were
cast down. The sense of Mark and Luke is just the same, that he
preached repentance unto remission of sins. For it is not true (as
some carelessly make out) that repentance is put in first place, as
though it were the cause of the remission of sins, or came before God's
starting to be well-favoured towards us, but men are told to repent
that they may perceive the reconciliation that is offered to them.
As first in rank comes the free love of God, in which He embraces
poor men, not imputing their sins to them, so we must note, that the
pardon of our sins is gained in Christ, not that God may use it to
foster His own generosity, but rather that we may find it our cure
from sin. Not without hating sin and turning against his faults shall
a man taste the grace of God. But we shall go on to recognize more
fully from the definition of repentance and faith how the two are
uniquely conjoint. Hence I can be more sparing in dealing with
this point of doctrine.

As far as concerns the sense of the present passage, it is proper to
note that the whole Gospel stands on two parts, Remission of sins,
and Repentance. As Matthew indicates the first part by the Kingdom
of Heaven, we may gather that there was a hostile divorce of men
from God, and they were utterly fallen from the heavenly Kingdom,
until God should bring them into His favour. And though John in
putting forward the grace of God encourages men to repentance, yet
we must hold that this too is equally the gift of God, as much as the

inheritance of the heavenly Kingdom. For just as He freely pardons our sins, and delivers us from the sentence of eternal death by His mercy, so He re-makes us after His image, that we may live in right-eousness. Just as He freely adopts us as sons, so by His Spirit He regenerates us, that our life may testify that it is no lie for us to call Him Father. No less does Christ, having crucified our old man, and crushed the weaknesses of our flesh, make us alive unto righteous-ness, since He washes away our sins by His blood, and by the sacrifice of His death wins us the favour of the heavenly Father. But this is the gist of the Gospel, that God having put away our sins in His Son embraces us, that we may deny ourselves and our own nature, and may live in holiness and sanctification, and so on the earth may think upon the life of heaven.

Luke 3.3. *Preaching the baptism of repentance.* This manner of ex-pression first gives a general indication of the right use of Sacraments, and then gives the reason for the institution of baptism, and its content. The Sacrament therefore is not a dumb ceremony, displaying some kind of parade without teaching, but contains attached to it the Word of God, to give life to the actual outward ceremony. By Word I mean, not the murmuring of magic undertones by some exorcist but the effect of a clear and distinct voice proclaimed for the building up of faith. For John is not said merely to have baptized unto re-pentance, as though the grace of God were wrapped in the visible sign, but he preached what was the benefit of baptism, that from the Word preached the sign might have effect. Now it is peculiar to baptism, that it is called a symbol of repentance unto remission of sins. Since the meaning of that baptism, and its power and purpose, were the same as ours, if we are to estimate a representation from the truth that is in it, it must be false to say that the baptisms of Christ and of John were different.

Matt. 3.3. *The voice of one crying in the wilderness, etc.* Though this passage of Isaiah (40.1), should not be confined to John alone, yet he is included amongst those to whom that speech applies. For when the Prophet had spoken of the fall of the city and the final ruin of the people, he promised a new restoration. The words are, 'The Lord will say again, Comfort ye, comfort ye my people.' For after the destruction of the temple and the abolition of sacrifices, after the people had been led into captivity, things were in a desperate condition. And as all ears had been deaf to the continuing voice of the Prophets the Lord for a time seemed to be silent. Lest godly minds should fail in that sad silence, the Prophet declares that new heralds of grace will again arise, to lift the people up to hope of salvation. Such were Zechariah, Haggai, Malachi, and the like. But as that promise is of a continuing restoration, not of a moment only, so Isaiah mainly looks to the redemption that was to be expected at the coming of Christ. John is rightly reckoned to be the leading minister of consolation. Then follows in the words of the Prophet, *The voice of one that crieth*. This voice is contrasted with that period of silence, which I have just mentioned, as over a certain time the Jews were to be deprived of teaching, which they had sinfully despised. The word *wilderness* is given metaphorically for the devastation, the unsightly ruin of the people, such as existed at the time of the exile. There was such a dreadful wastage as might well be compared with a wilderness. So the prophet expands God's grace, as if to say that, although the people be cast far out from their country, indeed sent far away beyond the concourse of men, yet the voice of God will resound even in the desert, to feed the weary with joyful comfort. At the time when John began to harangue the crowds, Jerusalem was the desert in this sense, for on all sides everything had come to a vast and appalling state of chaos. Slow and stupid men should have been the more impressed at the sight of the wilderness they saw, to reach out more eagerly for the promise of salvation out of death offered to them. We see now how aptly this oracle fits John, and how well it is matched with him.

Make ye ready the way of the Lord. There is no doubt that the Prophet is addressing Cyrus and the Persians, whose activity was used by God, and the sense is, that the Lord would work by wondrous power to open a way for His people through trackless glens, through sheer cliffs, through waterless deserts, because He would have at hand servants of His grace to remove every obstruction from the midst. But this was a preliminary foreshadowing of redemption. When the truth of the Spirit came to light, John was sent to remove its obstacles. The same voice sounds daily in our ears, to prepare a way for the Lord, that is, removing the faults that stop the way of the Kingdom of Christ, we may make access for His grace. With the same object the Prophet continues, *And the crooked shall be made straight*. For it means that there are rough places and twisting corners in the world, but the Lord makes Himself a road through such hard difficulties, so that He may, in a manner beyond belief, reach through to accomplish our salvation.

Luke 3.6. *And all flesh shall see.* The meaning is, that this salvation would not be at all obscure, nor only tasted by a few men, but radiant, and shared by all. So it follows that this oracle was not fulfilled in the return of the people (from exile). For even although God then gave memorable proof of His grace, yet He did not reveal His salvation to all the world. The purpose of the Prophet was to contrast the rare pre-eminence of the salvation now to be made manifest with God's earlier benefits, that the faithful might know that He had never dealt so famously with His Church, never in delivering His people had God's power shone out so splendidly. *Flesh* in this passage means 'men', without any connotation of fault.

Matt. 3.4. *John himself had his raiment.* The Evangelist does not consider it among his chief virtues that he adopted a severe and bare form of existence, indeed avoided even the common usual decencies, but as he had said before that he was a man of the hills, he now adds that his food and dress matched his habitation. And he relates this not only to tell us that he was content with country food and dress, and had no desire for luxury, but also that for all his sordid and mean appearance he was greatly valued by well-dressed and distinguished folk. Now as superstition makes perfect righteousness to be found in the outward covering, it has been commonly thought that such humility was the height of sanctity. This error is neighbour to another fault, that has made a man adopt a solitary state, and shrink from the ordinary round of existence, in the way that hermits and monks find excellence in this one point, so that they are apart from other men. Their excessively stupid ignorance has reached the point of making a whole coat from a few hairs. No doubt the Evangelist here described a man of the hills, removed from the gloss and luxury of the city, content with such food as came to hand, in fact eating only the fruits of the soil, as wild honey, which was there in plenty, and locusts, in which also the region abounded. He states all this because it was of benefit that a man of no account, graced with no easy charms, should come on the scene and allow the majesty of God alone to shine in him, which still would draw the amazement of all upon him. For we must take note of what is added, that there was a great gathering of people to him from all around. Thus we gather how greatly his fame was celebrated, either because God determined to set him up as a rare example of frugality, to induce the Jews by this means to reverence his teaching, or at least to convict them of ingratitude, according to Christ's words. 'For John . . . is come eating no bread,' etc. (Luke 7.33).

Matt. 3.6; Mark 1.5. *They were baptized of him . . . confessing their sins.* The evidence of their repentance was this confession, for as the Lord binds Himself to us in the sacraments as in His own writing, so in faithness should we in turn respond to Him. In Baptism, it is testified that our sins are remitted us, and He calls us to repentance. So that men may offer themselves properly for baptism, a confession of sins is required of them, otherwise the whole action would be nothing but an empty mockery. We must note that here adults are being spoken of, who we know are not to be admitted into the Church indiscriminately, nor to be initiated by baptism into the body of Christ unless they are first examined. It is obvious then how laughable are the Papists in twisting this to suit the practice of auricular confession, for there were no Priests there, for each to whisper his sins privately into their ears, nor are all sins referred to, nor do we read that John ordered a regular practice of confession for his disciples. Even so to allow the Papists what they ask, confession will belong only to catechumens, and after baptism it will have no place. Certainly it is contrary to John's example to prescribe from baptism a rule for confession.

But when he saw many of the Pharisees and Sadducees coming to his baptism, he said unto them, Ye offspring of vipers, who warned you to flee from the wrath to come? Bring forth therefore fruit worthy of repentance: and think not to say within yourselves, We have Abraham to our father: for I say unto you, that God is able of these stones to raise up children unto Abraham. And even now is the axe laid unto the root of the trees: every tree therefore that bringeth not forth good fruit is hewn down, and cast into the fire. (Matt. 3.7-10)

He said therefore to the multitudes that went out to be baptized of him, Ye offspring of vipers, who warned you to flee from the wrath to come? Bring forth therefore fruits worthy of repentance, and begin not to say within yourselves, We have Abraham to our father: for I say unto you, that God is able of these stones to raise up children unto Abraham. And even now is the axe also laid unto the root of the trees: every tree therefore that bringeth not forth good fruit is hewn down, and cast into the fire. And the multitudes asked him, saying, What then must we do? And he answered and said unto them, He that hath two coats, let him impart to him that hath none; and he that hath food, let him do likewise. And there came also publicans to be baptized, and they said unto him, Master, what must we do? And he said unto them, Extort no more than that which is appointed you. And soldiers also asked him, saying, And we, what must we do? And he said unto them, Do violence to no man, neither exact anything wrongfully; and be content with your wages. (Luke 3.7-14)

Matt. 3.7. *But when he saw many of the Pharisees.* Here Matthew and Luke tell how John's preaching was not repentance in a general sense, but was a call brought home to individuals. Indeed it will be an unattractive way of teaching, if the masters do not work out carefully what are the needs of the times, what suits the people concerned, for in this regard nothing is more unbalanced than absolute balance. Hence John is said to have handled the Pharisees and Sadducees more severely, as he believed their swelling hypocrisy and pride needed keener reproof than the crowd in general. Now, to grasp his purpose aright, we must realize that nothing is more stupid for hypocrites than deceiving themselves and others with an outward cloak of sanctity. While God thunders down often upon the whole world, their misguided imagination builds them a shelter, assuring them that they have nothing to do with the judgment of God. If any think that John took matters the wrong way, in tackling them so roughly at the first encounter, my answer is that they were not strangers to him, and the acquaintance he had with them was not habit or experience so much as the secret revelation of the Spirit. So there was no point at all in sparing them, or they would have gone home the more puffed up. If there is a further objection that men were not to be terrified with such harsh rebuke when afterwards they were professing themselves in baptism to be changed, then there is a ready answer; those who were in the way of lying to God and indulging themselves, put up a cloud of pretence over the realities, and therefore needed a sharper encouragement to true repentance. For the obstinacy of hypocrites, as I have said, is amazing. Until they are forcibly flayed, they cling to their pelts with their teeth. The way John takes them to task and rebuke in front of all is for the sake of others. In this sense Luke mentions that it was spoken *to the multitudes*. For though he chastised a few, yet he had them all in mind, to make them afraid, just as Paul says (I Tim. 5.20) that this good result may be looked for from public reproofs. So by tackling the Pharisees and Sadducees particularly, he gives warning in their persons to all, not to use a false appearance of repentance as a cover for real emotion. Besides it was greatly to the people's interest to know what kind of people the Sadducees and Pharisees were. By them, the worship of God had been wretchedly tarnished, the Church ruined, and all religion brought to a low ebb. Indeed they had, by their corrupt ways, quenched the light of God, and by their misdeeds they had spread evil on all sides. So it is likely that John ..ttacked the Pharisees in public to advise the whole Church of God that these people should no longer dazzle the eyes of the simple with a vain display, and keep the people under the grip of a godless tyranny. Truly this is a great mark of his constant will, that he did not spare the dignity of those who were exalted among them, but as they deserved brought them seriously to their account. Thus should all godly teachers be men of courage, not to fear the power of men, but to strive without fear to put down all high dealing that lifts itself up against Christ.

Now if this is the stern greeting given by the Holy Spirit's instrument to those who came forward for baptism, to subscribe to the Gospel, how are we to deal today with the professed enemies of Christ, who not only reject with contumacy every taste of sound teaching, but campaign for the ruin of Christ's Name by steel and fire and ever-growing violence? Truly, if you compare the Pope and his foul clergy with the Sadducees and Pharisees, the kindest thing that you can say is that they should be tossed into the same bundle. As their controversy is not with us, but with the Spirit of God, can our ears be so sensitive as not to bear any sharp criticism of the Pope? At the same time, let godly teachers take thought to themselves, that in their career against the Church's tyrants, in all holy zeal, they do not confuse the issue with fleshly emotions. Forcefulness cannot be approved by God unless it is moderated by the prudence of the Spirit. So they should both curb their own feelings, and also yield themselves and trust themselves to the controlling power of the Holy Spirit, that nothing may turn out lacking in consideration.

Offspring of vipers—he uses this term rather than vipers to rebuke the virulent malice of the whole caste, for he wished to condemn not only those few that were present but the whole body, as if to say that the offspring of each party were nothing but vipers. They were bitterly at odds with themselves, granted, but they all shared a contempt for God, a sinful lust for power, a hatred of sound doctrine, and a cess-pool of crimes of every kind. *Who warned you?* He was suspicious about their repentance, and asked them with doubt and amazement, whether it were possible that they repented from their hearts. Thus he stirs them to examine their inward conscience, that they may thoroughly shake themselves out, and with all compliments laid far aside apply to themselves severe criticism in their review of their sins. *Wrath* is taken here as in many other places of the judgment of God. As Paul says (Rom. 4.15 and 12.19), 'The Law worketh wrath,' and, 'Give place unto wrath.' *To come* he uses in the sense of hanging over their heads, that they may not go on with their manner of carelessly amusing themselves. For as the tide of God's wrath rises and His scourge lashes the earth on every side, still the hypocrites believe that they will come through unscathed. *To flee from the wrath of God* is here taken in good part, as meaning in effect to seek a means of pleasing God, that He may cease to be angry with us. For the most men, to escape the wrath of God, withdraw themselves from His hand and judgment, but in fleeing from God, the sinner succeeds so little that indeed he draws God's anger upon him all the more.

Matt 3.8; Luke 3.8. *Bring forth therefore fruit worthy of repentance.* This confirms what I said before, that penitence expressed in words counts for nothing, unless it is proven in real action. Action is more costly than to permit the passing of light and trifling judgments upon it. Thus John says, that the ritual testimony they gave was not enough, but that in the course of time it would finally be evident from their actual works, whether they had seriously repented. We must note that *good works* are called the fruits of repentance, for repentance is an inward thing, that has its seat in the heart and soul, but results in the production of fruit by a change of life. As under the Papacy this entire area of doctrine was dreadfully corrupt, we have to make the distinction, that repentance is a man's inward renewal, that comes into his outward life, just as the tree produces fruit from itself.

Matt. 3.9. *Think not to say.* Luke 3.8. *Begin not to say.* As it is certain that both expressions mean the same, we may readily gather what John intended. Until pressure is put on hypocrites, they shall either sleep on in their faults, or exult in their licence. Once they are hailed to God's tribunal, they anxiously look for subterfuges and escapes, or put up some kind of veil. So John addressed the Pharisees and Sadducees, Now you have been roughly scolded by me, do not do as your habit is, you and your type, and seek a remedy in an empty and fallacious pretence. The shameful confidence that they were so fond of is wrenched out of them. The covenant that God had made with Abraham had become in their hands a shield to ward off blows on their evil conscience, not that they put their confidence of salvation in one man, but as God had adopted the whole race of Abraham. And they never thought, that no-one is reckoned to be of Abraham's seed, unless he follow his faith, or that God's covenant is only valid in terms of faith, to be of use for salvation. The phrase *within yourselves* is far from superfluous. Although they did not boast themselves in speech as Sons of Abraham, inwardly they savoured this title, for hypocrites are so foolish as to be without shame in mocking God more than men.

God is able, etc. The Jews wrapped themselves comfortably in the same pretext, more or less, as the Papists today insolently trade upon, that there must be some Church in the world, for God wills to be recognized in the world, and to have His Name invoked. And the Church cannot be elsewhere than with us, with whom God has entrusted His covenant. This was the overweening arrogance of the Popes in particular, and others who were in government and authority

They reckoned the crowd as profane and accursed—as we read in John 7.49—but themselves as the sacred first-fruits. In the same way, the crested Bishops of today, Abbots, Canons, Monks, Sorbonnists, and any kind of priest, swollen with the proud title of clergy, look down on the lay folk before them. John picks up their error which is overmuch to restrict the promise of God, and refutes it, and he shows that although God had none of them, yet He would not be without a Church. So the meaning of the words is, God has struck an eternal covenant with Abraham and his seed. However, one thing deceives you, that though you are quite debased, you think you alone are the sons of Abraham, but God will raise up a new seed for Abraham, which now you cannot see. He speaks in the dative case, 'sons for Abraham,' that they may know God's promise will not be frustrated, nor will Abraham, who relied on Him, be disappointed, though his seed fail in them. Thus from the beginning of the world God has been true to His servants, nor has He ever failed to live up to the confidence He gave them, that He would extend His grace to their children, for all that He rejected the hypocrites. That some think that John spoke of the calling of the Nations does not seem to me quite certain. As it was incredible to proud men that the Church could be transferred to another, he warns them that it is in the Lord's hand to find ways of preserving the Church which they did not think of, as though He were to make His sons out of stones.

Matt. 3.10. Luke 3.9. *And even now is the axe, etc.* After John flung off the covering from their empty confidence, he declared the closeness of God's judgment. He had first said that with their removal God would not lack a people, but now He adds that God Himself is now at work driving the unworthy from the Church, as the barren trees are cut down. In sum, God's hand is now engaged in pruning the Church. For God's grace never works for the salvation of the godly without at the same time displaying His judgment upon this world, to destroy it: and this for two reasons, that God then divides His own from the reprobate, and the world's ingratitude provokes greater wrath. So there is no wonder that the preaching of the Gospel and the coming of Christ brought the axe to cut off the wasted branches, and daily hastened the vengeance of God upon the wicked.

Luke 3.10. *And the multitudes asked him.* Such concern is the fruit of a true feeling of repentance, when the sinner inquires eagerly, what is God's will and instruction. John's reply briefly outlines the fruits worthy of repentance, for the world ever wishes to perform ceremonies for God's benefit, and is always rushing to thrust concocted rites upon God, whenever He summons them to repentance.

So what fruits does the Baptist commend at this instance? The duties of charity, and of the second table of the Law, not that God overlooks the outward profession of worship and His service, but because this is a more certain criterion, and less often deceptive. Hypocrites make weary efforts to show themselves as God's worshippers in ceremonial, all the while leaving a concern for true righteousness unheeded; they are now cruel to their neighbours, now set on fraud and robbery. So they must be called back to a closer examination—do they foster fair dealing among men, or help the poor, or spare the wretched, or share with generosity, all that God has conferred upon them (Matt. 23.23)? On this basis Christ names the chief headings of the Law as righteousness, mercy, and truth, and Scripture frequently commends justice and judgment. The first thing to realize is that the *duties of charity* are named not because they are superior to the worship of God, but because they testify to men's devotion, so that pretence is revealed if any boast with their mouth what is far from their heart. The question is raised, whether this was a strict rule that John imposed upon all whom he prepared as Christ's disciples, that they should not have two coats. We must first note that this is an expression by synecdoche, in that under one example he includes a general lesson. Hence the sense we are to take must match the rule of charity that is prescribed by God, that each man from his own abundance should assist the needs of the poor. For God does not demand a tax for men to pay sadly and grudgingly, being forced to do something they would rather not, but He loves the cheerful and the willing givers, as Paul says at II Cor. 9.7. I stress this as of great importance, that men should be assured that the sacrifice that is welcome and of a sweet savour to God is that which men offer from their own resources. It makes consciences alarmed, indeed it casts them into despair, to make a law forbidding anyone to hold his own property. I do not need to make a long debate with revolutionaries of this sort, who fasten their teeth on the letter. If it is forbidden to have two coats, we shall have to say the same of pans, of salt-cellars, of underwear, and all our furnishings. But the context makes it obvious that nothing was further from John's thoughts than to subvert the order of society. So we infer that his whole instruction was for the rich, according to their means, to disburse to the poor, as their necessity demanded. In other words, See what basic necessities of life your neighbours lack, and which you have in plenty; let your supply meet their need. And the kinder God is to us the more we must beware of being kind to ourselves alone. Let the needs of our brothers press more upon us, and as often as God's favours come to our hands, so let them invite our generosity.

Luke. 3.12. *And there came also publicans.* He does not only give the *publicans* a general exhortation to repentance, but he touches them on the details of their calling, for we know that, beyond the general regulation of the Law, each man must consider what the manner of life to which he has been called demands. All Christians alike are given the commandment of love, but particular duties follow from this, relating the teacher to the Church, the magistrate or prince to the people, and the people in turn to the magistrate, the husband to the wife, and again the wife to him, lastly sons and parents mutually. Now the *publicani* (being a greedy, rapacious and cruel breed of men) often harassed the people with unfair assessments, and so the Baptist berates them for those vices under which that order chiefly laboured, forbidding them to exceed the norm in raising their tributes. Still we infer from this, that it is none the less permissible for a Christian man to exact tributes, as it is allowed to the magistrate to impose them. We must draw the same conclusion in regard to military service. John does not bid the soldiers throw away their arms, and renounce their oath, but bans them from using the pretext of service for pillaging the poor folk, bringing false charges on innocent people, stravaging like a gang of bandits, as many of them did: we can take from these words a clear acceptance of government. It is an unsubstantial plea, that these are mere elements taught to rough people, far beneath the Christian perfection. John's task was to prepare a perfect people for the Lord, and there is no doubt that he faithfully applied himself to this with all his means. It is a sacrilegious slander upon the Gospel to make it the opponent of human government, as if Christ were to destroy what the heavenly Father established. But laws are dead things, and judgments have no force or authority, without the sword. The magistrate must have both his executioner and his other servants besides, including soldiers, when peace can only be protected by their defence and might. But the end of it all must be borne in mind, that princes do not allow themselves to sport with human blood, nor may troops, hiring out their energies for slaughter through greed of gain, rush into savagery, for both parties must be impelled by necessity and regard for the public good.

I indeed baptize you with water unto repentance: but he that cometh after me is mightier than I, whose shoes I am not worthy to bear: he shall baptize you with the Holy Ghost and with fire: whose fan is in his hand, and he will thoroughly cleanse his threshing-floor; and he will gather

his wheat into the garner, but the chaff he will burn up with unquench-
able fire. (Matt. 3.11-12)

And he preached, saying, There cometh after me he that is mightier than
I, the lachet of whose shoes I am not worthy to stoop down and unloose.
I baptized you with water; but he shall baptize you with the Holy Ghost.
(Mark 1.7-8)

And as the people were in expectation, and all men reasoned in their
hearts concerning John, whether haply he were the Christ; John an-
swered, saying unto them all, I indeed baptise you with water; but there
cometh he that is mightier than I, the lachet of whose shoes I am not
worthy to unloose: he shall baptise you with the Holy Ghost and with
fire: whose fan is in his hand, thoroughly to cleanse his threshing-floor,
and to gather the wheat into his garner; but the chaff he will burn up
with unquenchable fire. With many other exhortations therefore
preached he good tidings unto the people. (Luke 3.15-18)

The Evangelists record the same words of the Baptist. Luke is
only fuller in one respect, that he first remarks on what occasion this
address was given, namely that there was a danger that the populace
might transfer allegiance to him by mistaken ideas. To cut off any
chance of error, in good time, he explicitly says that he was not
Christ, and so distinguishes himself from Him that he stresses his
own position before Him. He would have been doing this in any
case, in order to hand over (as they say) his disciples to Christ, but he
gets it in sooner, in case his silence should any longer confirm a false
idea in the people. When he says that a Mightier is coming, he means
One endowed with far different power and dignity, in respect to
whom he must himself be brought up short. He uses an everyday
expression that so well extols the glory of Christ as to make himself
as nothing before Him. The chief thing is, that he makes Christ
the Author of the baptism of the Spirit, while he is himself a minister
of the outward form. He also seems concerned, if anyone should
object, to show the intention of the baptism he had started. For it
was no small matter to make an innovation in God's Church, especially to put forward a new type of initiation, to make something more
perfect than the Law of God, and so he replies that he had undertaken
nothing inconsiderately, as he was still a minister only of the outward
symbol, and this diminished nothing of the power and glory that
were Christ's. Thus we infer that he had no intention at all to distinguish his baptism from that which Christ ordered His disciples,
the continuing practice which He wished to keep alive in the Church.

Nor did he contrast the visible sign with another sign, but comparing the persons of master and servant he explains the true character of the master and of the servant.

Do not be put off by an opinion which grew up variously and long since, that John's baptism differed from ours, but learn to make your judgment from the facts, and not from men's errors. The comparison they invent would be more than stupid, for it would follow from it that the Holy Spirit is today the gift of ministers. It would further follow that the baptism of John was a dead sign, and devoid of all effect. Thirdly, it would follow that we do not share in Christ's baptism, since it is agreed that the fellowship which He deigned to have with us is established by this token, when he consecrated baptism in His own body. Hence we must hold by what I said first, that John simply distinguishes here between the Person of Christ and himself, with all the other ministrants of baptism, that the Lord may be supreme over the servants.

A general lesson is drawn from this, as to what is the role of man in baptism, and what is particular to the Son of God. To men, there is only entrusted the administration of the outward and visible sign: the truth itself abides with Christ alone. Even Scripture occasionally ascribes to men, improperly, what here John claims for Christ alone, and denies as applying to men; but in these places it does not weigh up the status of man, in himself and of himself, but simply tells us what is the power and benefit of the signs, and how God works through them by His Spirit. Here however we are given the distinction between Christ and His ministers, in case the world should wrongly transfer to them, what uniquely and rightly is owed to Him, for there is nothing more liable to happen, than for the creatures to be decorated with God's awards. This same observation will clear us of many difficulties. We know what quarrels there have been in our century over the use and efficacy of signs, all of which we can settle with this one word, that the Lord's whole institution embraces the Author Himself and the power of the Spirit along with the expression of it and its minister, but when the Lord is compared with the minister, then to allow the former the possession of all, the latter must be reduced to nothing.

Matt. 3.11. *With the Holy Ghost and with fire.* It is asked why John did not also say, It is Christ alone, who cleanses our souls with His blood. But surely as the washing is in fact also done by the power of the Spirit, he did well enough to describe the whole effect of baptism under the single word *Spirit*. And the sense is clear, that Christ alone confers whatever grace the outward baptism seeks to express, for He makes consciences clean by His own blood. He also puts to death the old man, and confers the Spirit of regeneration. The term *fire* is added as an epithet: it goes with the Spirit, for it can only scour off our dirt as gold is refined with fire—as in other places the metaphor of *water* is employed (John 3.5).

Matt. 3.12. *Whose fan is in his hand.* In the last sentence John spoke about the grace of Christ, that the Jews might yield themselves to renewal, but now he speaks of judgment, to put fear into the scorners. For since many hypocrites ever proudly reject the grace of Christ offered them, it is necessary at the same time to lay before them the penalty that awaits them. For this reason John here describes Christ the severe Judge, set against the unbelievers. We too must keep to this order of teaching, that the hypocrites may know that they will not come off with impunity for their rejection of Christ; that they may be roused from their torpor and begin to tremble at the avenger, whom they had scorned as the Author of salvation. And I have no doubt that John wished to teach what Christ would bring to pass by His Gospel. So the preaching of the Gospel is that *fan* or winnow, for until the Lord shall shake us out, the whole world is involved in confusion. Everyone takes his own pleasures, the good are mixed with the evil, and in fact it satisfies them to be filled with chaff. But when Christ, with His Gospel, comes on the scene, examining consciences and summoning men to God's tribunal, the chaff is blown by the fan, that before filled a large part of the floor. Though the Gospel purges the chaff away from individuals, John here is comparing the chaff wholesale to the reprobate, and the faithful to the grain.

Threshing-floor is not used in the sense of the world (as some would think) but of the Church, for we must note at whom John directs his words. As the Jews boasted in the title alone, John warns them of their foolish pride, for it is only for a time that they hold a place in the Church of God, and shall soon be thrown out, just as the chaff from the threshing-floor. Thus he attacks the corrupt state of the Church as it then was, being choked with husks and scourings and all trash, but soon to be purged by the lively wind of the Gospel. But how is Christ said to divide the chaff from the grain, when He can find nothing in men but sheer chaff? The answer is easy: the elect are formed into grain, that free from chaff, they may be gathered into the barn. Now Christ began this purgation, and daily sees it through, yet the effect will not completely show until the final day. So John points us to that moment. But remember, today the faithful through hope enter into the barn of God, that there at last they may have their real abode, and the wicked now sense in their guilt the heat of that fire, whose actual burning they shall experience at the last day. On eternal fire, which is to be the wicked's torment after judgment, I know there have been ingenious arguments by many people, but we may gather from many passages of Scripture that it is a metaphorical expression: if it were a real and material fire, as they say, one must also agree that the *sulphur* and *blowing* are material, which are mentioned at Isaiah 30.33. *Fire* is to be understood in the same way as *worm*, for by general agreement the word *worm* is used as a metaphor, to be taken in the same sense as fire. So leaving aside speculations, over which vain men weary themselves without benefit, let it suffice that by these expressions, as far as our simple minds may grasp, a dreadful torment is indicated, beyond men's ability today to understand, beyond the power of words to express.

Then cometh Jesus from Galilee to the Jordan unto John, to be baptized of him. But John would have hindered him, saying, I have need to be baptized of thee, and comest thou to me? But Jesus answering said unto him, Suffer it now: for thus it becometh us to fulfil all righteousness. Then he suffereth him. And Jesus, when he was baptized, went up straightway from the water: and lo, the heavens were opened unto him, and he saw the Spirit of God descending as a dove, and coming upon him; and lo, a voice out of the heavens, saying, This is my beloved Son, in whom I am well pleased. (Matt. 3.13-17)

And it came to pass in those days, that Jesus came from Nazareth of Galilee, and was baptized of John in the Jordan. And straightway coming up out of the water, he saw the heavens rent asunder, and the Spirit as a dove descending upon him: and a voice came out of the heavens, Thou art my beloved Son, in thee am I well pleased. (Mark 1. 9-11)

Now it came to pass, when all the people were baptized, that, Jesus also having been baptized, and praying, the heaven was opened, and the Holy Ghost descended in a bodily form, as a dove, upon him, and a voice came out of heaven, Thou art my beloved Son; in thee am I well pleased.

And Jesus himself, when he began to teach, was about thirty years of age. (Luke 3.21-23)

Matt. 3.13. *To be baptized of him.* We may to some extent gather the reason why the Son of God wished to be baptized from His answer. The first cause presented is a particular one, that He undertook to share baptism with us (*communem nobiscum baptismum*), that the faithful might be more surely persuaded that they are ingrafted into His body, buried with Him in baptism, that they may rise again to newness of life. But there is a wider purpose displayed, as He now shows: thus it became Him to fulfil all righteousness. The word *righteousness* often has the same effect in Scripture as observance of the Law, and so this passage may be expounded thus: It was necessary for Christ, from His free submission to the Law, to keep it in every part. Yet I prefer to take it more simply to this effect, as if Christ had said: speak no more of worthiness in my regard, for it is not a matter of which of us is the more exellent, but we must rather look to the demands of our calling, what God the Father has laid upon us. For in general, the reason for Christ's undergoing baptism was to offer His father full obedience, while the particular reason, was to consecrate baptism in His own body, that it might be common between Him and us (*ut baptismum consecraret in suo ipsius corpore, ut nobis communis cum eo esset*).

Matt. 3.14. *I have need to be baptized of thee.* It is certain that Christ was not merely recognised as an outstanding Prophet by John, as some foolishly imagine, but as the Son of God, which He was, for otherwise John would have done injury to God, in offering to put God's holy calling under the hands of a mortal man. How he came to understanding, readers may learn from John 1.15. But there were reasonable grounds for refusing, namely that Christ had no need of baptism, but here John was deceived, for he did not realize that it was for the sake of others that He sought baptism. So Christ tells him to consider what suits the character of the servant that He has assumed (*susceptae servi personae*), for His voluntary submission takes nothing away from His glory. Though some part of His human mission lay concealed for the time, there was yet no particular error in his duly and lawfully fulfilling his duty as Baptist. The instance instructs us that we are not acting unwisely in fulfilling the task laid on us by the Lord, as far as it is revealed to us, even although there does not at once emerge what is the consequence of our call, or what depends on it. Note also his modesty, in yielding his own opinion and falling in at once with Christ.

Matt. 3.16. *And lo, the heavens were opened.* The regular meaning of the *heavens opening* is a manifestation of the heavenly glory, but here the meaning is a rending of the actual firmament, that John might see beyond the planets and the stars. There can be no other interpretation of *Mark's* words, when he says that he saw the heavens rent asunder. It is not greatly relevant, nor indeed useful to inquire more closely what this tearing apart could have been, for it is enough to know that it was a symbol of the presence of God. When the Evangelists say that the Holy Spirit was seen by John, it is likely that this was the chief reason for the rending of the heavens. Though I do not deny that Christ too, as far as He was a man, was made more certain of His vocation. This seems to be the object of *Luke's* words, when he says that the heavens were opened as Christ prayed. For though He always directed His prayers to the benefit of others, yet He had, insofar as His humanity required it, need of the defence of the Spirit's unique power, in embarking on such a rigorous campaign.

Two questions arise here. The first, why the Spirit *then* descended upon Christ, when it had *earlier* rested upon Him. This question is resolved by the passage in Isaiah 61.1, which will be dealt with elsewhere: 'The Spirit of the Lord is upon me; because the Lord hath anointed me, he hath sent me to preach good tidings unto the meek.' Though there was ever an amazing outpouring of the unique grace of the Spirit upon Christ, yet He contained Himself at home as a private individual right up to the time that He was to be brought out by the Father. So now, in the fulness of time, to equip Him for the fulfilment of the office of Redeemer, He is endowed with a new power of the Spirit, and this not so much for His own sake, as for others. And this is deliberately done to teach the faithful to receive and embrace with reverence His divine power, and not treat the weakness of His flesh with scorn. It was for the same reason that His baptism was put off till His thirtieth year. Baptism complemented the Gospel, and so it came together with the publishing of the Gospel. When Christ makes Himself ready to preach the Gospel, He was both initiated into His task by baptism, and directed by the Holy Spirit. Thus John sees the Holy Spirit descending upon Christ, to teach us that there is nothing carnal or earthly to be looked for in Christ as such, but rather He comes forth from heaven as a divine man, under the royal power of the Holy Spirit. We know that He is God, manifested in the flesh, but His heavenly power is also to be thought upon in His Person as minister, in His human nature.

The second question is, why the Spirit appeared in the form of a *dove* rather than fire: and the answer depends on the analogy or likeness of the thing signified and the sign. We know what Isaiah the prophet says of Christ (42.3). 'A bruised reed,' he says, 'shall he not break, and the smoking flax shall he not quench; he shall not cry, nor cause his voice to be heard.' It is for Christ's gentleness in calling sinners in kind and soft tones to hope for salvation, inviting them each day, that the Holy Spirit descended upon Him in the form of a dove. And in this symbol we have shown us a striking pledge of His most sweet consolation, that we should have no fear in approaching

Christ, for He meets us not in the dread power of the Spirit, but wearing His lovable and pleasant grace.

He saw the Spirit of God. John, that is, for he goes on to say that the Spirit descended upon Christ. Here a third question arises, how John could see the Spirit. I would answer that as the Spirit of God is diffused everywhere and fills heaven and earth, any descent there is improperly attributed. We must make the same conclusion regarding the appearance. Though in Himself invisible, yet He is said to be seen when He makes some demonstration of His presence. John does not see the essence of the Spirit, which does not fall within the sight of the eyes, nor does he see His actual power (which may be not apprehended by human intelligence, but only by the mind of faith) but he sees the form of a dove, under which God revealed the presence of His Spirit. So it is an expression in metonymy, where the name of a spiritual being is transferred to the visible sign. Whereas some press the literal sense foolishly and absurdly, to include the being in the sign, this form of words is used to indicate the conjunction of the being with the sign. It is in such a sense that the bread of the holy Supper is called the body of Christ, not that it is such, but that it testifies that it is truly given us for our food. At the same time we must remember what I have just said, that we are not to imagine a descent of the thing signified, as to seek it on the spot included in its sign. It should be enough for us, and more than enough, that God provides, by His hidden power, what He promises by outward expressions. Some look with more curiosity than usefulness into whether this dove were a solid body or a ghost. Though Luke's language appears to suggest that there was no substance to the body, but only a form, I prefer to leave the matter unsettled, and avoid provoking a dispute over it.

Matt. 3.17. *A voice out of the heavens.* A voice resounded from this tearing apart of the heavens, of which mention has just been made, in order that He might be all the more sure of His dominion. Further, Christ was presented to us by the Father with this proclamation, in His coming forth to fulfil His task of Mediation, that we might rely on this pledge of our adoption and without fear call God Himself our Father. The title of Son truly and by nature belongs to Christ alone, yet He was revealed as Son of God in our flesh, that He who alone claimed Him as Father by right, could win Him for us also. So God, in introducing our Mediator with words that praise Him as the Son, declares Himself to be a Father to us all. This is exactly the aim of the word *beloved*, for as in ourselves we are hateful to God, His fatherly love must flow to us in Christ. The best interpreter of this passage is Paul (Eph. 1.6), where he says that we have obtained grace in the beloved Son, that we may be loved by God. This is given further development in the phrase, *in whom I am well pleased.* For it suggests that God's love is so well content in Christ that from Him it may flow out upon us all: and not to us alone, but even to the angels themselves, not that they have need of reconciliation, as these never had any breach with God, but because not even they hold perfectly to God, except through the favour of their head. For this reason He is called the First-born of every creature. And Paul in another place again says that He came to gather in all things in heaven and on earth. (Col. 1.15 and 20).

Then was Jesus led up of the Spirit into the wilderness to be tempted of the devil. And when he had fasted forty days and forty nights, he afterward hungered. And the tempter came and said unto him, If thou art the Son of God, command that these stones become bread. But he answered and said, It is written, Man shall not live by bread alone, but by every word that proceedeth out of the mouth of God. (Matt. 4.1-4)

And straightway the Spirit driveth him forth into the wilderness. And he was in the wilderness forty days tempted of Satan; and he was with the wild beasts. (Mark 1.12-13)

And Jesus, full of the Holy Spirit, returned from the Jordan, and was led by the Spirit in the wilderness during forty days, being tempted of the devil. And he did eat nothing in those days: and when they were completed, he hungered. And the devil said unto him, If thou art the Son of God, command this stone that it become bread. And Jesus answered unto him, It is written, Man shall not live by bread alone. (Luke 4.1-4)

Matt. 4.1. *Then was Jesus led up, etc.* There were two motives for Christ's withdrawal into the wilderness: the first, that after a fast of forty days He should as a new, indeed a heavenly, man advance to the pursuance of His task, and the second, that only after He had been tested by temptations, after His preliminary training, would He be equipped for such an arduous and distinguished mission. So we may know that Christ, under the leadership of the Spirit, was taken away from the concourse of men, that He might come forth as supreme Teacher of the Church and Ambassador of God, more as one sent from heaven, than a man picked up from some town or from the common herd of humanity. Thus God took Moses up to Mount Sinai, when He wished to publish His Law by his hand, and when he was away from the sight of men, He received him in a kind of heavenly sanctuary (Exod. 24.13). It was right that Christ should shine with, at least, no less brilliant marks of the divine grace and power than Moses, or the majesty of the Gospel would be less than that of the Law. If the Lord accorded rare honour to doctrine that is the ministrant of death, how much more honour does the doctrine of life deserve? If the shadowy expression of God was so luminous, what should be the full radiance of the bright torch that we see in the Gospel?

The object of the fast was the same. Christ did not abstain from food and drink to give an example of temperance, but to gain Him more authority in being set apart from the common lot of men, that He might progress as an angel from heaven, not as a man of the earth. Let me ask you, what sort of virtue would there have been in abstinence, in not taking food, for one who would never have suffered pains of appetite from lack of food, if He had not been in the form of the flesh? So it is really quite foolish to institute the so-called forty-day (*Quadragesima*) fast in imitation of Christ. For there is no more reason today why we should follow the example of Christ, than ever there was for the holy Prophets and the other Fathers under the Law to imitate the fast of Moses. In fact we know that no-one ever had such a thought. Only Elijah, as being the minister of the restoration of the Law, was for a similar reason kept fasting by God on the mountain. They pretend to be imitators of Christ, when they fast every day of the forty, but really they so stuff their bellies at breakfast that they can easily go through dinner-time without food. What resemblance have they to the Son of God? The older generation were more frugal, but they too had nothing like Christ's fast. No more, I am sure, than man's abstinence approaches the angels' disregard of food. Besides, neither Christ nor Moses held a solemn fast every year, but both held one only, in all their lives. If they would only keep to harmless pranks like monkeys—but it was a wicked and detestable mockery of Christ to dare to train themselves with a pretended fast of His ruling. For them to persuade themselves that it is a work of merit, a part of religious devotion and the worship of God—this is the ultimate in superstition. And the least supportable feature of this insult to God is that it obscures His particular work of miracle. Moreover, it is insult to Christ, for they tear down His trophy, and dress themselves in His spoils, and then, to the Gospel, which loses no mean authority if Christ's fast is not recognized as His own seal. God worked a great miracle when He released His Son from the necessity of eating. It is surely mad audacity to rival God, and attempt the same by one's own efforts. Fasting brought Christ the distinction of divine glory. Is He not robbed of His glory and brought down to the ranks, when all mortals squeeze themselves in along-side Him? Did God not set the object of this fast of Christ as the seal of His approval on the Gospel? Then those who transfer it to another object are surely to that degree lowering the worth of the Gospel. Away then with that κακοζηλία (affectation), that perverts the purpose of God and the whole course of His works. Now I am not speaking of fasting in general, for I would wish its use (as long as it is sound) could be more frequent amongst us, but I had to show the aim of the fast of Christ.

Now Satan took the basis of his temptation of Christ from His hunger, just as will shortly be related. We must just look broadly at the reason why God willed Him *to be tempted*. That it was by God's firm decision that He was led to this conflict, is the sense of *Matthew's* and *Mark's* accounts, who state that for this reason He was led up of the Spirit into the wilderness. I have no doubt that God displayed in the Person of His Son, as on a brilliant screen, how hostile and persistent an adversary Satan is against the salvation of man. For how is it that he attacks Christ bitterly, throws all his force and onslaught upon Him at this precise moment which the Evangelists record, unless he saw that He was being trained for men's redemption? It was our salvation that he then attacked in the Person of Christ, just as today he fiercely persecutes the ministers of that same redemption, whose Author was Christ. But we must note at the same time, that the Son of God willingly underwent the temptations with which we are now dealing, and met the devil in a set trial of strength, that by His victory He might win us the triumph. So as often as Satan attacks us, let us remember that we can in no other way sustain and repulse his assaults than by the protection of that shield. Surely, it was for this cause that the Son of God suffered to be tempted, that He might intervene for us, whenever Satan brings any trial of temptation across our path. So we do not read of His being tempted, when He was running His own life at home, but when He had to enter on the career of the Redeemer, then He entered the lists in the name of His whole Church. But if Christ was tempted as the Representative of all the faithful, we should realize that the temptations that strike us are not fortuitous, or the turn of Satan's whim, without God's permission, but that the Spirit of God presides in all our trials, that our faith may be the better tried. So we may take sure hope, that God, who is the supreme Master of the ring, will not be unmindful of us, or fail to succour our weaknesses, as He sees we are unequal to them.

We have a slightly different impression from *Luke's* words—that Jesus *full of the Holy Spirit* returned from Jordan—which mean that, girded with a richer grace and power of the Spirit, He would be stronger to face the battles before Him, for it was not in vain that the Spirit had come down on Him in visible form. It has already been said that God's grace shone in Him the more, as the course of our salvation demanded. But at first sight it seems odd that Christ should be liable to the devil's temptations, as for temptation to strike a man, there must be underlying fault and weakness. This is the answer—first, that Christ took on our weaknesses, but without fault, and second, that it was no more loss to His glory to become exposed to temptations, than to put on Himself our flesh. On these terms He was made man, that He should bear our passion, as well as our flesh. All the difficulty comes in the first phrase. How could Christ have been encumbered with our weakness to the extent of lying open to the temptations of Satan, and yet remain pure and untouched by any fault? And the solution will not be hard to find, if we think of the nature of the perfect Adam, when God's image still shone there with a pure light, and how it was yet subjected to temptations. As many as are the appetites of the human body, so many are the occasions Satan leaps upon for his temptations. Now it is rightly considered a weakness of human nature, that our senses are stirred by objects presented to them, but in itself there would be no fault in this, if corruption did not find an entrance, with the result that Satan never approaches us without striking some wounding blow, or at least pricking us with some hurt. In this area, Christ's integrity separated Him from us; though we are not to reckon His state as a mere average, such as was Adam's, only allowed the possibility of not sinning. But we do know, that Christ was so defended by the power of the Spirit, that Satan's darts could not reach Him.

The tempter came. The Spirit deliberately gives Satan this name, that the faithful may the better look out for him. So we gather that the temptations which prompt us to evil, only come from him. For that God, in other contexts, is said to tempt man, is in quite another regard. He explores the faith of His own, or sets a penalty upon the unbelievers, or brings hypocrisy into the open in those who do not, from their heart, serve the truth (Gen. 22.1; Deut. 13.3).

Matt. 4.3. *That these stones become bread.* A former generation have amused themselves here with ingenuity, of no substance, when they said that the first temptation was gluttony, the second ambition, and the third greed, but it is ridiculous to speak of the immoderate display of gluttony, in the case of a hungry man seeking food to satisfy his nature. And what kind of high living is there in bread, to give a man the name of gourmandizing—when plain bread, as they say, is enough for him? However, not to waste words, Christ's answer alone makes very clear that Satan's plot was quite different. The Son of God was no unskilled or raw contestant, who did not know how to duck His opponent's blows, but let himself be struck on the right, then wildly held up his shield on the left! If Satan had tried to entice Him with the delights of gluttony, He had Scripture's testimony at hand with which to repel him. However, He uses none of this material, but produces the sentence that man does not live by bread, but by the hidden blessing of God. So we gather that Satan had made a direct attack on Christ's faith, that by overcoming it he might drive Christ into illicit and corrupt ways of finding food. Indeed, it was a blow aiming for a knock-out, to try to get us to lose faith in God, and to follow our own interests other than God's Word allows. Thus the sense of the words is: when you see yourself abandoned by God, necessity forces you to look out for yourself. So provide yourself with food, as God fails to provide it for you. Even if Christ exerts His divine power which turns the stones into bread, the sole object of his game is for Christ to move away from God, and follow the dictates of infidelity. Thus Christ aptly replies, 'Not by bread alone does a man live': in other words, You bid me seek some relief, to get myself provision other than God lets me have. But this would be to lose faith, which is quite beyond reason, as long as God promises that He will be my supplier. You, Satan, attach His favour to bread, but He Himself testifies to the contrary, that though all bread be lacking, yet His blessing alone is enough to nourish us. Now we see what kind of temptation this was, which Satan still uses every day in his attack upon us, for it was not an unusual temptation that the Son of God wished to undergo, but He wished to share our battles with us, that we must be armed with the same defence, and have no doubt that we have the palm of victory in our grasp.

Luke 4.4. *It is written, Man shall not live by bread alone.* The first thing worth noting is that Christ uses the Scripture as a shield against him, and this is the true way of fighting, if we wish to win a sure victory. Paul does well to call God's Word a spiritual sword, and bids us take up the shield of faith (Eph. 6.16-17). We may infer that the Papists, having come to an arrangement with Satan, cruelly to expose souls to their destruction for his delight, are by their malicious suppression of Scripture robbing God's people of their arms, with which alone they may manage to protect their salvation. As for those who willingly throw away this armour, and take no regular practice in the school of God, they deserve at any moment to be floored by Satan, in going out to meet him undefended. There is no other reason for Satan, who campaigns so feebly, to snatch up so many on all sides, except that God punishes men's apathy and contempt for His Word. Now we must examine this testimony of Moses which Christ quotes (Deut. 8.3). It is wrong to apply it to spiritual life, as if it meant that souls are not nurtured by visible bread, but by the Word of God. This is a truism, but it was not what Moses was intending. When there was no bread to hand, he records that Manna was an exceptional provision for the people, that by this sign, there might be affirmed to every age, that the life of man is not confined to bread but depends upon the command and pleasure of God. So *word* is not taken as being teaching, but for the decision that God made known, for the protection of the order of nature and the care of creation. For He does not cast off the men whom He established, but fills them with life, with a view continually to sustaining what He had once given. This means, that the whole world is animated, its separate parts keep to their condition, by His command and ordinance, whose authority reaches everywhere from the heights to the depths. Though it is bread that feeds us, we are not right to attribute the life we receive to bread in itself, but to the hidden grace which God breathes into the bread, that we may be fed. It further follows that God who now employs bread for our food will give other means, when He should so determine, for our life. Likewise by Moses' statement, is there condemned the dumb folly of those who take fulness and plenty to be life. Also, there is correction of the faithlessness and unworthy concern, which drives us to seek forbidden courses. This is the true direction of Christ's reply, for our livelihood and the other provisions of this present life, we must so trust in God, that none of us may transgress His appointed bounds. If Christ held it unlawful to make bread from stones against the will of God, much less may one make a living from fraud, raids, assault, or murder.

Then the devil taketh him into the holy city; and he set him on the pinnacle of the temple, and saith unto him, If thou art the son of God, cast thyself down: for it is written,
  He shall give his angels charge concerning thee:
  And on their hands they shall bear thee up,
  Lest haply thou dash thy foot against a stone.

Jesus said unto him, Again it is written, Thou shalt not tempt the Lord thy God. Again, the devil taketh him unto an exceeding high mountain, and sheweth him all the kingdoms of the world, and the glory of them; and he said unto him, All these things will I give thee, if thou wilt fall down and worship me. Then saith Jesus unto him, Get thee hence, Satan: for it is written, Thou shalt worship the Lord thy God, and him only shalt thou serve. Then the devil leaveth him; and behold, angels came and ministered unto him. (Matt. 4.5-11)

And he led him up, and shewed him all the kingdoms of the world in a moment of time. And the devil said unto him, To thee will I give all this authority, and the glory of them: for it hath been delivered unto me; and to whomsoever I will give it. If thou therefore wilt worship before me, it shall all be thine. And Jesus answered and said unto him, It is written, Thou shalt worship the Lord thy God, and him only shalt thou serve. And he led him to Jerusalem, and set him on the pinnacle of the temple, and said unto him, If thou art the Son of God, cast thyself down from hence: for it is written,
    He shall give his angels charge concerning thee, to guard thee: and,
    On their hands they shall bear thee up,
    Lest haply thou dash thy foot against a stone.
And Jesus answering said unto him, It is said, Thou shalt not tempt the Lord thy God.
    And when the devil had completed every temptation, he departed from him for a season. (Luke 4.5-13)

Matt. 4.5. *Then the devil taketh him.* There is nothing very remarkable in Luke putting in second place the temptation which Matthew places last, for the Evangelists had no intention of so putting their narrative together as always to keep an exact order of events, but to bring the whole pattern together to produce a kind of mirror or screen image of those features most useful for the understanding of Christ. It is quite enough to grasp that Christ was put to three temptations. Which test came second or third, is not a matter for anxious debate. In the exposition I shall follow Matthew's sequence. One is asked, whether He was really lifted up to a pinnacle or whether this was done in a vision. Many assert with determination that it was a true and (to use their word) concrete elevation in the body, for they think it would be improper for Christ to have been mixed up with Satan's wizardry. This objection soon disappears—there is nothing impossible in God allowing, and in Christ freely undergoing

139

it, as long as we do not imagine Christ to be in any way affected inwardly, that is, in His mind or soul. That it goes on to say, that all the kingdoms of the world were set in Christ's view, and Luke's similar note, that in a moment of time He was taken far away, belongs more to visionary experience. However, the matter is not certain, and there is no harm in admitting ignorance. Hence I prefer to leave it with judgment suspended, rather than give a loophole for contentious disputation. It may well be that the second temptation did not follow directly upon the previous one, nor the third upon the second, but only after some interval; indeed, this is more likely, though we gather from Luke's words that it was not a long period, as he speaks of relief being given to Christ 'for a season'. The really relevant matter is to know what Satan wanted to achieve from this kind of temptation, and we may learn this from Christ's reply, as I commented earlier. Christ, in meeting His enemy's plot and driving back his assault, takes up the shield that reads, 'Thou shalt not tempt the Lord thy God.' Obviously the aim of the enemy's attack was that He should over-reach the just limit, and wildly lift Himself up against God. Satan had first tried to bring Christ down to desperation, when He was destitute of food and the ordinary means of life, but now he urges Him to an inflated and vain assurance, to overlook the resources at hand and, without the need for it, to fling Himself into an open test, that would break all bounds. Now, we know we should not be shattered by the pressure of complete loss of means, but should depend on God's confidence. But neither may we be cocksure and lift ourselves up higher than God allows us. So we understand Satan's purpose, that Christ in trying out His divinity should intrude upon God, without thought or respect.

Matt. 4.6. *He shall give his angels charge concerning thee: And on their hands, etc.* Here note Satan's evil device of using Scripture's testimony falsely, to make life a source of death to Christ, to make His bread into poison. Daily he continues this abuse, and the Son of God has willed each to undergo this conflict as in His Person, for He is the common example all godly people enjoy, in order that all may learn to take good care not to fall into Satan's clutches by the fallacious pretext of Scripture. There is no doubt that the Lord allows our foe such licence to break our apathy, and keep us more alert upon our watch. Now we must not take the preposterous course of discarding Scripture for its so-called ambiguities, besides the distortions which the devil imports. For similar reasons, one would have to abstain from food, to stop the risk of being poisoned. Satan profanes God's Word, and strives to turn it to our ruin; yet, as it has been divinely appointed for our salvation, will it not be our own incapacity that spoils its saving power—if anything will? This is not a subject that requires long discussion; just consider what Christ tells us by His example, which we must follow as a rule. Does He yield to Satan when he criminally twists Scripture's sense? Does He allow Scripture, His earlier defence, to be shaken off Him or torn down? No—He gallantly throws back Satan's slander with a blow from Scripture in return. Thus as often as Satan throws up Scripture in his efforts to deceive, and godless men on this same pretext rise up against us, to circumvent our faith, let us borrow weapons for the defence of our faith from no other source than Scripture.

Now, though the promise, 'He shall give his angels charge,' etc. applies to all the faithful, it has particular relevance to Christ, as being the Head of the whole Church, and by right superior to the angels, to whom He entrusts our protection. So on this point Satan was not a liar, to show by this testimony that the angels were appointed to Christ's service, to guard Him, to bear Him in their arms, but the lie comes in leading the angels' protection out upon a vague and foolhardy cause, whereas it is actually promised to the Sons of God just as long as they keep to their bounds, and walk in their proper paths. If there is any stress on the phrase, *In all thy ways* (Ps. 91.11), then Satan is maliciously corrupting and mutilating the sentence of the Prophet, twisting it without concern or order into vague and misleading directions. God bids us walk in our ways, and then declares that the angels will be our guards. Satan presents the angels' protection, then urges Christ to plunge Himself into danger, as if to say, If you take a death leap against God's will, the angels will defend your life.

Matt. 4.7. *It is written, Thou shalt not tempt the Lord.* Most aptly, Christ replies that our hopes are to have no other basis than the promise of God, that He promises His assistance where the faithful humbly commit themselves to His governments, for we cannot have reliance upon God's promises other than by obedience to His commands. God is tempted in various ways. The word *tempt* is used here of neglecting the means which He reaches out to our hands. Those who overlook the means which God provides and attempt to try His power and strength are just behaving as if they lopped a man of his arms and hands, and then ordered him to work. In short, any who desire to experiment upon the power of God without necessity are tempting God by putting His promises to an unfair test.

Matt. 4.8. *The devil taketh him unto an exceeding high mountain.* Remember what I have said already, that it was not as the result of an enfeeblement of Christ's nature that Satan forced His eyes, but by His willing permission and consent. Also, His senses were so affected and beguiled by the presentation of the kingdoms in their glory as to allow no covetous affection to impress itself on His being—compared with the desires of the flesh, which like wild beasts are caught up by the objects that attract us, and pull us along with them, Christ shared our emotions, but not our unruly appetites. This was a different kind of temptation, for Christ to seek the inheritance which God promised His children other than at God's own hands. So the devil displayed sacrilegious audacity, snatching God's earthly dominion to himself as usurper. All these are mine, he says, and can only be gained by my favour. That we daily must fight the same imposture, is the experience of individual Christians, and the (more obvious) witness of the whole life of the godless. Though we set our defence, our resource, our supply upon God's blessing alone, yet our senses are continually titillated and seduced into finding extra means from Satan, as if God alone were not enough. The great part of the world, refusing God's right and rule over the earth, imagine to themselves that Satan is the giver of all good. Else how does it come to be, that practically all are addicted to evil crafts, thieving and swindling, unless they are giving Satan what belonged to God, the right to endow His own at His choosing? With their mouth they ask for their daily bread to be given them by God, but only with the mouth—Satan gets the job of distributing all the world's goods.

Matt. 4.10. *Get thee hence, Satan.* At this place Luke reads,[1] *Get thee behind me (Abi post me), Satan.* So some speculate vainly over the adverb, as Peter is told (Matt. 16.23), *Vade retro* ('Get thee behind'), as though Satan heard something different. Christ is simply telling him to be off. And in His same line of defence, He goes further, to use Scripture as no mere rushwork shield, but as a wall of bronze: and He draws the testimony from the Law, that God alone is to be worshipped and served. From His use of the text, and from the circumstances of the present passage, we may readily deduce what is intended in the worship of God and what is its worth. Papists, in denying that God alone is to be adored, dodge this and similar passages with a sophistical comment. The adoration of *latreia* (worship) they admit is allowed only to God, but *dulia* (service) is applied by them to the dead, and to their relics and statues. But without any regard for that cheap splitting of terms, Christ claims even προσκύνησις (reverence) for God alone. This warns us to take account of the substance rather than the word, whenever we are speaking of the service of God. Scripture bids us serve God alone, and we must see, to what purpose. If a man steals anything from His glory to apply

[1] Calvin's text differs here from that behind R. V.

it to created beings, this is a sacrilegious violation of divine service. That this is done, is more than plain, when we acknowledge good things received at the hands of creatures, when God alone willed to be known as the Author of these things. Now as the practice of religion is truly a spiritual thing and its external profession pertains to the body, so not only inward service is due to God alone, but also His outward testimony.

Matt. 4.11. *Then the devil leaveth him; and behold, etc.* Luke is more detailed: with the words, *when the devil had completed every temptation.* This means that Christ won no rest or truce until He was sharply tested by every sort of conflict. He adds that Christ was left only for a time, that we should know that the rest of His life was not altogether free of trials, but Satan's force was divinely restrained, that he should not persist in troubling Christ. Thus God deals with all His own. If at times He allows them to be sharply vexed, in due course He eases their undue struggle, that they may breathe a little, and gather their strength, yet He does not spare them to indulge in idleness, but only to prepare themselves for new battles. The following words, *angels . . . ministered unto him,* I would relate to Christ's comfort in knowing that God the Father cared for Him, and by His strong defence armed Him against Satan. For the loneliness itself could have increased His sorrow, as He passed His days without any of the intercourse of men, among wild beasts, as *Mark* explicitly related. We must not think that Christ was ever deserted by the angels, except to allow the opportunity of temptations, when God's grace, though present, lay hidden from Him, according to the perception of the flesh.

Now when he heard that John was delivered up, he withdrew into Galilee. From that time began Jesus to preach, and to say, Repent ye; for the kingdom of heaven is at hand. (Matt. 4.12 and 17)

Now after that John was delivered up, Jesus came into Galilee, preaching the gospel of God, and saying, The time is fulfilled, and the kingdom of God is at hand: repent ye, and believe in the gospel. (Mark 1.14-15)

But Herod the tetrarch, being reproved by him for Herodias his brother's wife, and for all the evil things which Herod had done, added yet this above all, that he shut up John in prison.
And Jesus returned in the power of the Spirit into Galilee: and a fame

went out concerning him through all the region round about. And he taught in their synagogues, being glorified of all. (Luke 3.19-20; 4.14-15)

Luke 3.19. *But Herod the tetrarch, etc.* Only Luke explains at this point why John was thrown into prison by Herod. Matthew and Mark refer to it in another place. Josephus (*Ant.* 18) says that because Herod was afraid of popular uprising and revolt, he had John shut up in the citadel of Machaerus, as the man's authority had become a source of suspicion to him. He says that Herodias was not given in marriage to Philip (whom he makes the husband of Salome), but to another Herod. However, this is a place where a lapse in his memory has been noted, and Philip's death also is not mentioned where it should be, which leads us to seek true information from the Evangelists, and confirms their testimony. It is generally agreed, that though Herod had as wife the daughter of Aretas, king of Arabia, he was beguiled by the beauty of Herodias, and wrongfully took her. He was able to do this wrong against his brother Philip with impunity, as the same Josephus tells us this was a mild and gentle-natured man. We can see clearly, in this history, what reward awaits those faithful and wise servants of the truth in this world, especially when they expose vice. Scarcely one in a hundred admits his correction, so that, if they are pressed more seriously, they burst into fury. If pride of this order is seen among the common folk, no wonder if tyrants rage the more bitterly against those who reprove them, for nothing grates on them more, than to be degraded. But consider the shining example of firmness that John displays, which all godly teachers should be possessed with, or they will hesitate to bring down the great and mighty on themselves as often as should be. No-one serves God with sincerity when he strives to please men. When Luke says that this was a culmination of evils, he means that the malice had reached a pitch of desperation when the sinner enraged by his cure, not only repudiates correction, but takes vengeance on his adviser, as upon a foe.

Matt. 4.12. *Now when he (i.e. Jesus) heard.* John's narrative does not appear to agree with these, for he records that John and Jesus began their teaching mission together at the same time. But we must note that our three Evangelists pass over that short period in silence, for the reason that John's career was not yet complete, that is, the preparation for the receiving of the Gospel of Christ. In fact, although Christ did act as Teacher during that time, He had not really started upon the preaching of the Gospel, until He succeeded John. There is then nothing amiss in the three Evangelists allowing and ascribing this time to John's ministry, in which he prepared disciples for Christ, as if to say that the light of dawn gave way to the risen sun. We must note the expression in Luke, that Jesus came into Galilee *in the power*—or through the power—*of the Spirit*: it is very important not to think about anything earthly or human in Christ, but to let His celestial and divine power impress itself upon us, and seize our imagination.

Mark 1.14. *Preaching the Gospel [of the kingdom] of God.* Matthew seems to have some difference from the other two, for only after he says that Christ left His home country of Nazareth, and came into Capernaum, does he say that He reached the beginning of His preaching. Luke and Mark, however, say that He taught publicly in His own country. But the answer is easy, for the adverb of time in Matthew should be referred not merely to the last part, but to the whole of his narrative. Thus, by His coming into Galilee, Christ embarked on a stage in His journey. The sum of His teaching, as recorded by Matthew, differs little from that we have just heard John use: it consists of two parts, repentance and the proclamation of grace and salvation. He urges the Jews to conversion, for the Kingdom of God is at hand: that is, that God takes His people into His rule, which is full and lasting prosperity. Mark varies slightly: *the kingdom of God is at hand: repent ye, and believe in the gospel*, but the sense is the same. Starting with the restoration of the Kingdom of God among the Jews, He urges them to repentance and faith. Yet it may be asked, as *repentance* depends on the Gospel, why Mark separates it from *the teaching* of the Gospel. There is a twofold answer. Sometimes God calls us to repentance in such a way as merely to say, that we should change our lives for the better, but afterwards He shows us that conversion and newness of life are the gift of His Spirit, that we may understand that we are not only being taught what is our duty, but are offered the grace and the power to obey. If we take in this sense John's sermons on repentance, the meaning will be, The Lord bids you be converted unto Him, but since you cannot do this by your own efforts, He promises the Spirit of regeneration, and therefore you must embrace this grace by faith. The faith, however, which Christ demands that we have in the Gospel should not be restricted to the gift of renewal, but chiefly has regard to the remission of sins. John links repentance with faith, for God reconciles Himself with us in order that He may as a Father receive from us the devotion of sanctity and righteousness. Now there is nothing wrong with saying that *believe in the Gospel* has the same force as embracing free righteousness, for the particular connection of faith and the remission of sins occurs often in Scripture, as when it teaches us that we are justified *by faith*. Whichever way you please to expound this passage, this principle must remain firm, that free salvation is offered us by God, in order that we may be converted to Him and live in righteousness. So He promises us mercy and calls us to denial of the flesh. We must note the designation ('of God') which Mark gives to the Gospel for, we learn from it that by His preaching the *kingdom of God* is lifted up on the earth and established, and in no other way does God rule over men. Thus it is evident, how wretched is the state of men without the Gospel.

Luke 4.15. *Being glorified of all.* This is expressly given by Luke to tell us that the divine power shone out from the first in Christ, to force men to Him in admiration, if they were not already hostile, through an evil passion of contradiction.

> *And he came to Nazareth, where he had been brought up: and he entered, as his custom was, into the synagogue on the sabbath day, and stood up to read. And there was delivered unto him the book of the prophet Isaiah. And he opened the book, and found the place where it was written,*
> *The Spirit of the Lord is upon me,*
> *Because he anointed me to preach good tidings to the poor:*
> *He hath sent me to proclaim release to the captives,*
> *And recovering of sight to the blind,*
> *To set at liberty them that are bruised,*
> *To proclaim the acceptable year of the Lord.*
> *And he closed the book, and gave it back to the attendant, and sat down: and the eyes of all in the synagogue were fastened on him. And he began to say unto them, To-day hath this scripture been fulfilled in your ears. And all bare him witness, and wondered at the words of grace which proceeded out of his mouth: and they said, Is not this Joseph's son?* (Luke 4.16-22)

Luke 4.16. *And he came to Nazareth.* The Evangelists lay emphasis on this one feature, to show by what proofs Christ became known, a notable instance of which is here related by Luke. He expounded a passage of Isaiah, and by His application of it to the present time, drew the eyes of all upon Himself. When he says that He came by custom into the synagogue, we may learn that it was not only on the routes and crossroads that he addressed the people, but, as He pleased, He used the ordinary practice of the Church. At the same time we may see that though the Jews had become degenerate, there was some good left, despite the confusion of the times and the wretchedly corrupt condition of the Church, for they read the Scripture in the face of the people, that from it they might take material for teaching and exhortation. This shows the true and rightful way of keeping the Sabbath. God did not order His people to hold holidays merely for taking a pleasant break from work, but rather applied them to the meditation of His own works. As men's minds grow dull at thinking over the works of God, they must be corrected by the standard of Scripture. Though Paul counts the Sabbath among the shadows of the Law, in this regard we share a reason for holiday with the Jews, that the people may come together for hearing the Word, for public prayers, and for the other exercises of devotion. For this purpose, the Lord's Day has succeeded the Sabbath of the Jews. But if we compare the periods, it will be apparent from the present passage that the corruptions of the Papal hierarchy today are more foul and more disfiguring, than they were under Annas and Caiaphas with the Jews. The reading of Scripture, that then was alive, has not only gone into decline under the Pope, but is driven from the temples by sword and fire, except what they chant in a strange tongue at their fancy, for a mockery. Christ stood up to read, not only that His voice might be better heard, but to approach His business with humility and respect.

Luke 4.17. *Found the place.* There is no doubt that Christ deliberately chose this passage. Some believe that it was divinely presented to Him, but as He had the gift of free choice, I prefer to assign it to His judgment, to pick out this passage before others. Isaiah now promises that after the Babylonian exile there will still be some witnesses of the grace of God, to gather the people out of ruin and the shadows of death, and to renew with spiritual power the Church, then struck with so many disasters. But as this redemption was only to be published in the name and auspices of Christ, it is written as of one person, and, so to speak, takes on the Person of Christ, the more effectively to strengthen the minds of the faithful unto sound confidence. And really, it is certain that what is written here properly applies to Christ alone, for two reasons. First, that only He was endowed with the fulness of the Spirit, to be a witness and ambassador for our reconciliation with God—and so Paul (Eph. 2.17) particularly assigns to Him what is common to ministers of the Gospel, namely His coming to proclaim peace, to them who were near and far. And second, that He alone, by the power of His Spirit, effects and provides the benefits promised here.

Luke 4.18. *The Spirit of the Lord is upon me.* This is said, that we may know that Christ both in Himself and in His ministers is not conducting a human or private affair, but is sent to restore the Church's salvation at a prompting of God, for He testifies that He does nothing by human instinct or design, but works all things by the direction of the Spirit of God, that the faith of the godly may be established on the authority and might of God. The following phrase, *Because he anointed me*, is added to fill out the sense: many falsely boast of having the Spirit of God, and all the time have none of His gifts at all. Christ, thinking of its effect, proves that He has the gift of the Spirit of God by anointing. Then he states the purpose for which He was awarded the graces of the Spirit, namely, to give good news to the poor. We may understand that those who are sent out by God to preach the Gospel are equipped with the necessary endowment first, as may suffice for the greatness of the task. So they make themselves quite ridiculous, who pretend to a divine calling and usurp the place of pastors, being more than useless for fulfilling the task—I mean those mitred bishops under the Papacy, who have less training than donkeys, but rudely shout about being vicars of Christ, the only rightful prelates of the Church. ... The Lord is expressly said to anoint His servants, as the true and effective preaching of the Gospel lies not in windy eloquence, but in the heaven-sent power of the Spirit, as Paul says (I Cor. 2,1 and 4).

Poor. The Prophet means the state of the Church as it will be before the rising of the Gospel, and the condition of us all apart from Christ. Thus he calls them poor, and contrite, and captive, and blind, and broken, to whom God promises renewal. Though the body of the people was oppressed by so many miseries, that these headings fitted each member, yet since many, for all their lack of means, their blindness, slavery, and death, indeed were in a blind state of folly, there were few who were in a right mind to receive this grace. The first lesson we learn is the perspective of the preaching of the Gospel, and what it brings to us: when we are altogether overwhelmed with every manner of evil, then God bursts upon us with His life-giving rays, to lead us out of the bottomless pit of death, and restore us to the fulness of bliss. Indeed this is no mean commendation of the Gospel, that we gather such a rare harvest from it. Secondly, we see who they are, whom Christ invites to Himself, and makes partakers of the grace entrusted to Him: those who are in all ways to be pitied, and destitute of all hope. At the same time we are warned, that the only way we may enjoy these benefits of Christ, is to be humbled by a serious realisation of our ills, and to seek for Him as hungry men seek their liberator. Those that are full of pride, and do not groan in their bondage, find no discomfort in their blindness, despite this oracle with deaf ears.

Luke 4.19. *To proclaim the acceptable year of the Lord.* Many have seen

148

his as a reference to the Jubilee, and I do not reject the idea. But it is worth noting that the Prophet is carefully anticipating the doubts that might disturb and shake weak minds, from the Lord putting off the promised salvation so long, and keeping them in suspense. Thus he fixes the time of redemption in God's purpose and good pleasure, as at Isaiah 49.8, 'In an acceptable time have I answered thee, and in a day of salvation have I helped thee. Paul (Gal. 4.4) speaks of the fulness of time, to teach the faithful not to follow curious research beyond the proper limit, but to abide by God's pleasure. And this one thing should be enough for them, that Christ was revealed for salvation, at the time when thus it seemed right *to God*.

Luke 4.20. *The eyes of all in the synagogue.* I have no doubt that God touched their hearts, that wonder might increase their attention, and thus they would give a hearing to Christ as He spoke. They had to be checked, or they would have shouted out at once, or at least interrupted the course of His sermon, since they were usually more ready to insult Christ, as we shall go on to see.

Luke 4.21. *Today hath this scripture been fulfilled.* Christ did not only use these three verses, but showed by actual fact that the time had come when God willed to restore His ruined Church, in order that His exposition of the Prophecy might bring more light and agreement among His hearers. This is the due and regular way of interpreters to handle Scripture, by applying it to the present occasion. He says it is fulfilled in their ears, rather than in their eyes, because the sight alone was of little value if the teaching did not have priority.

Luke 4.22. *And all bare him witness.* In first place, Luke here commends to us the truly God-given grace that breathed on the lips of Christ, and then he depicts to the life the ingratitude of men. *Words of grace* is a Hebrew expression he uses for those that had the evident power and favour of the Holy Spirit. Thus the folk of Nazareth were compelled to acknowledge, with wonder, God speaking in Christ, but at the same time, they stop themselves from giving Christ's heavenly teaching its own and its due honour. When they object that He is Joseph's son, they do not use the circumstance as they should, to enlarge on the glory of God, but maliciously use it to bring scandal onto the scene, to let them reject on plausible grounds anything spoken by Joseph's son. Today we may see many, however much convinced that what they hear is the Word of God, who still look for frivolous excuses to relieve themselves of the compulsion to obey it. Certainly, that we are not always affected by the power of the Gospel as properly we should be, results directly from the fact that we get in our own way, and by our own ill-will choke the light that leads us the way we would go.

149

And he said unto them, Doubtless ye will say unto me this parable,
Physician, heal thyself: whatsoever we have heard done at Capernaum,
do also here in thine own country. And he said, Verily I say unto you,
No prophet is acceptable in his own country. But of a truth I say unto
you There were many widows in Israel in the days of Elijah, when the
heavens were shut up three years and six months, when there came a great
famine over all the land; and unto none of them was Elijah sent, but only
to Zarephath, in the land of Sidon, unto a woman that was a widow.
And there were many lepers in Israel in the time of Elisha the prophet;
and none of them was cleansed, but only Naaman the Syrian. And they
were all filled with wrath in the synagogue, as they heard these things;
and they rose up, and cast him forth out of the city, and led him unto the
brow of the hill whereon their city was built, that they might throw him
down headlong. But he passing through the midst of them went his way.
(Luke 4.23-30)

Luke 4.23. *Physician, heal thyself.* We may readily deduce from the
words of Christ that He had a contemptuous reception from the
people of Nazareth, for He brings into the open the things that were
turning over in their minds, as He knew. He puts the blame on them
for His not working miracles amongst them, and convicts them of ill
will in granting God's Prophet no honour. The objection He anticipates is this—that it was no wonder that His fellow-countrymen had
little time for Him, if He did not grace His own place with miracles
as He did others, and so it was fair punishment if He was rejected by
His own folk, when He preferred everyone else to them. This is the
point of the common proverb, that the doctor should begin with himself, and his own circle, before demonstrating his skill in treatment upon
others. The gist of the objection is that Christ went the wrong way
about things, in blessing the other towns of Galilee with miracles, and
giving no regard to His own country. This seemed to the people of
Nazareth a fair excuse for them to reject Him in turn.

Luke 4.24. *Verily I say unto you.* He lays the burden of fault upon
them, that He did not exert the power He had in miracles with them, as
He had elsewhere: Men's incredulity blocks God's access, and prevent
Him working as He would wish for men's salvation (Matt. 13.58
Mk. 6.5). Therefore Christ could not show any sign amongst them
for they did not believe in Him. Not that it lies in men's choosing to
tie the hands of God, but that He takes away the fruit of His works from
those who make themselves unworthy by their lack of faith. Christ
response has the effect of saying, If you wish to be partakers in miracle
why do you not give God opportunity? Why do you proudly rebu
the minister of His power? Thus you have the right reward of you

contempt, that I pass you by and show to others with miracles that I am God's Messiah, entrusted with the work of the Church's renewal. Such ingratitude was indeed intolerable, that after God had decided to have His Son brought up in their city, they should spurn such a pupil. So He was right to draw back His hand from there, and not be laughed at by such godless scorners. We also learn the value which the Lord puts on His Word; when it is scorned, He orders a penalty to be paid, and this is the removal of the favours that testify to His presence. As for the saying that A prophet does not have honour in his own country, readers should refer to my commentary on John, the fourth chapter, towards the end.

Luke 4.25. *There were many widows.* After Christ had put the blame on them, for their being deprived of miracles, He now shows by two examples that it should not seem strange if God preferred foreigners to His own household, and He should not be complained against for complying with the calling of God, as Elijah and Elisha had in former days. It is an indirect criticism of their vain confidence, that they should find fault with Him, for having been brought up with them. He says that at the time the famine lasted for two and a half years, there were many widows in the land of Israel whose lack of food the Prophet Elijah was not ordered to help, but rather he was sent to a foreign woman in the territory of Sidon (I Kings 17.9). In a similar way, Elisha cured none of the lepers among his own folk, but Naaman, a man of Syria (II Kings 5.10). His words are particularly wounding to the people of Nazareth, but it is the ingratitude of the whole race that He attacks, that they had mostly become quite accustomed to treating their Lord with scorn, the nearer He came to them. How was it that God put a foreign woman above all in Israel? It was because His Prophet was thrown out by them, and forced to seek hospitality in pagan country. Why did God wish Naaman the Syrian to be healed by Elisha, but as a reproach to the people of Israel? Thus it means that the same as happened before, occurs again—God sends His power far afield to light on outsiders, for it is refused by the people of His household. Christ also means that it is no detraction from His glory, to be treated badly by His fellow-countrymen, for only by their disgrace and shame could God honour and extol His Son, as in former times He honoured His Prophets in the sight of all nations. The foolish boasting of the flesh is thus thrown back upon itself. We see how the Lord sends rain, not only where and when He will, but even on the furthest lands, passing over the land He had chosen as His resting-place. There is a general lesson to be drawn from this, that it is not for us to prescribe any rule to God for the dispensation of His benefits, for He may give recognition to the basest and most despised, at His choosing, and reject the first in line; nor may we complain, however much He alter the priority that appeals to our judgment. Granted we must keep the contrast between Israel and the pagan nations, but we must agree that none is preferred to another on account of its own worth, but all comes rather from the wonderful design of God, to whose height we must lift our eyes in adoration, though we are not able to see His reasons.

Luke 4.28. *They were all filled with wrath.* They saw the way these two examples which Christ adduced was leading, namely that God's favour was to be transferred elsewhere, and so they took it as an insult on themselves. Though their conscience should have been touched to the quick, to bring them to correct their faults and mend their ways, all they do is to turn furious. Thus the godless both reject God's judgments with contumacy, and rise against His servants with ferocity. Clearly the reproofs that have the force and backing of the Spirit of God have great power, for they drive the minds to madness which would gladly escape them. When we see that there is such a poison in men's minds that they go mad at God as soon as they are treated sharply, we must look for the Spirit to make us well-controlled, or a similar frenzy will speedily bring us to the same fatal conflict. When Luke says that Jesus went through the midst of the crowd, and thus slipped out of their hands, he means that He was snatched from imminent death by divine power, and by great miracle. The case shows us that however much our adversaries prevail, and our life appears to be at the mercy of their whim, yet the power of God will always succeed in saving us, as long as He wills to keep us in the world, or to tie their hands, or to strike their eyes with blindness, or to stupefy their minds and hearts.

And leaving Nazareth, he came and dwelt in Capernaum, which is by the sea, in the borders of Zebulun and Naphtali: that it might be fulfilled which was spoken by Isaiah the prophet, saying,
   The land of Zebulun and the land of Naphtali,
   Toward the sea, beyond Jordan,
   Galilee of the Gentiles,
   The people which sat in darkness
   Saw a great light,
   And to them which sat in the region and shadow of death,
   To them did light spring up. (Matt. 4.13-16)

Luke 4.13. *And leaving Nazareth.* It seemed right to adjoin this passage from Matthew onto Luke's narrative, as we may gather from the context that, while up to this time Christ had been used to go about in the town of Nazareth, He had now quite said Farewell to it, avoiding its threats, and had gone over to Capernaum and the neighbouring towns. This account has no difficulty, except that Matthew seems to have misused the Prophet's testimony by altering its sense. But if we grasp the true intention of the Prophet, it will appear readily and aptly suited to the present occasion. For Isaiah, after he has spoken of a most terrible disaster falling on the people, in order to console their grief, promises that when the people have been brought to their lowest point, a deliverance will at once ensue, dispelling the darkness and restoring the light of life. The words read, 'But there shall be no gloom to her that was in anguish in the former time, when he lightly afflicted the land of Zebulun and Naphtali: nor in the latter time, when they were more grievously afflicted by the way of the sea beyond Jordan in Galilee of the Nations. For the people that walked in darkness shall see a great light' (Isa. 9.1). The Israelites had now been oppressed by a double catastrophe: first, when four tribes, or thereabout, were led into exile by Tiglath-Pilesar and second, when Salmanassar cut off the whole kingdom of Israel (II Kings 15.29 and 18.9). The third disaster was yet to fall, which the Prophet, towards the end of his eighth chapter, said would be the cruelest of all. Now in the words that we have quoted, there follows a mitigation: because God stretches out His hand to His people, death will actually be more bearable, than the diseases that preceeded it. He says that even if all the people are to be destroyed, the bright rays of His light will make the darkness less at this final ruin, than it was at the fall of the ten tribes. I have no doubt that the promise should be extended to the whole people, which might well appear as much a case of ruin and despair. It is absurd for the Jews to confine it to the liberation of the city of Jerusalem, as if the life-giving light were restored to it, on the occasion when Sennacherib was put to flight and the siege lifted. From the context it is obvious, that the Prophet took a longer view. As it is the general restoration of the whole Church that he promises, it follows that the land of Zebulun, and the land of Naphtali, and Galilee of the Nations, are included in the number of those for whom the shades of death were to be turned into the light of life. The beginning of this light, its dawning as it were, came at the return of the people from Babylon. At length the fulness of its splendour emerged with Christ the Sun of righteousness, Who by His coming utterly scattered the shadows of death. So Paul (Eph. 5.14), says that there was fulfilled in Him what we read often in the Prophets, 'Sleeper awake, and rise from the dead'. As we know that Christ's Kingdom is spiritual, it must be that the light of salvation which He brings, and whatever aid we have from

Him must correspond to this nature. It follows that our souls must be plunged into the gloom of eternal death, until His grace enlightens them. Certainly the Prophet's words were related to the fall of the nation, but it is a portrayal of the state of the human race, previous to its deliverance by the grace of Christ. When they are said to have seen a great light, who before lay in darkness, it is the sudden and dazzling contrast that enhances the greatness of the divine salvation. Lower Galilee was called Galilee of the Nations, not only because of the vicinity of Tyre and Sidon, but because there Gentiles were mixed with Jews, especially from the time that David ceded some cities to King Hiram.

And walking by the sea of Galilee, he saw two brethren, Simon who is called Peter, and Andrew his brother, casting a net into the sea; for they were fishers. And he saith unto them, Come ye after me, and I will make you fishers of men. And they straightway left the nets, and followed him. And going on from thence he saw other two brethren, James the son of Zebedee, and John his brother, in the boat with Zebedee their father, mending their nets; and he called them. And they straightway left the boat and their father, and followed him.

And Jesus went about in all Galilee, teaching in their synagogues, and preaching the gospel of the kingdom, and healing all manner of disease and all manner of sickness among the people. And the report of him went forth into all Syria: and they brought unto him all that were sick, holden with divers diseases and torments, possessed with devils, and epileptic, and palsied; and he healed them. And there followed him great multitudes from Galilee and Decapolis and Jerusalem and Judaea and from beyond Jordan. (Matt. 4.18–25)

And passing along by the sea of Galilee, he saw Simon and Andrew the brother of Simon casting a net in the sea: for they were fishers. And Jesus said unto them Come ye after me and I will make you to become fishers of men. And straightway they left the nets, and followed him. And going on a little further, he saw James the son of Zebedee, and John his brother, who also were in the boat mending the nets. And straightway he called them: and they left their father Zebedee in the boat with the hired servants, and went after him. (Mark 1.16–20)

Now it came to pass, while the multitude pressed upon him and heard the word of God, that he was standing by the lake of Gennesaret; and he saw two boats standing by the lake: but the fishermen had gone out of them, and were washing their nets. And he entered into one of the boats, which was Simon's, and asked him to put out a little from the land. And he sat down and taught the multitudes out of the boat. And when he had left speaking, he said unto Simon, Put out into the deep, and let down your nets for a draught. And Simon answered and said, Master, we toiled all night, and took nothing: but at thy word I will let down the nets. And when they had this done, they inclosed a great multitude of fishes; and their nets were breaking; and they beckoned unto their partners in the other boat, that they should come and help them. And they came and filled both the boats, so that they began to sink. But Simon Peter, when he saw it, fell down at Jesus' knees, saying, depart from me; for I am a sinful man, O Lord. For he was amazed, and all that were with him, at the draught of the fishes which they had taken; and so were also James and John, sons of Zebedee, which were partners with Simon. And Jesus said unto Simon, Fear not, from henceforth thou shalt catch men. And when they had brought their boats to land, they left all, and followed him. (Luke 5.1-11)

Matt. 4.18. *And walking by the sea, etc.* Because this account appears in Luke after the two miracles that we shall shortly be dealing with, an opinion has grown generally that the miracle narrated by him was performed some time after they were called by Christ. But the logic they follow has in fact little weight, for the Evangelists did not definitely set down a fixed and distinct time sequence in their records. They neglected the order of days, and were content to put together the chief events in Christ's career as they saw them. They certainly took note of the years, to let the readers understand clearly how Christ pursued a three-year course, from the start of His preaching up to His death. But they freely confuse the miracles which occurred at much the same period, and this we shall see clearly from a number of cases. There are many indications that the same story is here given by all three: out of them all, this one should satisfy any non-contentious reader, that the three come to the one conclusion, in saying that Peter and Andrew, James and John, had been created Apostles. If they had been called earlier, it would follow that they had deserted and left their master, scorned their calling, and returned to their former mode of life. The only difference between Luke and the rest is the miracle, which they leave out and he alone records. But this, too, is not unusual for the Evangelists, to put down one part of an affair, and leave out many of the circumstances. There is nothing strange in saying that a miracle was omitted by two, and related by one. We must remember what John says, that from the innumerable miracles of Christ some part is chosen, to prove His divine power, and to serve to confirm our faith in Him. No wonder then, if Matthew and Mark touch rather sparingly

155

on the calling of the four Apostles, while Luke gives the occasion fuller treatment.

Luke 5.1. *He was standing by the lake.* Matthew and Mark speak of the sea of Galilee in the traditional way of their language. In Hebrew the name of the lake was really and originally כנרת (*Chinnereth*). With the corruption of the language, it declined into Gennesaret. Pagan writers speak of Genesar and the part that abutted on Galilee, they termed the sea of Galilee. The shore close to Tiberias took its name from that city. Of its size and setting there will be an opportunity to tell later, but now let us get down to the incident. Luke says, that Christ got into Peter's boat and went out a little distance from the land, in order to teach the crowds more conveniently from it, since they had poured together from various districts, in the desire to hear Him; and that when He had done His work of teaching, He displayed an instance of His divine power, in doing a miracle. Though it was common enough for fishermen to make many fruitless hauls, and then in one lucky catch to make up for all the wasted efforts, yet the miraculous element comes clearly to our eyes, in that they had caught nothing all night long (yet it is better suited to catches), and suddenly a vast heap of fish piled into their nets, filling their boats. Peter and his companions easily recognize that such an abnormal catch had not happened upon them by chance, but was a gift of God.

Luke 5.5. *Master, we toiled all night, etc.* No doubt Peter knew that Christ was used to fulfil the role of Teacher, and also was touched with a sense of awe, when he gave Him this title. He had not yet gone so far as to be numbered as a disciple. It is not enough to speak of Christ with respect, for we must also embrace what He teaches with the obedience of faith, and hold on to His will for us. Still, though he had none, or little, acquaintance of the Gospel, he shows how much he will do for Christ when, weary with toil, he starts again on a task which he had attempted to no effect. That Christ meant a great deal to him, and that His authority counted exceedingly, cannot be denied. But a particular response in faith to one order of Christ, and that over a private and earthly affair, would never have made a Christian out of Peter, or given him a place among the children of God, unless from this first service he had been led to full obedience in the long run. At the same time, when Peter was so quick to obey Christ's order, before he knew Him as Prophet or Son of God, then there is no excuse for our shame, who preach Him as our Lord and King and Judge, if we are commanded by Him ten times to do our tasks, but never move a finger.

Luke 5.6. *They inclosed a great multitude of fishes.* The particular object of the miracle was that, with Christ recognized in His divinity, Peter and others should attach themselves to Him as disciples. But the general lesson of this case is that we should not be afraid that God's blessing, and the desired success, will not match our labour, whenever we set our hands to a job at the bidding, and on the authority, of Christ. Now there was such a supply of fish that the ships were sinking, and the minds of all who watched were lifted to astonishment. Christ's divine glory had to be revealed in this miracle for His sure authority to be established for Him.

Luke 5.8. *Depart from me ... O Lord.* Though men may seek God's presence with unending prayers, yet they are bound to be struck with fear as soon as He appears, indeed made faint for terror and fright, until He gives relief. There is excellent reason for them to seek God so urgently, for they are bound to feel their condition without His presence as unhappy. Yet His presence is so terrifying, that they immediately begin to feel less than nothing, and with what a pile of evils they are overcome. For these reasons, Peter so reveres Christ at the miracle that he tries as best he can to escape Him, for fear of His Majesty. Nor is this Peter's feeling alone, as we may gather from the context, but fear caught them all up together. So we see this is an emotion inborn in all, to be alarmed at the presence of God. And it is of use to us, to humble any foolish confidence or pride, as long as comfort is quickly given, to lift us up again. So Christ puts fresh heart into Peter with a gentle and friendly answer, telling him not to be afraid of Him. The Lord brings His people down into the grave, that He may then give them life.

Luke 5.10. *From henceforth thou shalt catch men.* Matthew reads at this point, *I will make you fishers of men,* and Mark, *I will make you to become fishers.* The words inform us that Peter, and the other three, were not only brought in as disciples by Christ, but were made Apostles, or at least chosen in hopes of Apostleship. This is not merely a general description of the call to faith, but a particular one for a certain task. I agree that they are not yet given the role of teaching, but Christ brings them in and co-opts them to His inner circle, to prepare them for teaching. We must carefully consider the point, for it is not laid upon all that they leave their parents, and go after Christ on foot, in a primitive fashion of living. Others God is content to have in His flock and Church, and others He assigns to a particular station, but those who are appointed to a public role must realize that more is required of them than of the ordinary individual. Thus Christ makes no change in the everyday life of the others, but takes these four disciples away from the craft they had lived on to this time, in order to use their effort for a higher calling. Yes, Christ takes complete fools, both uneducated and ignorant of doctrine as subjects for His fine training, for renewal by the grace of His Spirit, that they may excel all the wise men of the world.

This was how he wished to put down the pride of the flesh, of course, and to make in the person of these men an outstanding example of spiritual grace, that we might learn to seek the light of faith from heaven, knowing that we cannot acquire it by our own industry.

Now, since He does not choose the unschooled and rough ones so as to leave them that way for ever, we should not force what He then did as an example, as though today also, Pastors were to be ordained and should thereafter be given the training to do their duties. For we know the rule He gives us from the lips of Paul (I Tim. 3.2), that only those who are apt to teach should be chosen. Nor in choosing such men does He prefer ignorance to learning, just as some crazy fellows applaud themselves for their ignorance, and reckon they are closer to the Apostles for being further from their books. At the start, He wished to choose men of no account, in order to bring down the lofty looks of those who thought heaven was closed to the uneducated classes—but later He makes Paul the colleague of the fishermen, a man who had been diligently schooled from childhood. Though there is no point in a very subtle discussion of the logic behind the metaphor, being taken from the occasion to hand, yet Christ's allusion to fishing is apt, in dealing with the preaching of the Gospel, for men drift and float about the world, as in a vast and troubled sea, and they are brought in by the Gospel. Now the story that is given in the first chapter of John is different from this. Andrew had been one of John's disciples, and when he was handed over to Christ by him, he brought his brother with him: for the time, they received Him as a teacher, but later they were admitted to a higher rank.

Matt. 4.22. *And they straightway, etc.* First, we see the forceful effect of Christ's voice, not only that His voice reaches effectively into men's hearts, but that the Lord inwardly compels men by His Spirit, when He wishes to draw and seize them for himself, to obey His voice. Secondly, there is praise for the meekness and readiness to obey which the disciples show, when they put Christ's calling before all their worldly business. We should particularly bring this instance before ministers of the Word, that they should neglect all their other concerns, and attach themselves, devote themselves, wholly to the Church to which they are appointed.

Matt. 4.23. *And Jesus went about in all Galilee.* The same things are related again in another place by Matthew, but there is nothing odd in a general reference being made twice or three times over to miracles, as Christ for some time did not cease to perform a countless number on all sides. The first thing to note in Matthew's words is that Christ took no rest in scattering the seed of the Gospel everywhere. Now Matthew speaks of the Gospel of the Kingdom, as by it the Kingdom of God was established among men for their salvation. Thus he distinguishes firm and eternal blessedness from the happy and prosperous things of this present life. When Matthew says that Christ healed all disease, you must understand sickness of every kind. For it is certain that not all were freed from their illnesses, but that there was no sort of disease which, offered to Him, He would not cure. He lists the chief types of sickness upon which Christ exerted His power. By *those possessed with devils* Scriptures does not indicate all who are harassed by the devil without distinction, but who by God's hidden reproof are enslaved to Satan, for him to possess their minds and senses. *Lunatici* (R.V. 'epileptics') is the term given to those in whom the force of the disease increases or declines according to the phases of the moon, for instance, those who suffer from epilepsy, and the like. Since we know that diseases of that sort are not curable by the means of nature, it follows that Christ's Godhead was given testimony when by miracles He healed them.

And they go into Capernaum; and straightway on the sabbath day he entered into the synagogue and taught. And they were astonished at his teaching: for he taught them as having authority, and not as the scribes. And straightway there was in their synagogue a man with an unclean spirit; and he cried out, saying, What have we to do with thee, thou Jesus of Nazareth? art thou come to destroy us? I know thee who thou art, the Holy One of God. And Jesus rebuked him, saying, Hold thy peace, and come out of him. And the unclean spirit, tearing him and crying with a loud voice, came out of him. And they were all amazed, insomuch that they questioned among themselves, saying, What is this? a new teaching! with authority he commandeth even the unclean spirits, and they obey him. And the report of him went out straightway everywhere into all the region of Galilee round about. (Mark 1.21-28)

And he came down to Capernaum, a city of Galilee. And he was teaching them on the sabbath day: and they were astonished at his teaching; for his word was with authority. And in the synagogue there was a man, which had a spirit of an unclean devil; and he cried out with a loud voice, Ah! what have we to do with thee, thou Jesus of Nazareth? art thou come to destroy us? I know thee who thou art, the Holy One of God. And Jesus rebuked him, saying, Hold thy peace, and come out of him. And when the devil had thrown him down in the midst, he came out of him, having done him no hurt. And amazement came upon all, and they spake together, one with another, saying, What is this word? for with authority and power he commandeth the unclean spirits, and they come out. (Luke 4.31-36).

It is likely that this demoniac was one of the crowd which Matthew remarked upon a little earlier. But the narrative of Mark and Luke is not superfluous, in relating the same circumstances, for they not only shed more light on the miracle, but also contain useful doctrine. The demon is clever to confess that Christ is the *Holy One of God*, so that men might be tempted to suspect that he had some necessary connection with Christ. This is the artfulness he has continually employed to make the Gospel suspect, and still attempts the same today. This is the reason why Christ checks him. It may perhaps be that this confession was forced from him with violence, but the two points are not contradictory, that he should be forced to yield by the power of Christ, and shout out that He is the Holy One of God, and yet craftily attempt to involve Christ's glory in his own dark realm. Yet we must note that he so flatters Christ as indirectly to withdraw himself from His hands, and thus he is at odds with himself. For to what purpose was Christ sanctified by the Father, if not to free men from the devil's tyranny and overthrow his kingdom? But as Satan cannot tolerate the power which he knows is fatal to himself, he wishes Christ would accept the mere title and lie down quietly.

Mark 1.22. *And they were astonished at his teaching.* The Evangelists mean that the power of the Spirit shone out in Christ to compel even the profane and unfeeling hearers to admiration. Luke says that His word was *with authority*, that is full of dignity. Mark goes more fully giving by contrast that it was *not as the scribes*. Seeing these were false interpreters of Scripture, their teaching was of the letter, and dead, breathing no virtue of the Spirit, with no grounding of majesty. We may sense this chill atmosphere in the speculative theology of the Papacy today. These teachers thunder out their chosen words in imperious tones enough, but when they gabble in common speech on divine things and show no sense of religion in their arguments, all they produce is rotten and useless: Paul was not far off the mark in saying (I Cor. 4.20), The kingdom of God is not in word, but in power. In short, the Evangelists mean that as at that time the mode of teaching was so degraded and utterly corrupt, that no respect for God could touch men's minds, the divine power of the Spirit was so evident in Christ's speech that it won faith for Him. This is the power, or dignity rather, and authority, at which the people gaped.

Luke 4.33. *A man, which had the spirit of an unclean devil.* This expression has the same effect as if Luke had said, he was stirred up by the influence of the devil. By God's permission, Satan had laid hold on

160

the faculties of his soul, to force him at his fancy both to speech and to movements of other kinds. So they are called demoniac in whom and through whom demons speak, as they are given licence to win control. The praise of the *Holy One of God* is probably taken from a manner of speaking, then common and accepted. It was a title given Messiah, as one who should be separated from all others, one endowed with singular grace, and Head of the whole Church.

Mark 1.26. *Tearing him.* Luke uses the gentler word (*thrown him down*), but agrees completely over the sense, as each intended to convey that the coming out of the demon was violent. He threw the poor man down on the ground as if he wished to tear him apart, yet Luke says he tried in vain, not that the force of his attack was without damage altogether, or at least without some painful sensation, but because afterwards the man was of one piece, freed from the devil.

Luke 4.36. *Amazement came.* The fruit of the miracle was that men were drawn to suspect something more than human of Christ. And they are sensible to relate the glory and power of the miracle to His teaching. What is this word, they say, which even the devils themselves are forced to obey? They call it *new teaching* (Mark 1.27) not in reproach, but as recognizing in it something unusual and extraordinary. They do not accuse it of novelty to weaken men's adherence to it, but it is rather part of their amazement, the opposite of the ordinary and the merely human. Their only sin is to stop in doubt, when Sons of God should go on to further advance.

And when Jesus was come into Peter's house, he saw his wife's mother, lying sick of a fever. And he touched her hand, and the fever left her, and she arose, and ministered unto him. And when even was come they brought unto him many possessed with devils: and he cast out the spirits with a word, and healed all that were sick: that it might be fulfilled which was spoken by Isaiah the prophet, saying, Himself took our infirmities, and bare our diseases.

Now when Jesus saw great multitudes about him, he gave commandment to depart unto the other side. (Matt. 8.14-18)

And straightway, when they were come out of the synagogue, they came into the house of Simon and Andrew, with James and John. Now Simon's wife's mother lay sick of a fever; and straightway they tell him of her: and he came and took her by the hand, and raised her up; and the fever left her, and she ministered unto them.

And at even, when the sun did set, they brought unto him all that were *sick and them that were possessed with devils. And all the city was gathered together at the door. And he healed many that were sick with divers diseases, and cast out many devils; and he suffered not the devils to speak, because they knew him.*

And in the morning, a great while before day, he rose up and went out, and departed into a desert place, and there prayed. And Simon and they that were with him followed after him; and they found him, and say unto him, All are seeking thee. And he saith unto them, Let us go elsewhere into the next towns, that I may preach there also; for to this end came I forth. And he went into their synagogues throughout all Galilee, preaching and casting out devils. (Mark 1.29-39)

And he rose from the synagogue, and entered into the house of Simon. And Simon's wife's mother was holden with a great fever; and they besought him for her. And he stood over her, and rebuked the fever; and it left her; and immediately she rose up and ministered unto them.

And when the sun was setting, all they that had any sick with divers diseases brought them unto him; and he laid his hands on every one of them, and healed them. And devils also came out from many, crying out, and saying, Thou art the Son of God. And rebuking them, he suffered them not to speak, because they knew that he was the Christ.

And when it was day, he came out and went into a desert place: and the multitudes sought after him, and came unto him, and would have stayed him, that he should not go from them. But he said unto them, I must preach the good tidings of the kingdom of God to the other cities also: for therefore was I sent.

And he was preaching in the synagogues of Galilee. (Luke 4.38-44)

Mark 1.29. *They came into the house of Simon.* We may deduce that Matthew has misplaced this story, from the fact that Mark explicitly names only four disciples as going with Jesus. Further, that they came straight out of the synagogue and went to Peter's home, shows that Matthew did not keep exactly to the time sequence. Now the Evangelists seem to have narrated this miracle with some emphasis, not for being in itself any more distinguished than the others, or more deserving to be remembered, but because in it Christ gave a homely and closer example of His grace to His disciples. Moreover, the healing of one woman gave Him the opportunity for many miracles, in that they came to Him from all sides for the sake of asking help. Luke accentuates the power that Christ displayed by one word—that it was a great fever that afflicted Peter's mother-in-law. It was a more sure and notable proof of divine power to remove a grievous and severe disease in a moment, and at a single touch. Though He could have done it

162

with a nod alone, He yet took her hand—either to give a sign of His feeling, or because He knew that the gesture would at the time have value. We know that by the standards of those days, there was a generous use of symbolic gesture.

Luke 4.39. *Rebuked the fever.* To a reader insufficiently acquainted with Scripture this might appear a severe form of expression, but it is not without reason. For fever and other diseases, famine, pestilence and every kind of hardship, are the forward troops of God, through which He works His judgments. By His decree and will we understand that He sends these messengers ahead, and then He restrains and calls them in, when He thinks right. How He healed the others, Matthew and Mark do not say, but Luke says, *he laid his hands on . . . them.* Under the Law this was a sign of reconciliation. Thus Christ is not hasty, but true to the case, to lay his Hands on those whom He absolves from the curse of God. It was also the solemn ritual of consecration, which we shall speak of more fully in another place. My interpretation simply is that Christ laid His hands on the sick to commend them to the Father, and to win them grace and deliverance from their diseases.

Matt. 8.17. *Which was spoken by Isaiah the prophet.* This oracle seems awkwardly cited, if not twisted into another meaning, for Isaiah spoke there not of miracles, but of Christ's death, not of temporal benefits, but of spiritual and eternal grace. Certainly he spoke of the failings of the soul, and Matthew has transferred this to bodily diseases. The solution is not difficult, if readers will only consider that the exposition is not only of what Christ gave to the sick, but the purpose of His healing their diseases. They in their bodies felt the grace of Christ, but we must look to the end in view, for it would be preposterous to tie ourselves to a fading benefit, as though the Son of God were a physician of the body. What do we say, then? He gave light to the blind in order to show Himself to them as the light of the world. He gave life back to the dead, that He might prove Himself to be the resurrection and the life; similarly with the lame and the paralysed. This is the analogy we must follow: whatever benefits Christ bestows on men in their flesh, we must relate to the aim which Matthew sets before us, that He was sent by the Father to relieve us from all our ills and woes.

Mark 1.34. *He suffered not the devils to speak.* There could be two reasons for not allowing them: one in general, that the full time of His complete revelation had not yet arrived; the other particular, as we have just mentioned, that He would not have them as the heralds and witnesses of His divinity, for by their praises they could only bring discredit and unwelcome reports on Him. This latter is beyond doubt, that there had to be testimony to the warlike divide that lay between the Author of eternal salvation and life, and the prince of death and his minions.

Matt. 8.18. *Now when Jesus saw great multitudes, etc.* I have no doubt that Matthew is giving a brief account of what the others deal with more fully and broadly. Matthew does not say, as the other two do, that it was for the sake of finding seclusion that Christ went away secretly to a solitary place, before the dawn. Mark says later that He was told by Peter that everyone was looking for Him. Luke says that the crowds came even out there to find Him. Where Matthew says that He crossed to the other shore, they both say that He traversed all Galilee to preach in every place. The other shore, in my opinion, is not that directly lying against them, but across the bay, which lay below Capernaum. Thus He crossed a part of the lake, but did not leave Galilee. We must notice what He says, that it was for that cause that He had come forth on His mission, for these words testify that He was so intent on fulfilling His task. Now if anyone should ask whether it is good enough for ministers of the Gospel to travel up and down, and only give portions of God's message in one place and another, in small measure and thin, or whether they should stick to the firm instruction of the hearers they have once acquired, I would answer that Christ's decision, being agreeable to the command and calling of the Father, was founded on the best reasons. Christ had to go through Judaea in a short time, to awaken men's minds on all sides to hear the Gospel, as with a trumpet call: and on this matter there will be more to write later.

And he goeth up into the mountain, and calleth unto him whom he himself would: and they went unto him. And he appointed twelve, that they might be with him, and that he might send them forth to preach, and to have authority to cast out devils: and Simon he surnamed Peter; and James the son of Zebedee, and John the brother of James; and them he surnamed Boanerges, which is, Sons of thunder: and Andrew, and Philip, and Bartholomew, and Matthew, and Thomas, and James the son of Alphaeus, and Thaddaeus, and Simon the Cananaean, and Judas Iscariot, which also betrayed him. (Mark 3.13-19)

And it came to pass in these days, that he went out into the mountain to pray; and he continued all night in prayer to God. And when it was day, he called his disciples: and he chose from them twelve, whom also he named apostles; Simon whom he also named Peter, and Andrew his

*brother, and James and John, and Philip and Bartholemew, and Matthew
and Thomas, and James the son of Alphaeus, and Simon which was
called the Zealot, and Judas the son of James, and Judas Iscariot, which
was the traitor; and he came down with them, and stood on a level place,
and a great multitude of his disciples, and a great number of the people
from all Judaea and Jerusalem, and the sea coast of Tyre and Sidon,
which came to hear him, and to be healed of their diseases; and they that
were troubled with unclean spirits were healed. And all the multitude
sought to touch him: for the power came forth from him, and he healed
them all.* (Luke 6.12-19)

Mark 3.13. *And he goeth up into the mountain.* In choosing men, He
does not yet ordain them as Apostles, to perform their task at once, but
takes disciples into His company in the hope of Apostleship to come.
Therefore interpreters are quite misguided to confuse these passages
with Matt. 10. The works clearly suggest that they are only set on the
way to the future mission, which is given them in Matthew. Mark and
Luke in fact relate their sending out in their narrative, as Matthew
records it in his. It is no wonder if the heavenly Teacher wished to
train and accustom them gradually to such an arduous career, for their
inexperience could not be put right, even with a long practice of
discipleship. Both Evangelists say that Christ went up into a mountain.
Luke gives the reason exactly, that He wished more freedom to pray on
His own, which we know from other passages He was often accustomed
to do. This example should be a kind of perpetual rule for us, to begin
with prayer as often as pastors are to be chosen for the Churches,
otherwise whatever we attempt will be inauspicious. Certainly the
Lord did not so much pray for His own sake, as to give us a rule. For
we lack prudence and deliberation, and however clear-sighted we may
be, nothing is easier than to be deceived in this matter. If the Lord
does not control our impulses to keep us clear of the risk of error, what
may not be the effect of favouritism to divert us, of obligation, or of
hatred or self-seeking—indeed, of violent means? Besides, though
everything in the election were done with utmost skill, yet all would
come to no good if the Lord did not take those who were elected into
His direction, and equip them with the necessary gifts. Well then?
Is anyone going to say that Christ's appeal to the Father was not made
in earnest, that He should preside over His choosing? I say, yes indeed,
and I would add that He declared by this testimony how much He was
concerned for His Church. Not in His daily fashion did He pray to the
Father, but all the night He spent in supplication. Now if He, who was
full of the Holy Spirit, besought the Father so warmly and so urgently
to be the overseer of His choice, how much greater is our need?

Calleth unto him whom he himself would. I am sure that Mark means by this expression that they were chosen for their great and honoured task, not on their own worth, but by the sheer grace of Christ. If you reckon that they were chosen as being more outstanding than the rest, this will not square with Judas. So the sense is that the Apostolate was not conferred on men's merits, but those who were raised to this degree by the mercy of God, were the least worthy, and thus was fulfilled what Christ declares in another place, 'You have not chosen me, but I have chosen you (John 15.16). In the same sense, Paul often commends God's purpose in His Apostolate (Eph. 3.7; Col. 1.25).

But several questions arise here. First, why did He with deliberate purpose choose Judas, a man He knew to be unworthy of the honour, one that would be a traitor. Second, why did the Father, after the Son's earnest appeals, permit a disloyal and wicked man to slip into the first rank of His Church, as though He had given Christ a rebuff? Third, why should He have wished the first fruits of His Church to be stained with such foul disgrace? Fourth, how did it come to be that Christ knowingly and willingly preferred Judas to good and faithful servants? The first objection, may be answered by saying that the Lord deliberately willed to anticipate future scandals, that we should not be too much put out when treacherous teachers seize office in the Church, or when men professing the Gospel turn apostate. And He also gave an instance of fearful betrayal in the person of one man, that those who are placed in a higher position of dignity should not become self-satisfied. At the same time, we must not say that Christ suffered a repulse. When the Father with His wonderful providence put one devil in with eleven angels, He yet kept such a grip on the event, that his failure gave the Church more strength than upset. This is the same solution that we must give to the third question. At the very outset, the future condition of the Church was shown early, that weak men should not collapse at the fall of one reprobate, as it is unworthy that the stability of the Church should depend upon men. As regards the last objection, Christ did not prefer Judas to the godly and holy disciples, but in setting him up high, to a point from which he would crash down, He wished him to be a spectacle for all, a proof to all generations, that no-one should abuse a divine honour conferred on himself: finally, even when pillars are falling, some may remain firm who appear to belong to the common company of the faithful.

Luke 6.13. *Whom also he named apostles.* This can be expounded in two ways: either that later, in installing them to their posts, He put the name upon them, or that in hope of their future dignity, He now awarded them this honour, that they should know to what purpose they had been separated from the common number, and to what employment they were appointed. The latter suits Mark's words, for he says that Christ made them, that they might be with Him, and that He might send them forth to preach. So He wished them to join His band, who later would be given a wider province. And when He says, to be with Him, and, that He might send them out to preach, He does not intend both parts to come into effect at the very same moment. as I have just remarked.

Mark 3.16. *Simon he surnamed Peter.* Though all Christians should be living stones of the spiritual temple, Christ gave the name particularly to Simon, according to the measure of grace He intended to fit upon him. It is no obstacle that, in denying His Lord, he was brought to shame for his weakness, for this title is the award given to his unconquered prowess and constancy, which lasted even to the hour of death. The Papists are just ridiculous in deducing from this that the Church was founded upon him, as will be more fully discussed at Matt. 16. Christ called the sons of Zebedee, *Sons of thunder*, since they were to receive a resounding voice to be heard over all the earth. Even today we hear thunder from the lips of John: that the earth was struck also by his brother, as long as he lived, we may have little doubt. However the word is corrupted, for its proper pronunciation should be בְּנֵי־רֶגֶשׁ (*Benai-regesh*), but there is no doubt about it, though there may be a flexible change in words, when they are translated into another tongue.

And seeing the multitudes, he went up into the mountain: and when he had sat down, his disciples came unto him: and he opened his mouth and taught them saying,

Blessed are the poor in spirit: for theirs is the kingdom of heaven.

Blessed are they that mourn: for they shall be comforted.

Blessed are the meek: for they shall inherit the earth.

Blessed are they that hunger and thirst after righteousness: for they shall be filled.

Blessed are the merciful: for they shall obtain mercy.

Blessed are the pure in heart: for they shall seek God.

Blessed are the peacemakers: for they shall be called sons of God.

Blessed are they that have been persecuted for righteousness' sake: for theirs is the kingdom of heaven. Blessed are ye when men shall reproach you, and persecute you, and say all manner of evil against you falsely, for my sake. Rejoice, and be exceeding glad: for great is your reward in heaven: for so persecuted they the prophets which were before you. (Matt. 5.1-12)

And he lifted up his eyes on his disciples, and said, Blessed are ye poor: for yours is the kingdom of God. Blessed are ye that hunger now: for ye shall be filled. Blessed are ye that weep now: for ye shall laugh. Blessed are ye, when men shall hate you, and when they shall separate you from their company, and reproach you, and cast out your name as evil, for the Son of man's sake. Rejoice in that day, and leap for joy: for behold, your reward is great in heaven: for in the same manner did their fathers unto the prophets. But woe unto you that are rich! for ye have received your consolation. Woe unto you, ye that are full now! for ye shall hunger. Woe unto you, ye that laugh now! for ye shall mourn and weep. Woe unto you, when all men shall speak well of you! for in the same manner did their fathers to the false prophets. (Luke 6.20-26)

Matt. 5.1. *He went up into the mountain.* Those who reckon Christ's assembly here to be a different one from that which is treated of in the sixth chapter of Luke, are swayed by an argument that is too weak and trifling—that Matthew tells how Christ spoke to His disciples on a mountain, while Luke appears to indicate that the sermon was given in the plain. It is absurd to put Luke's words into one context, that Christ came down into a level district, and that He lifted up His eyes, and thus spoke to His disciples. Both Evangelists had the intention of gathering into one single passage the chief headings of Christ's teaching, that had regard to the rule of godly and holy living. So though Luke earlier mentioned a level place, he did not pursue the same narrative without a break in time, but passed from miracles to teaching, without indicating time or place, just as in Matthew there is no record of time, but only of place. It is likely that only after the choice of the twelve did Christ hold this assembly. However, I have not wished to be over precise in calculating times, as I have seen them disregarded by the Spirit of God. It should be enough for reverent and humble readers that here, before their eyes, they have set a short summary of the teaching of Christ, gathered from many and various discourses, of which this was the first, where He spoke with His disciples on the true blessedness.

Matt. 5.2. *He opened his mouth.* This pleonasm picks up the underlying Hebrew expression. What in other languages would be a solecism was quite common in Hebrew, namely to say, He opened his mouth, for, He began to speak. Many believe the expression is used for emphasis, when something of weight or note is advanced, for better or worse, but as some passages of Scripture are against this, I really prefer the first explanation. Nor should we stay with their other clever idea, of suggesting that it was in a symbolic fashion that Christ led His disciples up a mountain, to lift up their minds far from the concerns and passions of earth, for it was a real retreat which He sought in climbing the mountain, to ease His weariness for a short time with His disciples away from the crowd.

We must first examine the object of His addressing His disciples on *true blessedness*. We know that it is not only the common crowd, but the philosophers also, who are caught in this error: that the happy man is he who, relieved from all troubles, in possession of all he asks, leads a happy and quiet life. Virtually every man judges happiness by his present state. So Christ, to accustom His men to bear the cross, corrects the common idea that those are the happy ones, who, according to the flesh, have it all good and prosperous. For clearly it is impossible for them to submit mildly to the yoke when there are pains and insults to be borne, if they assume that endurance is not the way of the life of blessedness. There is only one consolation by which the sharpness of the cross and all other evils are mitigated, even made sweet, and that is for us to be assured that we have blessing in the very midst of our miseries, for our endurance is blessed by the Lord, and a happier outcome will soon ensue. I admit that this doctrine is far from the general opinion, but it should be the philosophy of Christ's disciples, that they may set their happiness beyond this world, and above the desire of the flesh. Though the logic of the flesh will never allow what Christ is preaching here, yet it is no pipe-dream that He is propounding, like the paradoxical game which the Stoics used to play, but a real life demonstration of why those are the truly happy whose state is rated most unhappy. So remember, this is the main point of the sermon, that Christ says they are not wretched who suffer from the injuries of the wicked, and are oppressed by various pains. Christ not only contends that those who measure happiness by their present condition are on the wrong lines, because in a short time the woes of the godly are to be changed for the better; He also encourages His own to endurance, setting before them the hope of their reward.

Matt. 5.3. *Blessed are the poor in spirit, etc.* The metaphor in Luke is unadorned, but, as for many, poverty is accursed and to no good, Matthew expresses Christ's mind with more clarity. As many are caught up in troubles, but do not cease their inward passion of pride and temper, Christ pronounces blessed those who are humbled and subdued by their woes, to prostrate themselves at God's feet, and with interior submission to commend themselves to His protection. Others interpret *poor in spirit* as those who claim nothing for themselves, with all confidence in the flesh dispelled, confess their own lack of resource. But as the words of Luke and Matthew must have the same sense, there is no doubt that *poor* describes those who are afflicted and brought low by adversity. The only point is that Matthew, by adding an epithet, restricts blessedness to those who have learned humility in the school of the cross. *For theirs is the kingdom of heaven.* We may see that Christ is not stuffing His people's minds with some windy argument, or hardening them with iron-shod determination, like the Stoics, but encourages them to patience by recalling them to the hope of eternal life, as this is the way by which they will pass over into the Kingdom of Heaven. It is worth noting that no-one is poor in spirit, unless he has cancelled his own account and rested upon the loving kindness of God. Those who are broken by despair and shattered by it, and still cry out against God, must ever be high and mighty in spirit.

Matt. 5.4. *Blessed are they that mourn.* This sentence follows directly on the last, and is a kind of appendage or complement to it. As pains make a man wretched, the usual opinion follows that they always bring him grief and sorrow in their wake: nothing is more the opposite of happiness than mourning. But Christ says, the mournings are not only not wretched, but that the blessed life is aided by grief; that by this means they are trained to see the eternal joy, and by these stimuli induced to seek their abiding comfort in God, and no other. Thus Paul (Rom. 5.3), 'Let us also rejoice in our tribulations, for they work patience, and patience probation, and probation hope: and hope putteth not to shame.'

Matt. 5.5. *Blessed are the meek.* He means the calm and quiet ones, who are not easily provoked by wrongs, who do not sulk over offences, but are more ready to endure anything, than pay the wicked the same back. For Christ to promise the *inheritance of the earth* to such, might seem quite absurd, for the folk who really claim the control of the earth for themselves are those who rebuff injuries with energy, and, if ever they are hurt, are quick to raise a hand in vengeance. Certainly experience shows, that the wicked go on more audaciously and boldly, the more gently they are treated. Hence the devilish proverb, You must howl with the wolves—for whoever makes himself a sheep will soon come to be eaten by wolves. But Christ contrasts His and the Father's protection with the rage and violence of the evil ones, and effectively affirms that the meek will be lords and heirs of the earth. The sons of this generation believe that safety lies only in their sharp resistance to any wrong done them, and defend their lives by force of arms. But as we must be sure that Christ is the only guardian of our lives, then our only course is to hide under the shadow of His wings. Yes, we must be sheep, if we wish to be counted in His flock. If one objects that what is said here contradicts experience, I would have him first consider how the violent are so un-quiet that they are at odds with themselves. In all the tumults of life, though they were a hundred times lords of the earth, in possessing all things they yet possess nothing. On behalf of God's children I reply, that though they never find a place of their own to put their foot, they enjoy their residence on earth in quietness, and their possession is not illusory, for the earth which they inhabit they know to be granted them by God. Thus in the face of the wildness and rage of their enemies, they are covered by the protecting hand of God, and though exposed to all the slings of fortune, vulnerable to the evil-doing of the wicked, surrounded with every danger, they live securely under God's protection, and even now enjoy this grace of God. This is enough for them, until, at the last day, they reach the inheritance of the World.

Matt. 5.6. *Blessed are they that hunger.* *Hunger* and *thirst* I take to be an instance of synecdoche, for the toils of want, the lack of necessities, indeed the loss of one's rights. When Matthew writes *hunger . . . after righteousness* he gives a particular for the general. He heightens the indignity, that all their anxious sighs are straining after nothing but what is right. In other words, Blessed are they who confine their prayers to seek provision only of what is fair—and still languish like starving men. Though their torment of anxiety may bring them derision, yet is it a sure preparation for their blessedness, for they shall be filled at length. At the end God will hear their sighs, will satisfy their just desires, as it is His work to fill the hungry with good things, as we see in the canticle of the Virgin.

Matt. 5.7. *Blessed are the merciful.* Here there is a paradox set against human judgment. The world reckons those are blessed who are free of outside troubles to attend to their own peace, but Christ here says they are blessed who are not only prepared to put up with their own troubles, but also take on other peoples', to help them in distress, freely to join them in their time of trial, and, as it were, to get right into their situation, that they may gladly expend themselves on their assistance. He adds, *for they shall obtain mercy,* meaning not only with God, but also amongst men, as God turns men's minds to a sense of humanity. And though meanwhile the universe be ungrateful, and pay back the meanest reward to those who deserve the best, it should be sufficient that grace is laid up with God for the merciful and for the humane, that they in turn should find Him kind and merciful.

Matt. 5.8. *Blessed are the pure in heart.* Here Christ appears to introduce nothing that would not be agreed by general consent. All agree that purity of heart is the mother of all virtues, but there is scarcely a man in a hundred who does not put smart dealing in the place of the highest virtue. So it is, that those are generally reckoned blessed who are very clever at weaving schemes of deception, who craftily dodge round an issue, whenever they do business. Christ gives no endorsement to the currency of the flesh, when he calls those blessed who take no pleasure in cunning, but deal honestly with men, and put nothing in their words or expression but what they have also in their heart. As the simple dealers are mocked for their so-called lack of caution, for not looking out for themselves as they should, Christ raises their vision: if they are not so sharp-sighted on earth, they shall enjoy the sight of God in heaven.

Matt. 5.9. *Blessed are the peacemakers.* He means those who have an enthusiasm for peace, and, as best they may, avoid all quarrels, and also those who take pains to settle the dissensions that break out between others, being agents of peace to all, ready to stifle hatreds and rivalries. This is no light declaration: it is a matter of toil and trouble to pacify those who are at dispute. Men of moderation are compelled, in their efforts to foster peace, to bear hearing the insults and complaints and expostulations of both sides. The result is that each wishes to have everyone in his pay, to fight on his side. That we may not then depend on men's favours, Christ bids us look to the judgment of the Father, for as He is the God of peace, He reckons us among His sons as we work for peace, even though our efforts do not please men. To *be called* has the same force as to be reckoned.

Matt. 5.10. *Blessed are they that have been persecuted.* Of this teaching Christ's disciples have the greatest need, and the harder and more difficult it is for the flesh to accept, the more closely we must meditate upon it. We can fight Christ's battles on no other terms than for the majority of the world to be risen up in enmity against us, and to be our persecutors, even unto death. This is the situation, that Satan as prince of this world will never stop arming his ranks in a frenzy to assault the members of Christ, though it be monstrous and unnatural that those who serve righteousness should undeservedly suffer enemy attacks. Compare the words of Peter (I Pet. 3.13), 'If ye avoid the evil-doers, who is he that will harm you?' But in the misrule of a deranged world it too often occurs that the good, in their efforts for the right, inflame the hatred of the evil against themselves. Christians above all are virtually doomed to find the greater number of men their foes, for the flesh cannot abide the teaching of the Gospel, none endure the reproof of their own vices. He says, to suffer *for righteousness' sake*, meaning those who attract the ill-will of evil men and provoke their rage, because in their concern for equity and justice they oppose evil causes, and defend the good, to the best of their powers. Rightly, in this matter, God's truth has the ultimate word. This is the mark by which Christ distinguishes His martyrs from the wicked and the evil-doers. I repeat what I have just said, that all who wish to live a godly life in Christ are liable to persecution; Paul's testimony applies to all the faithful alike (II Tim. 3.12). It is proper, then, when God is gentle with us in our weakness, and does not allow the wicked to harass us at their will, to ponder this teaching in the time of shade and ease, that we may be prepared whenever needs arise to go out into the arena; let us not meet our trial ill-equipped. As throughout this life the way of the godly is most miserable, Christ duly lifts our thoughts to hope for the life of heaven. Christ's paradox here is vastly different from the commentaries of the Stoics, where men are told to be satisfied in their own judgment, and each to decide on his own happiness. But Christ does not tie happiness to empty imaginings, for He establishes it upon the reward of a future hope.

Matt. 5.11. *When men shall reproach.* For this, Luke (6.22) has, *when men shall hate you, and when they shall separate you from their company, and reproach you, and cast out your name as evil.* Christ wished these words to be a comfort to His faithful, that their spirits should not fail, though they saw themselves detested by all the world. It was no small temptation, being cast out of the Church as godless and profane characters. As He knew this was the worst venom of the hypocrites, He anticipated the time when the enemies of the Gospel should rise in mad assault against His tiny and contemptible flock, and determined to defend them firmly against collapse, though a huge tide of evil should threaten to overwhelm them. Here we may learn to have no fear of Papal excommunication, when those tyrants separate us from their synagogues, because we do not wish to make a divorce with Christ.

Matt. 5.12. *Rejoice, and be exceeding glad, etc.* He means we have a remedy to hand, to prevent our being shattered by unjust reproaches. Once our minds are lifted up to heaven, there unbounded ground for rejoicing opens out to us, and swallows up the sadness. Papists deceive us over the word *reward*, but there is no bother in clearing up the deception, for there is no mutual relationship between reward and merit (as they fondly imagine), but the promise of reward is gratuitous. If we consider how spoiled and faulty are the good works that come from the best of us, we shall never find anything that deserves God's reward. We must particularly note these phrases, *for my sake*, meaning, on behalf of the Son of man; likewise, *shall reproach you . . . falsely*, for no-one may rush to call himself a martyr of Christ who suffers persecution for his own fault, in the way that the Donatists of old were delighted simply with the record that they had been at odds with the magistrates. Today the Anabaptists plague the Church with their insane ideas, and bring dishonour on the Gospel by boasting that they bear the marks of Christ when they are justly condemned. Christ only declares that we are blessed when we are set on the rightful defence of His cause. *For so persecuted they.* This was deliberately added that the Apostles should not be hoping for triumphs without sweat and fight, and fail in times of persecution. As the renewal of all things under the reign of Christ is at various places promised in Scripture, there was a danger that they should boast of a false assurance and not think on the campaign. It is in fact obvious from other passages that they foolishly believed the Kingdom of Christ to be full of plenty and delights. So Christ has good cause to warn them that the same contests await them as in former days were faced by the Prophets, once they come onto their tracks. It is not only in respect of time that He says the Prophets went before them, but because, being of the same order, they should form themselves on their example. The common notion that makes out that there are nine beatitudes is too silly to need long refutation.

Luke 6.24. *But woe unto you that are rich!* As Luke presents only four orders of blessing, he now contrasts these with four orders of woe, to make the section balance. The antithesis is not only to strike terror into the godless, but to alert the faithful, in case they fall asleep under the vain and captious charms of the World. We know how easy it is to be intoxicated with success, to be ensnared in the flatteries of men, for it often happens that the sons of God envy the wicked when they see how everything turns out well for them and prosperously. This woe upon the *rich* does not apply to each and every one, but to those who take their comfort in the world, that is, who are so satisfied with their fortune that they forget the life to come. He means that riches are so far from making a man blessed that often they turn out to be his ruin. In other respects, God does not keep the rich away from His Kingdom, provided they do not get themselves caught up, or by fixing their hope on earth shut the door of heaven upon themselves. Augustine puts it neatly, showing that riches are not of themselves an impediment to the sons of God, when he tells how Lazarus the pauper was welcomed into the bosom of the wealthy Abraham. In like fashion, he curses the over-filled and sated, who are stuffed with the assurance of their present goods, to the extent of rejecting any good from heaven. Likewise with those who laugh: by these he means those devotees of Epicurean delight, soaked in the pleasures of the flesh, who run away from any trouble that would be involved in looking to the glory of God. His last *Woe!* is for the checking of ambition: as nothing is more common than to play to the applause of the crowd, or at least to be tempted on these lines, Christ shows how deadly men's favour will be, to scare His disciples off such a course. This is a warning that the teachers above all must note, who have no greater plague to fear than ambition, for inevitably they must adulterate the pure doctrine of God when they lean over to taste the favours of men. When Christ says, 'All men,' this should be related to the sons of this generation who only applaud the fakes and the false prophets. The faithful and true ministers of sound teaching have their appreciation and thanks with decent people. Such is the condemnation put on the favour of the flesh, that no-one could be Christ's servant and study to please men—as Paul teaches us (Gal. 1.10).

Ye are the salt of the earth: but if the salt have lost its savour, wherewith shall it be salted? it is henceforth good for nothing, but to be cast out and trodden under foot of men. Ye are the light of the world. A city set on a hill cannot be hid. Neither do men light a lamp, and put it under the bushel, but on the stand; and it shineth unto all that are in the house. Even so let your light shine before men, that they may see your good works, and glorify your Father which is in heaven. (Matt. 5.13-16)

For every one shall be salted with fire. Salt is good: but if the salt have lost its saltness, wherewith will ye season it? Have salt in yourselves, and be at peace with one another.
And he said unto them, Is the lamp brought to be put under the bushel, or under the bed, and not to be put on the stand? (Mark 9.49-50)

Salt therefore is good: but if even the salt have lost its savour, wherewith shall it be seasoned? It is fit neither for the land nor for the dunghill: men cast it out. He that hath ears to hear, let him hear.
And no man, when he hath lighted a lamp, covereth it with a vessel, or putteth it under a bed; but putteth it on a stand, that they which enter in may see the light.
No man, when he hath lighted a lamp, putteth it in a cellar, neither under the bushel, but on the stand, that they which enter in may see the light. (Luke 14.34-35, 8.16, 11.33)

Matt. 5.13. *Ye are the salt of the earth.* The character of the teaching is applied to the persons who are entrusted with its administration. When Christ calls the Apostles the salt of the earth, He means that it is their task to salt the earth, for in themselves men have no savour until they are seasoned with the salt of heavenly instruction. And once He has told them their vocation, He announces the heavy and appalling sentence that befalls them if they do not come up to their duty. The teaching which is put in their hands He shows to be so attached to the good of our conscience, and the life of godliness and integrity, that the wastage which might in others be tolerable, is in them detestable and indeed monstrous. In other words, If other men in God's sight lack savour, you will be given salt to win them sharpness of understanding, but if you are out of your senses, where will you find any cure which you may bring to others? The Lord cleverly pursues His metaphor in saying that other materials by their nature degenerate, but are still useful to some extent after they have gone off, but salt is positively harmful, and even makes compost unusable. In short then, it is an incurable disease when ministers and teachers of the Word waste themselves and render themselves without savour, for it is their savour that should season the rest of the world.

This warning is beneficial not only to ministers, but to all the flock of Christ. As God wishes the earth to be salted with His Word, it follows that anything that lacks that salt is tasteless in His mouth, however appetising to men. There is nothing better than that little seasoning which alone can improve our tasteless lives, but let the seasoners beware that they do not encourage the world in its own stupidity, and worse still, infect it with a mean and vicious savour. Thus Papistical ill-doing is not to be borne. They would have it, that Christ willed to allow The Apostles full rein, to make them tyrants over souls instead of counselling them on their office, in case they should wander off the right lines. Christ states what kind of teachers He would have for His Church. Those who set themselves up as Apostles with no authority, use it as a screen for bringing in any abominations they please, that Christ called Peter and his fellows *the salt of the earth*. They fail to take into account the solemn and serious condemnation attached thereto—that these are the worst of all men, if they *lose their savour*. This section is found rather abruptly set in Luke, but to the same intent as it has here, and needs no exposition of its own.

Mark 9.49. *For every one shall be salted with fire.* I have put these words of Mark onto the end of Matthew's, not that they entirely agree in sense, nor belong to the same place or time, but rather that readers may by comparison perceive better a different use of the same idea. When Christ spoke in Mark of eternal fire, He was urging His people, by contrast, rather to offer themselves now to God as holy sacrifices for the seasoning of fire and salt, than let their sins drag them into that fire which is never extinguished. *Salted with fire* is an inaccurate expression, but as salt and fire share the same function of purging and refining, Christ applied the same word to each. Notice now the occasion of this utterance: that the faithful should not refuse to be put through fire and salt, as without this treatment they could never be God's saints. He alludes to the precept of the Law (Lev. 2.13), where God expressly forbids any oblation being made without salt. He now tells us that the faithful should be salted with the Word of the Gospel, that they may find sanctification. When He adds that salt is good, He applies this in general to all whom God has once allowed to be touched with His Word, and urges them always to retain their savour. The metaphor becomes rather difficult when He calls salt something *to be seasoned*, but it does not cause any confusion in the sense that when those who were once acquainted with God's grace lose their tang, by their foolishness, they have no further means to use. Equally desperate are those who have lost the faith in which they were consecrated, and make fools of themselves, for they will find no other condiment to improve their savour: they are worse than unbelievers, for the grace of God has evaporated in them, and they are spoiled, even as salt spoils the earth—and the refuse heap.

Mark 9.50. *Have salt in yourselves.* This is an expression that allows various interpretations, meaning perhaps the savour of sweetness that comes with faith, the discretion of the Spirit: as when Paul tells us (Col. 4.6) that our speech should be seasoned with salt, meaning it should be purged and free of all profane follies and corruptions, and filled with spiritual grace, to give edification, and infuse a sweet odour upon all who hear. If you like this exposition, then you should take the second sentence as applying to the mutual harmony that derives from such salting, but as I think it is more likely that the second sentence depends on the first, I believe Christ is encouraging His people to preserve that vigour of faith, which rubs off on others too: as if He said, You must take care not only to be well-savoured within, but to give savour to others. But as salt has a biting edge, the use of it must be so restrained that peace is never disturbed.

Matt. 5.14. *Ye are the light of the world.* We are all children of the light, once we have received illumination by faith, and we are told to carry flaming torches in our hands, or we shall be lost in the darkness, and further to show others the path of life. Yet as the Apostles were the first to be given this task of preaching the Gospel, and the Church's pastors are today given it, it is to them that Christ gives this exceptional title, as if to say, This was the condition of their being put into that rank —to leave the rest behind and give light from a higher post. He adds two similes, that a *city* set on a hill cannot *be hid*, nor do men *conceal a lamp*, once it is lit, using language to express the idea that they must live as men exposed to the sight of all. Certainly the higher a man stands, the worse the effect of his bad example if he misbehaves. Christ wishes His disciples to be more keenly concerned to live in a godly and holy way, than the nondescript members of the crowd, for the eyes of all are turned on them as upon a beacon. They cannot be tolerated, if their decent behaviour and integrity of life does not correspond to the teaching, of which they are the ministers. In Mark and Luke, the application of the simile appears to be different. There Christ gives a general warning, that we are to take great care that no-one, relying on the darkness, should allow himself licence to sin, for what is temporarily hidden will come to the open eventually: it may be that they are both giving detached utterances, without respect to their context.

Matt. 5.16. *Even so let your light shine before men.* Once Christ has taught the Apostles that they are set on such a rank that both their virtues and their vices will shine out, to the good or evil example of mankind, He now tells them to arrange their lives that all may be prompted to give God the glory. 'Let men see your good works,' He says, for, as Paul testifies (II Cor. 9.12), the faithful win a good account in the eyes of men, as of God. Later, He will tell them to find a hiding-place, a corner, for their good works, but this is said to stop their self-seeking. Here His object is quite different, namely the glory of God alone. If the glory for good works may not duly be given to God without thanks to Him and recognition of Him as the only Author of them all, then to extol free will is a clear and crass example of bringing insult upon God, as to suggest that good works may in whole or in part spring from any other source than His goodness. Also we must notice how kindly God deals with us, to call good works ours, for the real credit should be ascribed to Him alone.

Think not that I came to destroy the law or the prophets: I came not to destroy, but to fulfil. For verily I say unto you, Till heaven and earth pass away, one jot or one tittle shall in no wise pass away from the law, till all things be accomplished. Whosoever therefore shall break one of these least commandments, and shall teach men so, shall be called least in the kingdom of heaven: but whosoever shall do and teach them, he shall be called great in the kingdom of heaven. (Matt. 5.17-19)

But it is easier for heaven and earth to pass away, than for one tittle of the law to fall. (Luke 16.17)

Matt. 5.17. *Think not, etc.* Christ's perfection of life might well provide justification for Him to boast that He had come to perfect the Law but the issue here is not life, but teaching. As He continually proclaimed that the Kingdom of God had come, and raised men to have new hope in their hearts—and gave disciples an initiation by baptism—it is likely that He had many people's minds in doubt and suspense, a they anxiously wondered where such novelty was leading. Now Christ declares that so far from there being any discord between His teaching and the Law, He intends there to be excellent agreement with the Law and the Prophets. Indeed He goes on to make it a full complement to them. He seems to have been led by two reasons to attest this agreement of Law and Gospel. As soon as any new form of teaching emerges, the commonalty at once jump on to it, as though it were the overturning of everything: such was the preaching of the Gospel (as I have just noted) that it gave hopes of a Church being established on a basis different from that previously. Therefore, they thought the old and customary régime was being abolished. Now this opinion was very dangerous in many ways. Pious worshippers of God would never have embraced the Gospel if it had been a defection from the Law, while triflers and trouble-makers would have laid hold on the Spirit's opportunity, eagerly to attack and to tear down the whole system of religion, for we know how wildly daring thrives on revolution. Besides, Christ saw that many of the Jews, despite their professed adherence to the Law, were leading a profane and shameful life. Affairs had sunk so low amongst that people, everything was so full of such corruption, the apathy or malice of the priests had dimmed the pure light of doctrine to such a degree, that no longer was there any great or lively respect for the Law. But if a kind of new teaching had been introduced, then the state of religion would have been sadly damaged. This seems to have been the first reason why Christ denied that He had come to undo the Law, and we may gather the same impression from the context. For by way of confirmation He shortly adds that it may not be that even a tittle shall fall out of the Law and He puts a curse on those teachers who do not faithfully strive to assert its authority.

Now the second reason was to do away with the base slander which He knew was laid against Him by the more untrained and ignorant. This was a brand stamped on His teaching by the scribes, as we see from His direct attack upon them. We must grasp Christ's intention, that in His invitation and encouragement to the Jews to accept the Gospel, He would still keep them in obedience to the Law: further, that He bravely refutes unworthy insults and slanders, with which His enemies had tried to make His preaching unpopular or suspect. If there is courage in restoring for the better a state of disorder, there must also be a use of discretion and moderation, that the people may realize that this is no reason for the eternal Word of God to be overturned, nor is any innovation brought in which will detract from Scriptures. No suspicion of contradiction must weaken the faith of the godfearing, and wild men must not grow insolent under the pretext of new affairs. Finally, profane contempt for the Word of God must be resisted, and religious practice keep its good name among the uneducated. So Christ's defence, by which He makes His teaching unimpeachable, should encourage us if we face slanders today. It was a charge laid against Paul, that he had fallen away from God's Law (Acts 21.21): so there is no wonder if the Papists use the same figment to whip up ill-feeling against us. But by Christ's example we may rid ourselves of false charges, and all the time the truth is freely to be professed however much it runs into unfair accusations

I came not to destroy. God had promised a new covenant at the coming of Christ, but had shown at the same time that it would not be different from the first, but rather this would be His object—the covenant that He had originally struck with His people would be confirmed for perpetuity. 'I shall write', He says, 'my Laws upon their hearts, and I shall forget their sins' (Jer. 31.33): these words do not at all depart from the former covenant, but rather declare that it will continue to be firm and valid, when the new has come upon it. This is exactly the intention of Christ's words, when He says that He has come to fulfil the Law. Truly He fulfilled the deadness of the letter by reviving it with His Spirit, and eventually displaying in actual fact, what had till then been indicated figuratively. As for doctrine, we must not make out that there has been any abrogation of the Law in Christ's coming, for as the rule of holy and devout life is eternal, it must be unchangeable, and likewise God's justice is one and constant, as He composed it therein. As regards ceremonies, if we allow that they may be reckoned somewhat incidental, it is only their practice that was abrogated: their significance was actually given more confirmation. So Christ's coming did not take anything away, even from the ceremonies, but rather the truth behind the shadows was revealed, and served to strengthen them; seeing the concrete fact, we recognize that they were not vain or useless. So let us learn to preserve this connection of Law and Gospel inviolable —but many erroneously try to break it. It has no small effect on consolidating our faith in the Gospel, if we hear that it is no other than the complement of the Law, both in mutual agreement claiming God as their common author.

Matt. 5.18. *Till heaven and earth pass away, etc.* Luke puts it rather differently, but in the same sense, *It is easier for heaven and earth to pass away, than for one tittle of the law to fall.* In both places Christ intended to teach that in all the structure of the universe there is nothing so stable as the truth of the Law, which stands firm, and that in every part Some play ingenious tricks with the word *until*, as though the passing of heaven and earth, which shall come at the last day of judgment, will mean the end of Law and Prophets. Certainly, as tongues shall then cease and Prophecies be done away, I consider the written Law and it exposition will then cease. But as I believe Christ spoke to simpler effect, I have no mind to feed my hearers' ears with such irrelevancies It is quite enough to understand that sooner will heaven crash, and all the fabric of the earth dissolve, than the fixity of the Law shall be shaken. But what does it mean for all the points of the Law to be observed to the last tittle? For we see how far men stand from the perfect observance of the Law, even those who are re-generate by the Spirit of God. I answer, that the word *accomplished* is not related to men's life, but to the solid truth of doctrine, as if He said: there is no variancy in the Law, nothing put there haphazardly; thus it is impossible for any letter of it to disappear.

Matt. 5.19. *Whosoever therefore shall break.* Christ is expressly speaking here of the rules of life, the Ten Commandments, by whose prescription all the sons of God should frame their lives. So He states that they are false and wrong teachers, who do not hold their disciples to the obedience of the Law, and not worthy of holding position in the Church, if they slacken the Law's authority in any part. But the good and true ministers of God are those who commend the observance of the Law, both by the example of their lives, and by their words. Now He speaks of the *least* observance of the Law, from the viewpoint of men, for though they have not all the same significance, indeed on comparison show some greater, some lesser, yet we may not rate any as tiny, when the heavenly Law-giver has deigned to give instruction upon it. For is it not great sacrilege, to treat with contempt anything that has proceeded from His holy mouth? By that means, His Majesty is reduced to nothing. Thus when Christ speaks of minute precepts, it is by way of concession. When He says, *he shall be called least*, it is in allusion to what had just before been said of the precepts. But the sense is clear, that there will be rejection to the very back of the queue, so to speak, for any who hold the Law's teaching up to contempt, even by one syllable. *The kingdom of heaven* is taken as the restoration of the Church, or the second state of the Church, as even then was coming to be at the preaching of the Gospel. Thus at Luke. 7.28 Christ makes him greater than John, who is least in the Kingdom of God. The logic of the expression is that God, in restoring the world by His Son's hand, firmly established His Kingdom. Thus Christ says that teachers are not to be admitted to His Church, when it had been restored, unless they shall be faithful interpreters of the Law, and shall study to assert its entire teaching.

It is asked whether ceremonies are not to be included among the precepts of God, and yet their observance is not demanded now. The answer is that we must consider the purpose and design of the Law-giver. As God gave rules for ceremonies on the basis that their outward use should last for a period, but their significance be everlasting, one does not do away with ceremonies, when their reality is kept, and their shadow omitted. When Christ keeps out of His Kingdom such men as accustom others to condemn the Law, then it is a fantastic folly for them not to be ashamed of remitting, by blasphemous indulgence, the absolute demands of God, and calling them venial sins, in order to do away with the justice of the Law. We must note again, that to good and holy teachers He gives praise. In the keeping of the Law, men are not encouraged by words alone, but especially by the living example.

For I say unto you, that except your righteousness shall exceed the righteousness of the scribes and Pharisees, ye shall in no wise enter into the kingdom of heaven.

Ye have heard that it was said to them of old time, Thou shalt not kill; and whosoever shall kill shall be in danger of the judgement: but I say unto you, that every one who is angry with his brother shall be in danger of the judgement; and whosoever shall say to his brother, Raca, shall be in danger of the council; and whosoever shall say, Thou fool, shall be in danger of the hell of fire. (Matt. 5.20-22)

Matt. 5.20. *Except your righteousness shall exceed.* He turns against the scribes, who struggled to besmear the teaching of the Gospel, as playing havoc with the Law. He makes no dispute over the facts, but merely gives a brief indication that nothing is less dominant in their minds than a zeal for the Law. It is as if He had said, They feign opposition to me, on the grounds of not wishing the Law to be violated, yet from their lives we may see how cold is their service to the Law, yes, how brashly they mock God, in parading before men their false and pretended righteousness: thus many interpreters. But consider whether He is not more arraigning them for the vicious manner of teaching, which the Pharisees and scribes had foisted upon the people. In attaching God's Law only to the outward duties, they trained their disciples in hypocrisy like monkeys. Now I do not deny that they lived badly, indeed worse than they taught. I willingly include their fake display of fictitious goodness with their perverse teaching. But it is this latter which Christ particularly attacks, as we may easily see from what follows, where He restores the Law to its purity, by ridding it of their degraded comments. In short, the very charge that was unfairly brought against Him by the scribes, He turns back vigorously upon themselves. See, He says, what able and efficient interpreters of the Law they are: they fabricate a righteousness, which closes the door of heaven upon its adherents. We must recollect what we have said elsewhere, that Pharisees are joined with scribes for a fuller expression, for that sect had won itself acclaim for holy living beyond the rest. But it is a mistake to think they were so named from separation, as if they claimed a rank for themselves by segregation from the common crowd, for they were called פרושים (*Perushim*), meaning, interpreters, for they were not satisfied with the plain text, but claimed to have a key to elicit hidden senses. This was the origin of that vast agglomeration they produced, when they pulled the teaching authority into their own court, and with godless licence and equal arrogance dared to obtrude their own figments into the place of Scripture.

Matt. 5.21. *Ye have heard that it was said.* This utterance and those following go with what He has just said. Christ proceeds to a fuller and detailed exposition of the distortions by which the Pharisees had mistreated the Law, making their righteousness of no more account than dross. It was wrong, though, to reckon this an ἐπανόρθωσις (revision) of the Law, or that Christ was wishing to lift His disciples to a higher level of perfection than Moses could achieve with his unenlightened and carnal folk, who were hardly ready to learn the rudiments. This has given rise to the idea that the beginning of righteousness was once handed down in the Law, but its perfection was taught in the Gospel. However, Christ in fact had not the least intention of making any change or innovation in the precepts of the Law. God there appointed once and for all a rule of life, which He will never repent of. But with the Law overlaid with extraneous commentaries, and distorted out of its proper intention, Christ champions it from out of the hold of all these excrescences, and demonstrates its true purpose, from which the Jews had departed.

That the teaching of the Law does not merely start, but completes the path of rectitude, may be inferred even in this section alone, where it demands the perfect love of God and of one's neighbour. Whoever is gripped with such a love as this has no want of perfection in the highest degree. So far as the rules for the good life are concerned, the Law takes men all the way in righteousness. Paul attributes its weakness not to itself but to the flesh we stand in. If anyone still wished to treat it as a preliminary to true righteousness, Moses' solemn appeal would have been meaningless, 'I call heaven and earth to witness against you this day that I have set before thee life and death' (Deut. 30.19). Or again (Deut. 10.12), 'And now, Israel, what doth the Lord thy God require of thee, but to cleave entirely to him?' And that promise would have been vain and empty, 'Which if a man do, he shall live in them' (Lev. 18.5). It is quite evident from other passages that Christ wished to make no alterations in its precepts: those who wish to enter upon life by the way of good works, must adhere to nothing else but the commandments of the Law. There is no other source either for Himself or for the Apostles to draw out rules for holy and godly living, indeed they would do cruel offence to God, the Author of the Law, if they alleged that eyes, hands and feet were only appointed for its benefit, to give a specious show of good works, while only the Gospel contained the teaching that God was to be loved from the heart. So let us have no more of that error, that here a defect of the Law is corrected by Christ: Christ is not to be made into a new Law-giver, adding anything to the everlasting righteousness of His Father, but is to be given the attention of a faithful Interpreter, teaching us the nature of the Law, its object, and its scope.

Now we must look into Christ's condemnation of the Pharisees, how their interpretation differs from His own instruction. Briefly, they had transferred the teaching of the Law to the political or civil sphere (*ad politicum ordinem*), to make the outward observance of its claims sufficient. It resulted in a man being cleared of homicide, where he did not kill a man by his hand, and leaving another to consider himself pure and innocent in God's eyes, where he had not stained himself with an act of adultery. This was an intolerable profanation of the Law, as it is certain that at all times Moses required the spiritual service of God, and God who handed it down by Moses spoke to the heart in accordance with its nature, as much as to hands and eyes. Christ cites the words of the Law, but suits His method to the general grasp of the folk, as if saying: So far it has been the literal exposition of the Law that has been spread amongst you by the scribes, namely, that it is enough for a man to keep his hands away from murder and violence, but I tell you, you must probe far more deeply, and as charity is the perfection of the Law, I say that your neighbour suffers assault as often as any unfriendly move is made against him. The last part, reading, 'whosoever shall kill shall be in danger of judgment', confirms what I have just said, that the fault which Christ takes them to task over is converting God's Law to a matter for the administration, when it was designed for guidance of the soul.

Matt. 5.22. *But I say unto you.* He does not set His answer against Moses, but against the popular fiction of the scribes. Now the Pharisees boasted of their antiquity (it is quite common for a long standing rule to be made a defence of mal-practice), but Christ recalls the people to His own authority, in the face of which all antiquity should rightly give way. Hence we may gather how far truth prevails over habit and length of years. *Whosoever shall say to his brother.* Christ marks three degrees of condemnation besides physical violence, meaning that that rule of the Law ties not only one's hand, but all emotions that are opposed to brotherly love, as if to say, Those who have only been angry at their brothers, or arrogantly insulted them, or wounded them with some word of abuse, are homicides. As it is certain that the word 'Raca' was meant to stand between anger and open insult, I have no doubt that it was an interjection of scorn or dismissal. Though Christ only sentences to the fire of hell those who break out into open abuse, it is not to exempt anger from this penalty, but in allusion to the judgments of earth He testifies that God will be the Judge of concealed anger, to punish that offence. Next in scale, the man who shows indignation in a bitter remark, is said to stand accused before the whole council of heaven, to receive a heavier penalty. While those who break out in streams of abuse—these He appoints to the hell-fire, meaning that hatred and all that is against charity will condemn a man to eternal death, even without any actual violence being used.

The word *gehenna* (*hell*) is doubtless a transliteration—גיא (gay) means a valley in Hebrew. Now the valley of Hinnom was an uncanny place with fearful horror attaching to it, for it was there that they used to sacrifice their children to idols. So it came to be that holy men, to increase the detestation of that criminal blasphemy, took it as a region of the underworld, for the people to abhor its very name was ill-omened and hateful. Clearly in Christ's age it was an accepted form of speech, and the underworld practically always got the name of gehenna, the word slightly altered from its original spelling.

If therefore thou art offering thy gift at the altar, and there rememberest that thy brother hath ought against thee, leave there thy gift before the altar, and go thy way, first be reconciled to thy brother, and then come and offer thy gift. Agree with thine adversary quickly, whiles thou art with him in the way; lest haply the adversary deliver thee to the judge, and the judge deliver thee to the officer, and thou be cast into prison. Verily I say unto thee, Thou shalt by no means come out thence, till thou have paid the last farthing. (Matt. 5.23-26)

For as thou art going with thine adversary before the magistrate, on the way give diligence to be quit of him; lest haply he hale thee unto the judge, and the judge shall deliver thee to the officer, and the officer shall cast thee into prison. I say unto thee, Thou shalt by no means come out thence, till thou have paid the very last mite. (Luke 12.58-59)

Matt. 5.23. *If . . . thou art offering thy gift.* This paragraph confirms and at the same time explains the previous teaching. Briefly, we have only satisfied the Law's commandment, which forbids killing, when we promote agreement and brotherly kindness with those who are nearest to us. To impress this more upon us, Christ states that the very claims of our religion are unwelcome to God, indeed repudiated by Him, if we are quarrelling amongst ourselves. When He tells those who have injured any of their brothers to return to a good understanding with him before offering their appointed gift, He means that as long as by our own fault we stand at variance with our nearest, there is no open access for us to God. But if men, by their acts of hatred, befoul and waste all the service that they pay God, we may deduce what a value He puts on mutual agreement between us. There is, however, a question that may be raised, Would it not be ridiculous to make the claims of charity superior to the worship of God? We would have to say that the order of the Law is reversed, or that the first table must retain priority over the second. The solution is easy: Christ's words are only directed at those who falsely and feebly profess themselves worshippers of God, and all the time proudly scorn the brothers whom they have wrongfully wounded. Taking one instance by synecdoche, He is describing the outward exercises of divine worship, in which men more often pretend to more godliness than the truth would tell. We must note that according to the use of that generation, He speaks of sacrifices. Our condition today is not the same, but the same teaching holds, that whatever we offer God is faulty if we are not in concord with our brothers, at least to the best of our means. Scripture calls almsgiving a Sacrifice of good odour, yet we hear from Paul's mouth that it is nothing for a man to spend all his substance on the poor, if he has not charity (Phil. 4.18; I Cor. 13.3). In all, God does not welcome or recognize as His children those who refuse to be brothers with their fellow men. Though Christ is only telling those who have done their brothers an injury to take care to make friends, He is using one case to show how precious fraternal harmony is to God. He says far more when He orders the gift to be left before the altar, than if He had said that it was vain for men to come to the temple, or dedicate sacrifices to God, as long as they were in disagreement with their brothers.

Matt. 5.25. *Agree.* Though Christ appears to take it further, and urge reconciliation not only on those who have hurt their brothers, but also on those who have been unjustly provoked, my interpretation suggests another objective, namely to take occasion to check strife and dispute, and point out the way to promote good-will. Where do all these hurts come from, except that individuals are too tenacious of their rights, over zealous, that is, for their own convenience to the detriment of others? Perverse love of self blinds almost every man, and gives false hopes in the worst of cases. So Christ, to prevent hatred and quarrels and contests and all kinds of injuries, restrains the persistence that is at the root of these evils, and tells His people to be inclined towards moderation and equity, not forcing their rights all the way, but winning an amicable settlement on such a basis of equality. It would be a great boon if no dispute of this sort ever occurred amongst us. Truly men would never rush into spite and strife, if the proper humility flourished in our lives, but as it can hardly be avoided that some contests come our way, Christ shows the remedy that may quickly compose them, to put a bridle upon our greed, and to be ready to settle even at our own loss, rather than pursue our rights with unyielding energy. But it is clear that Christ more than once used this same form of exhortation, as in Luke 12, where it is not the Sermon on the Mount which is being related, but a summary put together of various sayings of Christ. There, too, we understand this *agree . . . in the way*: meaning of course, before you come to the judge. *Lest the adversary deliver thee to the judge*. Some give a metaphorical turn to this section, that the heavenly Judge will deal with us to the fullest extent of His powers, and will give no remission, if we do not make efforts to settle peaceably the cases which we have with our neighbours. I would take it in a simpler sense, that Christ is telling us that in human terms it is to our advantage to settle with our opponents in good time, as their own greed is often ruinous for the contentious. At the same time I do not deny that the comparison transfers aptly to God who has a sense of justice untouched by pity for the man who is implacable towards his brother, and carries his case to extremes.

It is quite ridiculous for the Papists to build the structure of their Purgatory on the continuing allegory of this passage, for nothing is more obvious than that Christ spoke of the preservation of good-will amongst men. They have no sense of religion, to twist His words without shame, to force them into an utterly alien sense, a complete smoke-screen for the un-schooled. As they do not deserve a long refutation, let me show in a word, how shameful is their ignorance. They make out that the adversary is the devil. But Christ is telling His faithful to be kindhearted. So for the Papists to find their Purgatory, they must first have devils as friends and brothers. We know that the *quadrans* (farthing) was the fourth part of an *as* (penny): it is taken here as 'a quarter' or other tiny coin, as we may see from Luke. If you care to deal with trifles, the Papists' dimness is again shown up over this. If once a man enters Purgatory, he will never come out until he pays the last farthing, it follows that all the *suffragia* (prayers of the living), will be quite useless to the dead. Christ does not allow others to release the debtor from his bill, but demands precisely from each the quittance that he owes. Now if Masses and other propitiatory rites are useless, for all the burning fires of Purgatory, the kitchens of the priests and monks will run cold—their inducement to keep up their zealous efforts on the man's behalf.

Ye have heard that it was said, Thou shalt not commit adultery: but I say unto you, that everyone that looketh on a woman to lust after her hath committed adultery with her already in his heart. And if thy right eye causeth thee to stumble, pluck it out, and cast it from thee: for it is profitable for thee that one of thy members should perish, and not thy whole body be cast into hell. And if thy right hand causeth thee to stumble, cut it off, and cast it from thee: for it is profitable for thee that one of thy members should perish, and not thy whole body go into hell. (Matt. 5.27-30)

Matt. 5.27. *Thou shalt not commit adultery.* Christ continues His argument, that God's Law is not only a master in the public sphere of life to instruct us in our outward morality, but demands also the pure and untainted affection of the heart. Remember my first comment, that though Christ quotes the words of the Law, it is the insensitive and bogus sense which ill-minded commentators had put upon it that He is reprehending. For He started by saying, that He had not come as a new Law-giver, but as a faithful interpreter of a Law once given. Where it might be objected that this interpretation had the dignity of long usage, Christ frankly admits it. But he does so to anticipate prejudice, which should not stem from false acceptance of antiquity.

Matt. 5.28. *That looketh on a woman.* Christ's purpose is in general to condemn the lust of the flesh. So He says that they are adulterers in God's sight who not only have intercourse with others' wives, but who have stained their eyes with unchaste glances. It is an expression by synecdoche, for it is not only the eyes which convict men of adultery, but also the unseeing passions of the heart. So Paul places chastity (I Cor. 7.34) both in body and in spirit. But Christ was content to refer to the current foolish interpretation, for they thought that only outward adultery was to be guarded against. Since it is the eyes which most solicit souls by their panderings, and lust reaches through their portals, Christ used this form of speech in His will to condemn concupiscence: the word *lust after* shows this clearly. The lesson is, that they are rated adulterers in God's sight who not only by deliberate thought conceive harlotry in their minds, but admit even its slightest inducements. The hypocrisy of the Papists is quite stupid and dumb—to make concupiscence no sin, until assented to by the whole heart. But there is no wonder that the sin is so watered down by them, for you would expect that sort to be unintelligent and careless in reckoning sins, who ascribe righteousness to the merits of works.

Matt. 5.29. *And if thy right eye, etc.* Christ might seem, considering the weakness of our flesh and nature, to press men too severely, but He answers all objections of that kind. Briefly, He means that however difficult, arduous, troublesome or painful God's rule may be, we must

188

make no excuse for that, as the righteousness of God should be worth more to us, than all the other things which are chiefly dear and precious. In other words, You are not to object to me that you can hardly turn your eye this way and that, without some temptation creeping on it unpredictably. It would be better for you to do without your eyes, than depart from the commandments of God. However, it is not Christ's intention that we should mutilate our body to obey God, for as all would be glad for their passions to be under no restraint, but rather to give them free run, Christ in hyperbole bids us prune back anything that stops us offering God obedient service, as He demands in His Law. He does this deliberately, for men are too generous to themselves in the limits they allow over these things. If the mind were pure, it would find eyes and hands consistent; certainly they have no motivation of their own. We gravely sin in this respect, that we are not properly concerned to avoid temptations, but rather choose to excite our passions to evil with a headlong freedom.

It is said also, Whosoever shall put away his wife, let him give her a writing of divorcement: but I say unto you, that every one that putteth away his wife, saving for the cause of fornication, maketh her an adulteress: and whosoever shall marry her when she is put away committeth adultery. (Matt. 5.31-32)

Every one that putteth away his wife, and marrieth another, committeth adultery: and he that marrieth one that is put away from a husband committeth adultery. (Luke 16.18)

Matt. 5.31. *Whosoever shall put away.* As there will be a more convenient opportunity for a fuller treatment and explanation of this teaching at Matt. 19, I shall now run briefly over what Christ is saying here. As the Jews had come to believe, wrongly, that they had done their duty toward God if they kept the Law in the civil or political aspect, they also, foolishly, imagined that they allowed anything which the Law of the land did not forbid. The divorces which they were used to make with their wives Moses had not explicitly forbidden, but had only ordered, as a curb on their passion, that repudiated wives be given a certificate of divorce. It was a kind of testimonial of release, that the woman might thereafter be free from her husband's yoke and authority: at the same time the man declared that he did not send his wife away for any crime, but for not being agreeable. From this the error gained ground, that there was no blame attached to such repudiation, as long as it satisfied the Law. But then they were wrong in taking a rule for godly and holy life from the civil code. The laws of the state are deflected from time to time by human morality (*hominum mores*), but when God presents a spiritual law, He does not consider what men can do (*quid possint*), but what they ought to do (*quid debeant*). So perfect and complete righteousness is contained therein, although we may lack the means to live up to it. Hence Christ warns them that there is no direct guarantee that anything the civil Law of Moses tolerates is permissible in the eyes of God. On the pretext of the Law, He says, a man absolves himself who, in dismissing his wife, gives her a bill of divorce, but the chain of matrimony (*coniugii vinculum*) is too sacred for it to be dissolved at the choosing, rather, at the desire, of men. Though man and wife come together by mutual consent, God ties them in an indissoluble knot (*nodo indissolubili*) from which they may not afterwards freely depart. But He gives the exception, 'Except for fornication'. For a woman who treacherously violates her marriage, may well be cast out , as the bond is broken by her fault and the man gains his liberty.

Matt. 5.32. *Maketh her an adulteress.* As it was the object of the bill of divorce that a woman released from her first husband should go on to a new match, he is well condemned as an enticer, who prostitutes his wife to others, against all right and religion, when she has been given him in holy matrimony.

> *Again, ye have heard that it was said to them of old time, Thou shalt not forswear thyself, but shalt perform unto the Lord thine oaths: but I say unto you, Swear not at all; neither by the heaven, for it is the throne of God; nor by the earth, for it is the footstool of his feet; nor by Jerusalem, for it is the City of the great King. Neither shalt thou swear by thy head, for thou canst not make one hair white or black. But let your speech be, Yea, yea; Nay, nay: and whatsoever is more than these is of the evil one.* (Matt. 5.33-37).

Matt. 5.33. *Thou shalt not forswear thyself.* Here again there is no revision of the Law, but only its original interpretation. For God condemned in the Law both perjury and trifling with oaths, which take away from the reverence due to His Name. It is not only the perjurer who takes God's name in vain, but the man who in trivial matters and in everyday conversation rashly and contemptuously takes God's Name on his lips. While the Law condemns any kind of profanation of God's Name, the Jews pretended that the fault only lay in perjuries.

This is the crass error which Christ rebuts, that they should think it proper to abuse God's Name with impunity, as long as they do not lie on oath. It is a sacred injunction, that we should pay our oaths to God, for the man who takes God's Name to witness, and then deceives or defrauds his neighbours, does an injury not only to men, but also to God. But it is not right to attach to one part what has wider application. Some apply the word *perform* to such vows as when anything is promised God by way of devotion. But the word very well suits all contracts and promises, which are confirmed by taking God's Name on them, for then God is set as Sponsor between both parties, and to Him they pledge their faith.

Matt. 5.34. *Swear not at all.* The phrase *not at all* has deceived many, making them think that it was a general condemnation of every sort of swearing. Some men in former days were driven to this excessive rigour—not bad men, I may say—because of the unbridled freedom of swearing which they saw prevailing on all sides in their world. The Anabaptists, too, used this pretext for a great uproar, saying that Christ allowed no reason for taking oaths, in telling men to swear not at all. However, the exposition may be derived straight from the context itself. He goes directly on to say, 'Neither by heaven, neither by the earth'. Cannot we see that these particulars are added as explanation, to express precisely and categorically what the first part said? The Jews had round-about or indirect, if that is the expression, forms of swearing. When they swore by heaven or earth or altar, they made virtually nothing of it, and as one fault gives rise to another, they dressed over their (less obvious) profanation of God's Name. Christ faces this mal-practice, and states that there is to be no swearing at all in this or that way, neither by heaven, nor by earth, etc. So we gather the phrase *not at all* does not apply to the substance but to the form: in other words, Neither directly, nor indirectly. Otherwise it would be superfluous to set down these instances. Hence the Anabaptists reveal both their passion for dispute, and their total lack of intelligence, when they stress one word with great earnestness and lose the whole tenor of the discourse, with their eyes shut. Suppose a man objects that no oath-taking is allowed by Christ. I answer—what the Law's interpreter says should be understood according to the Law's intention. Briefly, it comes back to this, that there are other ways than perjury for God's Name to be taken in vain. So we must abstain from all unnecessary freedom in swearing, for when a right reason compels it, the Law not only allows the oath but explicitly enjoins it. Therefore Christ's sole purpose was that all oaths should be illicit which by any abuse profane God's holy Name, when they should enhance His respect.

Neither by the heaven, etc. It is wrong to expound that Christ checks these forms of swearing for being faulty in that it is by God alone that one must swear. The reasons that He adduces rather tend to the contrary, namely that one is actually swearing by God at the same time as one names heaven and earth: there is no part of the world in which God has not engraved the stamp of His glory. But this idea does not seem to agree with the Law's precept where God explicitly orders men to swear by His Name. Similarly, with the many passages of Scripture where He complains that wrong is done Him, when we swear by His creatures. The answer is, that there is corruption akin to idolatry when the power of judgment or the authority of attesting evidence is deferred to creatures. We must consider the actual purpose of swearing, which is for men to invoke God as the Avenger of perfidy and the Guardian of truth. This honour may not be transferred to another without His Majesty being infringed. For this reason, the Apostle says that we may not properly swear except by one greater, and it is peculiarly God's privilege to swear by Himself. So any who swore by Moloch, or any other idol, took as much away from God's right as to put another in His place, as the one who knows the hearts and judges the souls. Today also, those who swear by angels or by dead saints are robbing God and attaching an empty significance to them. It is a different matter when one swears by heaven or earth with respect to God their Creator. The religious effect of oaths does not subsist in the created things, but God Himself is called as sole Witness, with the signs of His glory brought into the midst of our minds. Now *heaven* Scripture calls God's throne, not that it contains Him, but to teach men to lift up their minds, whenever they think of Him, and not to imagine anything earthy or low about Him. *Earth* is called His footstool, to teach us that He is every where and not tied to the space of places. The holiness of *Jerusalem* depended upon the promise. So it was holy as the Lord had chosen it as the seat and abode of His dominion. When men swear by their *head*, they are as it were offering their lives, God's unique gift to them, as the pledge of their good faith.

Matt. 5.37. *But let your speech be.* Christ, in the second place, goes on to give a remedy, which is that men should have dealings with each other honestly and *bona fide*, for when no lesser form of speech than the taking of an oath will do, these are people who do not cultivate honesty as a virtue. It is certainly the best means of correcting faults to note the sources from which they flow. Why is there such a readiness to take oaths—if not because scarcely anyone find belief amidst such a welter of deceptions, shiftiness, empty living? Christ requires that our words possess candour and constancy, that we may not need to swear any more. Repeating the affirmation or negation makes the point that we should stand by our words, and thus display single-mindedness. As this is the true and rightful way of dealing, where men have nothing on their lips that is not also in their hearts, Christ declares that anything beyond this stems from evil. I do not agree with the exposition of some that the blame for oath-taking should rest with those who do not have faith in the speaker. Christ, as I see it, says that it is human failure that leads men to swearing. If good faith flourished amongst them, if they were not inconsistent and changeable in their speech, they would still preserve the simplicity which nature dictates. Yet it does not follow that we may not legitimately take an oath as often as necessity demand it, for the use of many things is innocent, though their source be vitiated.

Ye have heard that it was said, An eye for an eye, and a tooth for a tooth: but I say unto you, Resist not him that is evil: but whosoever smiteth thee on thy right cheek, turn to him the other also. And if any man would go to law with thee, and take away thy coat, let him have thy cloke also. And whosoever shall compel thee to go one mile, go with him twain. (Matt. 5.38-41)

To him that smiteth thee on the one cheek offer also the other; and from him that taketh away thy cloke withhold not thy coat also. Give to every one that asketh thee; and of him that taketh away thy goods ask them not again. (Luke 6.29-30).

Matt. 5.38. *An eye for an eye.* A further error is corrected here, that when God enjoined the judges and magistrates in His Law to pay back damages on an equal basis, each began, on that pretext, to take vengeance for himself. So they held it no sin, as long as they were not the aggressors, to pay back like for like when they were injured. Christ tells them to the contrary, that though the defence of the community is the charge of judges, who are appointed to avenge and restrain the wicked and check their force, yet each individual should bear with patience the injuries he has received.

Matt. 5.39. *Resist not . . . evil.* There are two sorts of resistance: one, when we ward off blows without causing hurt, the other, when we retaliate. While Christ does not allow His people to use force against force, He does not prohibit us from turning aside from undeserved attack. Paul is our best interpreter of this passage, at Rom. 12.17 (and 21), where he tells us rather to overcome evil with good than to struggle with those who wish us harm. We must note the contrast between the fault and the correction. Here He is dealing with requital, and to stop

193

His disciples making free with it, He forbids the repayment of evil for evil. Then He develops the rule of patience, that we should not only bear the injuries we receive in silence, but actually prepare ourselves to meet new ones. His whole lesson comes to this, briefly, that the faithful should learn to forget any evils done against them, in case their hurt drives them into sudden hatred or malice, or a desire to hurt back. They must be braced for greater endurance, in case the wicked passion of the wrongdoers should increase and annoy further still.

Whosoever smiteth. Julian and his like have absurdly slandered Christ's teaching, as though He made a complete reversal of law and order. As Augustine writes, with knowledge and discretion, in his fifth letter, Christ's purpose was purely to instruct the minds of the faithful in moderation and equity, in case after one or two knocks they should fail or weary. What Augustine says is true. The law is not confined to outward works, as long as you read it with intelligence. I grant that Christ holds back our hands from revenge, just as much as our minds, but where a man may, without taking revenge, protect himself and his own from injuries, Christ's words do not stop him from peaceably and non-violently deflecting the force as it runs onto him. Certainly Christ did not wish to urge His hearers to irritate the malice of those who were already over hot in their mood for trouble. Would it not be just such an irritation to turn the other cheek? Well, the fair and reasonable commentator will not strain at syllables, but concentrate on the intention that is in the speaker. It is quite unbecoming for Christ's disciples to trifle with turns of expression, when the Master's purpose is apparent. There is no doubt over Christ's aim, namely, that the end of one struggle would only be the beginning of another, and so in all the course of our lives the faithful must experience an unending succession of various hurts. Those who have been once wounded, He would have trained by that actual encounter to become tolerant, by their suffering to suffer more, with understanding.

Matt. 5.40. *And if any man would go to law with thee.* Damages of another sort are next referred to by Christ, when the wicked may harass us with lawsuits. He says that in this connection we are to have our minds steady and long-suffering, to the extent of being prepared to yield our overcoat if our jacket has been stripped off us. It will be stupid to stick over the details. We must give our adversaries what they demand, before ever it comes to court of law! Would not slackness of this order be like a fan incensing the hearts of the wicked to theft and fraud—which we know was far from the mind of Christ? So what does it mean to yield your coat, when a man on legal pretext tries to rob you of your jacket? This: if any man suffers an unfair judgment, and loses his property, and all the time is prepared to give away the rest (if need be), he deserves as much praise for his patience as the man who allows himself to be robbed twice, before coming to any tribunal. Briefly then, Christians should be ready, whenever anyone attempts to strip them of any of their goods, to lose the whole lot. So we infer that we are not entirely forbidden recourse to law, if we should be given the chance of a fair defence. Though they do not expose their fortunes to the snatching hand, men are not guilty of departing from the teaching of Christ, which urges us to bear nakedness with equanimity. It may be a rare occasion that a man may go to the law court to plead with a balanced and sincere motivation, but it is not altogether impossible to defend a decent case in the interest of the public good; so it is not right to condemn it out of hand, until we are certain that the motives are false. The differences in expression between Matthew and Luke do not alter the sense. An overcoat is usually of more cost than a jacket, and so when Matthew says we should give our coat when robbed of a jacket, he means that when we have had a small loss, we should be willing to put up with a heavy one. Luke's words agree with an old proverb about the jacket being nearer the skin than the coat.

Luke 6.30. *To every one that asketh thee.* We have the same words in Matthew, as we shall shortly see. We may soon infer from the context that Luke is not speaking here of prayers, where we ask for aid, but of lawsuits, which the wicked direct against other people to deprive them of their goods. He says, *Of him that taketh away thy goods ask them not again.* You may prefer to read these two parts separately, and I do not object: this it will be an exhortation to give generously. As regards the second part, where Christ forbids us to ask back what has been wrongly removed, here we must have an exposition of the previous teaching, concerning the way we should not take it harshly if we lose our goods. Hold on to what I have just said, that there is to be no ingenious forcing of words, to make it illicit for a godly man to get back his possessions, whenever a just occasion is given him by God of seeking redress. We are only given a rule to be patient, and not to be in a torment over our lost fortunes, waiting quietly till the Lord Himself demands an account from the thieves.

Give to him that asketh thee, and from him that would borrow of thee, turn not thou away. (Matt. 5.42)

And if ye lend to them of whom ye hope to receive, what thank have ye? even sinners lend to sinners, to receive again as much.
  Lend, never despairing; and your reward shall be great. (Luke 6.34-35)

Matt. 5.42. *Give to him that asketh thee.* Though the effect of Christ's words, as Matthew records them, is to enjoin us to give to all without distinction, we gather a different sense from Luke, who takes the matter a little further. First it is certain that Christ's purpose was to make His disciples generous, not prodigal. There is stupid prodigality, which pours away the Lord's gifts recklessly, but we see how elsewhere the Spirit gives us a rule for the gifts we make. Take this point then, that Christ is first urging His disciples to be openhanded and benevolent. And the measure of it is that they are never to reckon they have done their duty when only a few have been helped, but they are to be eager to reach all with their alms, and not to grow weary as long as their means last out. In case anyone should find a loophole in Matthew's words, compare what we have in Luke. Christ says that we are not performing our service towards God, if in our sharing of goods or anything else we are looking to our mutual benefit and so He makes a distinction between charity and fleshly affection. Profane folk have love for themselves, not for nothing, but for the reward they hope to get. Thus it happens that a man turns back the love he shows for others upon himself—just as Plato wisely remarks. It is gratuitous well-doing that Christ demands from His people—zeal to aid the help-less, from whom they can expect nothing in return. Now we see what it means to keep our hand open to those who seek: it is to be stretched out generously to those who need our help, and who are unable to repay our beneficence.

Luke 6.35. *And lend.* This utterance has been wrongly attached to usury, as though Christ were only forbidding His own to lend capital for interest. Clearly, from the earlier part of the speech, it has a wider application. Once Christ had explained how the godless behave, in loving their friends, and helping those from whom they expect some pay-back, and lend to their own kind in order to get as much from them again, He adds how much more He asks of His followers, namely to love their enemies, to give freely, to lend freely. So we see that the phrase, *hoping for nothing again* (R.V. 'never despairing') is wrongly taken as a reference to interest, added to the principal, for Christ is urging them only to services that are spontaneous, and saying that mercenary actions win no favour in God's sight. He is not utterly condemning a man who does good in hope of reward, but says that this has no effect towards the display of charity, for ultimately the man who is good to his neighbours is led to help them through no regard for his own benefit, but only through looking to the need of each. Now whether a Christian may from time to time make some profit on a loan, I shall not at this point discuss at any length, to avoid raising the question on false grounds (as I have just explained). I have already shown that Christ only wished that the faithful in lending should go further than profane men, meaning, that is, that they should aim at pure liberality.

Ye have heard that it was said, Thou shalt love thy neighbour, and hate thine enemy: but I say unto you, Love your enemies, and pray for them that persecute you; that ye may be sons of your Father which is in heaven: for he maketh his sun to rise on the evil and the good, and sendeth rain on the just and the unjust. For if ye love them that love you, what reward have ye? do not even the publicans the same? And if ye salute your brethren only, what do ye more than others? do not even the Gentiles the same? Ye therefore shall be perfect, as your heavenly Father is perfect. (Matt. 5.43–48)*

But I say unto you which hear, Love your enemies, do good to them that hate you, bless them that curse you, pray for them that despitefully use you.

And if ye love them that love you, what thank have ye? For even sinners love those who love them. And if ye do good to them that do good to you, what thank have ye? for even sinners do the same.

But love your enemies . . . and ye shall be sons of the Most High: for he is kind toward the unthankful and evil. Be ye merciful, even as your Father is merciful. (Luke 6.27–28, 32–33, 35–36)

Matt. 5.43. *Thou shalt love thy neighbour.* It is amazing that the scribes had fallen into the absurdity of restricting the word *neighbour* to one's friends, since there is nothing more clear or sure that God embraces the whole human race when He speaks of our neighbours. For as each is devoted to himself, whenever private interests separate one from another, mutual intercourse is abandoned—the course which nature herself dictates. To keep us in a fraternal bond of love, God testifies that our neighbours are all men in general, for the common tie of nature unites us. As often as I see a man, who is my bone and my flesh, I must necessarily see myself, as reflected in a glass. Though the majority may recoil from an association in holy things, yet the natural order is not ruined by this grievous fault of theirs, for we must consider God, the Author of the union. Thus we infer, that it is a general rule of the Law, that we are told to love our neighbour. Now the scribes, in assessing a man's neighbourliness by his particular attitude, denied that one should treat as neighbour any but those whose merits made them worthy of our love, or at least, who would in turn respond to the claims of friendship. This may well be the teaching of common sense, and the sons of this world are never ashamed to confess their hatreds, and to be able to boast of the reason for them. But charity, which God commends in His Law, does not regard an individual's merits, but pours itself out on the unworthy, the perverse, the ungrateful. Christ restores the true and original sense, and clears it of slander. Here also we see, as I said earlier, that Christ is not starting new laws, but correcting the degraded comments of the scribes, which had vitiated the purity of the divine law.

Matt. 5.44. *Love your enemies*. This one heading comprises all the previous teaching: the man who brings his mind to love those who hate him will readily restrain himself from taking any revenge, he will endure their hurts, he will be far more ready to aid the afflicted. Christ, in a summary, shows the logic and the means of fulfilling this rule, 'Love your neighbour, as yourself'. For no-one will ever attain to this precept until he puts self-love aside, or rather denies himself, and values men for their God-given unity with himself to the extent of actually loving those also who have hate for him. We learn from these words how the faithful should have no dealings with vengeance, of any kind, for they may not at all seek it from God, but are to let it go and be swept from their minds, that they may pray good things for their enemies. At the same time, they do not cease to commend their own cause to God, until He takes vengeance on the reprobate. They desire, as far as may be, the evil to return to a sound mind, and not to perish, and so they hope for their salvation. But they have this comfort to lighten all their pains, that they do not doubt, that God will be the Avenger of determined malice, that He may show that He has had a care for the innocent.

Now I grant that this is exceedingly difficult, quite the opposite of fleshly thinking, to pay back good for evil, yet we must not look for an excuse in our faults and weakness, but rather examine quite simply what are the demands of the rule of charity, in order that, relying on the heavenly power of the Spirit we may win the battle, however much against the impulse of our own emotions. This was the reason produced by the monks and such rogues, who pretended that these were words of counsel given by Christ, not rules, therefore our duty to God and to His Law was measured by human capacity. Now monks were not ashamed to claim perfection for themselves, in freely devoting themselves to keep His counsels. How faithfully they in fact display the claim that title makes, I here omit to say. But how ridiculous and unintelligent was that view of the 'counsels'! This is evident, first, from the fact that it must be damaging for Christ to have advised His disciples what was right, and not to have given it as a commandment. Secondly, it is more than stupid to make the claims of charity, that depend upon the Law, optional. Thirdly, the word *say* which here means declare or enjoin is wrongly explained as to 'advise'. Finally, the explicit confirmation of the necessity of the obligation is directly given in Christ's words, where He goes on to say, as follows. . . .

Matt. 5.45. *That ye may be sons of your Father.* As He definitely states that no-one shall be a *son of God* if he does not love those who hate him, who would dare to deny that there is a compelling necessity upon us to hold on to this teaching? For it is equivalent to saying, that whoever would be called Christian must love his enemies. What a terrible state of affairs, that the world should have been under such a dark cloud for three or four centuries that it did not see the plain direction, the neglect of which wipes our name off the roll of the sons of God. Now we should realize that the example of God is set for us to follow, not as though we would be right to do anything that He does: for He punishes the ungrateful, and frequently drives the wicked from the face of the earth, and in this area we do not have Him before us as an example to copy, for the judgment of the world does not rest upon us, but is His property. He wishes us to be imitators of His fatherly goodness and kindness. Not only have profane thinkers appreciated this point, but even the most worthless scorners of religion have been driven to admit, that in nothing are we more like God than in doing good works. In sum, Christ testifies that this will be the mark of our adoption, if we are kind to the bad and unworthy. Do not think that we are made sons of God by our kind deeds, but as the same Spirit (who is the Witness, and the Pledge and Seal, of our free adoption) corrects the base emotions of the flesh which contradict charity, Christ gives proof, from the effect, that the sons of God are precisely those who approach Him in their humility and tenderness. At this place Luke reads, *Ye shall be sons of the Most High.* No-one wins this distinction for himself, no-one begins to be a son of God from the time he loves his enemies—but this is Scripture's normal way of speaking, to present the free gifts of God as a reward, by way of encouraging us to do the right thing. And this is the reason for Him taking note of the end to which we are called: with the image of God restored in us, we are to live a godly and holy life. *He maketh his sun to rise.* He records two testimonies of the divine goodness, not only as being those most familiar to us, but as being shared by all, for the very sense of community makes the invitation stronger to us to give to each other the same mutual beneficence, in all directions. However, many other things too are comprised in the synecdoche.

Matt. 5.46. *Do not even the publicans, etc.* Luke uses the word *sinners* in the same sense, that is, wicked and criminal types. It is not the job itself that is condemned (the 'publicani' were the receivers of taxes: as rulers have the right to appoint taxes, so one may collect them from the people), but because this class of men was usually greedy and rapacious, indeed untrustworthy and hard of heart, and because among Jews they were reckoned as the agents of an unjust tyranny. So to deduce from Christ's words that they are the worst of men would be a false argument, for He is speaking in terms of the generally accepted fashion, as if to say, men who are virtually devoid of humanity, yet preserve some kind of mutual responsibility, for all that they aim at their own advantage.

Matt. 5.48. *Ye therefore shall be perfect.* Perfection here, not in the sense of equality, but in relation to its likeness. However far we are from God, yet we are said to be perfect as He is, as long as we aim for the same goal, that He presents us with in Himself. If you prefer to put it differently, there is no comparison made here between God and ourselves, but it is called God's perfection when we show, first, sheer and free generosity, not spurred by any thought of gain, then, exceptional goodness, such as tackles the ill-will and ingratitude of men. It comes out better in Luke's words, *Be ye merciful, even as your Father* in heaven. Mercy is contrasted with the mercenary, that which is tied to personal advantage.

> *Take heed that ye do not your righteousness before men, to be seen of them: else ye have no reward with your Father which is in heaven.*
>
> *When therefore thou doest alms, sound not a trumpet before thee, as the hypocrites do in the synagogues and in the streets, that they may have glory of men. Verily I say unto you, They have received their reward. But when thou doest alms, let not thy left hand know what thy right hand doeth: that thine alms may be in secret: and thy Father which seeth in secret shall recompense thee.* (Matt. 6.1-4)

Matt. 6.1. *Take heed, etc.* In this passage Christ is encouraging His hearers to have a sincere zeal for good works, that they should study to do good in God's sight with simplicity, and not make an exhibition of themselves to men. The warning is very needful, as there is always the danger of selfishness in virtuous action, and no work is so praiseworthy as not to incur from it many faults and stains. Now His general instruction is given under one heading, by way of synecdoche. He only discusses alms-giving, since He will shortly proceed with prayers likewise. That the word *righteousness* is used in many instances for *alms-giving*, is the rendering of former interpreters. There is nothing important about that, as in either case it is generally agreed that it is the disease of self-seeking which He is treating—the cases where men strive for glory by their good deeds.

Matt. 6.2. *When therefore thou doest alms.* Here He directly tackles a vice which was accepted by use and wont, where the vain lust for glory could not only be publicly seen, but actually be palpably felt. At crossroads and public places, where there were usually gatherings of the people, he used to hand out little baskets to the poor: this was manifest display, in seeking out crowded places where they would have many witnesses, and not content with that, they added the call of a trumpet. They pretended that it was to summon the poor (for excuses are never lacking), but there was never anything more sure than that they were out for applause and popularity. Now when we serve men's eyes, we do not ask for God to judge and approve our lives. So Christ is right to say that they have their reward now, who make this kind of show, for they cannot have eyes for God, whose sight is so full of vanity. For the same reason, all who are greedy for empty glory are called *hypocrites.* In the profane writers, hypocrite was the name for the stage performer, who acted out, in theatre and festival, fictitious roles, but Scripture transfers it to the twofaced personality, and the fake. There are various kinds of hypocrites, for there are some who in themselves have a fearful conscience, but have the face to go around in company as decent men, and try to conceal the vices, of which they are inwardly convicted. Others have such bland self-assurance, that even in God's eyes they dare to claim perfect righteousness. Others have no concern for good or for the glory of God, but do good deeds to win themselves a reputation and name for sanctity. It is this last kind which Christ now indicates, and rightly terms hypocrites, who in their good works have no object of real virtue before their eyes, but put on another character, to appear to be devout and honest worshippers of God.

Matt. 6.3. *Let not thy left hand know.* He means by this expression that we should be content to have God as our sole witness, and to be so anxious to obey Him, that no vanity should distract us. It often happens that men make sacrifices not so much to God, as to themselves. Christ does not wish us to be side-tracked by irrelevant considerations, but to keep aiming straight at the target—the service of God—with a pure conscience.

Matt. 6.4. *That thine alms may be in secret.* This utterance seems to contradict many passages of Scripture where we are told to build up our brothers with good examples. But if we grasp Christ's intention, we must develop the words more fully. He tells His disciples to pay heed to good works disinterestedly, with no personal ambition. To do this, our eyes must be turned away from the sight of men, that they may be content to have the approbation of God alone for their actions. Such single-mindedness is no check to our efforts and enthusiasm to build up the brotherhood. A moment before it was not exactly doing good in the sight of men that was forbidden, but the ostentation that was condemned. *Thy Father which seeth in secret.* It is a tacit criticism of the folly which often holds sway over men, to think they have wasted their efforts if their prowess is not watched by a crowd of witnesses. Thus God says, He does not need a great light to recognize a good action, for He can see the things that appear to be hidden in the dark. There is no reason why we should think things are lost when they escape men's sight, and do not get a testimonial, for the theatre of God is in the hidden corners, and it is a splendid cure He applies for healing the disease of ambition, to recall us to the powers of God's vision, who can make all vain-glory vanish from our hearts, and disperse it altogether. In the second part, that follows directly, Christ tells us in seeking the reward of good deeds to wait patiently for the final day of resurrection. Thy Father, He says, shall recompense thee openly. When? When the dawn rises upon that final day, when all that is now hidden shall be seen, out of the darkness.

And when ye pray, ye shall not be as the hypocrites: for they love to stand and pray in the synagogues and in the corners of the streets, that they may be seen of men. Verily I say unto you, They have received their reward. But thou, when thou prayest, enter into thine inner chamber, and having shut thy door, pray to thy Father which is in secret, and thy Father which seeth in secret shall recompence thee. And in praying use not vain repetitions, as the Gentiles do: for they think that they shall be heard for their much speaking. Be not therefore like unto them: for your Father knoweth what things ye have need of, before ye ask him. (Matt. 6.5-8)

Matt. 6.5. *And when ye pray, etc.* He now gives the same lesson on prayer as He had earlier given on alms-giving. It is an intolerably stupid and shameful profanation of the Name of God, for hypocrites, to get glory from men, to make their prayers in public, or at least to pretend to pray. But as hypocrisy is ever ambitious, no wonder that it is so blind, and so He tells His disciples that if they wish to pray properly, they must go into a withdrawn place. Though some think the instance given is absurd, and attempt an allegorical explanation about the interior precinct of the heart, there is no need for such ingenuity. We are told in many places to give prayer and praise to God in crowded gatherings and assemblies of men, in the face of all the people, and it is for the sake of attesting our faith and gratitude and also to encourage others by our example to do the same thing. Christ is not taking us away from such efforts, but only warning us to keep God before our eyes whenever we settle ourselves for prayer. So we must not press the words. *Enter into thine inner chamber*, as though He told men to hide away, and say that we cannot pray aright unless without witness. He is speaking comparatively, meaning that we should rather look for a corner, than go after a crowd of people so that they may see us at prayer. And it is useful for the faithful, in order to pour out their prayers and their appeals more freely in God's sight, to withdraw from human gaze. There is another advantage in a quiet place, that we may have our minds more free and unburdened of any outside calls. For this reason Christ Himself, more than once, went away to a secret place to pray. However, this is not the present issue. He is simply putting right a vain desire for glory. This is the sum of it: whether one is alone or in company at prayer the attitude to adopt is to think of God as one's witness, as though shut off in an inside room. When Christ says that a reward is given to our prayers, He is making plain that whatever reward the Scripture promises us in various places is given not as a due, but as a free gift.

Matt. 6.7. *Use not vain repetitions.* He reproves another fault in our prayer, namely, garrulity. He uses two words, with the same meaning: βαττολογία ('stammering on') is superfluous and futile repetition, πολυλογία ('much-talk') is a useless flow of words. Christ is checking the folly of those who, to persuade God, and to win Him over, pour out a great flood of speech. This is not opposed to the teaching that persistence in prayer wins frequent approval in Scripture. When we come to pray with serious intention, the tongue does not outrun the heart, nor is God's favour secured by an empty flow of words, but rather, the longings which the devout heart sends out like arrowshots are those that reach to heaven. This condemns, of course, the superstition of those who trust they will win merit with God for long mutterings: precisely the error we may see affecting the Papacy, where the highest virtue in speaking is reckoned to be wordiness. The more a man rumbles out the words, the more he is rated for his accomplished prayer. Long and drawn-out chants, supposedly to charm the ears of God, are ever echoing around their sanctuaries.

Matt. 6.8. *For your Father knoweth.* Here is the sufficient remedy to remove and to cleanse the superstition now condemned. Is not the source of the folly, which makes many think they shall succeed if they weary God with many words, that they imagine Him to be like a mortal man, who needs to be told and advised? Anyone who is persuaded that God not only cares for us, but also knows our necessities, and anticipates our prayers and our worries before He is told of them, this man will forget his long-windedness and will be content if he makes his prayers as long as it helps the practice of his faith. To approach God in a rhetorical fashion, in order to move Him by power of address, he will recognize to be absurd and laughable. But if God knows what we need before we seek it, there might appear to be no benefit in prayer. If of His own accord He is ready to help us, what need have we to interject our prayers that might get in the way of the spontaneous course of His providence? There is an easy answer, in the very purpose of prayer, for the faithful do not pray to tell God what He does not know, or urge Him to His duties, or hurry Him on when He delays, but rather to alert themselves to seek Him, to exercise their faith by meditating upon His promises, unburdening their cares by lifting themselves into His bosom, and finally to testify that from Him alone, all good for themselves and for others is hoped and asked. As for Himself, what He has determined to give, of His own free will and even before He is asked, He promises to give all the same, in response to our prayers. Keep hold of both points, then: our prayers are anticipated by Him in His freedom, yet, what we ask we gain by prayer. Why at times He puts us off for a long period, and at times does not give a kind answer to our prayers, there will be occasion to speak of elsewhere.

After this manner therefore pray ye: Our Father which art in heaven, Hallowed be thy name. Thy kingdom come. Thy will be done, as in heaven, so on earth. Give us this day our daily bread. And forgive us our debts, as we also have forgiven our debtors. And bring us not into temptation, but deliver us from the evil one. (Matt. 6.9-13)

And it came to pass, as he was praying in a certain place, that when he ceased, one of his disciples said unto him, Lord teach us to pray, even as John also taught his disciples. And he said unto them. When ye pray, say, Father, Hallowed be thy name. Thy kingdom come. Give us day by day our daily bread. And forgive us our sins; for we ourselves also forgive everyone that is indebted to us. And bring us not into temptation. (Luke 11.1-4)

We cannot be sure whether Christ handed down this form of prayer to His disciples once or twice. Some think the second more likely, as Luke says that He was asked, while Matthew shows Him offering it voluntarily. Yet as we have said that Matthew brings all the chief points of the teaching together, that readers may have a better perspective over the whole in an unbroken sequence, it may be that Matthew has omitted the introduction which Luke records, yet over this issue I should not like to argue with anyone.

Luke 11.1. *Even as John also taught his disciples.* That John should have handed on a particular form of prayer to his disciples was done, I believe, in view of the circumstances of that time. We know that the situation with the Jews was in a seriously deformed state. All religious practice had reached such a point of collapse that it is amazing that there was a habit of prayer preserved by some few, in due order. Now when the promised redemption drew near, the minds of the faithful had to be excited to hope and desire for it with prayer. So John could have put together from various passages of Scripture a particular, set prayer to suit the time, and come more near the spiritual Kingdom of Christ, which had now begun to be revealed.

Matt. 6.9. *After this manner therefore pray ye.* For this, Luke reads, *when ye pray, say,* although Christ is not telling His people to pray in His form of words, but only showing them the direction along which all their supplications and prayers should tend. Thus the petitions include everything that we may rightly wish from God. This is a lesson of incomparable value to us, for though it is the principal exercise of our devotion, yet when we come to frame prayers and form requests, all our ideas run out. So no-one will learn to pray aright whose lips and heart are not schooled by the heavenly Teacher. For this end, there is handed down to us this pattern, by which we must control our prayers, if we wish them to be in true form, and to be approved by God. God's Son did not wish (as I have just said) to lay down the words we must use, as though we could not move away from the formula that He dictated, but He did wish to direct and control all our vows, that they should not wander beyond these limits. Thus we conclude, that it is not in words, but in the matters themselves, that He gave to us an ordinance for correct prayer.

Now when I say that this form for prayer consists of six petitions, we must know that the first three set aside the thoughts of our own minds, and concentrate on the glory of God, while the second three are devised for those things which are of benefit to our salvation. As God's Law is divided into two tables, the first containing the claims of devotion, the second of Charity, so in prayers Christ tells us to consider and search out in one part the glory of God, and then allows us in another part to think of ourselves. Hence we must know, that we shall only be adjusted to pray as we should, when we are not anxious simply for ourselves, and for our own cause, but give prior place to the glory of God, for it is quite absurd if we only take care for own business, and neglect the kingdom of God, which is so much more important.

Our Father which art in heaven. Whenever we set ourselves to pray, there are two things of greatest moment to consider—that we may have an open access to Him, and that we may repose upon Him with firm assurance, and these consist in His fatherly love towards us, and His unbounded power. So we should have no doubt but that God has a mind to welcome us kindly, is prepared to hear our prayers, and is readily inclined to help us. He is given the name of *Father*. Now in this epithet alone Christ is supplying us with ample ground for our full assurance, but, as our dependence on God's goodness is only half of our situation, He commends His power to us in a further phrase. When Scripture says God is 'in heaven', it means that all things are subject to His command, the world and all that is in it are in the palm of His hand, His influence is spread on all sides, everything is ordered by His Providence. In Psalm 2.4 David says, 'He that sitteth in the heavens shall laugh at them.' Likewise Psalm 115.3, 'But our God is in the heavens: He hath done whatsoever he pleased'. Of course God is not located in the heavens as though He were included within them (*non ita locatur in coelo Deus, quasi illic sic inclusus*), for we must rather accept what is written elsewhere (II Chron. 2.6), 'The heaven and the heaven of heavens cannot contain him'. But this expression, separating Him from the order of created beings, reminds that when we deal with Him, we should not conceive of anything low-born or earthbound, for He is exalted beyond the entire universe. Now we see Christ's purpose, wishing at the very start of the prayer to fix His hearers' confidence on the goodness and power of God, for unless prayers are founded upon faith they shall never make any advance. For as it would be foolish, nay crazy, presumption to invoke God as Father, except as far as we know ourselves to be ingrafted into the body of Christ as sons, we conclude that there is no other means of prayer than to come to God relying upon His mediation.

Hallowed be thy name. Here we see more clearly what I have just said, that in the first three petitions we must lay aside thought of ourselves and seek the glory of God, not that it is divorced from our own salvation, but that God's Majesty deserves to be exalted far above all other concerns. It is salutary for us that God reigns, and this title is duly accorded Him, but no-one has enough of a burning passion for the divine glory unless he somehow forgets his own position, and raises himself to seek Him in His transcendence. Between these three petitions, now, there is a great affinity and likeness. The hallowing of God's Name is always attached to His reign, and the chief feature of His reign is to be acknowledged in the doing of His will. When you consider, however, how cold and apathetic we are in asking for the greatest things of all, such as these prayers here declare to us, you will agree that

206

there is nothing superfluous in this arrangement, that it is useful that the three things asked for are thus distinguished. For God's Name to be *hallowed* means exactly that God's Name is to be held in the honour which is deserved, that men may never speak or think of Him without the highest reverence. The opposite, is to use His Name in profanity, that is, when His Majesty is taken lightly, or men use it less reverently or honourably than is due. The glory, which is the manner of its hallowing, flows from and depends upon men's recognition of His wisdom, goodness, righteousness, power, and all the virtues that are in Him, for within Himself, God's holiness ever stays secure, but men partly obscure it by their malice and depravity, partly ravage and pollute it by their blasphemous contempt. So the sum of this petition is, that God's glory may shine out over the world, and its qualities be well spoken of amongst men.

True religion flourishes best when men accept firmly, that all which comes from God is right and laudable. full of justice and knowledge. For the result is that, according to the obedience of their faith, they embrace His Word, and acquiesce in all His pleasure and work, for the faith that we bring to God's Word (as John says, 3.33) is like our word of acceptance, testifying that God is true, just as unbelief and scorn for His Word are to show Him the most grievous insult. So we may tell how malignant are many of those who comment on the works of God, what bold and free tongues of criticism they allow themselves. Should He strike any of us, they object, they complain, they murmur at Him, and some indeed come out with open blasphemy. If He does not accede to our prayers, we do not think He has been sufficiently generous towards us. Many in fact make facetious remarks on the subject of His ineffable providence and hidden decrees and often His holy Name is taken up into a blatant mockery: yes, part of the world, as best they may, profane His holiness. So there is no wonder that we are bidden in the first place to ask, that He may have that reverence in the world which is His due. It is no mean condescension, that God should pass to us an interest in His glory.

Matt. 6.10. *Thy kingdom come.* Though the Greek verb is not compound, we shall still have the same sense if we read '*ad*-veniat', as former interpreters rendered it. We must first make sure of the definition of the Kingdom of God. He is said to be *reigning* over men, when they subdue their flesh to His yoke, and their own desires are laid aside, so that they willingly bind and give themselves over to His rule. For in this corrupt state of nature all our passions are so many soldiers of Satan, fighting against the righteousness of God, obstructing and disturbing His reign. So in this prayer we ask that, with all impediment removed, He may bring all mortals under His command, and lead them to consider the life of heaven. This is partly the effect of the Word of preaching, partly of the hidden power of the Spirit. He would govern men by His Word, but as the voice alone, without the inward influence of the Spirit, does not reach down into the heart, the two must be brought together for the establishment of God's Kingdom. So we pray that God will show His power both in Word and in Spirit, that the whole world may willingly come over to Him. The opposite of the Kingdom of God is complete ἀταραξία (disorder) and confusion: nor is anything in the world well-ordered unless He arranges its thoughts and feelings, by His controlling hand. So we conclude, that the beginning of the Kingdom of God in us, is the end of the old man, the denial of self, that we may turn to newness of life. God reigns in another fashion, too, when He overcomes His enemies, when He forces them all unwilling—with Satan at their head—to accept His authority, till all become His footstool. So the sum of this supplication is that God will illuminate the heart by the light of His Word, bring our hearts to obey His righteousness by the breathing of His Spirit, and restore to order at His will, all that is lying waste upon the face of the earth. His Kingdom's first effect is to tame the desires of our flesh. And now, as the Kingdom of God increases, stage upon stage, to the end of the world, we must every day pray for its coming. As far as iniquity holds the world in sway, so far is the Kingdom of God absent—for complete righteousness must come in its train.

Thy will be done. God's will, as far as concerns Himself, is one and simple but it is set before us in the Scriptures as twofold. God's pleasure is said to be done, when He executes the hidden decrees of His providence, for all that men contumaciously struggle to oppose Him. Here however, we are told to pray in another respect, for His will to be done, that all creatures may yield to Him, in quietness and without hostility. A comparison shows this more plainly. Just as He keeps the angels ready for all His errands (whence they are called the agents ever prepared for His service), so we wish that all the affections of men may be trained to fall in with the righteousness of God, that they may readily be turned wherever He should indicate. This is the prayer of duty, that we should submit to God's will, subscribe to His pleasure. But the prayer contains something more, that God, dispersing all the contumacy of men, which is always using up in His face, should make them compliant and governable to Himself, not wishing anything, nor seeking anything, but what is pleasing and acceptable in His sight. The question may be raised here, whether one should ask God for something which He states will never be, until the world come to an end. I reply, that there is no need to put every individual to the test, when we pray for the world to be obediently ordered at God's bidding. It is enough that we testify, by our request, that we do hate and lament all that we see to be opposed to the will of God, and that we wish it abolished, both that His will may govern all our passions, and that we, with due alacrity, may offer ourselves for its fulfilment.

Matt. 6.11. *This day our daily bread.* This is, as I said, like the second table of the form of prayer which Christ set out for us. It was in order to make this point that I drew the distinctions earlier. As the former of the two tables of the Law dealt with the proper service of God, and the latter with the claims of charity, so in this prayer He first fits us to seeking the glory of God, and in the second part shows us what we should ask Him on our own account. But we should note, at the same time, that the prayers we make for our own salvation or benefit must be related to that ultimate end. That is to say, we may not be so occupied in an enthusiasm for our own advantage, that God's glory fails to hold first claim. So whenever we pray, we must not drop our eyes from that target. But there is this difference between the two kinds of prayer we have indicated. When we deal with the Kingdom of God and the hallowing of His Name, we must lift up our imaginations, ignore self-interest, and wait only upon God, but then we come down to ourselves, and we attach our concern for our salvation to those earlier prayers, which only had regard for God. And though the remission of sins is to be preferred to food, as far as the soul naturally is superior to the body, Christ yet begins with bread and the supports of our earthly existence, in order to lead us higher from such elementary things. So we do not ask to be given our daily bread before we are to be reconciled to God, as though the passing diet of the stomach were worth more than the salvation of our eternal soul, but our thoughts ascend from earth to heaven, as by the rungs of a ladder. When God condescends to feed our bodies, certainly it is over our spiritual life that He is most concerned. Thus His kindly favour swells our confidence. Some take ἐπιούσιον (daily) bread in the sense of 'supersubstantial' (beyond what is necessary to support life); but this is quite absurd. The reasoning that Erasmus applies is both trifling, and contrary to religion, for he does not think it likely that when we approach God's sight, Christ should tell us to think about food. As though there were not frequent instances in Scripture of this way of teaching—that from the taste of present goods we should be induced to hope for heavenly ones. Ultimately, this is the real test of our faith, that we look to God for everything, recognize Him as the unique source of all benefits, and find the tokens of His fatherly goodness appearing even in the smallest matters, so that He will not refuse to consider the needs of the flesh also. That Christ here speaks of bodily food may first readily be deduced from the fact that His words would then be incomplete, not all-embracing. For we are told in many places to cast all our cares on the lap of God, and He Himself generously undertakes that He will fail us at no point, So, in a correct order of prayer, as it should be, there must be some instruction on the innumerable necessities of this present life. The phrase *this day* means that in this matter we must take care only to ask from God what the day demands. No doubt He intended to restrain and check that greed for earthly provision in which we are all too much involved. The use of synecdoche in the word *bread* is quite familiar. Hebrew employs it for all kinds of nutriment. Here perhaps it extends more widely. It is not only what we eat that is handed to us by God, for we ask Him to give us all that we need for our passage through this life. This makes the sense clearer. We are told first to pray that God will protect and favour the existence He has given us in this world, and, as it needs much assistance, that He Himself will bring to us whatever He knows to be essential. Because a continuous stream of loving-kindness flows from God to nourish us, the bread that He serves is called ἐπιούσιος, that is, that which follows (day by day), for this is how it should be interpreted. The word has the effect of saying: Lord, as our life has need of new nourishment every day, never grow weary of your continuing liberality. The adverb *this day* as I have just remarked, is added to stop excessive greed, that we should learn that God's benefits depend on each moment, and that we should be satisfied with such portion as will keep us (as they say in the trade) from day to day.

Now, the objection is raised, that since it is certain that Christ set this common rule of prayer before all godly people, and yet that there are some rich men in that number who have a capital sum saved up, how can He be telling them to ask for what they already have in their own homes, and to seek for one day what would do them very well for a year. The solution is simple. These words tell us that unless God feeds us, no amount of accrued capital will mean anything. Although grain, wine, and everything else be there to overflowing, if they do not have the dew of God's unseen benediction, these all vanish on the spot, or their enjoyment is taken away, or the power they have to nourish us is lost, and we starve in the midst of our great supply. So there is no wonder that Christ invites the rich and poor alike to the heavenly store. At the same time, no-one will take this prayer to heart until he has learnt from Paul's example to hunger and to abound, to bear his poverty and lean times with an untroubled mind, and not to be put off balance by the deceptive confidence of plenty.

Should anyone ask why the bread that we are asking to be given us is called *ours*, I should answer that it is not rightly so called except that by God's fatherly goodness it is appointed for our use. By this very means it becomes ours, that the heavenly Father, in case we should lack it in our necessity, freely gives it to us. Of course the fields are to be tilled, we must sweat over the gathering-in of the fruits of the earth, each must undergo and endure the labour of his own calling, to get himself a living, but this does not prevent us being fed by the gratuitous good-will of God, without which men vainly wear themselves out upon their tasks. So we are taught to acknowledge at His hand all that appears to be the proceeds of our own effort. At the same time, we may understand from this utterance, that if we wish to be fed at God's hand, we must not go to another's. God's family profess that they seek only such things as they may call their own, as often as they use this form of prayer.

Matt. 6.12. *Forgive us our debts.* This is a good place to recall what I said recently, that in arranging His people's requests, Christ did not take into account what should come first, or second. Since it is written, that our sins are like a dividing wall, which prevents God from coming close, and like a cloud, which stops His eyes from seeing us (Isa. 59.2 and 44.22; Lam. 3.44), we must always start our prayers with remission of sins, for at this point there appear the first rays of hope that our prayers reach God—that He is kindly favoured to us, and that He is only favourable towards us in that He freely pardons our sins. Now Christ has put in two petitions the objects of our soul's eternal salvation and spiritual life, as though these were the two headings of the divine cove-nant which comprise our whole salvation: He offers us free reconcili-ation, by not imputing our sins to us, and He promises the Spirit, to engrave upon our hearts the righteousness of the Law. We are bidden to ask for both, and in first place there is put the prayer for obtaining the remission of our sins. Sins are called *debts* in Matthew, for their guilt binds us to God's tribunal, and makes debtors of us. Moreover, they quite alienate us from God, till we have no hope of winning peace or grace unless by pardon. Thus is fulfilled the teaching of Paul (Rom. 3.19, 23), 'For all have sinned, and fall short of the glory of God, that every mouth may be stopped, and all the world may be brought under the judgment of God.' For though there is some glimmer of the righteousness of God in the saints, yet, all the time they are encumbered in the flesh, they lie under the burden of their sins. Thus no man will be found so innocent as not to need the mercy of God, and if we wish to be partakers of it, we must feel our wretched state for what it is. Those who dream up thoughts of perfection for themselves in this world, freedom from all fault, all blame, are not parting company with their sins so much as with Christ Himself, in separating themselves from His Church. As He bids all His disciples daily to have recourse to the remission of sins, He erases from that number those who reckon them-selves to have no time to waste on such treatment.

Now the remission which we are here asking to be accomplished is contrary to the satisfactions by which the world tries to redeem itself. A creditor is not said to give remission in accepting the payment, and demanding nothing further, but in freely and generously giving up his fair rights and releasing the debtor. There is no place here for the market-place distinction between blame and penalty, for there is no doubt that debts mean liability to penalty. If we receive remission on this, then all compensation flies out of the window. Luke's sense is exactly the same, although he says *sins*, for God only grants their pardon, by removing the liability.

As we forgive. (R.V. *have forgiven*). The condition is made to prevent anyone daring to approach God to seek forgiveness without being quite free and clear of hatred. Not that the pardon that we ask to be given us depends on that which we grant to others, but Christ decided to urge us in this way to put aside all injuries, and at the same time to have us confirm our own absolution, as by the imprint of a seal. There is no difficulty in Luke reading Καὶ γάρ ('for in fact'), which has the same effect as *siquidem* ('if indeed'/'since indeed') or *etenim* ('and in fact'): it was not Christ's intention to indicate a cause, but only to tell us the attitude we should have towards our brothers in the process of desiring to be reconciled with God. If the Spirit of God reigns in our hearts, then all ill-will and feelings of revenge must go. As we have the Spirit as the witness of our adoption, we see that this indication is simply put here to differentiate the sons of God from the outsiders. The word *debtors* here does not mean money, or any particular claim, but those who for wrongs done to us have crossed our paths.

Matt. 6.13. *And bring us not into temptation.* This petition has been wrongly divided by some into two parts, but the material itself shows it to be one and the same, and the connection of words proves the same. The adversative particle placed in the middle binds the two parts together, which is the point Augustine wisely makes. So the utterance should flow like this, In order that we may not be led into temptation, deliver us from evil. In brief, being conscious of our own weakness, we ask to be defended by God's protection, that we may have an impregnable position against all the devices of Satan. As we demonstrate in the last request, that no-one can be rated a Christian who does not admit that he is tangled up with sin, so we deduce from this one that our powers are not adequate to living well, except as far as God supplements them. Whoever beseeches God for aid in overcoming temptations, confesses that he needs Him as Deliverer too, or else he may fall away directly. Now the word *temptation* is often taken in a general sense, for any kind of test: in such a sense Abraham was said to have been tempted by God, when his faith underwent scrutiny. Thus we are tempted in good times and in bad, for it is the occasion for passions which were hidden before coming to light. But here is intended that interior temptation, which may aptly be termed the devil's lash, for whipping up our concupiscence. It would surely be absurd to ask God to keep us immune from every proof of our faith. So all the base impulses, which prick us on to sin, are comprised in the word *temptation*. It is inevitable that we feel such seductions in our hearts, for all through our lives we wage unending war with the flesh, but we ask the Lord not to bring us down with temptations, or to let us be overwhelmed. So that Christ could express better that we are ever on the brink of endless falls and catastrophes, unless God hold on to us, He uses the form of speech, 'Lead us not into temptation': or, as others translate, Carry us not in. Certainly everyone is tempted by his own lusts, as James tells us (1.14), but as God both allows Satan's whim to inflame the fire of lust, and also uses him as the agent of His wrath when He determines to drive men headlong into destruction, thus in His own way He actually leads men into temptation. In this sense, an evil spirit of God is said to have seized upon Saul, and there are similar arguments in several passages of Scripture, not that we are on this account to start to call God the Author of evil, for His sending men along the way of the wicked is not reckless tyranny, but the execution of His righteous—though obscure—judgments.

Deliver us from evil. (R.V. *from the evil one*). 'Evil' could here be read as either neuter or masculine. Chrysostom refers it to the devil, who is the architect of all evil, and inasmuch as he is the bitter enemy of our salvation continually wars against us. But it could just as conveniently be explained as referring to sin. There is no need to make a controversy over the matter, for the sense stays practically the same, that we are exposed to the devil and to sin, but God protects us and snatches us away.

For thine is the kingdom. It is strange that this doxology, closing the prayer, which it fits so well, has been omitted in the Latin. It was added not only to warm our hearts to press towards the glory of God, and warn us what should be the goal of all our supplications, but also to tell us that all our prayers, here set down for us, have no other foundation than God alone, in case we should put any weight upon our own merits.

For if ye forgive men their trespasses, your heavenly Father will also forgive you. But if ye forgive not men their trespasses, neither will your Father forgive your trespasses. (Matt. 6.14-15)

213

And whensoever ye stand praying, forgive, if ye have aught against any one; that your Father also which is in heaven may forgive you your trespasses. But if ye do not forgive, neither will your Father which is in heaven forgive your trespasses. (Mark 11.25-26)

Here Christ simply explains to what purpose the conditional clause had been intended, 'Forgive us, as we forgive.' God will not be affected by our prayers if we do not in turn show ourselves ready to give pardon, if any have hurt us. Certainly, unless we are harder than iron, this exhortation should soften us, and make us agreeable to remit offences. If God did not daily condone our various sins, we know that we should have died countless times. The only Law of admission to His forgiveness is that we pardon our brothers for any sin against us. Therefore it is nothing short of voluntary dedication to destruction deliberately to make God implacable to them, when men refuse to forget the wrongs done them.

Moreover when ye fast, be not, as the hypocrites, of a sad countenance: for they disfigure their faces, that they may be seen of men to fast. Verily I say unto you, They have received their reward. But thou, when thou fastest, anoint thy head, and wash thy face; that thou be not seen of men to fast, but of thy Father which is in secret: and thy Father, which seeth in secret, shall recompense thee. (Matt. 6.16-18).

Now he goes back to His earlier teaching. He had begun by reproving vain ostentation in almsgiving and in prayers, then interposed the proper pattern for prayer. Now he gives His men the same lesson on fasting as He had given before on prayers and alms-giving: they should not be so keen on playing to the gallery, as to have God the spectator of their works. Now telling them to anoint their head and wash their face is by way of exaggeration, for Christ is not leading us away from one kind of hypocrisy to lead us into another. He does not want us to put on a show of elegance, nor is He urging us to such an arrangement of our meals that may give us freedom for luxurious unguents and apparel, but He simply induces us to find a moderation where there will be no novelty or affectation: in other words, we must so leave room for fasts, that nothing in our accustomed way of life has to be altered. In promising God's *reward* for fasts, He uses an inexact expression, as was remarked a little before in connection with prayers, though there is a great difference between prayers and fasting. The former have a leading place in the duties of religion, but fasting in itself is a work of indifferent value, not of the sort that God requires and approves, in the way that almsgiving is. It pleases Him up to a point, as long as it is directed to an end beyond itself, namely, to prompt us to abstinence, to subject the lasciviousness of the flesh, to incense us to a desire for prayer, to testify to our repentance, whenever we are moved by the judgment of God. So the sense of Christ's words is that God will in time show that He was pleased with good works which seemed to have gone for nothing, as they escaped the sight of men.

Lay not up for yourselves treasures upon the earth, where moth and rust doth consume, and where thieves break through and steal: but lay up for yourselves treasures in heaven, where neither moth nor rust doth consume, and where thieves do not break through nor steal: for where thy treasure is there will thy heart be also. (Matt. 6.19-21)

Sell that ye have, and give alms; make for yourselves purses which wax not old, a treasure in the heavens that faileth not, where no thief draweth near, neither moth destroyeth. For where your treasure is there will your heart be also. (Luke 12.33-34)

Matt. 6.19. *Lay not up.* It is a major plague, which we find rampant amongst mankind, that they have a mad and insatiable desire for possessions. Christ convicts them of folly, for with all the effort they expend on piling up wealth, they are prostituting their fortune to worms and rust, leaving it open to the raids of thieves. What could be more senseless, than to put one's goods where either they will waste on their own, or be snatched up by robbers? But the greedy do not think of this. They hoard their wealth in well-sealed chests, yet they cannot avoid their riches being at the mercy of thieves or moths. So they are blind, and lack a right understanding, who strive to amass great sums of wealth with vast labour and vast trouble, for all of them shall be affected by decay, or theft, or the thousand other turns of fate, especially since God provides us with a place in heaven to lay up our treasure, and gently invites us to possess riches which shall never waste away. Those who *lay up treasures in heaven,* are those who rid themselves of earth's entanglements and direct their concern and zeal to consider the life of heaven. In *Luke* the contrast is not made, and another occasion is indicated, for Christ tells them to make for themselves purses that shall not grow old, for He had said, *Sell that ye have,* that you may give alms. Now as men find it hard and painful to strip themselves of their possessions, He proposes to them a full and splendid hope of recompense, as a way of relieving the difficulty, namely, that when they relieve their brother's need on earth, they are laying up for themselves treasures in heaven—according to Solomon's word, He that hath pity on the poor, lendeth unto the Lord (Prov. 19.17).

His instruction on selling our possessions, is not to be taken too exactly, as though it were not permissible for any Christian man to leave anything over for himself. The lesson He wished to give was that we should not donate to the poor in terms only of our superfluity spilling over onto them. No, we are not to spare our capital funds, if the interest available from these fails to meet their necessity. In other words, your liberality has to go as far as the diminution of your patrimony, and the disposal of your estates.

Matt. 6.21. *For where thy treasure is.* In this utterance, Christ proves how miserable men are who keep their treasure locked up on earth: their fortune is fading and transitory. The greedy say it does not stop their hearts aspiring to heaven, but Christ brings up the axiom, that where men reckon they have their highest good, there they are tied and there they are fixed. So it follows, that those who desire to be happy in this world, renounce the path to heaven. We know how much care philosophers have given to the *summum bonum*: indeed, it was the main heading of all their arduous labours, and rightly so, since the whole pattern of our life's course depends upon it, and to this point all our passions are related. If honour is rated the highest good, then ambition must take complete charge of a man; if money, then forwith greed takes over the kingdom; if pleasure, then men will certainly degenerate into sheer self-indulgence. By nature we are all drawn to seek the good, and thus it is that false notions pull us this way and that. But if we were well and seriously persuaded that our happiness was in heaven, it would be easy to knock the world aside, to scorn earthly goods (whose deceptive allurements captivate the majority of men), and ascend to heaven. This is the mind of Paul, who wishing to lift the faithful up to the heights, and to urge upon them zeal for the life of heaven, sets Christ before them, as in Him alone there is to be found the fulness of joy. It is as if He said, it would a strange thing, and less than worthy of them, if their souls should sink to the level of earth, when their treasure is in heaven.

The lamp of the body is the eye: if therefore thine eye be single, thy whole body shall be full of light. But if thine eye be evil, thy whole body shall be full of darkness. If therefore the light that is in thee be darkness, how great is the darkness! No man can serve two masters: for either he will hate the one, and love the other; or else he will hold to one, and despise the other. Ye cannot serve God and mammon. (Matt. 6.22-24)

The lamp of thy body is thine eye: when thine eye is single, thy whole body also is full of light; but when it is evil, thy body also is full of darkness. Look therefore whether the light that is in thee be not darkness. If therefore thy whole body be full of light, having no part dark, it shall be wholly full of light, as when the lamp with its bright shining doth give thee light.

No servant can serve two masters: for either he will hate the one, and love the other; or else he will hold to one, and despise the other. Ye cannot serve God and mammon. (Luke 11.34-36; 16.13)

Matt. 6.22. *The lamp of the body is the eye.* You must remember what I remarked before, that we have here a series of short utterances, not a continuing address. The gist of this section is that carelessness leads men astray, for they are not as intent as they should be on the right goal. For how is it that they come down in disgrace, or run into trouble, or have a breakdown, except that, in their corrupt judgment, they choose to obey their fancies rather than God, and so stifle the light of reason, which should have governed their path—indeed turn it altogether into darkness? Christ uses a simile, calling the eye the light of the whole body, as if He said that when men walk, it is not the hands or the feet or the belly that take first place in finding the road, but the eye is the competent member to lead all the other parts. So if our hands or feet run wild, out of all proportion, the fault for the error must be laid upon the eyes, for not doing their duty. Now transfer the simile to the soul. Individual passions are like its several parts, as they are blind in themselves, they have need of directions. So God provided reason, to bring them into line, and to do the work of a torch which shows the way ahead. And what is the most usual result? Men choose to corrupt and spoil that gift of a sane mind which they had received, until not even a flicker of light is left to it. He speaks of the *single eye*, as one unaffected by any hazing or inflammation, not suffering any kind of evil: πονηρὸν (referring to the *evil* eye) takes in the sense of faulty. The *body* is *full of light*, it has illumination, in the sense that all its actions are properly in order. *Full of darkness*, it is in a confused state and is drawn into a variety of errors.

We see then (as I have just said), that men's apathy is being brought home to them, when they neglect to open the eyes of the mind in order to govern their own emotions. That the Papists infer from this that men have a faculty of reason and discretion, whereby they enjoy a free choice of good or evil, is unfounded, for Christ is not speaking of any faculty with which we are endowed, but is telling us how we should conduct ourselves, by concentrating upon one sure goal. At the same time, He is showing how the whole course of human life is so shrouded in darkness, that no-one looks to his right end, but all take their own pleasure and eagerly chase after evil. I grant, that by nature, men have an inborn gift of reason, to discern between vice and virtue, but I say that it is so vitiated by sin, that it fails at every step. It follows from this that men consciously bring the darkness upon themselves, when they shut their eyes, so to speak, to the light that is offered them, and knowingly and willingly are captivated by their own lusts.

Matt. 6.23. *If therefore the light that is in thee, etc.* By *light*, He means reason, such little remnant as remains in men after the fall of Adam, by *darkness*, their stupid and beastly impulses. So the sense is, that it is no wonder that men should like cattle so foully wallow in the mire of their vices since there is no power of reason to control the blind and shadowy inclinations of the flesh. He says the light is *turned to darkness*, both as men, through the debased desires of the flesh, allow the judgment of their minds to be over-ridden, and as they yield their intelligence to perverse thoughts, and degenerate as it were to the level of beasts. We see the wicked thinking which men use to divert such prudence as they had into roguery, to construct for themselves great systems of speculation, as the Prophet says, seeking to make a wild assault on God (Isa. 29.15), and altogether to imagine innumerable ways of seeking their own destruction. For such reasons, Christ plainly states that there are bound to be fearful and unutterably dark shadows over that life where men deliberately choose blindness. The sense of Luke's words is the same, except that there Christ connects this idea with that expounded earlier, at the fifth chapter of Matthew, 'No-one lights a lamp and puts it in hiding etc.' Then, in place of the closing sentence, 'If the light that is in thee etc.', he gives the exhortation, *Look therefore whether the light that is in thee be not darkness.* In other words, See that your mind, which should shine as a lantern to guide your actions, does not throw a shadow and a perversion across your whole life. Then He adds, that when the body is lit by the eye, then the best harmony exists in all the parts, just as the lamp, when it is lit, scatters its rays and reaches into every corner of the room.

Matt. 6.24. *No man can serve, etc.* Christ returns to His previous teaching, where He pulls His disciples away from avarice. He had said before, that a man's heart is chained and bound to his treasure, and now He says that men's hearts are estranged from God when they devote themselves to riches. The majority are usually inclined to live in luxury, and at the same time imagine that it is possible to be divided between God and their own pleasures. Christ denies the possibility, that a man may together obey God, and his flesh, No doubt this was a proverb in common use at the time, No-one can serve two masters at once. As this was accepted by general opinion, He can take it for granted, and applies it to the case in hand—where riches sit upon the throne, God has lost His power. Granted, it is not impossible for men who are rich to serve God, but whoever hands himself over as a slave to riches must leave the service of God, since greed always engages us in bondage to the devil. I have brought into this context what Luke records at another. The Evangelists move Christ's utterances dispersedly as occasion demands, to different places, and we should feel no compunction in setting them together. What is said here particularly of riches, may be applied to all faults of any kind with equal propriety: as God always highly values sincerity, and abominates the two-faced character, men are entirely deceived if they think that He will be satisfied with half of their hearts. All profess with their lips, that God is only given true service by wholehearted devotion, but they deny it in their deeds, when they try to reconcile two contradictory principles. The ambitious man says, I shall not stop serving God, even though I apply the good part of my mind to pursuing positions of honour. Likewise the greedy, the pleasure-seekers, the hard drinkers, the sadists, all make the same pretence, as if it were possible for them to serve God in any part, when obviously they are dead set against Him. It is true that the faithful themselves are never so firmly devoted to God's obedience but that they are ever being drawn back by the sinful desires of the flesh. But as they groan under this wretched servitude, and are unhappy with themselves, and only serve the flesh with unwillingness and reluctance, these are not said to serve two masters, for their zeal and their efforts are being proven by the Lord, as surely as if the obedience they displayed were unsullied. This refutes the hypocrisy of those who go gaily on in their vices, as though they could bring together light and darkness.

Therefore I say unto you, Be not anxious for your life, what ye shall eat, or what ye shall drink; nor yet for your body, what ye shall put on. Is not the life more than the food, and the body than the raiment? Behold the birds of the heaven, that they sow not, neither do they reap, nor gather into barns; and your heavenly Father feedeth them. Are not ye of much more value than they? And which of you by being anxious can add one cubit unto his stature? And why are ye anxious concerning raiment? Consider the lilies of the field, how they grow; they toil not, neither do they spin; yet I say unto you, that even Solomon in all his glory was not arrayed like one of these. But if God doth so clothe the grass of the field, which today is, and tomorrow is cast into the oven, shall he not much more clothe you, O ye of little faith? (Matt. 6.25-30)

And he said unto his disciples, Therefore I say unto you, Be not anxious for your life, what ye shall eat; nor yet for your body, what ye shall put on. For the life is more than the food, and the body than the raiment. Consider the ravens, that they sow not, neither reap; which have no store-chamber nor barn; and God feedeth them: of how much more value are ye than the birds! And which of you by being anxious can add a cubit unto his stature? If then you are not able to do even that which is least, why are ye anxious concerning the rest? Consider the lilies, how they grow: they toil not, neither do they spin; yet I say unto you, Even Solomon in all his glory was not arrayed like one of these. But if God doth so clothe the grass in the field, which to-day is, and to-morrow is cast into the oven; how much more shall he clothe you, O ye of little faith? (Luke 12.22-28)

In all this speech Christ reproves the over anxious concern for food and clothing, over which men tear themselves with worry, and also prescribes the cure for treating this disease. When He forbids them to 'be careful', we should not exactly understand Him to intend that they were relieved of all care for their own. We know that men come into this world on condition that they assume some responsibility: indeed it is not the least part of the troubles which God lays on us for our chastisement, that He may make us humble. But excessive care He condemns, for two causes, that men wear themselves out and torment themselves in vain, when they are more busy than their calling permits or compels, and that they take more upon themselves than they should, relying too much on their own efforts, and neglecting to call upon God. We must hold onto the promise, for while the unbelievers go to bed late and rise early and eat the bread of sorrow, the faithful shall have peace and sleep, through the grace of God (Ps. 127.2). So the children of God, while they may not be immune from toil and care, are still not said really to be worried over their lives, for they rest on the providence of God, and have peaceful repose. We may readily infer, therefore, how far we should be concerned over food—which is that each of us should struggle just as far as our vocation takes us, and as God commands us, but after that, let each man's necessity prompt him to call upon God. Such concern is half-way between idle inactivity and useless torment, upon which the unbelievers waste themselves. If we think properly over what Christ says, it is not care in general which He forbids us, but such as is rooted in lack of faith. He says, do not be worried as to what you shall eat or what you shall drink, for this is the fate of those who tremble for fear of emptiness and failure, as though they who might at any moment be left without food.

Matt. 6.25. *Is not the life, etc.* The reasoning is from greater to less. He had forbidden men to be over-concerned with the business of putting up with this life; now He adds a reason, that the Lord who gave this life, will not allow the supports, which go to sustain it, to fail us. It is truly no small offence we do God, in not trusting Him to supply us with food and clothing, as though He cast us into the world without any heed. When a man is firmly persuaded that God clearly sees the state of our life—of which He is the Author—he will have no doubt that, in fact, He considers its necessities very well. So as often as any fear or worry creeps upon us, let us remember that our life will be God's concern, as it was His gift.

Matt. 6.26. *Behold the birds.* The remedy I spoke of lies in our learning to repose upon the providence of God: faithlessness is the mother of all immoderate cares. There is one means of correcting greed, which is, to embrace the promises of God, in which He testifies that He will take care of us. In such manner the Apostle (Heb. 13.5), determined to draw the faithful away from greed, confirmed this message with the quotation, 'I will not fail thee nor forsake thee.' Briefly, He urges us to have trust in God, for God neglects none of His own, however slight they may be. We must diligently note, that He says the heavenly Father feeds the birds. Though it is virtually a miracle that they sustain themselves, which one of us actually takes thought that their lives depend on God, who condescends to extend His providence even to their level? If it were firmly fixed in our minds that by God's hand nourishment is brought to the birds, it would be easy to take hope for ourselves, for we are founded on His image, and are reckoned among His sons. When He says, *the birds . . . sow not neither do they reap,* these words do not in the least invite us to be idle or lazy, but only mean that, even if every kind of assistance were to fail, God's providence alone would be enough for us, since it abundantly supplies the animals with all that they need. Luke has *ravens* instead of birds, possibly alluding to that passage in the Psalm (147.9), He giveth . . . his food to the young ravens which cry. Some believe that David expressly spoke of ravens, because they are immediately deserted by their parents, and so have to have food brought to them from God. Clearly, Christ's sole intention was to teach His people to cast their cares upon God.

Matt. 6.27. *Which of you by being anxious, etc.* Here Christ condemns another fault, which is almost always tied up with excessive concern for food, namely, that mortal man usurping more for himself than he is allowed, does not hesitate to everleap his finitude, in godless temerity.

'I know,' says Jeremiah (10.23), 'that the way of man is not in himself: it is not in man that walketh to direct his steps.' Yet you would scarcely find one man in a hundred who would not dare to make some promise to himself on the basis of his own efforts and potential. Thus God is put to one side, and men are actually bold enough at the start of schemes, to guarantee the successful outcome of events. Christ, to check such wild audacity, says that all which relates to the sustenance of our life depends upon God's blessing alone, just as if He said, that men foolishly weary themselves, for all their struggles are needless and unprofitable, their worries come to no good, unless and until God overrules them with His blessing. It is put more clearly in *Luke*, where Christ adds, 'If you cannot even do the least thing, why do you worry over the rest?' It is certain from these words, that not only is lack of faith brought up against them, but pride as well, in that men claim for their own cunning far more than is right and proper.

Matt. 6.26. *Even Solomon in all his glory*. The meaning is, that the blessing of God which glows upon the plants and flowers excels all that men may achieve by their wealth or influence, or by any other means: that the faithful may be positive, that nothing will be lacking to their perfect provision, even though all aids were to disappear, as long as God's blessing alone remains in force. *O ye of little faith*. Christ does well to charge them at this point with their failure, or weakness, of faith. The more we are affected with anxiety for this present life, because our intelligence is unenlightened, the more our lack of faith comes to the fore, if everything does not come out in answer to our prayers. So there are many, who in large issues appear to be endowed with at least a tolerable degree of faith, but who panic at the risk of a shortage in ordinary provisions.

Be not therefore anxious, saying, What shall we eat? or, what shall we drink? or, Wherewithal shall we be clothed? For after all these things do the Gentiles seek; for your heavenly Father knoweth that ye have need of all these things. But seek ye first his kingdom, and his righteousness; and all these things shall be added unto you. Be not therefore anxious for the morrow: for the morrow will be anxious for itself. Sufficient unto the day is the evil thereof. (Matt. 6.31-34)

And seek not ye what ye shall eat, and what ye shall drink, neither be ye of doubtful mind. For all these things do the nations of the world seek after: but your Father knoweth that ye have need of these things. Howbeit seek ye his kingdom, and these things shall be added unto you. Fear not, little flock; for it is your Father's good pleasure to give you the kingdom. (Luke 12.29-32)

His object is the same as in what precedes, that the faithful should trust to God's fatherly care, so that they should be full of hope that all things, which they know they need, shall come from him, so that they are not to torture themselves with useless anxiety. He forbids them to be *anxious*, or as Luke has it, *to seek*, meaning, of course, in the fashion of those who look this way and that, without regard for God, upon whom alone they should be intent. They are never at rest, except when they can see supply of corn before their eyes, and they give God no part in the world's government, but toss and turn in unending worries. When He says that the Gentiles seek after all these things, He is rebuking their crass ignorance, which is the source of all such anxieties. The reason that the unbelieving never stay in an untroubled state, is that they imagine that God sleeps in heaven unconcerned, or at any rate, takes His eyes off human affairs, neglecting to feed those whom He has taken into His household of faith. By this comparison, He is saying they have made little headway, indeed scarcely grasped the rudiments of religion, when they do not see, with the eyes of faith, that God's hand overflows with a secret supply of all goods, so that they may look to Him for their food, quietly, and with undisturbed minds. The heavenly Father, He says, knows you need these things: as if to say, that all those who are so greatly concerned for their food are giving no more credit to God's fatherly goodness and providence than do the unbelievers.

Luke 12.29. *Neither be ye of doubtful mind.* This clause corresponds to the last sentence we find in Matthew, *Be not therefore anxious for the morrow*: this is Christ's reproach for another fault, that men would gladly take in five centuries, in their passion to work out their future. The word μετεωρίζεσθαι which Luke uses, properly means to speculate from a great height, or as we say in common parlance, to take the long view. The intemperate rage of our flesh puts no limit on its labours, but keeps agitating heaven and earth, century upon century. Such unnecessary speculation is here given its precise censure, for by it, we bring needless troubles upon ourselves, and choose to be miserable before the event. Where Matthew says, *Sufficient unto the day is the evil thereof*, this is aimed at the faithful to put a check upon their worries, not to try to be far-sighted beyond the actual bounds of their calling. As I have said, this is not a condemnation of every kind of vigilance, but the sort that wanders beyond all the boundaries, into by-ways and vast digressions.

Matt. 6.33. *Seek ye first his kingdom.* He uses another argument to tackle undue concern for food, that it demonstrates a dumb and idle neglect of the soul, and the life of heaven. Thus Christ says that it is ridiculous for men, who were born for a better life, to occupy themselves completely with earthly things. Whoever puts God's Kingdom in first place, will only exercise himself over the provision of his food with moderate energy. And nothing was ever better suited to put a brake upon the appetite of the flesh, to stop it making a riot of this present life, than meditation upon the life of heaven. The word *righteousness* may be applied to God, and to His Kingdom, for we know that the Kingdom of God consists in righteousness, which consists in spiritual newness of life. When He states that the rest will be added, He means that the things which belong to this present life are in a way accessory, and so should take second place to the Kingdom of God.

Luke 12.32. *Fear not, little flock.* In this utterance, Christ confirms the confidence that He urged His people to possess. How would God deny plain, perishable food to His own, when He has made them, by adoption, heirs of His Kingdom? He deliberately picks upon the word *little* flock, that they should not rate themselves lesser in God's sight, for being counted as nothing in the view of the world for their smallness. By the word εὐδοκεῖν (good pleasure), he indicates that eternal life flows down to us from a spring of free loving-kindness. The word *give* adds to the force of the same message. When Christ openly declares that God has given us the Kingdom, and for no other reason than that it has so pleased Him, then it is more than evident that it is not acquired by any meritorious works. And so, as often as the Lord lifts us to the hope of life eternal, let us remember to have no fear for our daily food.

Judge not, that ye be not judged. For with what judgement ye judge, ye shall be judged: and with what measure ye mete, it shall be measured unto you. And why beholdest thou the mote that is in thy brother's eye, but considerest not the beam that is in thine own eye? Or how wilt thou say to thy brother, Let me cast out the mote out of thine eye; and lo, the beam is in thine own eye? Thou hypocrite, cast out first the beam out of thine own eye; and then shalt thou see clearly to cast out the mote out of thy brother's eye. (Matt. 7.1-5)

With what measure ye mete it shall be measured unto you. (Mark 4.24)

And judge not, and ye shall not be judged: and condemn not, and ye shall not be condemned: release, and ye shall be released: give, and it shall be given unto you; good measure, pressed down, shaken together, running over, shall they give into your bosom. For with what measure ye mete it shall be measured to you again.

And why beholdest thou the mote that is in thy brother's eye, but considerest not the beam that is in thine own eye? Or how canst thou say to thy brother, Brother, let me cast out the mote that is in thine eye, when thou thyself beholdest not the beam that is in thine own eye? Thou hypocrite, cast out first the beam out of thine own eye, and then shalt thou see clearly to cast out the mote that is in thy brother's eye. (Luke 6.37-38, 41-42)

Matt. 7.1. *Judge not.* These words of Christ are not to be taken exactly in the sense of condemning the function of judgment, but to cure a disease which nearly all grow up with. We see the way all treat themselves to seeing who can be the sharpest critic in the company. The fault is to some extent facilitated by an eagerness, which lights upon most of us, to inquire into other people's misdeeds. Everyone agrees, of course, that it is an intolerable evil to be so malicious towards our brothers, when they are ready to pardon us our faults. Pagan writers in their proverbs have long since condemned this: yet it has prevailed in all ages, and still prevails today. But there is another plague too, and a worse one, which is that a good number, by condemning others, reckon they have won freedom to sin themselves. This is the damnable desire to bite and tear and criticize which Christ is checking, when He says, 'Judge not.' The faithful should not be so blind as to notice nothing, but they should hold themselves in, and not go beyond the limit of strictness, should they ever have any occasion to make judgment upon their brothers. Compare the expression in James—'Be not many masters.' He is not frightening off the faithful, nor pulling them away from performing the role of teacher, but He is telling them not to seek after honour in a spirit of self-seeking. *Judge,* then, in this passage, simply means to inquire curiously into other people's affairs. It is a disease which always brings in its train an element of unfairness, so that we come to condemn a slight fault, as though it were a most heinous offence. Further, it breaks out into sheer arrogance, so that we form unfavourable judgments upon every issue with a haughty superiority, even when it might well have been taken in a good sense. Thus we see the object of Christ's intention, that we should not be too eager or ill-natured or malicious, or even over-curious, in judging those nearest to us. Whoever judges by the Law and Word of God, and directs his judgment according to the rule of charity, always begins his censure with himself, and this preserves in judgment a proper limit and order. Obviously men make false use of this testimony when they would make it a pretext to remove from the scene all discrimination between good

225

and evil. It is not only permitted to us to condemn all sin, it is an obligation—unless we wish to contradict God Himself, abrogate His laws, rescind His judgments, upset His tribunal. He intends us to be the heralds of the sentence which He pronounces upon the actions of men, but we must take care to use such discretion, that He alone remains the Lawgiver and the Judge.

That ye be not judged. He pronounces a penalty upon those rigid critics, who are so busy in shaking out others' sins: it will come to be, that they shall be treated with no more humanity, by others, but they in their turn shall feel the same severity against themselves, as they exercised upon others. As nothing is dearer or more precious to us than our reputation, so it is more than bitter to be condemned and subjected to the insults and disgrace of men. By our own fault, we bring the very thing upon ourselves which our natures so greatly abhor. Is there any one of us who does not pry into other folks' behaviour more than is reasonable? Who does not make a great fuss over slight faults? Who does not make a solemn row, out of a matter indifferent enough in itself? And what does all this come to, but deliberately to bring God down upon us as in vengeance, to pay us back in kind?

Now, though it belongs to the just punishment of God that we, who have judged others, should in turn suffer for it, yet this is a penalty which God uses men to prosecute. For Chrysostom and certain others to put this all onto the life to come, is a forced interpretation. Exactly as Isaiah threatens (33.1), that they shall be a prey who have made a prey of others, so Christ intends that instruments shall not be lacking to punish unfair and malevolent men, with an equal virulence and rigour. And even if the men should not appear, and they escape penalty in this world, those who have been so very keen on their brothers' condemnation shall not escape the judgment of God.

In Luke there is added a promise, *Release, and ye shall be released: give, and it shall be given unto you.* The sense of this is that the Lord will make that man, who has shown himself amenable, kind and fair to his brothers, experience the same kindness from others, and be treated gently and amicably by them. Now it often happens, that the sons of God are paid the worst recompense and suffer many unfair slanders, although they have done no harm to anyone's reputation, and have actually borne with their brother's vices—but this does not conflict with what Christ is saying: we know that such promises as have regard to this present life are not perpetual, and are not without exception. Though the Lord for a time allows the innocence of His people to be unworthily attacked and all but overcome, He still fulfils what He elsewhere declares, that their integrity shall shine forth as the morning (Isa. 58.8), and His blessing always rides high, above the undeserved reproaches. He causes His faifthul to endure unfair insult, that He may humble them, and vindicate their good cause in the end. Besides, the faithful themselves, when they do try to show fair treatment to their brothers are sometimes still involved in excessive severity against them, when they are in fact innocent, or at least not deserving of blame; thus by their own fault, they provoke a like judgment upon themselves. The fact that they do not receive a measure 'pressed down and running over'— even if this is due to the world's ingratitude—is in some degree to be accepted, for there is no-one who treats his brothers as kindly and generously as he ought.

Matt. 7.3. *Why beholdest thou the mote.* He explicitly indicates a fault under which hypocrites commonly labour. Though they have magnificent vision when it comes to seeing other people's faults, they turn their own sins behind their backs, or are so clever in extenuating them, that they try to find excuse even for the most blatant offence. Thus Christ checks both evils, the excessively sharp eye, which is begotten of a failure in charity, scrutinising our brothers' faults too closely, and the self-indulgence, which we use as a cloak and encouragement for our own sins.

Give not that which is holy unto the dogs, neither cast your pearls before the swine, lest haply they trample them under their feet, and turn and rend you. (Matt. 7.6)

Matt. 7.6. *Give not that which is holy.* I do not need to repeat too often that particular sentences are recorded by Matthew, which are not all to be taken as from one context. This utterance does not attach to the last discourse, but is quite separate from it. Christ is telling the Apostles, and in their person all the teachers of the Gospel, that they are to keep the treasure of heavenly wisdom only for the sons of God, not to prostitute it before the unworthy and profane scorners of God. But here a question arises, afterwards He tells them to preach the Gospel to every creature. And Paul says (II Cor. 2.16), that their preaching to the reprobate is a savour of death. And there is nothing more sure, than that it is daily set before the unbelieving as a testimony to render them the more inexcusable. I would reply: since the servants of the Gospel, and all who are called to teach the Gospel, are unable to discern between the sons of God and the swine, it is their role to set the doctrine of salvation indiscriminately before all. Even if from the outset they see many are thrawn and unteachable, charity does not let them assume that they are all desperate cases, for we must understand that those whom Christ calls *dogs* and *swine* are not any sort of unclean livers, or men who

227

have no fear of God, or such as have no part in true religion, but those who, by certain proofs, have displayed a determined contempt for God, thus showing that their sickness is incurable. In another place, Christ contrasts the dogs to the elect people of God and the household of faith, saying, 'It is not good to take the children's bread and give it to the dogs.' Here He means by dogs and swine, those so infected with an impious scorn for God that they admit of no healing. Thus we may see what a false distortion of Christ's words it is, to reckon that He restricts the teaching of the Gospel only to the docile and well prepared. How will it be, if godly teachers only invite those who anticipated the grace of God by their own obedience? But in fact, we are all impure by nature, and we are all inclined to be stubborn. So we must deny no-one the cure of salvation, except those who so foully reject it, when it is offered, that they are clearly reprobate and self-condemned, to use the word that Paul does of heretics (αὐτοκατάκριτοι Tit. 3.11).

There was a double reason for Christ forbidding the Gospel to be set before the ruined scorners. It is a blatant profanation of the mysteries of God, if we subject them to the mockery of the godless. Further, Christ willed to comfort His disciples, in case they should cease to attend to teach the Gospel to God's elect, when they see it rudely cast back at them by wicked and profane men—as if to say, lest this incomparable treasure become tawdry, the swine and dogs are to be kept away from it. We must notice the commendation Christ gives the teaching of salvation, calling it a *holy* thing, and comparing it with pearls. So we may deduce the value we should put upon it.

Lest haply they trample. Christ here seems to distinguish between the swine and the dogs, attributing brutish stupor to swine, and madness to dogs. Certainly experience teaches us, that there are two sorts of scorners of God. For example, whatever we are given in the Scriptures concerning the corruption of human nature, free justification, and eternal election, many turn their steps to idle acceptance, or pleasure-seeking: such are aptly and deservedly reckoned as swine. Others tear at pure teaching, and its ministers, with blasphemous abuse, to make it seem that the zeal for good works should make ruin of the fear of God, and of all care for salvation. Both terms are used by Christ to point the finger at the incurable opponents of the Word of God, but the simile, has double effect and briefly indicates how they differ one from another.

Ask, and it shall be given you; seek, and ye shall find; knock, and it shall be opened unto you: for everyone that asketh receiveth; and he that seeketh findeth; and to him that knocketh it shall be opened. Or what man is there of you, who, if his son shall ask him for a loaf, will give him a stone; or if he shall ask for a fish, will give him a serpent? If ye then, being evil, know how to give good gifts unto your children, how much more shall your Father which is in heaven give good things to them that ask him? (Matt. 7.7-11)

And he said unto them, Which of you shall have a friend, and shall go unto him at midnight, and say to him, Friend, lend me three loaves; for a friend of mine is come to me from a journey, and I have nothing to set before him; and he from within shall answer and say, Trouble me not: the door is now shut, and my children are with me in bed; I cannot rise and give thee? I say unto you, Though he will not rise and give him, because he is his friend, yet because of his importunity he will arise and give him as many as he needeth. And I say unto you, Ask, and it shall be given you; seek, and ye shall find; knock, and it shall be opened unto you. For everyone that asketh receiveth; and he that seeketh findeth; and to him that knocketh it shall be opened. And of which of you that is a father shall his son ask a loaf, and he give him a stone? or a fish, and he for a fish give him a serpent? Or if he shall ask an egg, will he give him a scorpion? If ye then, being evil, know how to give good gifts unto your children, how much more shall your heavenly Father give the Holy Spirit to them that ask him? (Luke 11.5-13)

Matt. 7.7. *Ask, and it shall be given you.* This is an exhortation to prayer. As we are so slow and lethargic in this exercise of devotion, which should hold first concern for us, Christ presses the same point in three expressions. He is not using superfluous words when He says ask, seek, knock, in case the plain lesson fail to impress, He brings it home to us with vigour. He has the same object in the promises that are added, you shall find, it shall be given you, it shall be opened. There is nothing better to stir us to make our prayers, than a firm assurance that we shall succeed in them, for those who have doubts are bound to pray defunctorily, indeed prayer without faith is an empty and deceptive ritual. So Christ, to excite us effectively towards this area of our duty, both teaches us what we should do, and promises that our prayers will not be in vain. We must note this carefully. First, we should know that this rule of prayer is set down and prescribed for us, so that we should be quite certain that God is propitious towards us, to hear our prayers. Also, whenever we come to prayer, or whenever we feel that there is not that live enthusiasm in our prayer that should be, we should bring this gentle invitation to our thoughts, where Christ gives us testimony of the fatherly affection of God. So it shall be that each of us, relying on the grace of Christ, will find assurance in prayer, and dare to call upon God with an open heart, as Paul teaches (Eph. 3.12). As we are unreasonably inclined to a lack of faith, Christ corrects this fault also, by repeating His promise in different forms. The metaphor of *seeking* has been used because we reckon that what our employment and needs demand is far from us, and *knocking*, because fleshly intelligence thinks that such things as are not available to hand must be shut away.

Matt. 7.8. *For everyone that asketh receiveth.* Some believe this is a proverbial expression, taken from the common usage of life, but I would prefer to take the other opinion, that Christ is extending the Father's grace to the praying people, as if to say that God of His own will is ready to hear us, if only we pray, while His riches are spread out for us, if only we ask. These words imply that men pay a fair penalty for their indolence, if when they are without necessities they fail to seek the remedy for their wants. However, it is certain that often, when the faithful are at sleep, God keeps watch over their salvation, and anticipates their requests. Nothing would be more unfortunate for us than if He were to wait for our great heaviness, our sheer apathy I should say, to turn to prayer, or if He should hide His face from our utter thoughtlessness. He is indeed His own incentive, to give us the gift of faith, which in rank and time antecedes all prayer. However, Christ is here addressing the disciples, and simply telling them how the heavenly Father wishes us to secure His gifts. While all comes of His free generosity, yet He tells us to pray in order to prompt our faith. To those who ask, He will give such things as flow from His sheer goodness.

Matt. 7.9. *Or what man is there of you.* The comparison moves from lesser to greater. First, Christ contrasts the malice of men with the unbounded goodness of God. It is φιλαυτία (self-love) that makes us evil, for when a man gets too fond of himself, he forgets to notice other people. But fatherly love overcomes this fault, for men forget themselves, and expend themselves with great generosity, upon their sons. And the only reason for this is that God, from whom all fatherhood descends (Eph. 3.15), instils a fraction of His own goodness into their hearts. But if these little drops have such effect, what may we hope to see from the inexhaustible ocean itself? Or would God be grudging, after thus enlarging the hearts of men? All the time we must remember the word of Isaiah, 'That even though a mother may forget her sons, the Lord will ever be consistent with Himself, and show Himself a Father' (Isa. 49.15).

Matt. 7.11. *Shall your Father . . . give good things.* Christ says this deliberately, to prevent the faithful giving too much free rein to foolish and unworthy fancies in prayer. We know that in this field there is a considerable lack of restraint, and a boldness in our flesh. There is nothing that we do not allow ourselves to ask from God, and if He does not fulfil our stupid ideas, we grumble at Him. So Christ subjects our prayers to the will of God, restraining Him from giving us more than He knows is for our good. We should not think that He has no concern for us when He does not answer our requests; He has the power to discern what is to our advantage. As all our emotions are blind, we must seek a pattern of prayer from the Word of God, for we are not adequate to assess such a matter for ourselves. Whoever wishes to approach God with confidence in his prayer, should learn to curb his heart, and ask for nothing which is not in accordance with His will, as James tells us (4.3). For *good things* in the last phrase, Luke reads *Holy Spirit*, not to the exclusion of other benefits, but showing what is to be sought above all else, for this should always come into our thoughts, 'Seek first the kingdom of God, and all other things shall be added unto you.' So the sons of God, to equip themselves in due fashion for prayer, should put off all earthly passions, and compose themselves to think upon the life of the spirit. Then they will rate food and clothing inferior to the assurance and pledge of their adoption. When God has given such a priceless treasure, He will not deny the little things besides.

Luke 11.5. *Which of you shall have a friend.* An illustration is given in Luke, which Matthew does not record. Briefly, there is no reason for the faithful to grow weary at heart, if they do not at once obtain their requests, or if what they ask for seems difficult to achieve, for, if you can put pressure on men by importunity in asking, when a man will not do a thing for you willingly, we should have no doubt that God will attend to our prayer, if we persist at it with resolution, and do not let our hearts faint through delay or difficulty.

> All things therefore whatsoever ye would that men should do unto you, even so do ye also unto them: for this is the law and the prophets.
> Enter ye in by the narrow gate: for wide is the gate, and broad is the way, that leadeth to destruction, and many be they that enter in thereby. For narrow is the gate, and straightened the way, that leadeth unto life, and few be they that find it. (Matt. 7.12-14)

> And as ye would that men should do to you, do ye also to them likewise. (Luke 6.31)

Matt. 7.12. *All things therefore whatsoever, etc.* We do not need to find any logical inference, since these utterances often consist of detached remarks. I have said before that it is not one discourse of Christ which Matthew here sets down, but an ordered summary of His teaching, taken from many speeches. So we must take this passage on its own, where Christ is setting His disciples a rule of fair-dealing, and is giving a short and simple definition of it, so that we should realize, that the only reason for there being such a reign of hatred upon the earth, men antagonistic towards each other for so many causes, is that they knowingly and willingly tread equity underfoot, yet every man demands its strict application for himself. Where our own advantage is concerned, there is one of us who cannot go into detail, chapter and verse, on the extent of our rights. Everyone shows himself an exact scholar of equitable dealing, when it suits himself. Then how is it that there is not the same immediate appreciation in questions of another person's benefit or loss, unless we only wish to be wise for ourselves, and nobody cares for his neighbour's interest? Not only that, but we maliciously and deliberately blink at the rule of fairness, which shines in our own hearts. So Christ teaches them, that the rule for each man to use, in living rightly and fairly with his neighbours, is for each to offer the other what he would have done to himself. This cuts across all empty pretence, which men think up for themselves, to cover and disguise all their injustice. No doubt, perfect equity would reign amongst us, if we were such faithful disciples of what I might call active charity, as we are so acute in the passive instruction we give on the subject.

This is the law and the prophets. Christ does not mean that this is the only heading of doctrine we receive in the Law and the Prophets, but that all that is taught there on charity, and all the laws and exhortations we find there to promote righteousness, must be related to this theme. So the sense is, that the second table of the decalogue is satisfied if a man behaves towards others, as he would have the other behave towards himself. In other words, there is no need of long and involved discussion, if we keep to the simple path, and do not follow a fantastically exaggerated self-love to obliterate from our hearts the standard of fairness which is engraved upon them.

Matt. 7.13. *Enter ye in by the narrow gate.* As Christ's teaching is at no point more opposed to the flesh, no-one ever makes any proper headway on this unless he has learned to get a real grip on his emotions, and on all his desires, so as to keep them in that narrow way which the heavenly Teacher prescribes for the restraint of our cravings. Men are so permissive towards themselves, so uncontrolled, and lax, that Christ here tells His disciples to get themselves onto the narrow and thorny road. As it is unpleasant to force our desires away from their free and unrestricted career, He relieves the pain, by the glad compensation of telling us, that by this narrow gate and path, we enter upon life. That we should not be trapped by the delights of a licentious and dissolute life, and drift along at the impulse of the desire of the flesh, He declares that men are rushing to their death, when they prefer to enter by the spacious way and the broad gate, rather than negotiate the straits which lead to life. He expressly says that *many* run by the broad way, since men lead each other to ruin by their evil example. How is it that men knowingly and willingly rush on, carefree, except that they cannot believe that they are perishing, when the whole crowd goes down at the same time? Contrarily, the small numbers of the faithful make many cowards, for it is hard to induce us to renounce the world, and to pattern our life upon the ways of a few. We think it unnatural to be forced out of the generality, as if we were not part of the human race. Although the teaching of Christ, as it were, takes us prisoner, compels our lives along the narrow road, separates us from the crowd, and attaches us to a few companions, yet this tough regime should not stop us from winning through to life. It is clear enough from Luke, that this was said by Christ on a different occasion from the time when He produced the paradox on the subject of the blessed life (which noted earlier), and gave them a rule of prayer. This is an instance of what I have several times remarked on, that what the other Evangelists record at various points, as the narrative requires, Matthew here gathers together in a summary form, the better to put under our eyes the kind of teaching that Christ gave His disciples. Where my readers have been carefully advised on the time-sequence which Luke followed, I hope they will pardon me if I am no more exact in assembling the doctrine than Matthew was.

And one said unto him, Lord, are there few that be saved? And he said unto them, Strive to enter in by the narrow door: for many, I say unto you, shall seek to enter in, and shall not be able. (Luke 13.23-24)

Luke 13.23. *And one said unto him, etc.* Though Matthew relates this answer of Christ as part of a series of utterances in the sermon, I think that the occasion of saying it was actually presented by the question we have here. The reason for the question being raised seems to be, that Christ who professed Himself to be the Author of life, had only just managed to attract a handful of disciples. It might appear, that after the salvation of only a few men the Church in general was on its way to disaster. God had adopted all that people, but now they gave little encouragement to Christ's teaching, and often in fact threw it back at Him. The same doubt occurs to us, when we see the perverse state of the world: what this can mean, that the greater part of men pursue a course foreign and contrary to that of the Gospel? So Christ directs His words to them all, and urges them to strive to enter *by the narrow door*. By these words, He intended to move His folk away from that foolish curiosity which hinders and complicates many who keep looking around to see whether other companions are joining them, as if they could only gain salvation in a great crowd. He tells them to strive, for He knows that they cannot win through to eternal life without great and heavy difficulties. The faithful should be more busily engaged upon this effort, and not be unduly curious about the crowd of stragglers.

Luke 13.24. *For many . . . shall seek to enter in.* This is added, to avoid our empty hopes letting us down, if we had imagined that a crowd of companions would help us, for under the gentle blandishments of the flesh, many promise themselves an easy access to life, and constantly indulge themselves. One deceives another, and they dream the time away, in a false state of security. Christ would have His people shake off such soft behaviour, and He tells them that those will be shut out, who devote themselves to an assured possession of life.

When once the master of the house is risen up, and hath shut to the door and ye begin to stand without, and to knock at the door, saying, Lord, open to us; and he shall answer and say to you, I know not whence ye are; then shall ye begin to say, we did eat and drink in thy presence, and thou didst teach in our streets; and he shall say, I tell you, I know not whence ye are; depart from me, all ye workers of iniquity. There shall be the weeping and gnashing of teeth, when ye shall see Abraham, and Isaac, and Jacob, and all the prophets, in the kingdom of God, and yourselves cast forth without. And they shall come from the east and west, and from the north and south, and shall sit down in the kingdom of God. And behold, there are last which shall be first, and there are first which shall be last. (Luke 13.25-30)

Luke 13.25. *When once the master of the house is risen up.* Although this is said later, on another occasion, as I have just remarked, I prefer to take account of teaching rather than of occasion, for it is a great help to our understanding to gather into one context matters which have a like significance. As Christ had denied that there was an open door for many who desire to enter into heaven, He now says that it does them no good that they hold a place in the Church, for at the last, God shall arise for judgment, to exclude from His Kingdom those who now claim a place in His household. He uses the simile of a *master of the*

234

house, who realizes that some of his wicked and depraved servants have slipped furtively out at night, and left the house open to thieves: so he rises himself, and locks the door, and he does not let these stray gad-abouts of the night back in, when they have had their wild career around the streets. He goes on to say, that we should use the opportunity we have, for as long as God invites us to Himself, we may use the open door, and come into the Kingdom of Heaven, but the majority do not condescend to move a muscle. Thus Christ declares that eventually the door will be shut, and there will be danger that those who wait for their friends, will be refused admittance.

Luke 13.26. *Thou didst teach in our streets.* Christ explicitly goes on to say that it will do the Jews no good that He has come nearer them, and made Himself closely available for them to enjoy, unless they reply to the call of that day. He does not go on with His comparison. Having spoken of the master of the house, He now speaks of Himself as Judge, without metaphor. Of course it corresponds only to His own Person to say, 'Thou didst teach in our streets.' We may grasp His purpose, which was to prevent sheer neglect stopping the Jews from attaining the salvation which lay in their reach.

Luke 13.28. *When ye shall see Abraham.* As the Jews—though they had nothing in common with their holy forebears—vainly boasted of their origins, and made a most regular practice of falsely claiming the title of Church, Christ testified that this degenerate mob, which had departed from the faith and religion of its fathers, was not within the Kingdom of God. There is also the implicit reproach, that, in their desire to have partners in their quest for salvation, they were not eager to take Abraham and the Prophets and the holy fathers into their company. Instead they looked around their contemporaries, by whose example they had fallen low, into countless corruptions. In other words, if at this time you do not choose to enter by the narrow gate, as the crowd of stragglers holds you back, do you not see that you are being cut off from the ranks of the faithful, when you are caught up with the unbelievers? But if the sight of the world now fascinates you, the last day will come to strip off this indolence too late for you. Then you will realize that you, and your like, are estranged from the Kingdom of God, and that you have nothing in common with Abraham.

Luke 13.29. *They shall come from the east.* The development stems from the fact that with the abdication of the Jews, who reckoned that they were the only rightful heirs of God, the Gentile nations are to enter into their place, to obtain the life promised to Abraham and his stock. He sets the Nations over against them, that a sanctified jealousy might stimulate them to faith: as Paul writes, that it will be the glory of his ministry, if he may provoke any from his own stock and blood to such rivalry (Rom. 11.14). The Jews certainly needed to be jabbed, as they were too pleased with themselves, and arrogantly despised God and His gifts. As this sentence will recur shortly in Matthew, I shall now touch on it lightly.

Luke 13.30. *And behold, there are last.* We shall see that Christ often used these words at other places, but in varying senses. Here, He simply intended to pull down that empty confidence the Jews had, who being chosen of God out of all the world, presumed upon that privilege to allege that God had an obligation to them. For this reason, Christ solemnly tells them that they will shortly change their fortune, that the nations who were then rejected shall obtain first place, and that the Jews, who have laid aside their honour, will not even occupy the furthest corner in the Church.

Beware of the false prophets, which come to you in sheep's clothing, but inwardly are ravening wolves. By their fruits ye shall know them. Do men gather grapes of thorns, or figs of thistles? Even so every good tree bringeth forth good fruit; but the corrupt tree bringeth forth evil fruit. A good tree cannot bring forth evil fruit, neither can a corrupt tree bring forth food fruit. Every tree that bringeth not forth good fruit is hewn down, and cast into the fire. Therefore by their fruits ye shall know them. (Matt. 7.15-20)

For there is no good tree that bringeth forth corrupt fruit; nor again a corrupt tree that bringeth forth good fruit. For each tree is known by its own fruit. For of thorns men do not gather figs, nor of a bramble bush gather they grapes. The good man out of the good treasure of his heart bringeth forth that which is good; and the evil man out of the evil treasure bringeth forth that which is evil: for out of the abundance of the heart his mouth speaketh. (Luke 6.43-45)

Matt. 7.15. *Beware of false prophets.* By these words, Christ taught that there would be various impostures for His Church to face, and so there would be the danger that many would lapse from the faith, unless they were active in taking precautions. We know the great propensity of men to vanity, for they have a natural appetite for deception, and indeed every man has a genius for deceiving himself. Satan is a great artist in falsehood, and never ceases to stretch his snares to catch the simple and incautious. The Jews, in general, hoped that things would go easy for them under the Kingdom of Christ, free of all struggle and distress. So He tells His disciples that if they will persevere, they must be equipped to ward off Satan's traps. For the Lord (as has been said) wills His Church to keep up an unending campaign in this world. To serve as His disciples to the end, it will not do merely to be naive, and to submit ourselves to His Word, but our own faith must be well-armed for resistance, for Satan will always be on the attack. Of course the greatest thing is to let ourselves be directed by true and faithful ministers of Christ, but false teachers will come out to meet us, and unless we keep careful watch, and stand firm in defence, we shall easily be abducted from the flock. This is the point of Christ's saying, 'The sheep hear the voice of the shepherd: they do not hear a stranger, but flee from him' (John 10.3). So we deduce, that there is no reason why the faithful should fail in heart or be upset, though wolves creep into the fold of Christ, though false prophets try with false teaching to subvert the pure faith: no, they should keep their eyes open, stay on watch—Christ's word to 'Beware' is not said in vain. So as long as our own carelessness does not get the better of us, we shall be able to escape every trap, and if we are not confident in this, we shall certainly not have the spirit to keep watchful. But, since we know that the Lord does not wish us to be ruined by Satan's assaults, whatever they are, we shall advance without fear, seeking from Him the Spirit of discernment; and using it to stamp upon our hearts the seal of faith, which is His truth, so as to uncover the fallacies and impostures of Satan, we shall not be tricked. When Christ says, that they come *in sheep's clothing* but inwardly are ravening wolves, He means that they do not lack a well got up exterior, if one does not prudently examine them through and through.

Matt. 7.16. *By their fruits ye shall know them.* If this criterion had not been added to tell them apart, then the whole authority of teachers of all kinds might have come up for examination. If there were fears of fatal dangers in the teaching body, and there were no accepted way of avoiding them, then all would inevitably become suspect, and there would be no better way out, than to shut one's ears to them all. We do actually see profane men reject every sort of doctrine with impunity and hold up this risk as their excuse—and at the same time the beginners, and those weak in faith, are caught in a state of perplexity. So Christ, not to rob His Church and honest ministers and teachers of their due respect, tells them that they must judge false prophets, by their fruits. It is therefore quite disgraceful of the Papists, in order to bring us into disrepute, to fling these very words of Christ at us, that 'one should beware of false prophets'; their upcry makes the untrained foolishly avoid us, without looking into the case. Any who wish to obey Christ's counsel must make a judgment, with prudence and selectivity. We are not simply pleased to preach, that false prophets are to be guarded against, but must actually urge the simple, painstakingly and insistently, to be on their guard against them. What we stress, however, according to the rule Christ laid down, is that there must first be a fair trial, for fear that these simple folk may one day pay a penalty for rashly rejecting the pure Word of God. There is a vast difference between timely warning and unreasoning contempt. The Papist's take-over of Christ's mandate is quite wicked, when they start false alarms to scare poor souls away from any inquiry. Grasp this point first, that those who, for fear, reject or run away from any doctrine which they do not examine, are acting wrongly, and quite other than Christ commanded.

Now we must see what *fruits* in particular Christ intends, for I believe it is wrong when people confine this to our way of life. Often, some of the worst impostors put on a fake holiness, and trade in all sorts of garbs betokening austerity in life—so this test would be quite ineffectual. I would agree, that in the long run their hypocrisy is exposed, for there is nothing more difficult than the pretence of virtue. But Christ did not wish His teaching to undergo such an unfair, and also uncertain, judgment, as to be reckoned by the life that men lead. So by fruits, it is the very *way of teaching* which we must understand, which in fact holds first priority. On these grounds indeed, Christ Himself proved His mission from the father, that He did not glorify Himself, but the Father who sent Him (John 7.18). If any object, that few have such penetrating judgment as to discern good fruits from evil, I would answer, as I have said already, that the faithful never lack the Spirit of discretion when they need it, as long as they have no self-confidence, but have in a real sense said farewell to self, and entirely submit themselves to His direction. At the same time remember that all teaching is to be examined by the Word of God, and so in judging false prophets, the analogy of faith is to be dominant: then go on to see what God enjoins upon His Prophets and the ministers of the Word, for here fidelity may easily be distinguished. As for example, if we take what Paul requires of bishops, that description alone would suffice to clear off the whole scum of the Papacy, for the papal ministrants seem deliberately to express the very opposite ideal. Hence there is no wonder that they forbid making judgment about false prophets. Moreover, this passage shows clearly that there is nothing to be made of titles, indeed vocation itself is of no great importance, unless those who are named pastors, and are called to the task of teaching, faithfully respond to their office.

Do men gather. By these proverbs, commonplace at the time and quite familiar, Christ confirms that no-one can be deceived by false prophets, unless he is willingly blind, for the fruits openly reveal the good servants of God, and the false workers, exactly as fruits reveal the tree. In *Luke*, the utterance appears to be general, Christ telling us that every single man should be judged by his fruits, as the tree is known by its fruits. For after giving reproof to those hypocrites who see the mote in the other's eye, and fail to see the beam in their own, He straight after says, *For there is no good tree etc.*, and the causal particle γὰρ seems to connect the two sentences. But as it is certain that in this sixth chapter Luke is relating various utterances of Christ, it may be that he has made a briefer note of what Matthew develops more fully. I shall not be put off by the causal adverb, for it is often superfluous elsewhere, as the conclusion in fact shows, for Luke closes his paragraph with, *The good man out of the good treasure of his heart etc.* I have no doubt that he is here describing, apart from metaphor, what kind of judgment it is that Christ orders them to make, by the fruits: that is, that the faithful are carefully to examine what exactly those professed servants of God have to offer; in other words, there is no value in titles, until the speaker proves by deeds that he has been divinely sent. At any rate, I do not deny that the passage could be suited to a general message. Certainly the last clause, *Out of the abundance of the heart his mouth speaketh*, has an application wider than to false prophets, as it is a well-used proverb. If any object that the tongues of men often lie, that men may speak very finely with the worst intentions, I would answer that Christ is here simply giving a lesson in what usually occurs. Though the hypocrites often present something in their words quite different from what is in the depths of their hearts, this does not prevent the tongue getting the appropriate and neat name of the mind's revealer.

Not every one that saith unto me, Lord, Lord, shall enter into the kingdom of heaven; but he that doeth the will of my Father which is in heaven. Many will say to me in that day, Lord, Lord, did we not prophesy by thy name, and by thy name cast out devils, and by thy name do many mighty works? And then will I profess unto them, I never knew you: depart from me, ye that work iniquity. (Matt. 7.21-23)

And why call ye me, Lord, Lord, and do not the thing which I say? (Luke 6.46)

Matt. 7.21. *Not every one that saith unto me, Lord, etc.* Christ takes His message further. Now He is dealing not only with the false prophets, who leap down on the flock to ravage and devour, but with those hirelings, who work their way in under the guise of pastors, falsely, without the slightest mind for devotion. Though He includes all hypocrites under this teaching, of whatever rank or status, He is particularly criticizing the pretended teachers who put themselves on a great pedestal. And directing His words at them, He is both awakening them from their fuddled composure in which they bask, and warning the faithful not to pay such shams any more respect than they deserve. All in all, He foretells that no sooner shall the teaching of the Gospel begin to bear fruit and gather many disciples, than there shall be many in the crowd who join the roll falsely, under pretence, and that even in the very ranks of the pastors there shall be the same treachery, men whose acts and lives deny the profession of their lips. So whoever would be rated among the disciples, must take pains to devote himself sincerely and wholeheartedly to the study of newness of life. In *Luke*, the rebuke is in general terms, *And why call ye me, Lord, etc*. This is a corruption mostly found among false teachers, and from them it penetrates more easily into the whole body. For this reason, in Matthew, Christ expressly inveighs against them. To do *the will of the Father* does not mean to adapt one's life and behaviour to the pattern of virtues, in the philosophic sense, but actually to believe upon Christ, as we read at John 6.40. These words do not cut out faith; in fact, they accord it first place, that from which the rest depends.

Matt. 7.22. *Many will say to me*. Again Christ calls the hypocrites to His judgment bench, as we have just recorded in Luke. As long as they have a place in the Church, so long will they be satisfied with themselves, and so long will they continue to deceive others in turn. So He says, the day will come, when the threshing floor will be swept, the refuse and chaff will be separated from the pure grain. To *prophesy in Christ's name* is to undertake the office of teacher on His authority and, as it were, with Him as Leader. For prophecy is here taken in the broad sense, as at I Cor. 1.14. He might simply have used the word 'preach', but chose to use the more distinguished term, to express better how the external profession counted for nothing, no matter what its appeal might be to the eyes of men. So *to do mighty works in Christ's name* means precisely the performance of miracles under His strength, His auspices, command, and direction: though the word *virtutes* (powers) is sometimes restricted to one sort of miracle, in this place, and in many others, it covers miracles in general.

Matt. 7.23. *Will I profess unto them*. In this word, Christ seems to allude to that fallacious boast which the hypocrites now make such play with, as if to say, They have confessed me with their tongue, and think they have done everything right: even now, the confession of my Name may be heard rolling from their lips, but I shall get up and answer them, that all their profession is empty and untrue. What does Christ's confession consist of? A declaration that He has never counted them amongst His people, even at the time when they were boasting that they were pillars of the Church. So He tells them to be off from Him, who for a time, with fake credentials, had robbed Him of the possession of His house. Paul seems to have taken from Christ's words what he says at II Tim. 2.19, 'The Lord knoweth them that are his: Let every one that nameth the name of the Lord depart from unrighteousness.' The first section was aimed at preventing the weak from being upset or put off by the defection of certain ones who had a great and famous reputation. He says, that the Lord did not know them, for all that their vain glamour held the eyes of men. Then he encourages them all, who wish to be reckoned disciples of Christ, to depart in good time from iniquity, lest Christ thrust them also from His presence, when He comes to divide the lambs from the goats.

Every one therefore which heareth these words of mine, and doeth them, shall be likened unto a wise man, which built his house upon the rock: and the rain descended, and the floods came, and the winds blew, and beat upon that house; and it fell not: for it was founded upon the rock. And every one that heareth these words of mine, and doeth them not, shall be likened unto a foolish man, which built his house upon the sand: and the rain descended, and the floods came, and the winds blew, and smote upon that house; and it fell and great was the fall thereof.

And it came to pass, when Jesus ended these words, the multitudes were astonished at his teaching: for he taught them as one having authority, and not as their scribes. (Matt. 7.24-29)

Every one that cometh unto me, and heareth my words, and doeth them, I will shew you to whom he is like: he is like a man building a house, who digged and went deep, and laid a foundation upon the rock: and when a flood arose, the stream brake against that house, and could not shake it: because it had been well builded. But he that heareth, and doeth not, is like a man that built a house upon the earth without a foundation; against which the stream brake, and straightway it fell in; and the ruin of that house was great. (Luke 6.47-49)

Matt. 7.24. *Every one therefore which heareth.* As it is very often hard to tell the true professors of the Gospel from the false, Christ gives an attractive simile, to show how they most greatly differ. He describes two houses, one of them built without foundation, the other well founded. The two have the same outward appearance, but the former, when it is hit by wind and storms, and dashed against by floods, tumbles at once, while the latter is firm enough to withstand all force against it. Christ compares the vain and frothy profession of the Gospel with a building which has an appearance, but no solidity, which for all its height is at any moment liable to collapse, because it lacks foundation. Similarly, Paul tells us to be well and truly founded upon Christ, and to have deep roots, that we may not topple at the first push. Ultimately, it comes to this, that true religion is not easily distinguished from a pretence to it, until it comes to the test. The temptations by which we are tried are like floods and gales, which readily overthrow the unstable spirits, whose poor stuff had passed unnoticed in times of calm.

Heareth these words. The demonstrative *hos* ('these)' does not denote one sort of utterances, but the whole sum of His teaching. Unless the Gospel be firmly bedded in our hearts it is, He says, like a wall which goes up high, without being supported underneath. It is just as though He said, really and truly, faith comes when it has deep roots in the heart, builds on a base of serious and enduring commitment, and so does not yield to temptations. Such is the vanity of human intelligence, that they build upon the sand, men who will not dig down to the point of utter self-denial.

Matt. 7.28. *When Jesus ended these words.* I take it there was a like impression over His address when He came down from the mount, as with the rest of His teaching—which had by now reached a number of the people. So the sense is that in all the various places, where He had given the people a taste of His teaching, astonishment had affected them all, as though a kind of new and unusual Majesty attracted men's minds to Him. What it is, to teach with authority, and not as the Scribes, I have explained above.

And when he was come down from the mountain, great multitudes followed him. And behold, there came to him a leper and worshipped him, saying, Lord, if thou wilt, thou canst make me clean. And he stretched forth his hand, and touched him, saying, I will; be thou made clean. And straightway his leprosy was cleaned. And Jesus saith unto him, See thou tell no man; but go thy way, shew thyself to the priest, and offer the gift that Moses commanded, for a testimony unto them. (Matt. 8.1-4)

And there cometh to him a leper, beseeching him, and kneeling down to him, and saying unto him, if thou wilt, thou canst make me clean. And being moved with compassion, he stretched forth his hand, and touched him, and saith unto him, I will; be thou made clean. And straightway the

*leprosy departed from him, and he was made clean. And he strictly
charged him, See thou say nothing to any man: but go thy way, shew thyself to the priest, and offer for thy cleansing the things which Moses
commanded, for a testimony unto them. But he went out, and began to
publish it much, and to spread abroad the matter, insomuch that Jesus
could not more openly enter tnto a city, but was without in desert places:
and they came to him from every quarter.* (Mark 1.40-45)

*And it came to pass, while he was in one of the cities; behold, a man full
of leprosy: and when he saw Jesus, he fell on his face, and besought him,
saying, Lord, if thou wilt, thou canst make me clean. And he stretched
forth his hand, and touched him, saying, I will; be thou made clean.
And straightway the leprosy departed from him. And he charged him to
tell no man: but go thy way, and shew thyself to the priest, and offer for
thy cleansing, according as Moses commanded, for a testimony unto them.
But so much the more went abroad the report concerning him: and great
multitudes came together to hear, and to be healed of their infirmities.
But he withdrew himself in the deserts, and prayed.* (Luke 5.12-16)

Matt. 8.1. *And when he was come down from the mountain.* Matthew
returns to the thread of the narrative. He had said before, that Christ
went up into the mountain, when he heaped together, so to speak,
many main points of Christ's teaching, but he now goes on to the healing
of the leper, around the time that he gave His Sermon on the Mount.
Mark and Luke give the same story, though they do not indicate the
time.

Christ's divine power was brilliantly shown in His immediately
cleansing the man of his leprosy, by word and touch of His hand alone.
Although we recognize that leprosy was a different kind of disease to
elephantiasis, it is agreed that it is difficult to cure. If it has persisted for
a long time, there were only rare instances of anyone recovering. Even
if we allow that physicians might have given some assistance from the
knowledge of their craft, it is quite evident that there was nothing of a
human order in this miracle.

Matt. 8.2. *There came . . . and worshipped him.* The meaning of the
word προσκυνεῖν, translated 'worship', may readily be inferred from
this passage: the other two Evangelists are our best interpreters, Mark
saying that he knelt down, and Luke, that he fell on his face. By this
gesture, that is, a bending of the knees, the leper showed Him a sign of
respect. We know that such prostration was a common thing with the
Jews, as the Eastern peoples are more inclined to such ritual. Thus
many believe that the leper had no thought in his mind of approaching
Christ in divine adoration, but merely saluted Him with honour, as an

outstanding Prophet of God. I do not argue over the state of mind in which he approached Christ, but I can see the force of his appeal—that He could heal him, if He wished. By these words, he demonstrated that he could recognize the divine power in Christ. And when Christ replies that He does so wish, He shows that the man has given Him credit for more than human force. A man must have supreme authority, to restore health to his fellows merely at his nod. Whether the leper believed that Christ was the Son of God, or that He possessed such virtue as Moses and the other Prophets, he has no doubt that in His hand and power there lies the gift of healing.

That he expresses himself in the conditional, *If thou wilt, thou canst*, does not contradict certainty of faith, as God demands it in our prayers, for men should not hope for more than God promises. The leper had not been informed of any oracle or promise from God of what Christ would do. He would have been foolhardy to have gone beyond these limits, for on the occasions when we read that some did simply make a prayer, we must recall that these were exceptional events, from which we should not draw any rule. I am not sure anyhow whether we would be quite right in saying that the leper made a prayer. He simply declares, that he is so convinced of Christ's power, that he has no doubt that it is in His decision to cure leprosy. So he presents himself to Him for healing, unsure of the outcome, as he had not yet come to know the will of Christ.

Matt. 8.3. *And he stretched forth his hand, and touched him.* In the Law, the touch of the leper was contagious, but as there is such purity in Christ he absorbs all uncleanness and pollution, He does not contaminate Himself by touching the leper, nor does He transgress the Law. For in assuming our flesh, He has granted us more than the touch of His hand, He has brought Himself into one and the same body with us (*in unum idemque corpus nobiscum coaluit*), that we should be the flesh of His flesh. He does not only stretch out His arm to us, but He comes down from heaven, even to the very depths; yet catches no stain thereby, but stays whole, clears all our dirt away, and pours upon us His own holiness. Now, while He could heal the leper by His word alone, He adds the contact of His hand, to show His feeling of compassion: no wonder, since He willed to put on our flesh in order that He might cleanse us from all our sins. So the reaching out of His hand was a sign and token of His vast grace and goodness. Here is a thing which we pass over without much impression at an idle reading, but must certainly ponder, with much awe, when we take it properly—that the Son of God, so far from abhorring contact with the leper, actually stretched out His hand to touch his uncleanness.

Matt. 8.4. *And Jesus saith unto him, etc.* Some, to excuse the leper, say that he was not seriously forbidden by Jesus from spreading the miracle, but rather was given an extra incentive to do so. But I think that others are more accurate in believing that the reason for the ban was that the time was not yet ripe. I grant that there was no necessity for the miracle to be suppressed, but the Lord did not wish its fame to be published at once, at least, not by the leper. Therefore I would say, that the leper, so far from deserving any credit for his misplaced well-doing, should really be censured for disobeying Christ's order. If he wished to show gratitude to the Author of his recovery, there was no better means than obedience, which in God's eyes is preferred to all sacrifices, and is the first principle and head of true worship (I Sam. 15.22). So we learn by this case that to give vent to ill-considered zeal is a wrong course, for the more men labour at winning God's approval, they only succeed in crossing His mandate.

Shew thyself to the priest. As the ceremonies of the Law were not yet abolished, Christ did not wish them scorned or overlooked. Now God had taught in the Law (as we find at Lev. 14.2), that if any man were cleansed from leprosy, he should take himself along to the priest, with a sacrifice of thanksgiving. The object was for the priest to approve God's favour, by his verdict: then, the man who was healed should perform his testimony of gratitude. When Christ therefore sends the leper away to the priest, He shows that He had no other purpose than to heighten the glory of God. The showing was connected with the examination, and the gift was a symbol of thanksgiving. He wishes the judgment to be given by the priests, that God's grace might be seen clearly and beyond doubt, while the leper is to acknowledge his gratitude to God for his recovery. At the same time, as I have just said, He tells them to keep the rituals prescribed by the Law till the time for their abrogation came. For the Papists to make this a proof text of their own confession is most unperceptive. They would make leprosy an allegory for sin, and the priests, appointed by the Pope, those who recognise the leprosy of the spirit. Granted, that priests in the Law were given their authority so that the people should know that all their purity, and its determination, depended upon the priesthood, never-theless the papal celebrants are making a blasphemous claim for them-selves herein. Such honour as was given to the priests of old, Christ now uniquely claims for Himself. He alone may diagnose that spiritual leprosy, and He deserves to receive the gift offered for cleansing, by those who have been purified. Purity was symbolised by the provision of a sacrifice under the Law because men could only be purged by the expiation of blood. It is criminal sacrilege to transfer to any other the right which God has given to His Son. That the servants of the Gospel pronounce their absolution (*mundities*) upon sinners, at Christ's command, is not at all to be confused with the fake jurisdiction that the Papists fancy, to give a verdict upon leprosy.

Mark 1.44. *For a testimony unto them.* Some take *testimony* as a law or ordinance, as it is used in the Psalm (122.4), 'God established this as a testimony for Israel.' But this does not appeal to me, and I have no doubt that the pronoun *them* refers to the priests. In my opinion, Christ had regard to the circumstances of the present case, for in this miracle there should have been a sufficiently clear proof to convict them of ingratitude. It is not a difficulty, that Christ told the leper to keep quiet, for He did not wish the record of this miracle to be concealed permanently. As the leper came into the presence of the priests at Christ's command, here was a testimony that made them inexcusable. If they were not willing to accept Christ as God's minister, at the same instant they lost all ground to complain about Him, for Christ had omitted no least detail of the Law. In short, if they had been open to cure, they could have been drawn to Christ. Such a solemn encounter with God had power enough to condemn their unbelief.

Mark 1.45. *That Jesus could no more openly enter.* We may gather from this why Christ did not wish the miracle to become common knowledge so quickly, for it would have been easier for Him to teach freely, not that enemies might have risen up against Him, in attempts to shut His mouth, but because the crowd became so importunate in demanding miracles, that He had no place left for teaching. For He wished them all to be more eager for the Word, than for signs. So Luke says, that He lived in remote areas. He avoided the crowds, for He saw that He would never satisfy the people's requests, without a quantity of signs completely swamping His teaching.

And when he was entered into Capernaum, there came unto him a centurion, beseeching him, and saying, Lord, my servant lieth in the house sick of the palsy, grievously tormented. And he saith unto him, I will come and heal him. And the centurion answered and said, Lord, I am not worthy that thou shouldest come under my roof: but only say the word, and my servant shall be healed. For I am also a man under authority, having under myself soldiers: and I say to this one, Go, and he goeth; and to another, Come, and he cometh; and to my servant, Do this, and he doeth it. And when Jesus heard it, he marvelled, and said to them that followed, Verily I say unto you, I have not found so great faith, no, not in Israel. And I say unto you, that many shall come from the east and the west, and shall sit down with Abraham, and Isaac and Jacob, in the kingdom of heaven: but the sons of the kingdom shall be cast forth into outer darkness: there shall be the weeping and gnashing of teeth. And Jesus said unto the centurion, Go thy way; as thou hast believed, so be it done unto thee. And the servant was healed in that hour. (Matt. 8.5-13)

After he had ended all his sayings in the ears of the people, he entered into Capernaum.

And a certain centurion's servant, who was dear unto him, was sick and at the point of death. And when he heard concerning Jesus, he sent unto him elders of the Jews, asking him that he would come and save his servant. And they, when they came to Jesus, besought him earnestly, saying, He is worthy that thou shouldest do this for him: for he loveth our nation, and himself built us our synagogue. And Jesus went with them. And when he was now not far from the house, the centurion sent friends to him, saying unto him, Lord, trouble not thyself: for I am not worthy that thou shouldest come under my roof: wherefore neither thought I myself worthy to come unto thee: but say the word. and my servant shall be healed. For I also am a man set under authority, having under myself soldiers: and I say to this one, Go, and he goeth; and to another, Come, and he cometh; and to my servant, Do this, and he doeth it. And when Jesus heard these things, he marvelled at him, and turned and said unto the multitude that followed him, I say unto you, I have not found so great faith, no, not in Israel. And they that were sent, returning to the house, found the servant whole. (Luke 7.1-10)

Matt. 8.5. *And when he was entered.* Those who believe that Matthew and Luke are telling different stories, are making a fuss over nothing. There is only this difference in the account, that in Matthew the Centurion is said to come to Christ, while in Luke he is said to have sent some of the Jews to speak on his behalf. Matthew quite reasonably attributes to him what was done at his request and in his name. In all the circumstances the two Evangelists agree so well, that it would be ridiculous to make two miracles out of the one. I have no doubt that the company of troops, which the Centurion commanded, was stationed in the town of Capernaum, for the legions were usually distributed for the defence of the towns. Though he could see that the behaviour of the people in that town was so shameful and sinful (we know that the town of Capernaum, on the sea shore, was more full of corruption than other places), this did not prevent him from condemning the superstitions of his fathers, and taking an interest in the true and sincere religion; for he had not built a synagogue for the Jews without a degree of unpopularity and risk, nor did he have an affection for that race unless he embraced the worship of the one God. So before Christ healed his servant, he himself had been healed by the Lord. And there was miracle in this: that a military man, who had crossed the sea in armed force to subdue the Jews into accepting the yoke of Roman tyranny, should submit himself to the God of Israel of his own accord, and devote himself to His obedience. When Luke says, that the servant was precious to him, he does so to check the hesitation that might come into the reader's mind. We know servants are not usually so well valued that their masters show great concern over their lives, unless they have won favour for their exceptional industry or loyalty or some other virtue. So Luke means that this was no common cheap slave, but a faithful servant of rare qualities, who enjoyed the highest favour with his master: hence the great anxiety for his life, and the urgent appeal. That it had been a sudden paralysis which, at its first onset, made them despair of his life, is agreed by both Evangelists. Chronic cases of paralysis involve no pain. Matthew says, that the lad was in grievous torment, and Luke, that he was near to death. I simply note that both tend to increase the splendour of the miracle, the grief and pain, and the critical situation, without venturing to assert anything definite about the nature of the sickness.

Luke 7.5. *For he loveth our nation*. There is no doubt that the Jews praised him on the score of religion, for there was no other source of love for such a generally hated people, than an enthusiasm for the Law and for God's worship. In building a synagogue, he had clearly testified to his appreciation of the teaching of the Law. So deservedly they call him worthy for Christ to show him favour, as a devout adherent of God. Yet it was incredibly stupid that they should, in the opinion they profess, transfer God's grace to a gentile, while they themselves contemptuously reject it. If Christ is to them the minister and dispenser of the gifts of God, why are they not the first to enjoy the grace that is offered, before bringing in the outsiders? But such is always the prevailing apathy of hypocrites, that they feel so sure that God is somehow obliged to them, and that they control His grace at their own choosing, as though they hold some rights. Ultimately, they become sated with it, and as they do not care to partake of it, they pass it over to others, as of little account.

Matt. 8.8. *I am not worthy that thou shouldest come under my roof*. Matthew is briefer, as he makes the man speak for himself, while Luke gives the fuller account, as he gives it through his friends, but both have the same sense. There are two parts to his message. The Centurion wishes to spare Christ, out of respect, and asks Him not to weary Himself, for he holds himself unworthy to receive Him. Secondly he ascribes to Him so much authority, that he reckons, that by His mere inclination and instruction, life may be restored to his servant. It is amazing humility, to place a man from a conquered, client race so far above himself. It is possible, that being used to the haughty manner of the Jews, his modesty prepared him to accept that he would be reckoned as a pagan, and was afraid he might cause offence to God's Prophet if he forced him to come to a gentile, unclean, man. However it is, for sure he speaks from his heart, and feels such reverence towards Christ that he dare not ask Him to approach him. Indeed it is evident from Luke's account that he does not think himself worthy of converse with Him.

It may be asked for what reason he was led to extol Christ so splendidly, and the difficulty is increased when he goes straight on to say, *But only say the word, and my servant shall be healed*, or as Luke says, *Say with a word*. Unless he had recognized Christ as God's Son, it would have been superstition to transfer the glory of God to a man. Yet it is scarcely credible that he had been properly instructed on Christ's divinity, which was virtually unknown to them all. Now Christ finds no error in his words, but testifies that they spring from faith. And this reason has compelled many commentators to believe that Christ was hailed, in the Centurion's words of acclaim, as the true and only God. I think that a God-fearing man, being informed of the exceptional and plainly divine acts of Christ, simply perceived that the power of God was upon Him. And no doubt he had heard something of the promised Redeemer. Though he has not yet any accurate understanding that Christ is God manifest in the flesh, yet he is well assured that the power of God is revealed in Him, and that He has been given the task of disclosing, by miracles, the presence of God. So there is no superstitious transference to man of what is God's own privilege, but, believing that Christ came by divine mission, he believes that He can heal his servant by His Word alone.

If anyone should object that nothing is more peculiarly God's own than the performance by His Word of what He may please to do, and that this supreme power cannot be entrusted to a mortal man without sacrilege, then again there is an easy answer. Though the Centurion did not make such subtle distinction, he did not in fact attribute this power to any word of mortal man, but to God's, whose minister he was fully persuaded Christ was. He had not the least doubt of this. So, since the grace of healing had been entrusted to Christ, and he recognized this heavenly virtue, he did not attach it to His bodily presence, but was content with the actual Word, from which he believed such effect would flow. The comparison which the Centurion adduces, saying that he is a man etc., is not an assumption of equal status, as they say, but a comparison of lesser with greater. For he rates the divine power which he acknowledges in Christ higher than the authority which he had himself, over his servants and troops.

Matt. 8.10. *Jesus . . . marvelled*. Though amazement is not appropriate for God, seeing it must arise from new and unexpected happenings, yet it could occur in Christ, inasmuch as He had taken on our human emotions, along with our flesh. When Christ declares, *I have not found so great faith, no, not in Israel*, He is speaking with some reservation, not in simple terms. If we take into account the full character of faith, Mary's faith at least was superior, for her believing that she would be with child by the Holy Spirit, to bring forth God's only-begotten Son: further, that she embraced the Son born to her as her Maker, as Creator of the whole world and as the unique Redeemer. But for two reasons in particular Christ preferred the faith of the gentile man, to the faith of all the Jews, for one thing, that he had, from such a mean and slight acquaintance with doctrine, produced such great and immediate fruit. It was by no means commonplace to speak so grandly of God's power, which had begun to shine out in Christ, to the extent of a few sparks. Further, while the Jews were excessively eager to see outward signs, this gentile man seeks no visible symbol, but declares that the bare Word is enough for him. Christ made to go to him, not because He had to, but to confirm his faith. So He commends his faith on this count explicitly, that he was content with the Word itself. What would even one of the Apostles have done? 'Come, Lord, see, touch.' This man neither asks for His bodily presence, nor for His touch, but believes that the Word contains such efficacy that he may expect from it the sure recovery of his servant. Such credit he gives not to man's word, but to God's, in determining that Christ is not a plain individual, but a Prophet divinely sent. From this we may take a general rule, that though God wishes our salvation to be secured by the flesh of Christ, and confirms it daily by sacraments, yet we must look to the Word for His assurance. Unless we allow such authority to the Word, for us to be certain that, once God has spoken by His ministers, our sins are forgiven us, and that we are restored to life, then all confidence in our salvation collapses.

Matt. 8.11. *Many shall come from the east, etc.* As Christ uses the person of the servant to present a first out-pouring, a kind of first fruits of His grace to the nations, so He says that his master will be an example of the future calling of the nations, and of the publishing of the faith throughout the entire world: and He says they will not only come from the neighbouring regions, but from the furthest bounds of the earth. Though this may have been the testimony of many an oracle in the Prophets, yet at the first it seemed absurd and incredible to the Jews, who imagined that God was confined to the seed of Abraham. So there was astonishment when they heard that those would belong to the house-hold and inheritance of God, who now were outsiders. And not that only, but that a covenant of salvation was shortly to be made known, which should draw the whole globe together into the one body of the Church; as He says that the gentiles who come to faith will be partakers of the same salvation as Abraham, Isaac, and Jacob. So we deduce, for sure, that it is the same once revealed in Christ which was also promised formerly to the fathers: nor would there be any shared inheritance, if faith itself were not one, seeing faith is the means to obtain it. The word *sit down* alludes to dining, yet since we know that the life of heaven needs no food nor drink, the expression has the same effect as to say, They shall enjoy the same life.

Matt. 8.12. *The sons of the kingdom.* How does He call those folk 'sons of the kingdom' who were anything but sons of Abraham? For certainly, those who are strangers to faith cannot in all fairness be reckoned in the flock of God. I answer that though they were not truly of God's Church, yet as they held a place in the Church He allows them this title. And we must note, that such was the worth of God's covenant, as long as it rested with the stock of Abraham, that the heavenly inheritance of the Kingdom did properly adhere to them. At least in the eyes of God Himself, they were still holy branches of holy stock. And certainly the renunciation that followed shows well enough, that they were then still retained in the Household of God. Secondly, we must note that Christ was not speaking of individuals, but of the whole race. What He had to say was far more grievous than the calling of the gentiles. For the nations to be ingrafted into the same body as the descendants of Abraham, by free adoption, would have been somehow tolerable, but for the Jews themselves to be expelled, so that the nations might enter upon a cleared space, was taken as nothing less than prodigious. Yet Christ declares that both shall come to pass; God, to admit the outsiders to Abraham's bosom, will actually put out the sons. In *outer darkness*, there is a tacit antithesis. God means, that beyond His Kingdom, which is the Kingdom of Light, there is nothing but the reign of darkness. Metaphorically, Scripture indicates by darkness a dreadful place of sorrow, which in this life, words cannot express, nor senses comprehend.

Matt. 8.13. *Go thy way; as thou hast believed, so be it done unto thee.* Here we see how courteously Christ pours out His grace, when He has come upon a vessel open to receive it. For although in these words He addresses the Centurion, yet there is no doubt that in his person He calls us all, to have good hope in Him. And by this too, we are taught why God should often be rather strict towards us, for our unbelief does not permit Him to be more forth-coming. So if by faith we open to Him an approach, He will hear our requests and prayers.

And it came to pass soon afterwards, that he went to a city called Nain; and his disciples went with him, and a great multitude. Now when he

*drew near to the gate of the city, behold, there was carried out one that
was dead, the only son of his mother, and she was a widow: and much
people of the city was with her. And when the Lord saw her, he had
compassion on her, and said unto her, Weep not. And he came nigh and
touched the bier: and the bearers stood still. And he said, Young man, I
say unto thee, Arise. And he that was dead sat up, and began to speak.
And he gave him to his mother. And fear took hold on all: and they
glorified God, saying, A great prophet is arisen among us: and, God
hath visited his people. And this report went forth concerning him in the
whole of Judaea, and all the region round about.* (Luke 17.11-17)

Luke 7.11. *And it came to pass . . . that he went, etc.* As in all Christ's
miracles, we should remember the analogy Matthew speaks of, and
understand that this young man, whom Christ raised from the dead, is
an example of the life of the Spirit to which He has restored us. The
naming of the city enhances the certainty of the story. So does Luke's
remark that a great crowd came from each direction. Christ had many
companions following Him, and many had also come to pay their
respects for the woman conducting her funeral. So the rising up of
the young man was seen by the eyes of so many witnesses that one
could scarcely fail to believe in it. Besides, there was the crowded,
public place—for we know that the gathering point was the gateway of
the city. As for the dead man being carried outside the city, this was
done by the custom of old times in all nations. Jerome says that the city
of Nain still survived to his day, two miles below Mount Tabor, to the
south.

Luke 7.12. *The only son of his mother.* The reason which led Christ
to raise up the boy was that, when He saw a widow deprived of her
only son, He felt pity. He did not hold back His grace till any should
ask Him, as at other times, but anticipated all their prayers and returned
the son to his mother—who expected nothing of the sort. Here we
have a shining example of His free mercy, in reviving us from the dead.
By touching the bier, perhaps He wished to show that death and the
grave would have less terror for Himself, His means of winning life for
us. Indeed, He has not just granted us the touch of His hand, but to
raise us into heaven, He has descended Himself into the sepulchre.

Luke 7.14. *Young man, I say unto thee.* In these words, Christ testifies
to the truth of Paul's teaching (Rom. 4.17), 'God . . . calleth the things
that are not, as though they were'. He calls up the dead and gets Himself a hearing, so that death itself is instantly turned into life. Here we
have the first, splendid instance of the resurrection to be, as Ezekiel was
bidden to say to the dry bones, 'Hear the word of the Lord' (37.4). We
are also taught how Christ spiritually revives us by faith, by instilling His

secret power through His Word, that it may reach even to the dead souls, as He Himself declares in John (5.25), 'The hour cometh... when the dead shall hear the voice of the Son of God; and they that hear shall live.'

Luke 7.16. *And fear took hold on all.* A sense of the divine presence is bound to bring fear with it, but one may distinguish between the kinds of fear, for unbelievers go virtually dumb with panic, or, terror-struck, rage against God, but the godly and devout, touched with awe, spontaneously bow their heads. *Fear* on this instance is therefore to be taken in good part, for in allowing God the honour due to His power, as they saw it, they not only gave Him reverence, but thanksgiving besides. In saying *God hath visited his people* I doubt if they mean just any sort of visit, but such a one as restored wholeness to themselves. The state of Judaea was indeed tottering, and they lay under a wretched and ugly servitude, as if God had no regard for them. Only one hope remained, that God had promised Himself as their coming Redeemer once they had suffered the affliction of extreme distress. I have no doubt, that warned by the miracle they hoped that the restoration of their state was near: they only err over the manner of the visitation. For although they recognize, and praise, an unusual grace of God in it, yet their praises are far below the worth and glory of the promised Messiah. So it appears, that the faith which was then in that people was in a great confusion, and was complicated by many accretions.

And there came a scribe, and said unto him, Master, I will follow thee whithersoever thou goest. And Jesus saith unto him, The foxes have holes, and the birds of the heaven have nests; but the Son of man hath not where to lay his head. And another of the disciples said unto him, Lord, suffer me first to go and bury my father. But Jesus saith unto him, Follow me; and leave the dead to bury their own dead. (Matt. 8.19-22)

And as they went in the way, a certain man said unto him, I will follow thee whithersoever thou goest. And Jesus said unto him, The foxes have holes, and the birds of the heaven have nests; but the son of man hath not where to lay his head. And he said unto another, Follow me. But he said, Lord, suffer me first to go and bury my father. But he said unto him, Leave the dead to bury their own dead; but go thou and publish abroad the kingdom of God. And another also said, I will follow thee, Lord; but first suffer me to bid farewell to them that are at my house. But Jesus said

unto him, No man, having put his hand to the plough, and looking back,
is fit for the kingdom of God. (Luke 9.57-62)

Matt. 8.19. *And there came a scribe.* Matthew presents us here with
two men, and Luke with three. All prepared to enrol with Christ, yet
as all are hindered from the proper course by various failings, they each
receive appropriate answers. It might seem odd, at first sight, that
Christ sends away the one who offers himself to follow at once and
without delay, and refuses him as a fellow, while the other who asks for
leave to go back for a time and is slower, less ready, He should keep by
Him. But there is an excellent reason in each case. How could the
scribe be so prompt in hurrying to attach himself to Christ's company,
unless he had taken no thought whatever for the hard and unpleasant conditions of His companions? We realize that he was a scribe,
a man accustomed to a quiet and easy existence, treated with respect,
who would be no match for hard words or hard times, for persecution,
or the cross. He wishes to follow Christ, but he imagines to himself a
soft and pleasant path, lodging with all good things provided—while
Christ's road is a thorny one for His disciples; it leads through endless
pains to a cross. So the greater his haste, the less his preparedness. He
is exactly like the man who fancies a battle in cool and attractive settings,
no sweat, no dust, and beyond the range of the artillery. There is no
wonder that such men are rejected by Christ; wildly they rush in, and
they are the first to break under any emergency, at the first test they
faint and draw back their foot, shamefully deserting their post. Besides, this scribe could have been seeking a place with Christ merely to
feed at Christ's table freely and idly, in all comfort. So we should
learn that, in his person, we are all being told not to make wild and
irresponsible claims to be Christ's disciples, without taking any thought
for the cross and the hardships. Let us take thought in good time of the
conditions we must encounter. This is the basic training which admits
us to His school, denying ourselves and lifting up our cross.

Matt. 8.20. *The foxes have holes.* God's Son reveals the conditions of
His own life, while He lived on earth, and further prescribes for all His
disciples the pattern of living by which they should learn. It is only
surprising that Christ says He has no foot of earth on which to lay His
head, while He had many godly and kindly men, who would readily
have given Him hospitality. But note that this was said as a warning
that the scribe should not look for an ample and wealthy reward, as
from a master of great means, since the master himself lived a precarious
existence in other people's homes.

Matt. 8.21. *And bury my father.* As we said, the scribe is refused by
Christ as a fellow-traveller, because he had pushed himself forward

without thought, imagining that he would have a comfortable kind of life for himself. This one now, whom Christ holds on to, laboured under the opposite fault, for the trouble that prevented him from instantly obeying Christ's call was that it was hard for him to leave his father, and we may well believe that he was in extreme old age, from the words, 'Allow me to bury.' The expression surely means that there was not much time left to him. *Luke* says, that he was commanded by Christ to follow Him. And so, *Matthew* says, that he was one of His disciples. At any rate, he does not refuse his calling, but asks for temporary leave to be granted him to fulfil the obligation which a son owes his father. His excuse has the effect of saying, that he was not a free man until his father should die. Now we learn from Christ's reply that sons are so to observe their duties towards their parents, as to be able to lay them aside when God's call leads elsewhere, and to give first priority to His orders. All obligations to men come to an end, I say, when God asks attention for Himself. Individuals must see what God asks of them, what is the demand of the vocation to which they are tied, and not let earthly parents prevent them from having God retain His rights, who is the supreme and unique Father of all.

Matt. 8.22. *Leave the dead to bury their own dead.* In these words, Christ is not condemning the obligation of burial. It would be disgraceful and cruel to throw away the corpses of the dead without sepulture, and we know that the rite of burial was divinely imposed upon men, accepted by the usage of the saints, in confirmation of the hope of a final resurrection. He only wished to teach us that anything which diverts us from the straight course, or hinders us, will savour only of death. In other words, the only ones who are really living are those who concentrate their efforts, and all the activity of their life, upon God's obedience, while those who sink back into the world, and for the sake of keeping up an appearance of custom before men overlook God, are like dead folk, who occupy themselves in attentions to the dead, vainly and uselessly.

Luke 9.60. *Go thou and publish abroad.* Matthew only reads, *Follow me.* Luke makes more explicit to what end he was called, namely to be a minister and herald of the Gospel. If he were to be left to his private life, then there was no compulsion upon him to leave his father, as long as he did not for his father's sake let down the Gospel, but as the preaching of the Gospel will not allow him to stay at home, Christ is right to pull him away from his father. At the same time as we wonder at the goodness of Christ, which grants such an honourable calling to a man of no previous strength, we should be right to notice that the weakness which still affected him is not given indulgent treatment, but is put right.

Luke 9.61. *And another also said.* Matthew does not mention this third man. He appears to have been more attached to the world, than to be free and set to follow Christ. He presents himself as a companion of Christ, but adds the proviso that he should say farewell to his household, that is, when he should have his affairs in order at home, as men do when they are going on a journey. This is the reason why Christ rates him so severely. He professes verbal attachment to Christ, yet turns his back on Him until he has satisfied his earthly business. When Christ says that those who look back over their shoulder are not fit for the Kingdom of God, we must look carefully to see what He means. They are said to *look back*, who become tied up in the world's business, and so allow themselves to be taken off the proper course; especially those who plunge themselves into concerns which makes them useless for following after Christ.

And he entered into a boat, and crossed over, and came into his own city. And behold, they brought to him a man sick of the palsy, lying on a bed: and Jesus seeing their faith said unto the sick of the palsy, Son, be of good cheer; thy sins are forgiven. And behold, certain of the scribes said within themselves, This man blasphemeth. And Jesus knowing their thoughts said, Wherefore think ye evil in your hearts? For whether is easier, to say, Thy sins are forgiven; or to say, Arise, and walk? But that ye may know that the Son of man hath power to forgive sins (then saith he to the sick of the palsy), Arise, and take up thy Bed, and go unto thy house. And he arose, and departed to his house. But when the multitudes saw it, they were afraid, and glorified God, which had given such power unto men. (Matt. 9.1-8)

And when he entered again into Capernaum after some days, it was noised that he was in the house. And many were gathered together, so that there was no longer room for them, no, not even about the door: and he spake the word unto them. And they come, bringing unto him a man sick of the palsy, borne of four. And when they could not come nigh unto him for the crowd, they uncovered the roof where he was: and when they had broken it up, they let down the bed whereon the sick of the palsy lay. And Jesus seeing their faith saith unto the sick of the palsy, Son, thy sins are forgiven. But there were certain of the scribes sitting there, and reasoning in their hearts, Why doth this man thus speak? he blasphemeth: who can forgive sins but one, even God? And straightway Jesus, perceiving in his spirit that they so reasoned within themselves, saith

*unto them, Why reason ye these things in your hearts? Whether is
easier, to say to the sick of the palsy, Thy sins are forgiven; or to say,
Arise, and take up thy bed, and walk? But that ye may know that the
Son of man hath power on earth to forgive sins (he saith to the sick of the
palsy), I say unto thee, Arise, take up thy bed, and go unto thy house.
And he arose, and straightway took up the bed, and went forth before
them all; insomuch that they were all amazed, and glorified God, saying,
We never saw it in this fashion.* (Mark 2.1-12)

*And it came to pass on one of those days, that he was teaching; and there
were Pharisees and doctors of the law sitting by, which were come out of
every village of Galilee and Judaea and Jerusalem: and the power of the
Lord was with him to heal. And behold, men bring on a bed a man that
was palsied: and they sought to bring him in, and to lay him before him.
And not finding by what way they might bring him in because of the
multitude, they went up to the housetop, and let him down through the
tiles with his couch into the midst before Jesus. And seeing their faith, he
said, Man, thy sins are forgiven thee. And the scribes and the Pharisees
began to reason, saying, Who is this that speaketh blasphemies? Who
can forgive sins, but God alone? But Jesus perceiving their reasonings,
answered and said unto them, What reason ye in your hearts? Whether
is easier to say, Thy sins are forgiven thee; or to say, Arise and walk?
But that ye may know that the Son of man hath power on earth to forgive
sins (he said unto him that was palsied), I say unto thee, Arise, and take
up thy couch, and go unto thy house. And immediately he rose up before
them, and took up that whereon he lay, and departed to his house,
glorifying God. And amazement took hold on all, and they glorified
God; and they were filled with fear, saying, We have seen strange
things today.* (Luke 5.17-26)

Matt. 9.1. *Came into his own city.* This passage shows that the town of
Capernaum was popularly believed to be Christ's birth-place, because
He came so often to it. There is no doubt that the same incident is being
told by the three, though there is a slight variation on points of detail
between them. Luke says that scribes came from various corners of
Judaea, and in their sight Christ healed the paralytic, yet there is a
suggestion that others also were restored to health, thanks to Christ.
For before turning to the paralytic, Matthew speaks in the plural
number of God's power being revealed there for the healing of their
diseases. There was exceptional glory in this miracle—the fact that a
man, struck in all his parts, whom they lowered by ropes lying upon a
stretcher, should suddenly have risen up, fresh and fit. But there is
another particular reason why the Evangelists give this miracle more

emphasis than others, the fact that the scribes were so offended at Christ for assuming the right and authority to remit sins, but Christ in fact determined that this should be confirmed and sealed to him by a visible sign.

Matt. 9.2. *Seeing their faith*, Only God can recognize faith, but the example of faith they gave in their tremendous effort is evident from the fact, that they would never have taken such trouble or struggled to overcome such odds, if their spirits were not supported by the firm confidence that they would succeed. The fruits of their faith were shown, in that, when their access was blocked on all sides, they were still not beaten. The way some reckon that Christ had a divine insight into their faith, while it lay hidden inwardly, seems to me a forced interpretation.

Now, as Christ conceded to their faith the benefit which He would do to the paralytic, one usually asks at this place, how far another person's faith may prevail. First, we may be sure that Abraham's faith had advantage for his successors, when he embraced, for himself and for his stock, the freely offered covenant of salvation. And we may think the same of individual men of faith, that they, by faith, propagate to their children and grandchildren, even before they are born, the grace of God. Further, there is the place it holds in infant children, who for their age are not yet capable of faith. For adults of course, who have no faith of their own (whether we are speaking of outsiders or of blood relatives), the faith of another is only directly of benefit, as far as concerns eternal life. For as prayers are not without avail, wherein we ask God that He may turn the unbelievers to repentance, we may reckon our faith helps them only so far as that they shall not win to eternal salvation, until they gain the fellowship of that same faith, but where there is an agreement in faith between us, our salvation is mutually assisted, more than we realize. It also will not be disputed, that the unbelievers are often awarded earthly benefits, by the goodwill of the godly. As regards the present passage, even though Christ is said to have been moved by the faith of others, the paralytic could not have gained the forgiveness of sins, unless he had his own faith. Christ often restored health of body to the unworthy; even today, God makes His sun rise on the good and on the evil, yet the only way by which He reconciles Himself to us is by faith. So there is a synecdoche in the word *their*, for Christ did not so much attend to those who carried the paralytic, as He looked at the faith of the man himself.

Thy sins are forgiven. Christ here appears to promise the paralytic something he had not asked, but as He intends to give health of body, He makes a start by removing the cause of the sickness, and further warns the paralytic of the source of his disease, and how he should

258

frame his requests. Commonly, men do not think that the pains they bear are the chastisement of God, and only wish for a relief to the body, while all the time they are careless over their sins, just as though an invalid neglected his disease, but asked a cure for the pain he felt at the moment. But there is one only deliverance from all evils, which is to have the favour of God. It often happens that the godless survive their troubles, and God is just as much their foe as ever; then, while they think it is over, the same thing comes back again, or a worse and repeated attack, to show that there will be no limit or end, until God's wrath be appeased—as He testifies Himself through the Prophet Amos (5.19), 'As if a man did flee from a lion, and a bear met him: or went into the house . . . and a serpent bit him.' Hence the repeated and regular expression in Scripture, 'He promises pardon from sins,' when they seek relief from their pains. Such is the priority we should keep in prayers—warned by a sense of our afflictions of the sins we have, we should first be anxious to obtain pardon, that being reconciled to God, He may then withdraw His hand from chastising us.

Matt. 9.3. *And behold, certain of the scribes.* They accuse Christ of blasphemy and sacrilege, for usurping to Himself what is properly God's, and the other two add, 'Who can forgive sins, but God alone?' Now there is no doubt that they were drawn to this unfair judgment by their passion for malicious criticism. If they do think there is anything that deserves reproof, why do they not ask out? Since the words were ambiguous, and Christ presented nothing that was not the practice of the Prophets in their testimonies to the grace of God, why should they take something in a bad sense which could be interpreted far more reasonably? Thus we agree, that they were already affected with malice and hatred, in being so hasty to snatch up an excuse to condemn Christ. Now they say nothing, but think over in their hearts what they shall say against Him in His absence, among their own sort. It is perfectly true that the right and authority for forgiving sins belong to God alone, but they are quite wrong to deduce that it does not belong to Christ, for He is God manifested in the flesh. They should have inquired, by what right Christ assumed such authority, whereas, without any inquiry, they imagine Him to be just somebody out of the crowd, and rush straight in to condemn Him.

Matt. 9.4. *And Jesus knowing.* Here He gave an instance of His Godhead, that He brought their hidden thoughts out into the open, for no-one knows what is in a man save his spirit (I Cor. 2.11). So Mark adds, that He perceived in His Spirit, as if to say, that humanly one could not see what lay in their hearts, but Christ had reached even to those depths by His Spirit. He says they have evil thoughts, not because it grieved them that what God claims for Himself alone is transferred to a mortal man, but because they are proudly and maliciously rejecting God in His self-offering.

Matt. 9.5. *Whether is easier.* The sense is: as it is by no means easier for a body, which was virtually dead, to become alive again at a word, than it is for sins to be remitted, it should not astonish them that when He performs the former sign He also remits sins. But Christ's reasoning seems to lack solid foundation, for as the soul excels the body, so does remission of sins excel bodily health. However, there is a ready solution, that Christ is suiting His words to their intelligence, for they are like animals, more impressed by outward signs than by all the spiritual power of Christ which works for our eternal salvation. Thus John (5.28) proves the efficacy of the Gospel, in making men alive again, by the fact that at the last day He shall raise the dead from their tombs by His voice. So the argument was certainly valid for refuting them well enough, seeing it was of no more significance to them than the outward miracle; they could not rightly deny His remitting the sins of the paralytic when He restored him his strength and well-being, for the remission of sins was made evident by the effect in question.

Matt. 9.6. *Hath power on earth.* This power is quite different from that which was entrusted to the Apostles, and which today the pastors of the Church exercise, for they do not so much remit, as testify that they are remitted, in declaring the mission they are enjoined to fulfil. Christ uses these words to assert Himself not only as Witness and Minister of his grace, but also as Author. What then is the aim of His restrictive word, *on earth*? For what good will it do us to have gained pardon here, if we do not have it guaranteed in heaven? Surely, Christ intended to say that we are not to seek the remission of sins at long range, but that, in His person, it was (so to speak) set at the hand's reach of every man. For (such is our propensity to faithlessness), we should never dare to affirm that God is merciful towards us, unless He should come near and open Himself out to us at close quarters. Now as it was for this reason Christ came down to earth, that He should offer to men the very present grace of God, He is said to remit their sins to their face, for in Him and through Him has been revealed God's will, which previously (according to the sense of the flesh) had been hidden beyond the clouds.

Matt. 9.8. *But when the multitudes saw it.* For the *amazement* that Luke records, the other two speak of ἔκστασιν, or stupor, and in fact Luke adds *fear*. They all intended to teach us that God's power was not merely recognised but that all were struck with wonder, so as to be made to give glory to God. The fear which ensued upon their wonder had the effect that they did not shout against Christ, but submitted reverently to Him as to God's prophet. Matthew expressly says, that they

glorified God, who gave such power to men, in which they seem somewhat off the point, for although they see a man with their eyes, they
ought in their minds to perceive something loftier than man. They are
quite right to this extent, that they preach the honour given to man's
nature in Christ to the common benefit of the human race, but as they
do not yet appreciate God revealed in the flesh, their confession is not
free of a certain error. All in all, it was true that God had given such
power to men, but they had not yet grasped the means and the reason of
its giving, for they did not know the link between God's majesty and
the flesh (*Dei maiestas cum carne coniuncta*).

*And as Jesus passed by from thence, he saw a man, called Matthew,
sitting at the place of toll: and he saith unto him, Follow me. And he
arose, and followed him.*

*And it came to pass, as he sat at meat in the house, behold, many
publicans and sinners came and sat down with Jesus and his disciples.
And when the Pharisees saw it, they said unto his disciples, Why eateth
your Master with the publicans and sinners? But when he heard it, he
said, They that are whole have no need of a physician, but they that are
sick. But go ye and learn what this meaneth, I desire mercy, and not
sacrifice: for I came not to call the righteous, but sinners.* (Matt. 9.9-13)

*And he went forth again by the sea-side; and all the multitude resorted
unto him, and he taught them. And as he passed by, he saw Levi the son
of Alphaeus sitting at the place of toll, and he saith unto him, Follow me.
And he arose and followed him. And it came to pass, that he was sitting
at meat in his house, and many publicans and sinners sat down with Jesus
and his disciples: for there were many, and they followed him. And the
scribes of the Pharisees, when they saw that he was eating with the
sinners and the publicans, said unto his disciples, He eateth and drinketh
with publicans and sinners. And when Jesus heard it, he saith unto them,
They that are whole have no need of a physician, but they that are sick:
I came not to call the righteous, but sinners.* (Mark 2.13-17)

*And after these things he went forth, and beheld a publican, named Levi,
sitting at the place of toll, and said unto him, Follow me. And he forsook
all, and rose up and followed him. And Levi made him a great feast in his
house: and there was a great multitude of publicans and of others that were
sitting at meat with them. And the Pharisees and their scribes murmured
against his disciples, saying, Why do ye eat and drink with the publicans
and sinners? And Jesus answering said unto them, They that are whole*

*have no need of a physician; but they that are sick. I am not come to call
the righteous but sinners to repentance.* (Luke 5.27-33)

Matt. 9.9. *He saw a man sitting at the place of toll.* That Matthew from
his tax office (a position usually addicted to grasping and unjust exaction,
and then particularly ill-famed) should have been received into Christ's
fellowship, yes, and called to the office of an Apostle, is an illustrious
example for us of the grace of God. It was Christ's will, not only to
choose simple and blunt men for that rank, to bring down the world's
wisdom, but also this tax-officer (*publicanus*), who had followed a
career of small credit, which involved a great many corrupt deeds, to
make him an instance of His free goodness, and in his person to teach
that the calling of us all depends not on the merits of our own righteousness, but on His sheer generosity. So Matthew is a witness and spokes-
man of the grace revealed in Christ, and also a testimonial and example
of it. And he shows his gratitude for it, in not being ashamed to put
down for perpetual memory what kind of man he was, and from
whence he was taken, that he might display all the more in his person
the grace of Christ. Compare Paul (I Tim. 1.15), 'Faithful is the saying
. . . that Christ Jesus came into the world to save sinners; of whom I am
chief.' When Mark and Luke call him *Levi*, they apparently use his
tribe's name, but being a tax-officer was the reason for him taking a
foreign name to himself. *Follow me.* There is no doubt that Christ
used many words to say where and why He called him, and of this we
can be more sure from Luke, who says he left everything and rose up in
order to follow Christ. To leave everything behind, was not a necessity,
except for such as were called to close discipleship with Christ, and to
the hope of Apostleship. Now we may see, in his eager enthusiasm to
obey, the divine effect of Christ's voice; not that He affects all alike in
their hearts when He touches their ears, but that in this man Christ did
determine to give an exceptional example, for us to realize that he was
not called by human means.

Luke 5.29. *And Levi made him a great feast.* What Luke says here does
not seem to agree with his having left everything behind him, but the
answer is easy., Matthew put aside all hindrances, and gave himself
wholly to Christ, but he did not throw away his household interests.
Paul, when he urges on the ministers of the Word, like soldiers, to give
their efforts for the Church free and unencumbered of all hindrances,
says (II Tim. 2.4), 'No soldier on service entangleth himself in the affairs
of this life, that he may please the commander': he certainly does not
mean that all who enrol in a military career must divorce their wives,
renounce their children, completely cut themselves off from their houses
and turn their back on all their interests, so as to devote themselves

entirely to the army. Matthew had nothing which would keep him from following Christ, wherever He might lead, yet, as far as the manner of his calling allowed him, he freely used both his home and his means. He had to resign from the tax office, for he could never have been a companion of Christ if he were engaged with this. The greatness of the feast consisted not so much in the crowd of diners, as in the supply and splendour of the repast, for we know that Christ was not so austere as not at times to allow a rich reception to be given Him by the wealthy, so long as there was no extravagance. At the same time, there is no doubt that being Himself a singular example of moderation He would have encouraged His guests to a frugal and restrained diet, and He would never have tolerated a wasteful profusion of expense. Matthew says that sinners came, that is, men of wicked life, or notorious for their ill-doing, and this is because the tax-officers, being themselves generally open to hatred and insult, did not abhor the company of such, for as a light correction may shame and humble sinners, by the same token extreme severity may drive some to desperation, where all shame is driven from their thoughts, and they run riot into degraded habits. To exact tribute or revenues was no crime, but when the *publicani* saw how they were cast off as pagans, and abominations, they took comfort from the company of those who shared the same weight of ill-favour and disgrace, and so did not despise them. So they mingled with adulterers and drunkards and the like—whose crimes they would have condemned, men from whom they were quite dissimilar, because they were forced to it, by the hatred and rejection of the public.

Matt. 9.11. *Why eateth your Master with publicans?* The scribes turn on Christ's disciples, and by way of getting them to desert Him, make a charge which at first sight was very disagreeable and shameful. Why should they take this man as their Teacher, unless they wished to withdraw themselves from the generality, and lead a more holy life? But now He had led them down to the level of pagan licentiousness, away from the decent and proper orders of living, to pollute them with company that was unclean. It was a charge which might well hurt untrained, and still very impressionable disciples, and make them abandon their Master. They do well, being insufficiently equipped to deal with such a slander, to take their complaint to their master, for Christ, by His encounter with it, gives them strength for the future.

Matt. 9.12. *They that are whole have no need, etc.* It is clear from Christ's answer, that the scribes had sinned on two points—they had not taken account of Christ's mission, and though they spared their own vices they proudly looked down upon all others. And we have to note, that this has ever been a widespread sickness. Hypocrites, sated and intoxicated with windy confidence in their own righteousness, never think over the purpose of Christ's mission to earth. The depths of the labyrinth of evils into which the human race has plunged, the dread wrath of God, and the curse which lay over all, the chaotic aggregation of vices which load us down—none of this do they acknowledge. They are insensitive to man's woes, and they take no heed for his cure. They satisfy their own interests and will not wake up to reality, indeed, take it as insulting when they are ranked with the sinners. Here Christ tackles that second error, when He replies that the well need no physician. The admission is ironical, by which He tells them that the reason for their being offended at the sight of sinners is that they are claiming to be righteous themselves. Because you are well, He says, the sick are objects of scorn to you; you find them distasteful, you are troubled to look their way, but the doctor must take quite a different approach. Then he demonstrates the role of physician which He must undertake, for His Father has sent Him to call sinners.

Though Christ starts with the words of rebuke, we who wish to advance in His teaching must give first place to what He put second, namely, that He came to revive the dead, to justify the guilty and the convicted, to cleanse the foul and filthy livers, to rescue the perishing from hell, to dress in His glory men who were covered with uncleanness, to renew to blessed immortality those who were wasted with the stench of vice. If we consider that this was His mission, this was the object of His coming, if we take to heart that for this reason He put on our flesh, shed His own blood, fulfilled the sacrifice of death, went down to the depths beneath, it will never seem to us out of place that He draws into the embrace of salvation the very dregs of humanity, people entirely swamped in the morass of crime. Does the man you detest seem unworthy of the grace of Christ? Then why was Christ Himself made a propitiation, and a curse, unless it was to stretch out a hand to accursed sinners? If we feel with some insinuation of disgust, that Baptism and the holy Supper alike bring us into association with unclean persons, that their company seems in some way to stain us, we should at once look into ourselves and mercilessly examine our own evil deeds. Such a scrutiny will readily bring us to let ourselves be washed at the same spring as the most foul, in case we should cast away the righteousness which He offers to all the godless without discrimination, and the life He offers to the dead, and salvation to the desperate.

Matt. 9.13. *But go ye and learn.* He dismisses them, and clears them off, for He sees they are not men willing to be taught, but obstinate. But He certainly gives them the hint that they have a case to settle before God and His Prophet, when their cruel pride makes them take offence over assistance to the unfortunate healing brought to the sick.

This testimony is taken from Hos. 6.6 where the Prophet gives an address on the judgment of God against the Jews. They should not assume they had done everything by their outward worship of God, after the manner in which they used smugly to pride themselves upon their rituals. He says, that God turns sacrifices aside, where hearts are empty of pious feeling. and lives are estranged from integrity and righteousness. When God declares He does not wish sacrifices, we may plainly see from the second clause that this is said comparatively, that the knowledge of God is more to Him than holocausts, for He does not explicitly reject burnt-offerings in these words, but subordinates them to piety and faith. We must get this into our heads, that faith and spiritual devotion are of themselves pleasing to God, and charity and the claims of humanity towards our neighbours are demanded on their own right, but sacrifices are nothing but auxiliary, as they say, deserving no reward or position unless they have a firm basis in truth. I have dealt with this subject more extensively at Hebrews (ch. 10). In the word *mercy*, note the synecdoche: the Prophet embraces under one part all that we owe to our brothers in humanity.

For I came not, etc. Though this is said to rebut the pride and hypocrisy of the scribe, it contains a general and most useful lesson. We are told that the grace of Christ is only of benefit to us when we are conscious of our own sins, and come to Him in humility, groaning under their weight. Again the weak consciences are moulded into a position of firm assurance, for there is no fear that Christ will reject sinners, since it was to call them that He came down from His heavenly glory. At the same time, we must hold onto that phrase *to repentance*,[1] informing us that pardon is achieved for us, not to foster our sins, but to recall us to a desire to live in holiness and sanctification. On these terms He reconciles us to the Father, that, redeemed by His blood, we should offer ourselves as true sacrifices, as Paul says (Titus 2.12), 'In this have the mercy and kindness of God been revealed, that denying worldly lusts we should live righteously and godly,' etc.

Then come to him the disciples of John, saying, Why do we and the Pharisees fast oft, but thy disciples fast not? And Jesus said unto them, Can the sons of the bridechamber mourn, as long as the bridegroom is with them? but the days will come, when the bridegroom shall be taken away from them, and then will they fast. And no man putteth a piece of undressed cloth upon an old garment; for that which should fill it up taketh from the garment, and a worse rent is made. Neither do men put

[1] This is omitted by R.V. in Matthew and Mark.

*new wine into old wine-skins: else the skins burst, and the wine is spilled,
and the skins perish: but they put new wine into fresh wine-skins, and
both are preserved.* (Matt. 9.14-17)

*And John's disciples and the Pharisees were fasting: and they come and
say unto him, Why do John's disciples and the disciples of the Pharisees
fast, but thy disciples fast not? And Jesus said unto them, Can the sons
of the bridechamber fast, while the bridegroom is with them? As long as
they have the bridegroom with them, they cannot fast. But the days will
come, when the bridgeroom shall be taken away from them, and then will
they fast in that day. No man seweth a piece of undressed cloth on an old
garment: else that which should fill it up taketh from it, the new from the
old, and a worse rent is made. And no man putteth new wine into old
wine-skins: else the wine will burst the skins, and the wine perisheth,
and the skins: but they put new wine into fresh wine-skins.* (Mark
2.18-22)

*And they said unto him, The disciples of John fast often, and make
supplications; likewise also the disciples of the Pharisees; but thine eat
and drink. And Jesus said unto them, Can ye make the sons of the bridechamber fast, while the bridegroom is with them? But the days will
come; and when the bridegroom shall be taken away from them, then will
they fast in those days. And he spake also a parable unto them; No man
rendeth a piece from a new garment and putteth it upon an old garment;
else he will rend the new, and also the piece from the new will not agree
with the old. And no man putteth new wine into old wine-skins; else the
new wine will burst the skins, and itself will be spilled, and the skins will
perish. But new wine must be put into fresh wine-skins. And no man
having drunk old wine desireth new: for he saith, The old is good.*
(Luke 5.33-39)

Matt. 9.14. *Then come to him the disciples of John.* Luke represents the
Pharisees as speaking, Mark seems to bring the two parties together.
And there is certainly no doubt, that by this trick the Pharisees maliciously attempted to bring the disciples of John over into their camp, and
to start a confrontation with Christ's disciples. Similar practice in
prayer and fasting made a tempting suggestion of common purpose.
The quite different manner of Christ gave an occasion for dispute and
rivalry, to men who were too gloom-ridden and turned in upon themselves. The case teaches us to take discreet warning against wicked and
crafty men sowing quarrels amongst us, for some trifling pretext.
Satan is a wonderful planner at constructing these devices. It is easy for
us to be upset over nothing.

We must especially beware that the consensus of the faithful is not split over an issue of external ceremony, and so the bond of charity is broken. Practically all of us labour under the affliction of attributing to the rites and worldly elements far more than they deserve (cf. Paul, Col. 2.8 and Gal. 4.9). Thus they have no hesitation in setting the first rudiments to a great extent above the highest perfection. Gloom and prudery bring another evil in their train, that individuals compel the whole world to follow their example. If we find something to our liking, we immediately desire it to be put into the Law, that others may live by our judgment. When we read that John's disciples were ensnared in these coils of Satan, let us first learn that we do not assign sanctity to outward things and means, and that we must exercise the restraint of moderation and reasonableness, so as not to attempt to coerce others by our decision, but leave everyone his own liberty. We must understand, on fasting and prayers, that John had trained his disciples to a fixed régime, and to this end had determined on days for fasting, and prescribed a form of prayer and set hours: this is why I count these prayers among outward rites. Though the invocation of God holds first place in spiritual worship, yet the means in question, being arranged for men's rudimentary instruction, have their right place among the ceremonial and indifferent matters, whose observance is not to be stressed too strictly. We have said in another place why the discipline of John was more austere than Christ's, and there will be a further place to treat of this more opportunely.

Matt. 9.15. *Can the sons of the bridechamber mourn.* It is on the grounds of time that Christ excuses His disciples, that God wishes them to express such joy in their manner, as though they were guests at a wedding. He compares Himself to the bride-groom, whose presence delights his friends. Chrysostom believes this simile is taken from the testimony of John Baptist, 'He that hath the bride is the bride-groom' (John 3.29), which I do not dispute, but do not believe to be sufficiently established. Enough for us that Christ affirms that He spares and lets off His disciples just as long as He may be with them. Lest any should grudge them this leave, for the short period, He tells them that soon after they will have it more hard and tough. On this hangs the excuse, that fasting and prayers belong to sad and difficult times: I mean the exceptional prayers, of which mention is here made. Christ wished to accustom them gradually to a greater endurance, and not to put much burden upon them, until they gained more strength. From this we may take a double lesson, that if ever the Lord relieves our brothers' weakness, and treats them kindly, while He deals with us more grimly, we are not to complain. And if we are granted a relaxation of sadness and troubles, we must beware not to dissipate ourselves in soft living: rather we must remember that the wedding will not last for ever. *Sons of the bridechamber* (*filii sponsi*, or *thalami nuptialis*) is a Hebrew expression for wedding guests.

Matt. 9.16. *No man putteth a piece.* He takes two similes to confirm His last utterance, one from clothing, the other from wine-skins. There is no plausibility in comparing worn clothes and rotten wine-skins to the Pharisees, and new wine and new cloth to the teaching of the Gospel. The comparison suits the present issue very neatly and agreeably, if we expound it as referring to Christ's weak and raw disciples, and a discipline that was too rigid for them to match up to. It is no matter that old age does not compare with young recruits, for Christ does not compare His disciples to old skins, and old tears, because they were worn out with long use, but because they were not strong, not toughened. In brief, not all are to be compelled to lead the same pattern of life, for their conditions are not the same, and everything does not suit everybody, and one must be especially sparing on the infirm, that they are not shattered by violent usage, or broken under a weight of responsibility. Note that Christ speaks in terms of the ways of the region, in talking of skins, not jars or pitchers.

Luke 5.39. *And no man having drunk old, etc.* This is only inserted by Luke, and it agrees doubtless with what has gone before. Although it receives various turns from the interpreters, I would simply take it in the sense of a warning to the Pharisees not to attribute more weight than they should to accepted custom. For how is it that wine, without changing its savour, is not equally agreeable to every palate, except that use and custom shape our tastes? Thus it follows, that the way Christ deals with His disciples, is not to be denigrated for having less pomp and display, just as old wine, for all that it gives off no fresh aroma, is none the less sweet and just as suitable for nourishing the body.

While he spake these things unto them, behold, there came a ruler, and worshipped him, saying, My daughter is even now dead: but come and lay thy hand upon her, and she shall live. And Jesus arose, and followed him, and so did his disciples. And behold, a woman, who had an issue of blood twelve years, came behind him, and touched the border of his garment: for she said within herself, If I do but touch his garment, I shall be made whole. But Jesus turning and seeing her said, Daughter, be of good cheer; thy faith hath made thee whole. And the woman was made whole from that hour. (Matt. 9.18-22)

And there cometh one of the rulers of the synagogue, Jairus by name; and seeing him, he falleth at his feet, and beseecheth him much, saying, My little daughter is at the point of death: I pray thee, that thou come and lay thy hands on her, that she may be made whole, and live. And he went with him; and a great multitude followed him, and they thronged him.

And a woman, which had an issue of blood twelve years, and had suffered many things of many physicians, and had spent all that she had, and was nothing bettered, but rather grew worse, having heard the things concerning Jesus, came in the crowd behind, and touched his garment. For she said, If I touch but his garments, I shall be made whole. And straightway the fountain of her blood was dried up; and she felt in her body that she was healed of her plague. And straightway Jesus, perceiving in himself that the power proceeding from him had gone forth, turned him about in the crowd, and said, Who touched my garments? And his disciples said unto him, Thou seest the multitude thronging thee, and sayest thou, Who touched me? And he looked round about to see her that had done this thing. But the woman fearing and trembling, knowing what had been done to her, came and fell down before him, and told him all the truth. And he said unto her, Daughter, thy faith hath made thee whole: go in peace, and be whole of thy plague. (Mark 5.22-34)

And as Jesus returned, the multitude welcomed him; for they were all waiting for him. And behold, there came a man named Jairus, and he was a ruler of the synagogue: and he fell down at Jesus' feet, and besought him to come into his house; for he had an only daughter, about twelve years of age, and she lay dying. But as he went the multitudes thronged him.

And a woman having an issue of blood twelve years, which had spent all her living upon physicians, and could not be healed of any, came behind him, and touched the border of his garment: and immediately the issue of her blood stanched. And Jesus said, Who is it that touched me? And when all denied, Peter said, and they that were with him, Master, the multitudes press thee and crush thee. But Jesus said, Someone did touch me: for I perceived that power had gone forth from me. And when the woman saw that she was not hid, she came trembling, and falling down before him declared in the presence of all the people for what cause she touched him, and how she was healed immediately. And he said unto her, Daughter, thy faith hath made thee whole; go in peace. (Luke 8.40-48)

Matt. 9.18. *While he spake these things unto them.* Those who reckon that Matthew gives a different incident from Mark and Luke, are clearly refuted by the very context, and the issue does not need any long argument. The three say with one accord that Christ was asked by the ruler of the synagogue to come to his house and heal his daughter. The only difference is that the name Jairus is passed over by Matthew, but expressed by Mark and Luke; and that he represents the father as saying

269

that his child was dead, while the other two say that she was critically ill, and her death was announced on the way, as he brought Christ along. But this is nothing strange, if Matthew aiming at brevity mentions in one breath what the others space out more accurately, as it took place. All the rest is so entirely consistent, so many circumstances agree precisely, that they may be seen as three fingers pointing out of the course of one incident, and there is no reason which permits the narrative here to be split into different occasions. The Evangelists tell with one voice, that Christ was asked by the ruler of the synagogue to come to his home, that on the way a woman secretly touched His garment, and was healed of haemorrhage, and that afterwards Christ came to the ruler's house and raised the girl from her deathbed. I am quite sure there is no need for a long drawn-out discussion to prove that the same thing is related by all three.

Now to attend to the details. *Behold, there came a ruler.* Though we may see from the other two that he had not yet reached such a point of confidence as to hope that the life of his daughter might be restored, yet there is no doubt, that at Christ's rebuke, he conceived a greater measure of hope than he left the house with. But Matthew, as I have said, aiming at brevity, set down as occurring at the very beginning, what actually happened with the passing of time. So we must see the shape of the incident thus—first, Jairus asked for his daughter to be healed of her sickness, and then, to be restored from death to life, once, that is, Christ had given him the courage . By *worshipped*, we understand a genuflexion, as is shown by the words of Mark and Luke. This was not divine respect that Jairus showed Christ, but the reverence due to a prophet of God. This bending of the knee is quite common with Easterners, as we know well enough.

Come and lay thy hand upon her. Here we have a magnificent example of the kindness of God towards us: if we compare the ruler of the synagogue with the Centurion, the gentile man, you may say that in the latter there was the full splendour, and in the former the merest trickle, of faith. He allowed Christ no power, except in actual touch, and when he gets word of her dying, he panics, as though there were no hope now of any more relief. Thus we see his faith was feeble, virtually exhausted. That Christ falls in with his prayers, and encourages him to hope well, is a proof that his faith, however small, was not rejected outright. So though we are not yet trained to the full degree of faith that one would wish, there is no reason for our weakness to stop us, or hold us back from calling on His aid.

Matt. 9.20. *A woman, who had an issue of blood.* The Evangelists expressly say, that the issue of blood had lasted twelve years without remission, and yet the woman had not been idle in seeking out remedies to the extent of spending all her substance on physicians—all this, to highlight the glory of the miracle. Quite clearly, an incurable disease was not shifted by human means, as immediately as that, and at the mere touch of His clothing. That the woman thought that only by touching Christ's garment, she would be at once healed, was a unique prompting of the Holy Spirit, one which should not be forced into a general rule. We know how wildly superstition delights to play at foolish and unthinking emulation of the saints, but these are apes, not imitators, who usurp some exceptional case without God's orders, and take it in their own sense, not in the direction of the Spirit. And it may be that there was some grain of fault or error involved in the woman's behaviour, which Christ's forbearance accepted and forgave. Certainly when she afterwards trembled, and shook for bad conscience, this was a kind of hesitation which is contrary to faith and cannot be excused. But why did she not go straight up to Christ? If reverence held her back, where did she think she would get help, if not from His mercy? How was it that she feared to offend, when she was sure of the favour? Christ marks her faith with a notable word of praise, and surely because, as I have just remarked, God deals kindly and gently with His own; to accept their faith, though it be imperfect and weak, He does not impute to them the failures and faults which are involved in it. With faith to lead her, the woman approached Christ. But that she stopped at His argment, rather than present herself to Him with prayers for healing, was perhaps to lapse a little from the right course, through unthinking zeal, especially as she soon afterwards reveals, that she made her venture in doubt and perplexity of spirit. Yet, if we allow that this was the Word of the Spirit to her, yet the standard rule remains that our faith should not be led off this way and that by individual instances, for it should be thoroughly established by the Word of God, as Paul says, 'Belief cometh of hearing, and hearing by the word of God' (Rom. 10.17). This is a most useful warning, to stop any rashly conceived notion being taken into acceptance with us as a matter of faith.

Who is it that touched me? Mark puts it more distinctly, that Christ looked round to discover who it was. It might seem absurd that Christ poured out His grace without knowing whom He was helping. There is also some difficulty where He says, a little later, that He realized that power went out of Him, as though it were just flowing out, not by way of free gift, as such time and upon such persons as He should choose to allot it to. There is assuredly no doubt that He healed the woman knowingly and willingly, indeed there is no doubt that He drew her to Him by His Spirit, to restore her health, but He asks her to come out into the open of her own accord. If Christ had testified to His own miracle, perhaps they would not have credited His words, but now that the woman, in a fit of alarm, tells what happened to her, her confession makes more effect.

Matt. 9.22. *Daughter, be of good cheer.* Her weakness of faith is proven by this Word, for if her fears had not been wrongly conceived, Christ would not have checked her with a call to gather her confidence. At the same time, He commends her faith: whence we deduce what I have said before, that though she sought Christ by the leading of His Spirit, and an honest desire for devotion, she still faltered, so as still to require to be given assurance. Thus we see that faith, to be pleasing to God, must have forgiveness and the support of fresh aids, in order to grow more sturdy. Now we must draw an analogy, from the health of the body, to the salvation of the soul. As Christ attributes it to faith, that the woman was freed from her disease, so it is certain that by faith we obtain the remission of our sins, which reconciles us to God. When He tells her to go in peace, and to be cured of her scourge, we may infer from this, that her benefit was then truly ratified, when she heard from Christ's lips, what she had already discovered by experience. Nor can we in any other way, or with a quiet conscience, enjoy God's benefits, than by entrusting them to the safe custody of the treasury of His promises.

And when Jesus came into the ruler's house, and saw the fluteplayers, and, the crowd making a tumult, he said, Give place: for the damsel is not dead, but sleepeth. And they laughed him to scorn. But when the crowd was put forth, he entered in, and took her by the hand; and the damsel arose. And the fame hereof went forth into all that land. (Matt. 9.23-26)

While he yet spake, they come from the ruler of the synagogue's house, saying, Thy daughter is dead: why troublest thou the Master any further? But Jesus, not heeding the word spoken, saith unto the ruler of the synagogue, Fear not, only believe. And he suffered no man to follow with him, save Peter, and James, and John the brother of James. And they come to the house of the ruler of the synagogues and he beholdeth a tumult, and many weeping and wailing greatly. And when he was entered in, he saith unto them, Why make ye a tumult, and weep? the child is not dead, but sleepeth. And they laughed him to scorn. But he, having put them all forth, taketh the father of the child and her mother and them that were with him, and goeth in where the child was. And taking the child by the hand, he saith unto her, Talitha cumi; which is, being interpreted, Damsel, I say unto thee, Arise. And straightway the damsel rose up, and walked;

for she was twelve years old. And they were amazed straightway with a great amazement. And he charged them much that no man should know this: and he commanded that something should be given her to eat. (Mark 5.35-43)

While he yet spake, there cometh one from the ruler of the synagogue's house, saying, Thy daughter is dead; trouble not the Master. But Jesus hearing it, answered him, Fear not: only believe, and she shall be made whole. And when he came to the house, he suffered not any man to enter in with him, save Peter, and John, and James, and the father of the maiden and her mother. And all were weeping, and bewailing her: but he said, Weep not; for she is not dead, but sleepeth. And they laughed him to scorn, knowing that she was dead. But he, taking her by the hand, called, saying, Maiden, arise. And her spirit returned, and she rose up immediately: and he commanded that something be given her to eat. And her parents were amazed: but he charged them to tell no man what had been done. (Luke 8.49-56)

Mark 5.36. *Fear not, only believe.* The messenger of death brought despair upon him; as he had only sought from Christ that He should come to the aid of the sickness. So Christ forbids him to obstruct, by fear or lack of faith, the advance of grace, for death was to be no barrier to it. For He means by this word, *only believe,* that His power will not be lacking, if Jairus will but admit Him, and He urges him too, to think more freely and bravely, for there is never any fear that his faith will range more widely than the unbounded power of God. And this indeed is how it is with us all: God would deal far more expansively with us, if we were not so narrow, but our contracted minds check Him from pouring out His gifts more richly upon us. Briefly, we are taught at this place, that we cannot go beyond the limit in believing, for our faith will not grasp one hundredth part of the goodness of God, however full it be.

Mark 5.37. *He suffered no man to follow with him.* He forbade them to come in, either because they were unworthy to use as witnesses to the miracle, or because He did not want the miracle crowded out with a host of noise all around. It was quite enough to bring out the girl, whose body had been on view, suddenly in life and full vigour to the sight of men. Mark and Luke say that only three disciples were admitted, and the two parents. Mark, alone, includes those who came with Jairus, when he came to ask Jesus. Matthew is briefer, and omits this detail.

Luke 8.52. *And all were weeping.* The Evangelists record the mourning, to make our faith in the resurrection more certain. Matthew

273

explicitly says, that the *flute-players* were on the scene, which was only the case when death had occurred, and showed that they were by then arranging the obsequies. 'And o'er the sorry rite, the flute's sad notes ascend', as the poet says. Though their idea was to attend their dead with some form of respect and, as it were to adorn, their burial, yet we can see how the world tends, not merely to foster, but actually to provoke error. The right thing was to use all means to assuage their grief, as if they had not sinned enough with their wild lamentations, they take new steps to set it urgently under way. The Gentiles thought this was a way of placating the shades. Thus we may gather what a state of corrupt practice infested Judaea.

Mark 5.39. *The child . . . sleepeth.* *To sleep* is often used in Scripture for 'to die'. And there is no doubt that by this simile, taken from the passing time of quietness, we have an indication of the resurrection to come. Here Christ carefully distinguishes between sleep and death, to give them hope of life. In other words, You will soon see her awake, whom now you take to be dead. That he was laughed at, by stupid and dumb persons, is no wonder, for they were so full of their godless mourning that they did not follow His intention. This too gives the miracle commendation—the fact that they had no doubt left, but she was dead.

Mark 5.41. *And taking the child by the hand, he saith unto her.* Although in the way of nature all the noise here did nothing to arouse the senses of the dead girl, Christ determined marvellously to display the force of His own voice, that He might the better accustom men to hear His teaching. Thus it is obvious how effective is the choice of Christ, which even reaches the dead, to give life at the very place of death. So Luke says that her spirit returned, as if to say, that, wakened at Christ's command, it was at once ready.

Mark 5.43. *And he charged them.* Although Christ had not fallen in with their desire to come in and see the rising again, the miracle could not long remain concealed. Nor would it have been reasonable to suppress the power of God, by which the whole world was to be made ready for life. So why does He impose silence upon the parents of the girl? Perhaps it was not so much the event, as the means, He wished to conceal, and that only for a time. For we see in other places too, that He chose to seize His occasion. Those who think that He refused them to speak, in order to sharpen their enthusiasm, are being forced into a solution, as a let-out. I would agree that the miracle was not done without Him wishing it to be known abroad, but perhaps at a more suitable time, and when the crowd had been sent away, for there was no normality or restraint with them. He wanted to have a space, in which they could ponder God's work, in peace and order.

*And as Jesus passed by from thence, two blind men followed him, crying
out, and saying, Have mercy on us, thou son of David. And when he was
come into the house, the blind men came to him: and Jesus saith unto them,
Believe ye that I am able to do this? They say unto him, Yea, Lord.
Then touched he their eyes, saying, According to your faith be it done
unto you. And their eyes were opened. And Jesus strictly charged
them, saying, See that no man know it. But they went forth, and spread
abroad his fame in all that land.*

*And as they went forth, behold, there was brought to him a dumb man
possessed with a devil. And when the devil was cast out, the dumb man
spake: and the multitudes marvelled, saying, It was never so seen in
Israel. But the Pharisees said, By the prince of the devils casteth he out
devils.* (Matt. 9.27-34)

Matt. 9.27. *And as Jesus passed by from thence.* The other Evangelists
say nothing of these two miracles, for as we have said elsewhere, and
John makes perfectly clear, they did not plan to gather every single
deed of Christ, but to put together a compact case, that would show
Him to be the Messiah. Now here, Matthew tells how two blind men
had their sight restored, but Christ did not bring the unfortunates help
as quickly as He was, at other times, used to do. When they shout on
the road He does not respond, but, as though He noticed nothing, lets
them follow Him to the door of the house. Then at last, He asks them
what they think about His power. He wished to test their faith in deed
and in word. He kept them in suspense, in fact. He walked past, as
though He did not hear, and so made trial of their patience, and the
firmness of the roots which faith had planted in their hearts. Later, in
asking what they believe, He went on with the same scrutiny. But it
may be asked, whether it be enough to be persuaded of the ability of
God, and of Christ, for a man to be faithful. For this is the implication
of the words, *Believe ye that I am able to do this?* However it is clear
from other passages of Scripture that the knowledge of what He can do,
is of little weight or import, if there is not also the knowledge of what
He wills to do. Yet Christ is satisfied with their answer, and praises
their faith, as clear on all counts. The answer is, that as they had first
confessed Him son of David, they had understood something about
grace, for by this title they dignified Him with being the Redeemer of
His race, and the Author of all good. So when He asks about His own
power, He is interrogating them more deeply to see if their belief is
serious. Faith in God embraces His mercy and fatherly love, with His
power; faith in Christ takes in His purpose of good will, along with His
virtue. As men often ascribe less than is right to God's might and
Christ's power, the question is relevantly put to the blind men, whether

275

they believe that Christ is able to do what they, with their mouths, have professed. Though here, Christ simply wished to know whether they whole-heartedly gave Him the honour of Messiah. For this reason, their faith is praised, in that for all His humble and lowly appearance, they took Him as the Son of David.

Matt. 9.29. *According to your faith.* Though the narrative here is of a particular favour done to the two blind men, we may well take a general lesson from this utterance of Christ, that we (as long as we pray from faith) shall never suffer rejection in our prayers. If these two men, of slight and scarcely formed faith, gained what they wished, much more today shall the faith of those men avail who come to God with the gift of the adoption of the Spirit, and in reliance upon the sacrifice of the Mediator.

Matt. 9.30. *Strictly charged them.* Either He wished to have other witnesses to the miracle, or He wished them to delay their report to another time. That they went straight out, and published it everywhere, deserves blame: for the idea which some have invented that Christ made the prohibition to add some excitement to events, is refuted elsewhere in this commentary. Certainly there was some reason for the ban. We do not know what it was, but their zeal in spreading the account prematurely was irresponsible.

Matt. 9.32. *There was brought to him a dumb man.* It is probable that this man was not naturally dumb, but being in the grip of the devil was the reason for his losing his speech—not all mutes are demoniac. Therefore it was the affliction of the penalty that he should show, in clear signs, that his tongue was in the grip of an evil spirit. The way the crowd exclaim at his healing—'that it was never so done in Israel'—seems exaggerated, for in former days God had revealed His glory to that people by greater miracles. It may be they are looking to the deeper significance of the miracle, that the minds of them all were then keyed up to hope for the coming of Messiah. Certainly, in wishing to extol the present grace of God, they did not mean to detract from previous days. We must note too, that it was not a considered reaction, but a sudden burst of astonishment.

Matt. 9.34. *By the prince of the devils, etc.* Here we may see what an attack of rage had befallen men who did not fear with downright insult to slam the door against so outstanding an action of God. Note the contrast between the people's acclamation, and their own blasphemy. The people say, that never was it so done in Israel, making clear expression of their sense of the divine glory: to make it all the plainer, then, that the opposition were completely out of their wits in daring, as I may say, to curse God to His face. At the same time, we learn that when godlessness comes to the extreme point of blindness, there is no work of God, however plain, which will not be distorted in its eyes. Indeed this is an amazing portent, for mortal men to rise against their Maker, and from it all the more are we to fear the blindness I speak of, for which God takes vengeance upon the wicked, after long years of patience.

And Jesus went about all the cities and the villages, teaching in their synagogues, and preaching the gospel of the kingdom, and healing all manner of disease and all manner of sickness. But when he saw the multitudes, he was moved with compassion for them, because they were distressed and scattered, as sheep not having a shepherd. Then saith he unto his disciples, The harvest truly is plenteous, but the labourers are few. Pray ye therefore the Lord of the harvest, that he send forth labourers into his harvest. (Matt. 9.35-38)

Matt. 9.35. *And Jesus went about.* This is a comprehensive view, to tell us that here is no point by point narrative of Christ's ministry, but that He continued to exercise His task, in preaching the doctrine of salvation, and confirming it with miracles over and above. *The gospel of the kingdom* is named from its effect, as we have already said, for to this end God gathers to Himself the sadly wasted people, that He may reign in their midst; and indeed, He raised up His judgment seat, that He might award all His folk with the fulness of joy. But remember, that we must be subjects of God, to be lifted up by Him into the glory of heaven.
Matt. 9.36. *He was moved with compassion.* The first thing we can deduce from this is the lazy state of the priesthood, for although they were distributed all over the ground to be the leading lights in teaching about heaven, they were just idle bellies. They were so proud of being the front men of the people, and there was quite a crowd of them who boasted of this title. Yet Christ found no pastor amongst them. The same wilderness greets our eyes today in the Papacy, for all that it is crammed with nominal Pastors. What a vast flood of them there is, who gulp down the populace under the name of Clergy! And though they are dumb dogs, yet they are not ashamed to yap fiercely about their own hierarchy. But it is Christ's voice we must hear, which declares them to be no pastors, when they are not workers: the sheep are straying and scattered, who are not gathered into God's fold by the teaching of the Gospel. That He is touched with compassion shows Him to be the faithful Minister of His Father, in caring for the salvation of His people, for whose sake He had put on the flesh. And although, now that He is entered into heaven, He may not have the same emotions as He then willed to feel and suffer in this mortal life, He has not

cast off His concern for His Church, but looks at His wandering sheep, and gathers in His flock, which the wolves had cruelly scared and ravaged.

Matt. 9.37. *The harvest truly is plenteous.* By the metaphor, He means that many of the populace were ready to receive the Gospel. Though in due course the majority in base ingratitude refused, to their shame, the salvation that was offered them, He deliberately compares the moderate number of the elect who were mixed in with the unbelievers to a full harvest, because God rates His small handful more highly than all the world. As many put themselves forward, but very few showed faithfulness in their lives, He does not reckon them among the *labourers.* This word has a good significance for Him. When Paul speaks of evil workers (2 Cor. 11.13; Phil. 3.2), he is thinking of their boastfulness. He would not have allowed them this title, since their labour was all being expended on ruin and devastation, except that they were trading under false pretences. *Pray ye therefore the Lord of the harvest.* As no true and acceptable minister of the Gospel will ever advance on his own, nor can any properly fulfil their teaching office unless they are such as the Lord calls forth, and equips with the gifts of His Spirit, so whenever we see a lack of good pastors, we must lift up our eyes to Him, to bring us the remedy. The burden of such prayer was never greater than in the appalling devastation of the Church, as we see it everywhere today.

And when he was entered into a boat, his disciples followed him. And behold, there arose a great tempest in the sea, insomuch that the boat was covered with the waves: but he was asleep. And they came to him, and awoke him, saying, Save, Lord, we perish. And he saith unto them, Why are ye fearful, O ye of little faith? Then he arose, and rebuked the winds and the sea; and there was a great calm. And the men marvelled, saying, What manner of man is this, that even the winds and the sea obey him? (Matt. 8.23-27)

And on the day, when even was come, he saith unto them, Let us go over unto the other side. And leaving the multitude, they take him with them, even as he was, in the boat. And other boats were with him. And there ariseth a great storm of wind, and the waves beat into the boat, insomuch that the boat was now filling. And he himself was in the stern, asleep on the cushion: and they awake him, and say unto him, Master, carest thou not that we perish? And he awoke, and rebuked the wind, and said unto the sea, Peace, be still. And the wind ceased, and there was a great calm. And he said unto them, Why are ye fearful? have ye not faith? And

*they feared exceedingly, and said one to another, Who then is this, that
even the wind and the sea obey him?* (Mark 4.35-41)

*Now it came to pass on one of those days, that he entereth into a boat,
himself and his disciples; and he said unto them, Let us go over unto the
other side of the lake: and they launched forth. But as they sailed he fell
asleep: and there came down a storm of wind upon the lake; and they were
filling with water, and were in jeopardy. And they came to him, and
awoke him, saying, Master, master, we perish. And he awoke, and
rebuked the wind and the raging of the water: and they ceased, and there
was a calm. And he said unto them, Where is your faith? And being
afraid they marvelled, saying one to another, Who then is this, that he
commandeth even the winds and the water, and they obey him?* (Luke
8.22-25)

There will shortly after be further mention of a lake, where we are told
swine charged in and were drowned, but there is no general agreement
whether this is one and the same lake. All agree that the waters of
Gennesaret were sweet to taste and safe to use, but the Gadarene lake is
said by Strabo to be so noxious and unhealthy that beasts lost their
hooves and hair from drinking it. So there is no doubt that there were
two different lakes, and separated from one another by an appreciable
distance. Now there is no dispute about this being the lake of
Gennesaret understood here, which Christ crossed, and reached the land
of the Gadarenes, whom Matthew calls Gergesenes. Those who infer
from the variety of names that there are various narratives given, try to
appear highly ingenious, but actually fall into total nonsensity. The
region of the Gergesenes was also called Gadarene, after the well-
known town of Gadara. In the time of Jerome, the name was changed,
and so he calls them Gerasenes, according to the usage then prevailing.
Yet I do not deny that it was into lake Gadarene that the swine were
driven headlong by devils. However, when Christ says, 'Let us cross
to the other side', this can only be expounded as of lake Gennesaret.
Now we must look into the matter of time, which we cannot deduce
from Matthew, nor from Luke. Only Mark notes, that it was the
evening of that day on which Christ had spoken of the preaching of the
Gospel, under the parable of the seed. Clearly they did not preserve
the time-sequence, as Luke clearly states when he says, that it happened
'on one of those days': the words show that he was not very worried
which came first or second.

Matt. 8.23. *And when he was entered into a boat.* Mark says that other
little boats made the crossing, while Christ took His own boat, with
His disciples. Luke actually gives His words, and Matthew is more

brief. But, all in all, they agree that Christ settled down for repose, and while He slept a tempest suddenly sprang up. The first thing we may be sure of is, that it was no casual storm which disturbed the lake. For how would God have allowed His Son to be tossed by the blind fury of the winds? But He took the occasion to show His Apostles how slight and feeble their faith was at this stage. Though Christ's sleep was natural enough, it too had the effect of making the disciples realize their own weakness better. I do not say, as many do, that Christ pretended to sleep, in order to test them. I really think He slept, as the state and needs of His human nature affected Him. But all the time His Godhead was on the watch, so that His disciples should not have been afraid for themselves, without immediately finding comfort in the knowledge that assistance from heaven was at hand. So we should know, that all this was governed by God's hidden providence, that Christ should sleep, that a violent storm should rise, and the waves cover the ship till the vessel seemed little short of disaster. Hence we may learn, that as often as adversity arises, our faith is being tested by God. If ills weigh heavily on us, so as almost to overwhelm us, this is done by the same purpose of God to try our endurance, or to bring our hidden weakness, by this means, into the open; just as we see, when the waves broke over the Apostles, their infirmity was disclosed, which before had been hidden.

Matt. 8.25. *Save, Lord.* A godly prayer, you might think: what better could they do than ask deliverance of Christ, in all their disaster? But, as Christ censures their lack of faith, we must see in what part they sinned. For myself, I am convinced they were too attached to the carnal presence of their master: for in Mark, they do not simply pray, but expostulate with Him, Master, carest thou not that we perish? Luke records their confusion and alarm, Master, master, we perish. They should have been sure, that Christ's Divinity was not overcome by the slumber of the flesh, and have taken recourse to that: but they lie quiet, until the extremity of the crisis forces them: then they are in a panic of wild consternation, and reckon they cannot be saved if Christ does not wake up. This is the reason why He accuses them of lack of faith: that they asked Him to lend assistance, was, of course, a testimony to faith, if they had relied in confidence on His divine power, and hoped for the aid they sought quietly and without such alarm.

This answers the question which might come from His words of rebuke—surely all fear cannot be wrong and contrary to faith? First of all, He does not simply rebuke them for being afraid, but for being men of fear. In Mark, there is added the particle οὕτω (so much), meaning that they were afraid beyond limit. Further, in contrasting faith with their fear, He shows that He is speaking of an excessive upset, which is not just stirring their faith, but in fact knocking it clean out of their minds. Fear, in the ordinary sense, is not opposed to faith. This is obvious, for if we fear nothing, the idle apathy of the flesh is creeping in, then faith languishes, the mood for prayer turns drowsy, and at last the very thought of God is extinguished. Besides, those who are not touched with a sense of evils to the point of fear, are more stupid than firm. So we see, that fear which arouses faith is not a vicious thing in itself, until it goes beyond the limit. The excess comes if the tranquillity of faith is broken or spoiled; this should find its peace in the Word of God, but as it never happens that the faithful are in such control of themselves that their faith does not have to struggle, they practically always sin in their fears. But we must be sure that nervousness is not a proof of a failure in faith, but only such anxiety as disturbs the peace of our conscience, and stops it from resting upon the promise of God.

Matt. 8.26. *Rebuked the winds.* Mark gives Christ's words, with which He addressed the sea and bade it 'Peace', that is quietness; not that the lake had any means of comprehension, but that He might show the power of His voice in reaching the dumb elements. Not only do the sea and winds obey God's command without senses, but so do even the godless, for all their contumacy. When God determines to settle the tumults of wars, He does not always mollify and mould the wild spirits to obey Him, but makes the weapons actually fall from the hands of the savage contenders: in fulfilment of the words of Psalm 46.9, He maketh wars to cease unto the end of the earth; He breaketh the bow, and cutteth the spear in sunder; He burneth the chariots in the fire.

Matt. 8.27. *And the men marvelled.* Mark and Luke seem to assign this to the Apostles. After telling that they were rebuked by Christ, they add that they cried out in fear, *Who then is this?* yet this is more appropriate for others who had not yet known Christ. Whichever way we take it, the fruit of the miracle comes to light, now that Christ's glory is praised. If you believe that the Apostles are speaking, the sense of the words will be that His divine power is sufficiently proven by the fact that the winds and sea obey Him. Yet as it is more likely that it was others who spoke, the Evangelists are teaching us by these words that their hearts were so impressed by the miracle that their awe at the sight of Christ was a kind of preparation for faith.

And when he was come into the other side into the country of the Gadarenes, there met him two possessed with devils, coming forth out of the

281

tombs, *exceeding fierce, so that no man could pass by that way. And behold, they cried out, saying, What have we to do with thee, thou Son of God? art thou come hither to torment us before the time? Now there was afar off from them a herd of many swine feeding. And the devils besought him, saying, If thou cast us out, send us away into the herd of swine. And he said unto them, Go. And they came out, and went into the swine: and behold, the whole herd rushed down the steep into the sea, and perished in the waters. And they that fed them fled, and went away into the city, and told everything, and what was befallen to them that were possessed with devils. And behold, all the city came out to meet Jesus: and when they saw him, they besought him that he would depart from their borders.* (Matt. 8.28-34)

And they came to the other side of the sea, into the country of the Gerasenes. And when he was come out of the boat, straightway there met him out of the tombs a man with an unclean spirit, who had his dwelling in the tombs: and no man could any more bind him, no, not with a chain; because that he had been often bound with fetters and chains, and the chains had been rent asunder by him, and the fetters broken in pieces: and no man had strength to tame him. And always, night and day, in the tombs and in the mountains, he was crying out, and cutting himself with stones. And when he saw Jesus from afar, he ran and worshipped him; and crying out with a loud voice, he saith, What have I to do with thee, Jesus, thou Son of the Most High God? I adjure thee by God, torment me not. For he said unto him, Come forth, thou unclean spirit, out of the man. And he asked him, What is thy name? And he saith unto him, My name is Legion; for we are many. And he besought him much that he would not send them away out of the country. Now there was on the mountain side a great herd of swine feeding. And they besought him, saying, Send us into the swine, that we may enter into them. And he gave them leave. And the unclean spirits came out, and entered into the swine: and the herd rushed down the steep into the sea, in number about two thousand; and they were choked in the sea. And they that fed them fled, and told it in the city, and in the country. And they came to see what it was that had come to pass. And they come to Jesus, and behold him that was possessed with devils sitting, clothed and in his right mind, even him that had the legion: and they were afraid. And they that saw it declared unto them how it befell him that was possessed with devils, and concerning the swine. And they began to beseech him to depart from their borders. And as he was entering into the boat, he that had been possessed with devils besought him that he might be with him. And he suffered him not, but saith unto him, Go to thy house unto thy friends, and tell them how great things the Lord hath done for thee, and how he had mercy upon thee. And he went his way, and began to publish in Decapolis how great things Jesus had done for him; and all men did marvel. (Mark 5.1-20)

And they arrived at the country of the Gerasenes, which is over against Galilee. And when he was come forth upon the land, there met him a certain man out of the city, who had devils; and for a long time he had worn no clothes, and abode not in any house, but in the tombs. And when he saw Jesus, he cried out, and fell down before him, and with a loud voice said, What have I to do with thee, Jesus, thou Son of the Most High God? I beseech thee, torment me not. For he commanded the unclean spirit to come out from the man. For oftentimes it had seized him: and he was kept under guard, and bound with chains and fetters; and breaking the bands asunder, he was driven of the devil into the deserts. And Jesus asked him, What is thy name? And he said, Legion; for many devils were entered into him. And they intreated him that he would not command them to depart into the abyss. Now there was a herd of many swine feeding on the mountain: and they intreated him that he would give them leave to enter into them. And he gave them leave. And the devils came out from the man, and entered into the swine: and the herd rushed down the steep into the lake, and were choked. And when they that fed them saw what had come to pass, they fled, and told it in the city and in the country. And they went out to see what had come to pass; and they came to Jesus, and found the man, from whom the devils were gone out, sitting, clothed and in his right mind, at the feet of Jesus: and they were afraid. And they that saw it told them how he that was possessed with devils was made whole. And all the people of the country of the Gerasenes round about asked him to depart from them; for they were holden with great fear: and he entered into a boat, and returned. But the man from whom the devils were gone out prayed him that he might be with him: but he sent him away, saying, Return to thy house, and declare how great things God hath done for thee. And he went his way, publishing throughout the whole city how great things Jesus had done for him. (Luke 8.26-39)

I have earlier refuted the mistake of those who think a different miracle is related by Mark and Luke. Since the three Evangelists describe the same district, across from Galilee—as Luke expressly states it to be—and all the circumstances agree, who is going to be persuaded that all these same things happened on separate occasions?

Matt. 8.23. *There met him two possessed with devils.* This single difference has been the cause of the interpreters' error, in distinguishing Matthew from the others in that he names two men and the others name one. But Augustine's conjecture is probably right, who held that there were two, but excused the mention of only one on the ground that this was the more notorious, and, because of the savagery of his affliction, was the subject of a more striking miracle. Certainly we see how Luke and Mark go to great length to describe to the full the devil's fury, to make us realise the misery of this man, of whom they speak, and the distress he suffered from his utter incapacity. Seeing then that it is the outstanding example of Christ's power which they are publicising, there is no contradiction in Matthew's narrative, when he adds the other man, who was presumably less well known.

When Luke says that a man 'out of the city' met Him, we cannot tell whether he means that he was a citizen of Gadara, or that after leaving that town he encountered Christ. For when he was told to go home and preach the grace of God to his own folk, Mark says that he did this around Decapolis, which was the neighbouring district, bordering on Galilee, from which we deduce, that he was not a native of Gadara. Besides, Matthew and Mark expressly say that he did not come out from the city, but from the tombs, and the whole context of Luke indicates that he lived in the solitary places. So I interpret these words, *there met him a certain man out of the city*, as saying that before Christ reached the city, a demoniac stood in His path, from that quarter.

Now, those who think that the man lived in the tombs because evil spirits enjoy the stench of corpses, or find sweetness in the savour of the offerings, or because they are after the souls which they seek to have close to their bodies—all this is quite insubstantial, indeed foolish speculation. Rather, the unclean spirit kept the poor man at the tombs, to rend him with unending terror at the gloomy spectacle of death, as though, cut off from the company of men, he were already leading his life among the dead. We also learn that the devil does not torture men only in this present life, but pursues them even in death, where indeed his reign flourishes.

Mark 5.3. *No man could any more bind him.* By his natural force, he could not burst his chains. We may gather that sometimes extra-ordinary energy is given to Satan, whose power goes beyond our understanding and the accustomed course. We may often observe in the deranged far more strength than they would possess in their normal state, and we cannot deny that the devil also plays his part there, as God may permit, but the violence which the Evangelists describe was far greater. Indeed, it makes a gloomy and awful scene, yet one which warns us of the misery and horror of being subject to Satan's tyranny. The distress of the soul is as much to be feared as the torment of the body, however fierce and cruel it be.

Mark 5.6. *Worshipped him.* This is the sequence of the narrative. When the demoniacs came out and met Him, Christ commanded the unclean spirits to depart from them; whereupon they begged Him, on their knees, not to torture them before the time. So the worship did not come before Christ's words, nor did they complain of Christ troubling them before He forced them to go out. We must realise that they had not really come voluntarily into Christ's view, but were drawn by Christ's hidden command. Just as they were used previously to snatch men off to the tombs in a wild attack, so now a higher power compels them unwillingly to come to the tribunal of their Judge. So we see that the whole kingdom of Satan is under the command of Christ. No more were the demons then in charge of their affairs, when Christ haled them before Himself, than those poor men were shortly before, whom they had tossed all ways under their domination. Further, they are brought to a halt in mid-career by Christ's secret force, that by their expulsion He may reveal Himself as men's Deliverer. Under duress they worship Him, and their spiteful complaints are witness to their confession not being free, but forced out of them.

What have we to do with thee? they say. They would have been glad to have put Him to flight with this cry, but when they see that they are held in a grip, and that it would be vain to attempt an escape from His command, they complain that they are being tormented before the time, and they put up a plea for Him to cease. So we see, how the devils breathe nothing but fury against God, and yet with all their swelling pride they fall like broken creatures in a twinkling: for their malice and perversity is never tamed, never ceases to resist God's rule, and yet it meets its match and surrenders. Christ does not openly rebut the devil's confession as He does elsewhere, and the reason seems to be that their confrontation was right out in the open, and there could be no place for any false imputations being raised. Besides, Christ took account of men. Hence when evil-minded and spiteful observers were present, He took more care to refute slanders, and thus would check the evil spirits more sharply. But as regards this present case, it is entirely beyond question that with their supplications and prayers, the demons were in a wild rage against Him.

Matt. 8.29. *Art thou come hither . . . before the time.* Some explain their torment, as being forced to let the man, whom they possessed, go free and unrestrained. Others relate it to the last day of judgment. I consider that they were alarmed by the presence of their Judge and came to think of their punishment, for their evil conscience told them, without any word from Christ, what their deserts were. As criminals brought to trial think of their sentence, so must devils and all the ungodly tremble at the sight of God, just as if they sensed the underworld, the fire which never dies, and the torment to come. As the devils knew that Christ was Judge of the world, there is no wonder if the sight of

Him struck fear into their minds, for the pains which threatened them. The question raised by some, as to whether they understood that there was a day of ultimate judgment, is superfluous. What does that phrase *before the time* imply? Simply, that for the wicked, the time to pay the penalty is never ripe, and they would gladly prolong it from one day to another. Any postponement they treat as gain, as long as God lets them go on, and so they turn their tails, and run from His judgment, though quite without success.

Mark 5.9. *My name is Legion.* Christ makes the devil come out with this name, the better to display the greatness of His grace. We cannot overlook the severity of the affliction with which the man was assaulted, that he had a virtual horde of demons residing in Him. Who was to show him the compassion that would snatch him out of so many deaths, after a thousand defeats? What a magnificent exhibition of Christ's power, that in an instant He routed by His voice not one, but an entire colony. *Legion* is not really taken for a finite number of men, but just as a great crowd. Well do we see what a poor creature man is when He loses the protection of God. Each individual lies exposed not to one devil, but gives lodging to a vast crew. This also refutes the common error, which Jews and Christians have taken over from pagan sources, that each man is assaulted by one demon at once. Scripture clearly affirms that according as it may please the Lord, sometimes one devil is sent to afflict a whole nation, sometimes one man is given over to a large number for punishment. Similarly, sometimes one angel watches over an entire people, sometimes to one individual there are assigned many guardians of his safety. So we should keep more careful watch, else a huge crowd of foes may get the better of us.

Mark 5.10. *And he besought him.* Luke says that they entreated Him not to be sent *into the abyss*, which is explained by some as meaning that they shunned solitude. But I refer it to their lust for destruction, for the one enthusiasm of devils is to go about amongst man, as a lion seeking prey. It grieves them to be cast into the abyss, where they lose the means of causing pain and damage. That this is the right sense may be inferred from Mark's words, when he says, that they prayed Him not to be sent *out of the country.* Altogether the way they show their mind working is in an overpowering desire for the ruin of mankind.

Matt. 8.31. *Send us away into the herd of swine.* Some make the guess that they wished to rush into the swine, since they hated all God's creatures. I grant that it is true, that their whole motive was to waste and upset the entire order of nature, as composed by God, but certainly, their purposes looked further, namely to drive the inhabitants of the region by the loss of the swine to bring curses down upon God. When the devil strikes Job's house with lightning, he does not act out of hatred for wood or stone, but in order that the holy man, by bearing his loss with impatience, may rage against God. Christ agrees, but not in answer to their prayers, for He wills to take the occasion to see what kind of people they are at Gadara. Or perhaps it was to correct their wickedness, that He allowed the devils such freedom to set upon the swine. Anyhow, we have no definite reason, and we should accept God's hidden judgment with reverence, and worship Him with religious awe.

The passage also teaches us what stupid nonsense it is to say, with some ungodly folk, that devils are not real spirits (*essentiales spiritus*), but only the depraved passions of men. Well now, how do you transfer avarice, self-seeking, cruelty, perfidy . . . into swine? No, we should realize that unclean spirits (being doomed to destruction) are the foes of the human race, and aim to drag whom they may into the same pit as themselves.

Mark 5.15. *And they come to Jesus.* Here we have a remarkable proof that not all who recognise God's handiwork profit from it as they ought, and submit themselves to Him in true devotion. After seeing the miracle, the Gadarenes were afraid, presumably bacause the Majesty of God shone upon Christ. And this was good. But what could be worse than their action in driving Him out of their territory? They too had gone astray. Here was the Pastor who gathers men in, yes God by His Son reaches out His arms, to lift them to heaven in His embrace, when they had been overwhelmed by the shadows of death. But they prefer to do without the offered salvation, rather than tolerate the presence of Christ any more. They seem annoyed at the loss of their swine, but Luke notes a deeper reason, that they were gripped with a great fear, and indeed, if they had been so bitter over the loss they had suffered, they would not have come up with a request, but would have flung Him out pretty sharply.

Now though they respect Him as God's Minister, yet, in their fit of alarm, they wish Him to be far from them. Thus we see how they are touched with no sense of the divine grace. It is true that all the wicked turn to God in prayer, and spend much effort in placating Him, but if the chance were given them, they would get as far away from Him as they could, for His aspect is too terrifying to men who see Him more as Judge, than as Father. Hence the teaching of the Gospel, though you can imagine nothing more sweet, is often unhappy and bitter, and makes a good part of the world wish that it were buried. At the same time, it is true that part of their alarm was occasioned by the stock lost. Thus today, when men, in public or private affairs, reckon that Christ is not favourable to their interests, are seized with a mean, fleshly fear and will not taste the grace He offers. So believing that God at His coming

287

will be more angry than welcoming, they try their best to have Him move elsewhere. This is a sign of disgusting stupidity, that they are made more afraid by the loss of swine, than delighted at the salvation of the soul.

Luke 8.38. *But the man . . . prayed him.* The Gadarenes are not able to endure Christ's presence, but he who has been delivered from the evil influence wishes to abandon his country, and follow Him. Clearly, what a great difference there is between the knowledge of God's goodness, and of His power, for the latter instils fear, scares men from God's sight and thrusts Him far away, while His goodness gently induces men to decide that nothing could be more desirable than to be united with God. Why Christ refuses to have this man as a companion is uncertain, except that He hoped that richer fruit might come from that source if he should be a witness among his own race To the famous and extraordinary benefit which he had received—exactly as Mark and Luke say was the case. Christ bids him speak of the work of God, not His own, intending by this that He should be accepted as a true Minister and Prophet of God, and so win authority. This was the way an uncouth people had to learn the elements, little by little, for they had not yet any understanding of His divinity. Christ is in fact the ladder by whom we ascend to God the Father, but as this had not yet been revealed, He started with the Father, until a better opportunity should arise. We may add a higher interpretation (*anagoge*). Christ, in the person of one man, gave an example of His grace, which is extended to the whole human race. For albeit we are not tormented by the devil, yet he holds us as his slaves, until the Son of God claims us from his domination. Naked, torn and unsightly, we wander afar, until He restores us to our sane and ordered mind. It remains for us, in praising His grace, to testify to our gratitude.

And he called unto him his twelve disciples, and gave them authority over unclean spirits, to cast them out, and to heal all manner of disease and all manner of sickness.

Now the names of the twelve apostles are these: The first, Simon, who is called Peter, and Andrew his brother; James the son of Zebedee, and John his brother; Philip, and Bartholomew; Thomas, and Matthew the publican; James the son of Alphaeus, and Thaddaeus; Simon the Cananaean, and Judas Iscariot, who also betrayed him. These twelve Jesus sent forth, and charged them, saying,

Go not into any way of the Gentiles, and enter not into any city of the Samaritans: but go rather to the lost sheep of the house of Israel. And as

ye go, preach, saying, The kingdom of heaven is at hand. Heal the sick,
raise the dead, cleanse the lepers, cast out devils: freely ye received, freely
give. (Matt. 10.1-8)

And he called unto him the twelve, and began to send them forth by two
and two; and he gave them authority over the unclean spirits. (Mark 6.7)

And he called the twelve together, and gave them power and authority
over all devils, and to cure diseases. And he sent them forth to preach the
kingdom of God, and to heal the sick. (Luke 9.1-2)

Here the calling of the Apostles is described for us, not the earlier
occasion, when the Lord chose them as fellow-travellers, meaning to
prepare them for their task. Now they are summoned to immediate
action, they are told to get set for the job, instructions are given them,
and, in case they should lack authority, they are accorded the power of
the Spirit. Formerly, they were charged with the hope of their future
task: now Christ declares the hour has come, in which they are to put
their hands to the wheel. Yet we must note, that there is at this stage no
word of the continuing Apostolate, but only of the proclamation of
that time, when men's minds had to be stirred and awakened, to be
more ready to listen to Christ. At this time they are sent to announce
in Judaea that the season of the promised restoration and salvation has
arrived: later, Christ will ordain them to spread His Gospel throughout
the world. Here He takes them only as auxiliaries, to prepare Him an
audience, where His voice could not reach: afterwards He will assign to
them the role of teaching, which He had undertaken. It is worth noting
carefully, that we are not to believe that a regular and fixed rule is prescribed for all the ministers of the Word, when the Lord instructs the
heralds of His message about what, in this short period, He wishes them
to do. Failure to understand this has deceived many, and led them to
force all ministers of the Word, without making any distinction, to
keep to this norm.

Matt. 10.1. *And he called unto him his twelve.* The number twelve
indicated the coming restoration of the Church. For as the people had
its origins in twelve Patriarchs, so Christ now recalls the scattered
remnant to remembrance of its origins, and to find sure hope that it
would get renewal. Though there had been no flourishing of the
Kingdom of God in Judaea as would preserve the integrity of the
people's position—in fact the race had now come so low, that by
spurning the offer of grace it deserved for its ingratitude to perish twice
over—yet this did not prevent the birth of a new people. It later came

to pass, that He extended the sceptre of His Son's power more widely from Zion, that from its source rivers should flow to spread their waters at large over the four corners of the earth. Then God gathered in His Israel, from all sides, that they should form into one body, not only the torn and scattered fragments, but those men who before had been quite estranged from the people of God. So the Lord makes sure that He testifies to the restoration of the Church by this institution of twelve, as the Patriarchs were twelve. Besides, by this number a warning was given to the Jews of the reason for His coming. Since they did not allow any place for God's grace, He engendered a new Israel for Himself. To look at the origins, it might seem laughable that Christ should have appointed such distinguished roles, for men of obscurity, and of no repute, but the amazing success, and such fruitful increase to the Church, shows that the Apostles, so far from yielding to the Patriarchs in rank of honour, or in propagation of children, did in fact far exceed them.

Gave them authority. As in men's eyes the Apostles held virtually no position, the appointment Christ gave them was divine. They were not outstandingly clever or fluent, but the excellence and novelty of their mission demanded more than human gifts: they had to have authority from elsewhere. When Christ charges them with performing miracles, He equips them with the tokens of heavenly power, with which they may gain faith and reverence among the poeple. Hence we infer the legitimate use of miracles, that as Christ appoints them at one and the same time to be heralds of the Gospel and ministers of mighty acts, He makes miracles nothing other than seals to His teaching, and we are not allowed to break this unique bond. The Papists are false, therefore, and criminally wasteful of the works of God, when they separate the Word from miracles.

Matt. 10.2. *The first, Simon.* The Romanists are foolish to deduce their primacy from this. We readily agree, that Simon Peter was first among the Apostles, but there is no place for letting the rule, which applied to a few men, be extended to all the world. Anyhow, the fact that he is named first does not immediately advance him to domination over his colleagues. Let them have all they wish, concerning Peter's position, but until they can show how these godless and sacrilegious apostates are successors of Peter, his merits have no connection with the see of Rome.

Matt. 10.5. *Into any way of the Gentiles.* This makes more clear what I have already remarked, that the mission then laid on the Apostles was directed only at exciting the Jews to hope for the salvation which was at hand, and to make them eager to listen to Christ. At this time, He confines their speaking to the territory of Judaea, while later it was to resound in the uttermost parts of the globe. And the reason is, that He had been sent by the Father as a minister of the Circumcision, to fulfil the promises which had once been given to the fathers—cf. Rom. 15.8. God had made a peculiar alliance with the stock of Abraham. Naturally Christ began by continuing the grace of God to the chosen people, until the time was ripe to publish it abroad. From the resurrection, we may definitely see the second stage, the blessing promised to all nations being shed forth, even as then the veil of the temple was rent, the partition wall of strife pulled down. So if any should think the prohibition lacking in humanity, that Christ does not grant the Gentiles to be partakers in the Gospel, his quarrel is with God for excluding the rest of the world at the time when He confirmed His covenant with Abraham's seed alone, for it is on this that Christ's command has its basis.

Matt. 10.6. *Rather to the lost sheep.* As I said, He gave the Jews priority, as being the firstborn, for God then reckoned them the sole members of His household, while others were outsiders. And He calls them the lost sheep, that the Apostles might be touched with compassion, and go to their aid the more keenly, with more ardent feeling, as well as that they should realise that there was a plentiful supply of work for them to do. And yet, in the character of that one race, Christ is telling them what is the condition of all the human race. The Jews, being close and covenanted with God, were still so far from being true heirs of eternal life, that they might actually be called lost, until they came to find their salvation in Christ. So how will it come out for us, who are far below them in honour?

The name of *sheep* He also ascribes to the wicked, who were not truly of God's flock, for the adoption availed for all the people: and elsewhere, He calls those sons of the Kingdom, who were eventually to be expelled by reason of their false profession (Matt. 8.12). Briefly, Christ commends the Jews to the Apostles under the term sheep as a way of making His work over to them, since they were unable to acknowledge any as being of God's flock who had not been brought into the same fold.

Matt. 10.7. *Preach, saying, etc.* This is the announcement I spoke of, by which Christ intended to stir up the minds of the people to hope for the near redemption. For *kingdom of heaven*, Luke reads, *kingdom of God*, with the same sense. The Jews had to know first that they were restored divinely, not by men's favour, then, that their state would be prosperous with God as their king, and thirdly, that it was no earthly and passing prosperity that was promised them, but one from heaven, which would never pass away.

Matt. 10.8. *Heal the sick.* As He equipped them with power, so He told them to be His faithful and generous ministers, and forbade them to suppress what was entrusted to them, for the common good of all.

Further, He demonstrated by these miracles the end for which He was sent by the Father, and what shall be the result of His Gospel. He is quite deliberate in telling them to raise the dead, and heal the sick, rather than afflict healthy men with sickness, or bring death upon the living. Miracles have an analogy and likeness to Christ's work and calling, telling us that He came to us as the author of all good, to deliver us from the tyranny of Satan and of death, to heal our diseases and faults, and to give aid to all our distresses.

Freely ye received. To make them share more generously the gifts He had conferred upon them, He indicated that they had not been entrusted to them for their personal glory, but to make them as it were, channels of God's free beneficence. In other words, Consider the source of the power that has come to you, and as it has flowed from the sheer grace of God, and not from any merit of yours, it should now flow freely by your ministry to others. We know how difficult some people are at sharing with others what each may reckon belongs to him alone, and also when one of the brethren outshines the rest, how quickly he comes to despise them all. The kindly sharing of spiritual gifts could have no better commendation, than for Christ to say that no-one excels by his own efforts, but by the free liberality of God. Now in His ministers Christ displayed an instance of that grace which had been foretold by Isaiah, 'Ho, everyone that thirsteth, come ye to the waters, drink, take without price wine and milk' (Isa. 55.1). At the same time He makes plain that no-one will be an honest minister of His Word and dispenser of His grace, who is not prepared to expend all his labours freely, while all the hirelings corrupt and shamefully profane the sacred office of the ministry. Now it is no contradiction to free dispensation, that the teachers of the Church are provided for by public stipends, as long as they serve Christ and His Church willingly and generously, and take their living as an appendage to their task.

Get you no gold, nor silver, nor brass in your purses; no wallet for your journey, neither two coats, nor shoes, nor staff: for the labourer is worthy of his food. And into whatsoever city or village ye shall enter, search out who in it is worthy; and there abide till ye go forth. And as ye enter into the house, salute it. And if the house be worthy, let your peace come upon it: but if it be not worthy, let your peace return to you. And whosoever shall not receive you, nor hear your words, as ye go forth out of that house or that city, shake off the dust of your feet. Verily I say unto you, It shall be more tolerable for the land of Sodom and Gomorrah in the day of judgment, than for that city. (Matt. 10.9-15)

*And he charged them that they should take nothing for their journey, save
a staff only; no bread, no wallet, no money in their purse; but to go shod
with sandals: and, said he, put not on two coats. And he said unto them,
Wheresoever ye enter into a house, there abide till ye depart thence. And
whatsoever place shall not receive you, and they hear you not, as ye go
forth thence, shake off the dust that is under your feet for a testimony unto
them.* (Mark 6.8-11)

*And he said unto them, Take nothing for your journey, neither staff, nor
wallet, nor bread, nor money; neither have two coats. And into whatsoever house ye enter, there abide, and thence depart. And as many as
receive you not, when ye depart from that city, shake off the dust from
your feet for a testimony against them.* (Luke 9.3-5)

Matt. 10.9. *Get you no.* This was a kind of mission where Christ
willed His disciples to go through the whole of Judaea in the space of a
few days, and to return directly to Himself. Hence He tells them to
take no luggage, which would delay the speed of their progress. It is
not intelligent thinking to say that a continuing rule is here being
prescribed for the ministers of the Word, or the Apostles. A little
later, there will be some utterances which have a longer perspective,
but these instructions about not taking extras are certainly related only
to the period of proclamation which we have spoken of. Further, we
must take in one context all that is said about the ban on gold, silver,
wallet and change of coats, as we find it in Matthew, and is easily
found in the other two. I have chosen simply to take *get you no* as the
heading for the Lord's simple desire to forbid them to take anything
for the road. They might have wallets at home, and shoes, and other
coats, but for the sake of being better set for the journey He tells them
to leave every burden behind. There seems to be a discrepancy over
the *staff* or stick, for in Mark, the *baculus* is allowed, but in Matthew and
Luke it is denied. But as there is ambiguity over the Hebrew word
שֵׁבֶט (*shebet*), the Evangelists, granted they wrote Greek, also used
ῥάβδον in various senses. Matthew and Luke mean the heavy sticks,
which would be a burden to carry, but Mark means the light stick that
gives travellers support and comfort, It is well known that there was a
practice of carrying a stick for making journeys: hence the saying, 'With
my staff I passed over this Jordan' (Gen. 32.10). By these words,
Jacob affirms that he had come into Syria empty, with no burden of
wealth.

Matt. 10.10. *For the labourer is worthy.* Christ anticipates some reluctance: the terms might seem severe, going through all Judaea, without any provision for the journey. So Christ says, they are not to be

afraid that they will have to contend with hunger, for wherever they come they shall at least deserve their provisions. He speaks of *labourers*, not implying that they are like the ordinary ministers, who husband the vineyard of the Lord, whose efforts of planting and watering are all for its increase, but only as being the fore-runners of that richer and complete message. For at that time there was laid on them no other teaching task, than to make the Jews ready for the preaching of the Gospel. And in case they should object that they would lose their pay due to them, as no-one would recognize them as labourers, Christ anticipates their difficulty by telling them to inquire in every town who may be worthy of this message of salvation. By these words, He tells them to find out if there are any godly and decent men, who have still some lively signs of the fear of God and of religion, upon whose readiness to learn there may be good reason for hope, in order that they may devote their attention to them in particular. As they were not allowed to stay very long in any one place, it was right for them to start off wherever there was some favourable preparation.

Matt. 10.11. *There abide till ye go forth.* This again applies to their haste. If they should spend too long anywhere, they would have had to change lodging, so as not to be too much burden upon any one. Christ tells them to stay with their first host until they move to another town, meaning that they are to hurry, and, once the Gospel has been declared in one town, they should run on directly to the next.

Matt. 10.12. *Salute it.* As they cannot distinguish the true worshippers of God from the scorners, He tells them to make a friendly approach when they meet any family. The salutation is a kind of introduction to conversation. Now while they had been warned to betake themselves to such hosts as were known and generally reputed for their zeal for religion, it might sometimes occur that those who were given outstanding praise by report, would at close quarters reveal their ungodliness. Hence this rule should be kept to scrupulously. And this is what it means. Discover at your first approach, whether the host will bear to hear you, and those who are glad to welcome what you teach. Stay with such, and so endorse the greeting you gave, but those who reject it, leave them at once, and, as best you may, take back your greeting. His words exactly have the effect of saying, that as their ingratitude makes them undeserving of the enjoyment of God's blessing, which you called down upon them, you are to break off every bond of communication.

The word *peace*, derives from the style of greeting which was in common use with the Jews. As peace meant to them a state of prosperity, they call down peace on those whom they wish to live well and happily, whose lives they wish to stay secure. I agree, that it was a different peace that the Apostles brought to men, but it is rather over-ingenious speculation to force this passage into the sense of God's free atonement with men.

Matt. 10.14. *And whosoever shall not receive you.* Here is a serious denunciation of vengeance upon the scorners of the Gospel, by which Christ willed to hearten His disciples, in case the world's ingratitude should cause them any hindrance. He instructs the Apostles what He wants them to do, if they fall in with scorners, but the chief point of His counsel, is to give some relief to them for their natural sorrow and dismay, whenever their teaching may be flung back upon them, for fear that they might give up in mid-career. We may compare Paul, who, relying on this comfort, vigorously despises all men's contumacy, forces his way forward in the midst of obstacles, and glories that he is a sweet savour to God, however lethal he may be to them that perish (II Cor. 2.15). The passage also tells us how greatly the Lord values His own Gospel, and as it is indeed an incomparable treasure, those who repudiate its offer are too shamefully ungrateful. Since it is the very sceptre of His throne, it cannot be rejected without causing Him open insult.

Shake off the dust. As the Lord here commends the teaching of the Gospel, that all may receive it with reverence, and with a heavy sanction of punishment strikes fear upon the rebellious, so He orders the Apostles to be the spokesmen of that vengeance which He pronounces. And this they may do, only if they are on fire with a most urgent zeal to bring home the message which they preach. We must understand, that no-one is a sufficient instructor in the heavenly teaching, if he does not feel pain and burning, at its being condemned. To *shake off dust* was probably a usage of the Jews of those days, a sign of anathema, as though they made testimony that the inhabitants of the spot were so foul that their contagion infected the earth whereon they stood. I conceive this to have been a normal practice, as Christ speaks of it as of a familiar event. This form of curse adds all the more emphasis to what I have just said, that God is offended by no crime so much as by contempt for His Word: not for murder, or adultery, or for any other crime, are we told to show detestation in so serious a rite.

Matt. 10.15. *Verily I say unto you.* Should this mark of terror seem insignificant, Christ declares that those who reject the Gospel will pay a heavier penalty than did the people of Sodom. To take *judgment* here, as some do, of the destruction of Jerusalem, is foreign to Christ's thinking: He must mean that common day of judgment, where they shall render their account together, and the penalties may be compared. Christ named Sodom, before other towns, not only because it went beyond other towns for its gross wickedness, but because it had been

295

burnt up in an exceptional kind of divine catastrophe, to be an example to all ages, for its very name to be an abomination. Yet there is no wonder that Christ declares it will go more easily with them, than with those unbelievers who have refused to hear the Gospel. For when men refuse authority to their Creator and Maker, and grant His voice no audience, but repel His kind invitation, and undermine confidence in Him who promises all ready gifts, such impiety reaches the utmost peak of all possible wrong-doing. If such terrible vengeance followed the rejection of that twilight teaching, what terrible penalty now awaits those who repulse Christ who speaks with open voice? If God takes such dire note of the scorners, what shall be done to those wild enemies who resist the Gospel with blasphemies, with poisoned speech, or cruelly persecute it with fire and sword?

Behold, I send you forth as sheep in the midst of wolves: be ye therefore wise as serpents, and harmless as doves. But beware of men: for they will deliver you up to councils, and in their synagogues they will scourge you; yea and before governors and kings shall ye be brought for my sake, for a testimony of them and to the Gentiles. But when they deliver you up, be not anxious how or what ye shall speak: for it shall be given you in that hour what ye shall speak. For it is not ye that speak, but the Spirit of your Father that speaketh in you. (Matt. 10.16-20)

And when they bring you before the synagogues, and the rulers, and the authorities, be not anxious how or what ye shall answer, or what ye shall say: for the Holy Spirit shall teach you in that very hour what ye ought to say. (Luke 12.11-12)

The instructions which Matthew has so far recorded apply only to that first mission, which was to be completed within a few days. Now Christ goes further, and equips them for the future period, to make them realise that they are chosen, not only for that brief task of heralding the news roundabout, but that they have a field of work to come far more difficult, far longer in extent. For although they are not immediately involved in the conflicts which Christ speaks of, yet it was useful to them to be warned before the event, that if they should encounter difficulties on this round, they should know that these were like an overture to a more severe campaign, for which they were set down. It was true enough for the first mission, that the Apostles went as sheep into the midst of wolves, but as the Lord spared their weakness, and restrained the wolves' savagery so that they should not hurt them, He is really referring to the future time, when the Lord treated them more roughly. Before the resurrection, in the company of the bridegroom, they still enjoyed wedding conditions, but when the groom left them, then the ease and gentle living stopped, and so tough was the going then that they would feel that it was not in vain that they had been provided with this re-inforcement in good time. Of course, it may be that Matthew put together into this one passage speeches spoken at different times. For Luke (as we shall see shortly) tells us that the same things were said to the seventy disciples, who came in after the Apostles. One thing is beyond dispute, that in these words we are not given a prediction of the outcome of the journey on which they were then setting out, but an advance warning to cover the whole course of their Apostolate.

Matt. 10.16. *Behold, I send you forth.* The point of this warning is clearly shown by the exhortation which directly follows. Therefore the thread of the argument runs—You need to have prudence and simplicity, for you shall be as sheep in the midst of wolves. The reason springs from necessity, for if they do not take careful heed to themselves, they may soon be devoured by wolves, but if they panic at the wolves's fury, or start to get careless, they will at once stumble, and ultimately fall down completely on their mission.

In first place, let us consider what He means by saying that they are sent *as sheep in the midst of wolves.* However cruel and bloodthirsty men are, the Lord is able to mitigate their ferocity, who may, when He pleases, make angry beasts tame and amenable. So when He does not humble the greater part of men to the obedience of His Gospel, but leaves them in the wild state of their nature, He is acting deliberately to train His ministers. Though all men are wolves by nature (such as God does not regenerate by the Spirit of humility), Christ denotes as the fiercest of all the enemies of the Gospel those who, so far from being quietened when they hear the voice of the pastor, blaze up into a greater rage. These are the terms on which the Lord sends out the ministers of His Word, that they are to go in the midst of the wolves; that is, to find many bitter foes against them, to be beset by many perils on every side, to perform their task with difficulty, and in the teeth of obstruction. To make their trial more searching, He does not provide weapons of violence to use in self-defence, but exposes them to the fangs of the wolves naked and unarmed. The comparison with sheep does not refer to their pacific and gentle natures, or to their softheartedness, but simply means that they will have no more force, or be any more equal to throw back the assault of the enemy, than sheep are against the rage of wolves. Christ does ask of His disciples sheeplike minds, to strive against the malice of the wicked with patience, to receive hurts quietly, but in essence this passage is simple: many mighty and savage enemies lie in wait for the Apostles, but they have no armament to defend themselves. If any object, that the contrast beween sheep and wolves is not on these lines, there is an answer to hand. For although the Lord, by calling the enemies of the Gospel wolves is expressing more their power to harm, than their will, yet as no-one is reckoned a wolf unless he turns his frenzy against the Gospel, there is reason for Him to put the two ideas together; men are drawn to a thirst for blood in cruel onslaught, and at the same time they possess violent energies.

Be ye therefore wise. Briefly, discretion is so to be tempered with caution, that they are not to be excessively timid, nor yet over slow in their work. For we see men who wish to be rated circumspect and provident, who are very often meticulous and slow. It is right for the disciples of Christ, when dangers threaten on all sides, to be keeping a cautious look-out, but as the greatest danger is that they may be hindered by sluggish action, He tells them to advance frankly, where their call leads. He expresses this in a double simile. Serpents know how they are loathed, and are anxious to slide off and escape whenever anything gets in their way: thus the faithful are told to look out for their lives, not to leap rashly into danger, and expose themselves to all sorts of accidents. On the other hand, doves, though timid by nature, liable to countless forms of attack, still fly around naturally enough, as though they did not care when they were shot, and quite often cast themselves into the hunters' snares. Such simple living Christ urges on His disciples, that no excessive alarm may check them from finishing their course. Some speculate very learnedly over this, on the nature of the serpent and of the dove, but the comparison does not go any further. We see how Christ condemns the prudence of the flesh—or rather its roguery, wherein the better part of mankind indulges itself far too much, peering around this way and that, how far it may be safe to proceed. They do not want to take any risks, and so they renounce the call of Christ.

Matt. 10.17. *But beware of men.* Erasmus added 'those' (men), for he believed that the article had the force of a demonstrative pronoun. But in my opinion, it is quite satisfactory to read it indefinitely, as if Christ had said, one must tread carefully with men, since everything is full of deception and harm. Yet that seems self-contradictory, for the best way to take care would be to stay at home, and not go out to face the world. I would answer, that another sort of caution is intended here, not where a man is so struck with terror that he refrains from his task, but where a man is not unduly shaken by sudden adversity. We know how men, caught unexpectedly, lose heart and give up. Christ wants

His men to take a long view of what the future may hold, that they may compose their minds in good time to the conflicts they must undergo. In fact, He blows the call to arms, to have them dress for battle with more eagerness. For as foresight may go to extremes, and start worries beyond all reason, thus making many exhausted, so many also are drugged with apathy and carelessness, rush in without preparation, and fail in the first moment.

They will deliver you up to councils. We may readily gather from these words, that the trials which here Christ states shall fall on the Apostles, should not be confined to that first mission, on which they experienced nothing of the kind. The scope of this prediction, is to stop them being shattered at any time, for it takes rare mettle for slight men, when they come into the sight of princes, to keep a level head and not to be put off by worldly spendour. He warns them that they will have to fight, not only in Judaea, but in distant lands; so that, by taking long thought, they might be prepared for such campaigning, and also, as professed and confirmed masters, should know beyond doubt that they travelled under the direction of heavenly powers. Adding, *for a testimony to them and to the Gentiles,* He means, that the Will of God must be given its testimony, before foreign chiefs and far-off nations, in order that they be without excuse. Hence it follows that the work of the Apostles will not be vain, as it will display the judgment of God, where men shall be convicted of their stubborn resistance.

Matt. 10.19. *Be not anxious.* A consolation is added. Christ might have exhorted His disciples a hundred times to no avail, if He had not at the same time promised them that God would be with them, and that by His sure power they would be victorious. So we see that it was by no means Christ's purpose, in stating all the dangers, to lower the temperature of their enthusiasm, for they had to be white-hot disciples, if they were to fulfil their task in the right fashion. It is a big thing to face the eyes of princes, for not only fear, but also some respect, may at times overthrow good minds. And what if the princes break out into angry tirades, and storm down on us? Christ tells His men not to be anxious, for the Spirit will speak words to them. The more a man is conscious of his own weakness, and distrusts himself, the greater his alarm, if he does not look elsewhere for aid. And we see that many fail for this reason, that they measure the outcome of their undertaking by the means they possess themselves, and these are very slight, indeed nil. So Christ tells His men, to take no regard for what they are strong in, and orders them to depend upon the confidence of heaven's grace alone, Here, He says, there is no question of your resources, but of the power of the Holy Spirit, who trains and prompts the tongues of the faithful, to make a pure confession of faith.

In case they should be frightened that they may fail on the spot, He declares that assistance will reach them in that very instant. The Lord often robs the faithful of the gift of ready speech, for as long as He does not ask testimony from them, but when it comes to the crisis, He makes them more than fluent—though before they appeared to be speechless. Thus in our days, we have seen some martyrs, who though they were virtually primitive men, yet, when they were called to proclaim their confession of faith, were wonderfully fitted with outstanding powers of speech, apt and incisive. Now Christ did not wish the Apostles to take no care at all, for there was benefit in their being concerned enough to plead, in their prayers, for that Spirit to be granted them, but it was the vexing thoughts, by which men often hinder themselves, that Christ wished to dismiss. For as long as men go on wondering what is going to happen if this or that occur, and fail to rest upon the providence of God, they toss in wretched insecurity. We may say they deserve torment of this kind, if they do not allow such dignity to God's providence, that He will, in due time, come to the support of their incapacity.

And brother shall deliver up brother to death, and the father his child: and children shall rise up against parents, and cause them to be put to death. And ye shall be hated of all men for my name's sake: but he that endureth to the end, the same shall be saved. But when they persecute you in this city, flee into the next: for verily I say unto you, Ye shall not have gone through the cities of Israel, till the Son of men be come.

A disciple is not above his master, nor a servant above his lord. It is enough for the disciple that he be as his master, and the servant as his lord. If they have called the master of the house Beelzebub, how much more shall they call them of his household! (Matt. 10.21-25)

The disciple is not above his master: but every one when he is perfected shall be as his master. (Luke 6.40)

Matt. 10.21. *And brother shall deliver up brother.* First He warns them of the grave times of distress that await them; then He gives a remarkable word of comfort, to soften all the pain. He declares that what others find to be their protection, or at least a source of some help, will fail the disciples, and so their misfortunes will be the greater. Their own brothers, who should aid the oppressed and reach out a hand to the afflicted, and look to their safety—these will be their declared enemies. But it is wrong to think that this only happens to the faithful, to be

300

handed over to death by their brothers. It may be that in holy zeal a
father will prosecute his son, should he see him going back upon the
true worship of God. In fact, on this point, the Lord commands us to
forget flesh and blood and to direct all our efforts to vindicate the glory
of His Name. And indeed, when God's fear and religion flourish in all
places, a man will not spare his kinsfolk, but will rather have them all
perish, if need be, than have Christ's Kingdom spoiled, the message of
salvation extinguished, the worship of God abolished. If man's motives
were all directed aright, this would be the only fair reason for hating
our kin. But when Christ is restoring God's Kingdom, restoring
religion to its original true growth, and recalling men from ruin to
salvation, then nothing is more unfitting than for the ministers of this
kindest of doctrines to be exposed to hatred on His account. This is an
unnatural prodigy, which might easily shatter the minds of the simple.
Yet Christ says that this will come to pass.

Matt. 10.22. *He that endureth to the end, the same shall be saved.* This
promise alone should be quite enough to sustain the hearts of the godly,
that though all the world should rise against them, they are promised a
happy and safe outcome. If firmness of resolve carries men even to
their death, when they fight the uncertain issues of war under earthly
leaders, should any hesitate to risk their all for Christ, when they are
given the assurance of victory?

Matt. 10.23. *But when they persecute you.* He anticipates their possible
objection. If they are to face the hatred of all the world, what will ever
be the end of it? Although there will be nowhere to lie back, in safe
retreat, Christ says there must be no despair, but when they have been
expelled from one place, they must try if they cannot get better results
elsewhere. Interpreters are deceived when they take this as a licence
with no terms stated, for in fact Christ is telling the Apostles precisely
what He wants them to do. The man who had gone through one
persecution might be glad to retire, like a pensioned-off soldier. But
this is not the calling Christ gives His men, for He would have them
finish their course, with unwearied zeal. Briefly, the Apostles are
commanded always to face new conflicts as they come, and not to
draw back after meeting one or two. They are not allowed to slip off
into hiding, where they may have a quiet repose, but, however un-
fortunately their labours may have come out in one place, the Lord
urges them to advance further.

Now these orders include permission to leave a conflict. What we
are to realise about fleeing from persecution, is that not all who flee are
to be censured indiscriminately; and at the same time, not every kind of
running away is permissible. In former days, there was too much
passion over this issue, and flight was condemned as being none other

than a kind of desertion. If that were really true, some part of the disgrace would fall even on Christ and the Apostles. On the other hand, if one were allowed to run off without limit, there would be no telling in time of persecution which was the good pastor and which the hireling. So we must take the moderate line, which Augustine set out for Honoratus, that no-one should desert his post for fear, or treasonably betray his flock, or give an example of cowardice, and yet no-one should throw himself forward heedlessly. If the whole Church should be under attack, or a part be haled off to death, it would be wrong for the pastor to keep out of the way, since his role is to put his life in front of the people's, but it will sometimes happen, that by his absence, the rage of the enemy may be appeased, and he will be acting in the Church's best interests. So this is where the simplicity of the dove should shine forth, that comfort-loving men should not make an excuse of their timidity, for the flesh is ever too clever at finding ways to avoid trouble.

Verily I say unto you. Some take this of the first mission, but it will not do, for it really embraces the whole Apostolate. But the difficulty lies in this point, as to what is the meaning of the *coming of the Son of man.* Some speak of there being such a progress of the Gospel, that all men shall recognise that Christ truly is King, and that one may hope from Him for the restoration of the reign of David. Others refer to the fall of Jerusalem, where Christ was seen to bring vengeance upon their ingratitude. The former is a tolerable exposition, but the latter is rather forced. I think this is a word of comfort, particularly given to the Apostles. Christ is said to *come,* when He brings relief in time of desperation. The vast mission is now almost upon them, when they shall spread the teaching of the Gospel throughout all the world. So Christ promises that He will come, before they have traversed all Judaea, as by the power of His Spirit, He shall display His Kingdom, to make His Glory and Majesty truly shine upon the Apostles, which till that point lay hidden.

Matt. 10.24. *A disciple is not.* Now He urges them by His own example to be patient, and assuredly the consolation He gives is of such fashion as to dry up all our tears, if we think that we share in the lot of the Son of God. Yet to make us feel more shame, He borrows a two-fold comparison from the normal ways of men. The disciple reckons it a mark of honour to be counted equal with his master, but does not dare seek more honour than this. Further, the conditions which their lords accept with patience, shall not be for the servants to refuse. As the Son of God is exalted above us on both accounts, being given supreme authority by the Father, and commissioned with the role of Master, we should be ashamed to dodge anything that He Himself has not been unwilling to accept for our sakes. These things are matters more for meditation than for explanation, for they are sufficiently clear in themselves.

Luke, in his sixth chapter, produces this utterance out of context, set in the midst of other remarks quite abruptly, but as Matthew expresses the tenor of the words very well in this passage, I say that it cannot be better placed anywhere else. Note that in translation, it is preferable not to follow Erasmus, or older interpreters, and for this reason: the participle κατηρτισμένος (Luke 6.40) means perfected, and also trained and well-fitted. Now in the comparison He is making, Christ is not speaking here of perfection, but would rather say that nothing is more appropriate than for the disciple to model himself in the example of his master; hence it is the latter sense that appeared most appropriate.

Matt. 10.25. *If they have called the master of the house, etc.* It is just as though He were calling Himself Lord of the Church, as the Apostle (Heb. 3.1), comparing Him with Moses and the Prophets, says that these were His servants, and He was the true Son and heir. Even though He accords us the honour of brothers, yet He is the First-born and Head of the whole body, and ultimately, the supreme goverment and power are in His hands. So there is nothing more absurd than to wish to be ranked in the order of the faithful, and all the time grumble against God, who shapes us to the image of His Son, whom He has appointed Chief of the whole estate. What kind of high living do we seek, if we wish to have a place in His house and rise above the Lord Himself? In short, we are too soft and feather-bedded, if we think it is a hardship to endure insults, which our captain willingly underwent.

The word *Beel-zebub* is a corruption: it should properly be Baal-sebub. Thus did the Philistines name the principle deity out of their false gods, as was worshipped by the state of Accaron (or Ekron). Baalim is the term for the minor divinities, which the Papacy today refers to as local *patroni*. Since the patronal influence of Baalsebub only covers the fly, or flies, some believe the name derives from the temple which seethed with swarms of flies over the heaps of sacrificial victims. I would rather think that they sought help from the idol to save them from the flies, which infested the district. When Ahaziah (II Kings 1.2), in his superstition, asked an answer from him about his health, he gave him this title. Evidently then the name was not a term of insult. Further, as religious men have applied the name of Gehenna to hell, to give that place a name of infamy, so in their hatred and detestation of the idol, they have called the devil Beelzebub. Hence we may gather that the wicked, to make Christ generally of ill repute, put the worst insult they could upon Him, making Him the devil, the greatest foe religion could have. So if it should befall us to feel the sting of similar

303

opprobrium, it should strike us as nothing new; what began at the head, shall come down to the members.

Fear them not therefore: for there is nothing covered, that shall not be revealed; and hid, that shall not be known. What I tell you in the darkness, speak ye in the light: and what ye hear in the ear, proclaim upon the housetops. And be not afraid of them which kill the body, but are not able to kill the soul: but rather fear him which is able to destroy both soul and body in hell. Are not two sparrows sold for a farthing? and not one of them shall fall on the ground without your Father: but the very hairs of your head are all numbered. Fear not therefore; ye are of more value than many sparrows. (Matt. 10.26-31)

For there is nothing hid, save that it should be manifested; neither was anything made secret, but that it should come to light. If any man hath ears to hear, let him hear. (Mark 4.22-23)

For nothing is hid, that shall not be made manifest; nor anything secret, that shall not be known and come to light.

But there is nothing covered up, that shall not be revealed: and hid, that shall not be known. Wherefore whatsoever ye have said in the darkness shall be heard in the light; and what ye have spoken in the ear in the inner chambers shall be proclaimed upon the housetops. And I say unto you my friends, Be not afraid of them which kill the body, and after that have no more that they can do. But I will warn you whom ye shall fear: Fear him, which after he hath killed hath power to cast into hell; yea, I say unto you, Fear him. Are not five sparrows sold for two farthings? and not one of them is forgotten in the sight of God. But the very hairs of your head are all numbered. Fear not: ye are of more value than many sparrows. (Luke 8.17; 12.2-7)

Matt. 10.26. *Fear them not.* When the Apostles saw the Gospel so much despised, and the small number of believers came to their minds, they might well have abandoned hope for the future. Christ now meets this doubt, when He asserts that the Gospel is to be more widely published, and that whatever may be the obstruction of men, it will rise superior to it and in the end come out in full view. Though the saying seems to be proverbial, that *there is nothing covered that shall not be revealed*, here it does actually seem to be particularly applied to the teaching of salvation which Christ promises shall prevail, however men may fashion plots to suppress it. Though there had been some open harangues in the temple, His teaching had met with rejection, and still

304

lay hidden in obscure corners, but He declares that the time of its revelation will come, and, as we know, this was shortly after fulfilled. For never was so great a clap of thunder heard in any corner of the globe, than the sound of the voice of the Gospel over the whole world. While such a promise ought to put heart into them, Christ gives them the stimulus to apply themselves to this thought, with courage and energy, and not to be terrified if the Gospel still appeared of little account—they must still be its outspoken heralds.

My reference to *Mark* may perhaps be taken at another time and in another sense, but as we read a series of short utterances at that place, I have taken the line which I think more probable. When Christ there taught the Apostles that they should show a clear light from a distance, like flaming beacons, He adds directly, 'Nothing is hidden that shall not be manifested'. The lamp of the Gospel was lit by the Apostles, as it were in the darkness, so that by their ministry it should be lifted up high, and shine the world over. This is exactly the context of *Luke*, ch. 8.

As regards the passage in the twelfth chapter, there is no doubt that it corresponds to this, although it is somewhat different in expression, for there Christ bids them bring into the open all that the Apostles have spoken in the darkness, meaning that till now, they have merely whispered the Gospel message, but so distinguished shall be the proclamation which they undertake, that it shall cover the utmost corners of the globe.

Matt. 10.28. *And be not afraid of them which kill the body.* Christ puts the best reason of all for scorning death into His disciples' hearts, namely that men who are created for the immortal life of the skies, should count this changing and passing existence as a feather's weight. In the end it all comes down to this, that the faithful should consider for what they were born, and what are the terms of their life. Thus, they would have no call to desire the life of earth with such concern. The words have, of course, a fuller and richer sense, for Christ shows how the fear of God has died in men who depart from the profession of the faith from fear of tyrants, and that brute stupidity reigns in the hearts of men who, for fear of death, do not hesitate to abandon this same confession. We must note the contrast between two opposed fears. If for fear of men, the fear of God be stifled, is it not plain that they ascribe more to them, than to God Himself? From which it follows, that by throwing away the life of heaven and eternity, we only leave ourselves to an existence on the level of beasts. In God's hand alone is the power of life and death. It is on Him we turn our backs, when the fear of men tears us aside. Does this not make evident, that this shadowy life of the body has become more worth to us than the eternal state of the soul; indeed, that the heavenly Kingdom of God is of no value with us, compared with the fleeting, vanishing shade of this present life? So this is how we should resolve Christ's words, Recognise that you have been given immortal souls, which being under the judgment of God alone, do not come under the authority of men. So let your faith succumb to no threats or terrors of men. For how is it that in the time of stress, the dread of men should prevail, unless the body is given priority over the soul, and immortality is put in second place, behind this transitory life? So there is the emphatic repetition in Luke, *Yea, I say unto you, Fear him:* as if Christ had said, that there is no respect for God in us, when we succumb to the dread of men, but if we revere God, then there is an easy victory in His grasp for us, to prevent any human force distracting us from our calling.

Now the experience of history shows us how necessary such an exhortation was to Christ's ministers, and to all the faithful in general, for there never was any period when men did not rise up against God with violence, and try to overthrow the Gospel. Granted, not all are armed with equal might to instil the terror of death, but in the great number there reigns such a Cyclopean ferocity as will surge up at the given opportunity. Often indeed, Satan raises up giants, at whose sight the servants of Christ would fall to the ground in collapse, unless this lesson gave them a firmness that could not be broken. Further, as the two sections are united in one band, it is completely ignorant to take this one part on its own, as some do, that we are not to be afraid of men. For Christ (as has already been said) contrasted the perverse fear of men, which takes us off the right road, with the devout and holy fear of God, which serves as our remedy: otherwise the consequence would lose its effect. If we fear God, who is the Lord of body and soul, men, whose power does not go beyond the body are not to be feared. That Christ ascribes to men the power to kill, is said as a kind of concession. This is how God gives the wicked free rein, that, puffed up in the confidence of their own power, they may dare anything, and batter the weak hearts, as though they could do as they pleased. Of course it is to no avail that the godless grow so insolent, as though they had control over the life of the god-fearing, and God also holds them so sure, that whenever He wills He forces back their brutality and violent assaults; yet they are said to have leave to kill, by His consent, for often He allows their rage to spread, in its impotence. Ultimately Christ's instruction has two parts: first, to teach us to bear with equanimity the loss of our bodily life, He recalls us to the vision of eternal life, and death; second, He arrives by stages at the point of revealing to us also, that the protection of our lives is in the hand of God.

Matt. 10.29. *Are not two sparrows, etc.* As I have just said, Christ takes us further and shows that however tyrants may rave, they do not even have power over the body. So they are wrong, who fear the violence of men, and behave as though they were not under the protection of God. Here then is a second consolation given us in our dangers: as God is the defence of our lives, we may rest safely upon His providence, in fact, we do Him injury if we do not commend our lives to Him, since He has deigned to take them into His care. And He extends the providence of God in a general sense to all creatures, that by arguing from greater to less He may prove that we are kept under His special defence. There is practically nothing cheaper than sparrows (for two were then sold for a farthing, or as Luke says, five for two farthings) and yet the eye of God is alert to watch over them, that nothing accidental may happen to them: will He then neglect men's lives, seeing He is so careful over sparrows'?

Now there are two points to note. First, Christ defines God's providence quite differently from many who care more like philosophers, and though they agree that the world is under divine government, conceive of a diffuse kind of providence, as if God had no concern for individual creatures. But Christ asserts, that each single creature is distinctly under God's hand and protection, that nothing may be left open to chance. For the Will of God is opposed to contingency. However we do arrive in this way at the Stoic concept of fate, for it is one thing to devise a necessity constructed from a nexus of various causes, but quite another to set the whole world and its separate parts under the judgment of God. In the nature of things itself, I agree there is contingency, but I say that nothing occurs by the blind turn of fortune where God's will holds the cords. Secondly, we must consider God's providence, not in the way that the curious and empty-headed used to do, but in such a way as to make it the ground of our assurance, and the incentive to bring us towards God. He does not tell us that all the hairs of our head are numbered, to foster trifling speculations, but that we may learn to depend on God's fatherly care, which He exercises over our fading flesh.

Matt. 10.31. *Ye are of more value.* This in general is true of all men, and for their sakes the sparrows were made, yet properly speaking, it concerns the sons of God, whose excellence is of an order higher than creation. Worth is attached to men only as God in His freedom may reckon it.

Every one therefore who shall confess me before men, him will I also confess before my Father which is in heaven.

Think not that I came to send peace on the earth: I came not to send peace, but a sword. For I came to set a man at variance against his father, and the daughter against her mother, and the daughter in law against the mother in law: and a man's foes shall be they of his own household. Matt. 10.32-36)

For whosoever shall be ashamed of me and of my words in this adulterous and sinful generation, the Son of man also shall be ashamed of him, when he cometh in the glory of his Father with the holy angels. (Mark 8.38)

For whosoever shall be ashamed of me and of my words, of him shall the Son of man be ashamed, when he cometh in his own glory, and the glory of the Father, and of the holy angels.

And I say unto you, Every one who shall confess me before men, him shall the Son of man also confess before the angels of God: but he that denieth me in the presence of men shall be denied in the presence of the angels of God.

Think ye that I am come to give peace in the earth? I tell you, nay; but rather division: for there shall be from henceforth five in one house divided, three against two, and two against three. They shall be divided, father against son, and son against father; mother against daughter, and daughter against her mother; mother in law against her daughter in law, and daughter in law against her mother in law. (Luke 9.26; 12.8-9, 51-53)

Matt. 10.32. *Every one therefore who shall confess me.* Christ now fits what He had previously said about the disregard for death to His present purpose, that we should resist the fear of death, in case it should divert us from that frank confession of our faith, which God strictly demands, and which the world cannot endure. So the reason why Christ's disciples must be brave and stout-hearted is that they must ever be ready for martyrdom. Now the confession of Christ, though it be treated by the majority of men as a negligible thing, is here reckoned in the forefront of the honour paid to God, and as a unique practice of religion; and deservedly so. If earthly kings call their subjects to arms to defend the fulness of their glory, and to increase their resources, why should not the faithful, with their tongues at least, assert the glory of their heavenly King? It is certain that men (as best they may) extinguish the faith, when they suppress it inwardly, and pretend that the open profession of it is an irrelevancy. For it is not in vain that Christ here calls us His witnesses, on whose lips His Name has praise in the world. Christ wills, I say, that the profession of His Name be set in confrontation with the false religions. This goes against the grain, and so He states categorically, that no man's faith is to be stuffed away secretly in his heart, but is openly to be produced in the sight of men. If a man runs away or keeps silence, is he not, by frustrating the work of the Son of God, taking himself out of the family of God?

Now a more distinguished profession of the faith is required of the teachers, than of ordinary men. As all are not endowed with an equal measure of faith, each should give a lead by his own example of whichever gift of the Spirit he may be superior in. But there is not one of the faithful whom the Son of God does not wish to have as witness. As to the where, when, how often, in what way, and to what extent, we are to confess our faith, this is difficult to define with any exact rule, but we must look to the occasion, that none of our people fail in his calling at his time. We must ask of the Lord, the Spirit of discretion and fortitude, and with His direction we shall know what is expedient, and boldly carry through what we are sure is laid upon us.

Him will I also confess. The promise is added, to inflame our zeal in this regard. We must note the antitheses. If we compare ourselves with the Son of God, is it not shameful for us to deny Him our testimony, when He offers His for us in return, by way of recompense? If we compare men, mortal, mere nothings, with God and the angels and all the glory of heaven, how much more excellent is what Christ promises, than what He asks? For though men are unbelieving and perverse, yet simply for making our testimony before them, Christ rates it as though it were the assembly of God and the angels. Thus in Mark and Luke there is said for amplification, *in this adulterous generation,* in case we should think that our efforts are wasted, because the audience is unfit.

Now if any man should not feel the force of this promise, a dire curse follows it, that when Christ shall appear to judge the world, He will deny all those who have falsely denied Him before men. Let them carry on now, let the enemies of the cross amuse themselves in their fake show, while Christ deletes their names from the book of life. For whom shall God recognise as His sons at the last day, but those who are presented to Him by Christ? But he declares that He will testify against them, and stop them creeping in by deceit.

That Christ is said to be *coming* in the *glory of His Father with the holy angels,* means that His divine glory will then be clearly displayed, and the angels who now surround the throne of God will be at His side, to adorn His Majesty. The passage from Luke 12 corresponds to the context in Matthew. As for that in ch. 9, and the reference in Mark, this seems to have been spoken on another occasion, but as the teaching was very much the same, it was best to add it on.

Luke 12.51. *Think ye that I am come to give peace?* What Christ had just asked of His disciples, each of us would for himself provide with no difficulty, if all the world were to subscribe with one accord to the teaching of the Gospel. But as the majority is not only opposed, but actually in bitter conflict, we are not able to profess Christ without strife and the hatred of many. So Christ tells His people to be ready for battle, for there must needs be war over the testimony of the truth. This involves a double offence, which otherwise would have caused weak minds much perturbation. Since the Prophets always promise that under the reign of Christ there will be peace and tranquil times, what else would the disciples have hoped for, but that everything would at once be pacified, wherever they should travel? As Christ is called *our peace*, and the Gospel reconciles us with God, it follows that a state of brotherly concord is established amongst us. So for battles and strife to be started in the world, where the Gospel is preached, does not seem to agree with the oracles of the Prophets, and far less with the role of Christ and the nature of the Gospel. But that peace which the Prophets extol, being linked with faith, only flourishes amongst the pure worshippers of God, and in godly consciences. It does not penetrate to the unbelievers, although it is offered to them, and no more can they bear to return into a state of grace with God but are excited by the very message of peace into a higher degree of unrest. For as Satan, who has his throne with the wicked, goes mad at the very Name of Christ, so once the teaching of the Gospel is produced, the godless mood of these people, which before lay in a trance, comes sharply to life. Thus it is, that Christ, who is truly the Author of peace becomes, on account of the malice of men, an occasion for disturbance.

This teaches us how great is the depravity of our corrupt nature, that not only blemishes such an incomparable gift, but actually converts it to a vicious bane. At the same time, if tumults arise at the dawn of Christ's Kingdom, we are not to be upset, as though we faced a new or strange phenomenon, since He Himself compares His Gospel to a sword, and speaks of διαμερισμόν (division). Some believe this is the description of the penalty inflicted upon scorners of the Gospel, that they rise up against one another in battle, but the context shows that Christ here is urging His disciples to constancy, in a case where the greater part of the world is at odds with them, and they find His voice, like the soldiers' bugle-call, stirs up countless hosts to arms.

Matt. 10.35. *To set a man at variance.* This makes what we have recently said more clear, that, quite against the nature of the Gospel, it happens that wars and tumults arise, through the fault of the wicked. For what Malachi (4.6) says of John the Baptist, suits all the ministers of Christ, that to this end was He sent, to turn the hearts of the fathers to the children, and the hearts of the children to the fathers. But the malign spirit of the godless makes those who were originally tied together separate into opposing sides when they hear of the voice of Christ, to the point of bursting all the bonds of essential kinship. Ultimately Christ says the world will come to such a state of confusion, that all the rights of nature will be discarded, and humanity will be heeded no more. For when Micah complains (7.6) that a man's enemies are in his own house, he is deploring an extreme and ruined state of corruption. The same future is affirmed by Christ, looking to the time when His doctrine would enter upon the scene: it would otherwise not have been believed. But He does not understand this as a perpetual state of affairs—contrary to the fashion of some gloomy folk, who fancy they can only be His true disciples if they cut themselves off from parents, children, and wives. No, in the unity of faith every honest tie is sanctified. Christ is only warning His men not to be alarmed when it does happen.

He that loveth father or mother more than me is not worthy of me; and he that loveth son or daughter more than me is not worthy of me. And he that doth not take his cross and follow after me, is not worthy of me. He that findeth his life shall lose it; and he that loseth his life for my sake shall find it.

He that receiveth you receiveth me, and he that receiveth me receiveth him that sent me. He that receiveth a prophet in the name of a prophet shall receive a prophet's reward; and he that receiveth a righteous man in the name of a righteous man shall receive a righteous man's reward. And whosoever shall give to drink unto one of these little ones a cup of cold water only, in the name of a disciple, verily I say unto you, he shall in no wise lose his reward. (Matt. 10.37-42)

For whosoever shall give you a cup of water to drink, because ye are Christ's, he shall in no wise lose his reward. (Mark 9.41)

Now there went with him great multitudes: and he turned, and said unto them, If any man cometh unto me, and hateth not his own father, and mother, and wife, and children, and brethren, and sisters, yea, and his own life also, he can not be my disciple. Whosoever doth not bear his own cross, and come after me, cannot be my disciple. For which of you, desiring to build a tower, doth not first sit down and count the cost, whether he have wherewith to complete it? Lest haply, when he hath laid a foundation, and is not able to finish, all that behold begin to mock him, saying, This man began to build, and was not able to finish. Or what king, as he goeth to encounter another king in war, will not sit down first and take counsel whether he is able with ten thousand to meet him that cometh against him with twenty thousand? Or else, while the other is yet a great way off, he sendeth an ambassage, and asketh conditions of peace. So therefore whosoever he be of you that renounceth not all that he hath, he cannot be my disciple. (Luke 14.25-33)

Matt. 10.37. *He that loveth father.* As this is a very painful thing, to make ourselves enemies out of those who should be closest to us, and as it is repugnant to natural sense, Christ now states that there are no other terms on which to be His disciples. He does not tell them to shed human affections, He does not forbid each to show kindness as is due to his own people, but He merely wishes to bring into step all that concerns the mutual friendliness of men, so that pride of place may go to godliness. So let the husband love his wife, the father his child, and in turn the child the father, as long as human love does not overwhelm the attention that is owed to Christ. For if among men themselves (where we are tied to each other in tighter bonds) some get the better of others, it is not right if Christ is not preferred above all. Certainly our thoughts are lacking in gratitude for what it should mean to be a disciple of Christ, if our appreciation of His worth does not move us to put all affections of the flesh under control. The expression is more severe in Luke—*If any man . . . hateth not his own father.* But the sense is the same, If love for our kin prevents us from following Christ, it must be bravely resisted. Thus Paul says, that he counted all things to be loss for Christ's sake, which before he had reckoned as gain, and he willingly suffered the loss of all things (Phil. 3.8).

Matt. 10.38. *And he that doth not take his cross.* He proceeds from the particular to the general, to teach us that by no other way may we be rated among His disciples than by setting ourselves to bear much hardship. If it causes us torment and pain, that for the sake of the Gospel, we must have discord with father or wife or children, let these terms come to our minds, whereby Christ appoints all His disciples to the cross. At the same time, let us be open to this word of comfort, that in bearing our cross we are the companions of Christ, and so it shall be, that every bitterness shall be eased. To their cross the wicked also are bound, nor can their struggles ever get it off them, but as apart from Christ the cross is accursed, the end which awaits them is a sorry one. Thus we should learn to keep these two things together, that the faithful are to take up their cross, in order to follow their Master. That is, they are to shape themselves by His example, and like His companions stick to His tracks.

Matt. 10.39. *He that findeth his life.* In case the teaching given above (and it is by all accounts difficult and disagreeable to the flesh) should not be effective enough in itself, Christ backs it up in this utterance by two means. He says that the over cautious and provident, who believe that they have taken every step to secure their own lives, shall be disappointed, and find they have lost them; on the other hand, those who have neglected their lives shall make no loss, for they shall win them back. We know that all is done or not done in the interests of our lives: we have such an inborn love of them. So Christ, to press His men to despise death, had to give them these threats and promises. In this passage, *to find life* means to possess it, so as to keep it in safe custody. Those who are too fond of earthly life, are pleased when they take precautions against all risks with the empty assurance that they have made the best provision for themselves, yet their soul will slip away from all its stout defence-works, for one must die at last, and death will be the end for them. But when the faithful meet death, their soul which seemed for the moment to fade away will be restored to a better life. Now, as we occasionally find men who throw their lives away rashly, for a dare or a mad scheme, Christ explicitly gives the grounds upon which we are to seek death. It is hard to say whether the speech Luke records was given at another time: there also the Lord urges His men to suffer the cross, but not in such a long discourse. Then He proceeds to add two similes, in confirmation of this utterance, of which Matthew makes no mention, and as the gist of the matter is completely congruent, I have had no scruples in attaching Luke's sayings to this passage.

Luke 14.28. *For which of you, etc.* In case any should find it hard going, to follow Christ on these conditions—that a man should renounce all his own desires—a useful word of warning is presented to them, that they should consider before the event what the profession of the Gospel may demand. It often turns out, that many succumb to the slightest test, because they imagined to themselves a state of pure delight, as if they would forever be in the shelter, or a life of ease. No-one will ever be a fit soldier of Christ who does not equip himself, a long time before, for the campaign. The similes focus on this point very sharply. Building is a business full of labour and frustration, and in terms of costs far from satisfying. As for war (which involves so many upsets, in fact virtually threatens to destroy the human race) no-one starts this unless by compulsion. Yet the very convenience of having a house induces men to have no hesitation in pouring out their substance, while necessity also forces us to spare no expense in waging wars. But the prize that awaits the builders of the temple of God, and the recruits to Christ's army, is of far greater excellence: for Christians are not engaged upon the construction of a building of limited survival, nor are

313

they fighting for a short-lived triumph. Christ says, that if any king be incapable of sustaining the impetus of war, he seeks peace with his opponent, in case he should suffer the shame of defeat. This is not to be applied to our present case, as if we were to come to terms with our spiritual foe, or our resources or energies should fail us. It would be foolish to force particular details of parables upon the matter being dealt with. The Lord simply means that we should be so prepared, that we shall not be overtaken without proper protection, and so be shamefully turned back in flight: we are none of us our own king, waging war on our own account.

This teaching demonstrates the temerity of those who brazenly go beyond their limits, or indulge themselves, without any thought of taking up the cross. At the same time, we must beware that this thoughtfulness which Christ urges upon us should not deter or delay our enthusiasm. There have been many who failed to give themselves a fixed rule of patience at the starting-blocks, and fell out of the running, because they were out of training: their only programme for running as Christians is one which by-passes the cross. There are others, who, when the prospect of service strikes them as over-strenuous and unpleasant to the flesh, will not dare to approach Christ. Yet there is no reason why the awareness of our feebleness should take the heart out of us, for the Lord hastens to our assistance. I agree, if we count up the cost, we are so destitute that we cannot lay one stone, or put a sword in the enemy's path. But as the Lord provides us from heaven with material, costs, arms and supplies, our sluggishness and hesitancy will find no excuse on the score of difficulty. Christ's counsel is to advise His men of the cross to be borne, so that they may equip themselves bravely.

Luke 14.33. *So therefore whosoever he be of you that renounceth not.* This sentence shows what this reckoning-up of costs, which Christ tells His men to start from, really means, namely, that they should quite clearly settle their intention to renounce all things. Those who advance to the profession of Christianity will be disappointed if their delight is in the sweet and leisured life, which knows nothing of the cross. Now by 'renouncing all things', you must understand that they are to give Christ such priority over their own lives, and over all the demands of the flesh, that nothing impedes their straight path. It would be a ridiculous proceeding to insist exactly on the literal sense, as if no-one could be a disciple of Christ who did not throw all he possessed into the sea, divorced his wife and said farewell to his children. This sort of fiction has led many stupid men into Monasticism, wishing to come nearer Christ by forfeiting their humanity. The truest way to renounce all one' spossessions is to be ready at any instant to abandon everything, to entrust oneself wholly to the Lord as a free and unattached man, and to pursue one's own vocation, rising above every obstacle. Thus, true abnegation, which the Lord asks of His people, is sited not so much in deed (*in actu*, as they say), but in intention (*in affectione*), that each man should live by the day, and not fasten his heart on the matters to hand.

Matt. 10.40. *He that receiveth you receiveth me.* Another word of comfort, that although the great part of the world be hostile to Christ's disciples, and though by their confession of faith they provoke the hatred of all men upon themselves, yet the Lord, in order to prompt as many as possible to show kindness towards them, condescends to take to His own account whatever may be given them. This shows how dearly He holds them, in allowing all the services accorded them, to be imputed to Himself. And He is speaking not so much of their treatment of the message, but of the men. I grant that the latter depends upon the former, but we must consider Christ's mind, for as He saw it would be most helpful to support their infirmity, He willed to testify, that any who treated them kindly, and gave them friendly assistance, would be doing Him as welcome a duty as though He had in His own Person enjoyed their generosity: more than that, they would have offered a sacrifice of good behaviour in the sight of God the Father.

Matt. 10.41. *He that receiveth a prophet, etc.* He starts with the Prophets, but goes all the way down to the lowest level, to take in all His disciples. So without exception He commends the true worshippers of God, and adherents of the Gospel. *To receive in the name of a Prophet and a righteous man* has the effect of saying, to do them a kindness in honour of their teaching, and in respect of their devotion. Although God bids us perform the duties of charity towards the whole of the human race, He deservedly elevates His own people a higher degree, for them to have a particular care and attention.

Shall receive a prophet's reward. Interpreters give this phrase various explanations. To some it appears as a mark of mutual recompense, God's Prophets returning spiritual for earthly goods. But if we accept this solution, what are we to make of *the reward of a righteous man?* Others take it, that those who have been generous to them will be partakers in the same reward which is laid up for the Prophets, and for the righteous. Some refer this to that mutual sharing among the saints, whereby we testify, by our beneficence, that we are one body with the servants of Christ, and by this means are made to share in all the good things which Christ dispenses among the members of His body. I consider it simply to be a reward which corresponds to the worth of the person to whom the action was performed. Christ indicates, that this will be a notable proof of the value in which Christ holds His Prophets and ultimately all His disciples, of any sort, for the fulness of the reward will show that no action which was done for them, has gone for nothing. By way of amplifying the point, He promises a reward for the cheapest services, such as giving a glass of cool water. He calls them, *these little ones*, partly as being the least in the Church, and most despised, partly as all His disciples are trodden down by the pride of the world.

INDEX TO THE HARMONY

Matthew

1.1-17	52
1.18-25	61
2.1-6	81
2.7-12	86
2.13-18	99
2.19-23	104
3.1-6	110
3.7-10	119
3.11-12	125
3.13-17	127
4.1-4	133
4.5-11	138
4.12	143
4.13-16	152
4.17	143
4.18-25	154
5.1-12	167
5.13-16	175
5.17-19	178
5.20-22	182
5.23-26	185
5.27-30	188
5.31-32	189
5.33-37	190
5.38-41	193
5.42	195
5.43-48	197
6.1-4	200
6.5-8	202
6.9-13	204
6.14-15	213
6.16-18	214
6.19-21	215
6.22-24	216
6.25-30	219
6.31-34	222
7.1-5	224
7.6	227
7.7-11	229
7.12-14	231
7.15-20	236
7.21-23	239
7.24-29	241
8.1-4	242
8.5-13	246
8.14-18	161
8.19-22	253

Matthew (contd.)

8.23-27	278
8.28-34	281
9.1-8	256
9.9-13	261
9.14-17	265
9.18-22	268
9.23-26	272
9.27-34	275
9.35-38	277
10.1-8	288
10.9-15	292
10.16-20	296
10.21-25	300
10.26-31	304
10.32-36	307
10.37-42	311

Mark

1.1-6	110
1.7-8	126
1.9-11	129
1.12-13	135
1.14-15	143
1.16-20	154
1.21-28	159
1.29-39	161
1.40-45	242
2.1-12	256
2.13-17	261
2.18-22	266
3.13-19	164
4.22-23	304
4.24	224
4.35-41	279
5.1-20	282
5.22-34	268
5.35-53	272
6.7	289
6.8-11	293
8.38	308
9.41	311
9.49-50	175
11.25-26	214

Luke

1.1-4	1
1.5-13	3

Luke (contd.)

1.14-17	9
1.18-20	14
1.21-25	17
1.26-33	20
1.34-38	26
1.39-45	31
1.46-50	34
1.51-55	37
1.56-66	41
1.67-75	43
1.76-80	49
2.1-7	70
2.8-14	73
2.15-21	78
2.22-32	88
2.33-39	93
2.40-47	106
2.48-52	109
3.1-6	111
3.7-14	119
3.15-18	126
3.19-20	143
2.21-23	129
3.23-38	52
4.1-4	133
4.5-13	139
4.14-15	143
4.16-22	146
4.23-30	150
4.31-36	159
4.38-44	162
5.1-11	154
5.12-16	243
5.17-26	257
5.27-33	261
5.33-39	266
6.12-19	164
6.20-26	168
6.27-28	197
6.29-30	193
6.31	231
6.32-33	197
6.34-35	195
6.35-36	197
6.37-38	224
6.40	300
6.41-42	224

Luke (contd.)		Luke (contd.)		Luke (contd.)	
6.43-45	236	9.26	308	12.51-53	308
6.46	239	9.57-62	253	12.58-59	185
6.47-49	241	11.1-4	204	13.23-24	233
7.1-10	247	11.5-13	229	13.25-30	234
8.16	175	11.33	175	14.25-33	311
8.17	304	11.34-36	217	14.34-35	175
8.22-25	279	12.2-7	304	16.13	217
8.26-39	283	12.8-9	308	16.17	178
8.40-48	269	12.11-12	296	16.18	189
8.49-56	273	12.22-28	220	17.11-17	251
9.1-2	289	12.29-32	222		
9.3-5	293	12.33-34	215		

INDEX OF SCRIPTURE REFERENCES
(including further refs. to Matthew, Mark, and Luke)

GENESIS

12.3	58
13.15	20
17.7	36
17.10	81
17.17	15
18.10	15
22.1	136
32.10	293
43.12	88
49.10	60
49.26	106

EXODUS

24.13	134

LEVITICUS

2.13	176
12.6	90
14.2	245
18.5	183

NUMBERS

3.13	90
6.4	105
12.6-8	63
36.6	29

DEUTERONOMY

6.12-17	68
7.9	36
7.21	69
8.3	138
10.12	183
13.3	136
22.13	21
30.19	183
33.16	106

JUDGES

6.17	15
13.5	105

I SAMUEL

8.5	59
10.6	11
15.22	245
21.4	18

II SAMUEL

7.13-14	55

I KINGS

6.5	18
17.9	151

II KINGS

1.2	303
5.10	151
9.27	56
11.1	56
15.29	153
18.9	153
24.6	60
24.15	60

II CHRONICLES

2.6	206
22.9	57
22.11	54
23.3	57

JOB

7.1	77

PSALMS

2.4	206
2.7	24
22.7	59
46.9	281
72.5	58
72.10	83
89.29	58
91.11	141
103.17	37
107.40	39
110.2	25
115.3	206
122.4	246

PSALMS (contd.)

127.2	220
127.3	20
130.4	48
132.11	55
132.14	69
132.17	45
147.9	221

PROVERBS

19.17	216
30.19	68

ISAIAH

7.11	17, 66
7.14	65
8.13	96
8.14	95
9.1	153
9.2	50
9.6	76
11.1	27
28.16	96
29.15	218
30.33	129
33.1	226
40.1	116
42.3	131
44.22	211
49.8	149
49.15	230
55.1	292
58.8	226
59.2	211
59.16	38
60.2	50
60.19	51
61.1	131

JEREMIAH

10.23	222
27.20	60
30.9	25
31.9	93
31.15	103
31.33	180

319

LAMENTATIONS
3.44   211

EZEKIEL
3.24   25
37.4   252
37.24   25
44.21   21

DANIEL
2.21   39
7.14   26

HOSEA
2.23   17
3.5   25
6.6   265
11.1   101

AMOS
5.19   259
9.11   25

MICAH
5.2   86
7.6   311

ZECHARIAH
9.9   76

MALACHI
3.1   12, 111
4.2   50
4.6   310

MATTHEW
1.21   23
8.12   291
11.11   10
13.58   150
16.23   142
23.23   124

MARK
1.27   161
6.5   150

LUKE
7.28   181
7.33   118
10.16   16
16.16   111

JOHN
1.15   130
1.16   11
3.5   128
3.29   267
3.33   207
4.22   55
5.25   253
5.28   260
6.40   240
7.18   238
7.49   123
10.3   237
12.47   23
15.16   166

ACTS
21.21   179

ROMANS
3.4   33
3.19   211
3.23   211
4.15   121
4.17   252
4.19   15
4.20   30
5.3   170
8.15   25
10.17   12, 271
11.14   236
11.16   89
11.25   26
12.1   48
12.17   193
12.19   121
12.21   193
14.5   2
14.17   75
14.23   48
15.8   25, 55, 93, 291

I CORINTHIANS
1.14   240
1.21   21
1.25   74
2.1   148
2.4   74, 148
2.11   259
4.20   161
7.34   188

I CORINTHIANS
(contd.)
8.5   33
12.11   11
13.3   186

II CORINTHIANS
2.15   295
2.16   227
3.6   12
3.18   92
9.7   178
9.12   178
11.13   278

GALATIONS
1.10   175
4.4   81, 149
4.5   25
4.9   267

EPHESIANS
1.4   115
1.6   22, 132
2.17   68, 75, 147
3.7   116
3.15   230
4.7   11
5.14   153
6.16-17   137

PHILIPPIANS
2.7   59
2.9   24
3.2   278
3.8   212
4.18   186

COLOSSIANS
1.15   133
1.20   133
1.25   166
2.8   267
2.9   69
3.3   115
4.6   177

I THESSALONIANS
5.19   44

I TIMOTHY
1.15   262
3.2   158
3.16   67

I TIMOTHY (contd.)		TITUS (contd.)			HEBREWS (contd.)	
5.20	120	2.12	265		13.5	221
		3.4	47		13.8	56
II TIMOTHY		3.9	58			
1.12	30	3.11	228		JAMES	
1.14	1				1.14	213
2.4	262	HEBREWS			4.3	231
2.19	241	1.5	24		5.13	35
3.12	172	2.2	16			
3.14	1	3.1	303		I PETER	
		4.15	106		2.4-8	96
TITUS		12.25	16		3.13	172
2.11	47, 49	13.4	19		5.6	38

INDEX OF NAMES

Africanus, 56
Augustine, 174, 194, 283, 302

Bucer, 105

Chrysostom, 83, 105, 213, 226, 267

Demosthenes, 3

Epiphanius, 60, 72
Erasmus, 3, 60, 209, 298, 303
Eusebius, 56, 73

Helvidius, 70
Hieronymus (=Jerome), 70, 252, 279

Irenaeus, 107

Josephus, 72, 105, 113, 114, 144
Julian, 194

Maccabaeus, 4
Macrobius, 102
Manichaeus, 23
Marcion, 23

Nicodemus, so-called, 3

Origen, 21
Osiander, 103

Plato, 48, 196
Pythagoras, 13

Robertus Stephanus, 60

Servetus, 24
Strabo, 279

Virgil, 3
Vulgate, Latin, 78, 213

GENERAL INDEX

Abraham, 15, 30, 47, 55, 58, 66-7, 235, 258
seed of, 13, 20, 25, 29, 37, 40, 44, 113, 122, 250, 291
ad Abraham, 40
Adam, 55-6, 89, 107, 136
adoption, 24-5, 41, 132, 199, 206, 251, 276
alms-giving, 200-1
Anabaptists, 173, 191
anathema, sign of, 295
ἀνατολή, 50
angel, 8 *seq*, 16, 21 *seq*, 62, 74, 79, 112
anima, animus etc., 34-5
anti-type, 105
apostles, 3, 155, 157, 165-6, 173, 175-6, 260, 262, 289 *seq*, 296 *seq*
assent (to concupiscence), 188
ἀταραξία, 208
αὐτοκατάκριτοι, 228

baculus etc., 293
baptismum etc., 130
βαττολογία, πολυλογία, 203
Beel-zebub etc., 303
Bethlehem, 70 *seq*
blame and penalty (sc. *culpa, poena*), 212
blindness, spiritual, 87, 149, 152, 218, 276
blood, 47, 69, 116, 127, 245
Boanerges (Heb.), 167
bread, 210
burial rites, 252, 255, 274

capital and labour, 210-11, 215-16
celibacy, 18-19
ceremonies, 80-1, 245, 267
Chinnereth etc. (Heb.) (cf. Gadara), 156
CHRIST, 11, 13, 21, 23-4, 28, 45, 60, 65, 69, 75, 81, 85, 91, 106, 112, 130, 147, 156, 159, 163, 244, 249-50, 259-60, 264, 280, 288, 315
baptism of Spirit, 126
coming, 302
genealogy, 52-7
head of church, 101, 141, 161, 303
Immanuel, 65-6
judge, 128, 236, 285, 309

CHRIST (*contd.*)
king, 65, 88, 91
lord over life and death, 49-51, 96, 154, 157, 252, 274, 291
mediator, 8, 29, 69, 107, 132, 276
minister, 288
priest, 69, 91
prophet, 150, 244, 249, 288
representative, 135
teacher, 133, 144-5, 156, 165, 205
(and cf. redemption, salvation, etc.)
Christ and Mary, 32
church, 11, 13, 24, 46, 64, 75, 95, 98, 101, 118, 120, 126, 128, 146, 165-6, 179, 181, 233, 236, 251, 260, 278, 289, 302
confession, 118-19, 245
conflict (and endurance), 77, 94, 135, 169, 172, 194, 213, 280, 301, 313
conscience, 6, 48, 63, 121, 127, 175
contingency—cf. fortune
corruption, 13, 39, 108, 120, 146, 264, 274, 311
counsels—cf. monasticism
cross—cf. salvation
cross, sinners bound to, 312
elements of, 104

Daniel, 61
David, 4, 5, 7, 21, 25-6, 45, 53 *seq*, 59, 63, 113
διαμερισμόν, 310
δικαιώματα, etc., 6
disciples, 156-7, 166, 177, 240-1, 254-6, 263, 268, 280, 302, 312
divorce, 189-90
Donatists, 173
dreams, 63
dulia, latreia, 142
duties of charity, 124, 171, 186, 196, 198, 209 *seq*, 232, 315

ἔκστασιν, 260
elements, as signs, 76, 132
Elijah, 13
Elisabeth, rel. to Mary, 29, 53
ἐμνηστευμένην, 21
ἐν, 77

ἐπανόρθωσις, 183
Epicureans, 174
ἐπιγραφή, 58
ἐπιούσιον, 209
essentiales spiritus, 287
εὐδοκία, etc., 78, 224
εὐλογίαν, 94
ex ordine naturae, 83
ex parte Dei, 34
exinanitio etc., 59, 74, 100, 106, 110

faith, 1, 2, 3, 12, 15, 26, 30-1, 63, 69,
    76-7, 79-80, 94, 128, 145, 177, 207,
    238, 249-50, 258, 270, 271 seq,
    275, 308
  lack of, 14, 17, 30, 37, 84, 95, 138,
    150, 220-2, 230, 280
  unity of, 13-14, 33, 251, 311
fasting, 98, 134, 214, 267
fear, sinful, 281, 287, 306
fire, 128-9, 176
fortune, 38, 307
free will, 178, 217

Gadara, etc., 279, 284
Gehenna (Heb.), 185, 303
GOD, author of good works, 178
  calling of, 3, 110, 130, 255, 315
  conversion to, 11, 13, 208
  covenants, 36-7, 40, 45-6, 55 seq,
    65-6, 89, 122, 250
  creator, 12, 143, 192, 221
  elect of 11, 44, 91, 97, 228, 278
  father, 20, 25, 28, 109, 170, 202-3,
    206, 209-10, 223, 230, 244, 302
  fear of, 37
  hand of, 43, 71, 208, 259, 306
  holy, 36, 206
  image of, 199
  judgments, 15, 121, 163, 172, 185,
    199, 213, 225, 295
  kingdom, 115, 145, 158, 178, 181,
    205, 207, 224, 256, 301
  love of, 1, 22, 132, 206
  mercy, 40
  omnipotent, 30, 206
  ordinances, 6, 138
  peace with, 14
  presence, 8, 23, 68-9, 131, 151, 157,
    253
  promises, 15, 141
  providence, 62, 71, 112, 166, 208,
    220-1, 300, 307

GOD (contd.)
  purposes, 2, 12, 21, 81, 82, 88, 99,
    135, 149
  'tempting man', 136, 212
  Word of, 2, 17, 23, 29-30, 34, 40,
    46, 66, 79-80, 90, 92, 116, 137-8,
    149, 151, 176, 179, 207, 228, 231,
    238, 246, 249-50
  works of, 3, 19, 23, 28, 31, 43, 135,
    146, 150
  worship of, 6, 13, 34, 76, 88, 90, 98,
    108, 124, 142, 186, 301
gospel, 1, 3, 111-12, 114, 128, 144-5,
    148, 176, 179 seq, 227, 241-2,
    277, 289, 297, 304
grace, 7, 9, 11, 13, 22, 27, 46, 77, 115,
    117, 123, 127, 145, 166, 177, 230,
    244, 252, 262, 265, 285

happiness, 169, 216
heaven, 26, 73, 81, 130, 172, 206, 215
Hebrews, epistle to, 8, 16, 24, 265, 303
heresy (sc. adoptionist), 28
Herod, 4-5, 72-3, 84, 87, 102
  Tetrarch, 144
holiness, 47, 116, 145, 174, 244
hypocrites, 120-1, 173, 182, 201, 214,
    219, 227, 238 seq, 248, 263

ignorance, inexcusable, 80, 88, 246
in unum idemque corpus etc., 244 (cf. 261)
incense, 7
indulgences, 182
Isaac, 7
Isaiah, 65-6, 68, 147, 163

Jacob, 4, 58, 60, 293
James, 225
Jesus (Heb.), 23, 64
Jews, 25-6, 46, 58, 67-8, 72, 75, 84, 87,
    95, 117, 122, 128, 145, 179, 183,
    189-90, 235-6, 243, 247-8, 251,
    265, 291
John (Heb.), 9
joy, 10, 74, 170
jubilee, 149
Judas, 166

κακοζηλία, 135
κατεσκευασμένον, 22
κατηρτισμένος, 303
kingdom of Christ, 25-6, 46, 63, 93,
    117, 153, 174, 310

kingdom of heaven, 20, 115, 170, 234

law, 5, 6, 7, 18-19, 24, 29, 47, 48, 53 *seq*, 81, 89-90, 91, 105, 108, 109, 111, 126, 142, 163, 176, 178 *seq*, 205, 244
levites, 7
life, 46-7, 115, 232, 274, 305, 313
lunatici, 159

Maccabaeans, 4
magistrates, 125, 173, 193
merit, 7, 37, 47, 59, 134, 173, 213, 224
Messiah, 4-5, 25, 40, 57-8, 66-7, 91, 150, 161, 253, 276
μετεωρίζεσθαι, 223
μετοικεσία, 60
ministers, ministry, 3, 12, 19, 126-7, 148, 158, 164, 238, 250, 255, 278, 289 *seq*
miracle, 28, 68, 135, 150, 155-6, 158, 160-1, 240, 243, 246, 252, 257 *seq*, 271, 273-4, 275 *seq*, 281, 287, 290
moderation, 186, 214, 263
monasticism, 118, 198, 214
mundities, 245
mystery, 22, 26, 27, 63, 110, 228

naming, 42, 81
nations, 75, 82, 93, 123, 154, 235, 250, 291, 299
nature, common tie of (cf. 171), 197, 265, 311-12
Nazaraean (and Heb.), 10, 104
non ita locatur Deus, 206

oaths, 191
obedience, 6, 16, 47, 63, 69, 74, 79, 100, 130, 156, 189, 208, 245
original sin, 89, 107

papists, pope, 7, 10, 11, 14, 18-19, 22, 27, 35-6, 82-3, 85, 119, 121-2, 137, 142, 146, 148, 160, 167, 173, 176, 180, 187, 188, 203, 217, 237-8, 245, 277, 290, 303
παρακολουθεῖν, 3
παρεστηκώς (past for present), 16
patroni, 303
Paul, 1, 12, 22, 24-5, 58, 59, 74, 98, 132, 146, 158, 179, 183, 193, 210, 216, 235, 242, 262, 295, 312
peace, 51, 77, 172, 294, 310
Peter, 156, 167, 290

Pharisee (and Heb.), 120-1, 183-4, 266, 268
φιλανθρωπία, 47
φιλαυτία, 230
πληροφορία, 2
politicum ordinem (of Law), 184, 189
πονηρόν, 217
potentiam, primates etc., 38
poverty, spiritual, 148, 169
prayer, 9, 94, 98, 131, 165, 171, 202 *seq*, 229, 244, 258, 267, 278
preaching, 81, 119, 128, 148, 177, 208, 294
priesthood, 5, 8, 85, 114, 245, 277
princes, 38, 125, 299
prophecies, 23, 25, 45, 64, 71, 84, 101, 103, 250, 310
prophets, 4, 7, 10, 12, 44, 49, 97, 105, 111, 116-17, 151, 153, 174, 238, 259, 270
προσκυνεῖν, 142, 243, 270
publicani, 125, 199, 262
puer, 40
punishment, instruments of, 226
purgatory, 187
purification (of Mary), 89

quiescente divinitate, 107
Quirinius, 72

rabbinic teaching, 23
reason, 217
redemption, 44-5, 90, 98, 101, 105, 149, 291
regenita (spiritualiter), 32
remission of sins, 46, 49, 65, 115, 145, 211, 214, 259-60
repentance, 115, 119 *seq*, 123 *seq*, 145, 265
reprobate, 123, 128, 198, 227
revolutionaries, 124
righteousness, 5, 47, 50, 61-2, 65, 116, 130, 145, 182, 189, 224, 264

Sabbath, 146
sacraments, 116, 118, 127, 250, 264
sacramentum, 42
sacrifice, 16, 90, 116, 186, 265
Sadducees, 120-1
salvation, 23, 33, 35, 45, 64, 75, 77, 92, 103, 110, 117, 135, 137, 145-6, 228, 233, 250, 264
salvator etc., 35, 76
Sanhedrin, 4, 102

Satan, 1, 3, 16, 21, 29, 36, 46, 135 *seq*,
    159, 160, 172, 207, 212-13, 236-7,
    266-7, 284-5, 306, 310
scribes, 85, 160, 182, 197, 254, 263
scripture, 40, 70, 77, 85-6, 92, 103, 105,
    111, 127, 137, 140-1, 145, 146, 163,
    168, 179, 183, 199, 209, 274
sermonis ministri, 3
sicera, 10
soldiery, 125
Solomon, 55 *seq*, 216
soul migration, 13
SPIRIT, 28, 51, 61, 74, 82, 121, 131-2,
    135, 148, 160, 208, 231, 271, 299
  discernment, 237, 309
  gifts, 1, 11-12, 107, 145, 149, 292
  regeneration, 7, 116, 127, 145, 181, 252
  revelation by, 32-3, 51, 62, 83, 91
  seal, witness, 63, 87, 199, 212
sponsi filii, 268
stipends, 292
Stoics, 169-70, 173, 307
subiecta (ignorantiae), 106

suffragia, 187
συμβάλλειν, 80, 110
summum bonum, 216
suscepta (publica persona), 9, 39, (cf.
    110, 130)
symbol, 8

teachers, teaching, 1, 3, 94, 108, 144,
    157, 174, 179, 181, 227, 237, 289,
    309
temple, 8, 18, 98
twelve, 289-90

usury, 196

venial sin, 182
virgin (Heb.), 67
virginity, perpetual, 27, 70
virtutes, 240
visions, 18

witnesses, 74, 79, 82, 84, 262, 288, 308
'word', Heb. use, 29